BILL BRANDT
A LIFE

Self-portrait with mirror, East Sussex coast, 1966

PAUL DELANY

BILL BRANDT

A LIFE

JONATHAN CAPE

PIMLICO

LONDON

Contents

Introduction

Bill Brandt was a man who loved secrets, and needed them. The face he presented to the world was that of an English-born gentleman, someone who could easily blend in with the racegoers at Ascot whom he liked to photograph. Behind this façade – which he would defend with outright lies if he had to – lay an inner self that was walled-off behind a deep reluctance to explain himself. Today, many people are eager to discover their roots and make an identity from them. Brandt did the exact opposite: he buried his true origins and presented himself as a completely different person from the one he had been, in reality, for the first twenty-five years of his life.

To understand Brandt, one has to begin by tracking down the substantial facts about him. In the world of espionage, cover stories are most effective if they make use of parts of the truth, and fit in with the temperament of the person living in disguise. This is what Brandt did, at times shuffling the facts, at others simply creating blank spaces. But to do more than correct the record, and get down to the level of Brandt's deeper self, is more difficult. He can certainly be recognised as a type: the kind of sensitive, artistic young man who is a product of the German high bourgeois family, even in his rebellion against it. 'Well, that was him,' his sister-in-law has said, 'Him who was feeling apart, him who was not really strong.'[1] Such young men keep turning up in the Freudian case histories, with their nervous habits and sexual troubles. They are staples of Thomas Mann's fiction: gentle misfits like Tonio Kröger and Hanno Buddenbrooks, or the bewildered Hans Castorp in *The Magic Mountain*. It is tempting to find the key to Brandt's north German upbringing in Mann; yet he was so hostile to Mann that his friends learned never to mention him. Does this mean that Brandt knew how much about himself was exposed in Mann's writings? Or did he feel belied by those texts, the superficial resemblances only false clues to his true self?

The foundation for this biography has been a series of interviews with Brandt's widow, Noya Brandt, and with surviving friends and relatives whose memories go back to the late 1920s. These interviews have provided the main features of his life, cutting through his own mystifications, and have identified emotional patterns in both his personal relations and his photography. Still, the biographical evidence remains tantalisingly incomplete. We know that Brandt was twice psychoanalysed, in 1927 and in the late 1950s, but little about his reasons for going or what consequences followed. With other crucial events, such as his divorce from his first wife, his relationship with

Man Ray in 1930 and the death of his younger brother in a raid on Germany, we are still ignorant of his motives or responses.

In writing this biography of Brandt, I have had to build a house of straw rather than bricks. But this need not be a reason to despair; perhaps it only sharpens the fundamental dilemma of any biographer. In Anthony Powell's *Hearing Secret Harmonies*, the character X. Trapnel holds forth on the problem:

> People think because a novel's invented it isn't true. Exactly the reverse is the case. Because a novel's invented, it is true. Biography and memoirs can never be wholly true, since they can't include every conceivable circumstance of what happened. The novel can do that. The novelist himself lays it down.[2]

There is an understanding that comes from seeing the places that shaped Brandt: the mansions by the Alster Lake in Hamburg, the sanatoria of Davos, the street life of Vienna or Paris. There is the tone of voice in which he is remembered by his friends, and the bafflement of those who worked with him but never felt they knew him. But whatever scaffolding of facts one can erect, whatever the narrative plan that ties events together, there will always be impenetrable areas of ignorance, which the biographer cannot just fill out of his own imagination.

The closest thing to a solid foundation for this book are the 5,000 or more pictures taken by Brandt between 1927 and 1983. They are hard evidence, in the sense that they can usually be given a subject, a place and a date. But photographs do not speak; they have to be 'read', to be placed in one or another pattern. The great variety of Brandt's work is a help here, since his photographic interests were so responsive to shifts in artistic or personal agendas. Brandt also had a marvellous eye for the photographic work going on around him, in Vienna, Paris or London. Putting him against the background of Surrealists in Paris or photo-journalists at *Picture Post* helps to bring out the distinctive qualities of his vision. That background also includes the whole tradition of the Western visual arts, which Brandt knew intimately and constantly drew on for inspiration. His first ambition was to be a painter and he remained a Pictorialist photographer all his life, someone whose composition, lighting and atmosphere were inspired by painting. One of his nineteenth-century precursors was Oscar Rejlander, who photographed staged scenes and put out a series called 'Every Picture Tells a Story'. In his time, Brandt's preference for artifice over the hunt for Cartier-Bresson's 'decisive moment' made him, arguably, the first postmodernist in English photography. He drew on English and French literature also, which he knew intimately (he remarked that he could not get much visual inspiration from Italy because he did not know its literature). In his many visual essays on writers, he assumed that one needed to include the buildings and landscapes that were their spiritual home. Buildings brought in architecture: Brandt thought of becoming an architect as a young man, and photographed architecture from the beginning to the end of his career.

One might guess that Brandt chose photography, in part, because of all the arts it reveals the least about its creator's personality. The objects of photography already exist, out there in the world, and the photographer only needs to frame a composition and press the shutter. But Brandt was someone who managed to construct the world he photographed, and to impose his personality on almost every picture he took, across his whole range from photo-journalism to landscapes or nudes. 'He wasn't interested in anything that didn't lend itself to mystery,' said Tom Hopkinson. 'The mystery was in Bill, and he projected it on whatever he photographed.'[3] Brandt's pictures arrest your gaze, but also make you wonder what is hidden behind the surface.

That Brandt planted messages in his scenes is most evident in the staged pictures of the late 1930s, where he collaborated with his brother Rolf and other friends to construct moments in a narrative. It could be said that all photographs had been staged before Oskar Barnack invented the 35mm Leica in 1925. Early cameras required long exposures and control of lighting; any subject needed to be arranged before the shutter was opened, whether it was a society group or the Union dead that Matthew Brady laid out in noble repose. In 1914, André Kertész used his brother when he wanted a sinister passer-by for a street scene in Budapest; Brassaï, using long exposures at night, could both take a picture and be one of the figures in it.[4] Brandt's interest in staging came from nineteenth-century Pictorialism, from the photographic story-magazines of Paris in the early 1930s and from the Surrealist fascination with the miniature dramas of street life.

However, few such pictures would supply biographical evidence about the photographer who took them. Brandt was distinctive in making use of the visual vocabulary of street pictures to express symbols and obsessions peculiar to himself. To document the night life of Paris, Brassaï went to live in a hotel frequented by prostitutes and took his classic pictures of them on the street outside, where they stood on the cobbles in the lamplight. Brandt looked at one of those pictures and re-staged it off the Reeperbahn in Hamburg, getting his wife to dress up in clothes almost identical to Brassaï's original. This picture must have had a private meaning for Brandt, something quite different from Brassaï's aim of capturing an authentic image of a prostitute's life. Similar personal fantasies underlie Brandt's pictures of drinkers at Charlie Brown's pub in the early 1940s, or his raffish nudes for *Lilliput* later in the decade. Throughout his career, Brandt used the photographic conventions he saw around him to construct a personal mythology.

It could be argued that such myths and mysteries should be left unresolved, since to reveal them might also take away a picture's evocative power. But often enough, we cannot get further than to suggest what kind of a mystery is present, and leave the rest to imagination. Brandt's picture of Robert Graves with Beryl Pritchard and Judy Campbell, for example, echoes Brandt's own obsession with possessing two women at once. Behind the commissioned portrait, an effective piece of work for *Picture Post*, lies Brandt's secret life in a *ménage à trois*. His great nudes of the late 1950s can be linked thematically with Kertész's distorted nudes of thirty years before, but more directly to some kind of psychic crisis that led Brandt to psychoanalysis after he began taking them. His landscapes are not tributes to the immediacy of the natural world – like, say, those of Ansel Adams. The pictures are saturated with the spiritual influence of writers associated with those scenes, such as Wordsworth, Hardy or the Brontës. Some photography may deserve to be called an impersonal art, but not the kind practised by Brandt.

Hidden within Brandt's personality were sexual eccentricities, rejection of his

German origins, secretiveness that ended in outright paranoia. But as an artist, he was the opposite of a one-dimensional obsessive, and his photographic art went through a series of transformations. Some of the changes in his photography reflect wider changes in British photo-journalism from 1935 to 1957. Some came from his eagle eye for innovations by other photographers, such as Man Ray or Brassaï. But most of Brandt's inventiveness came from the inner logic of his art, as he explored the possibilities of so many different kinds of photography, from studio photography in 1920s Vienna to his late nudes and portraits, taken with a Hasselblad shortly before his death.

To place Brandt in these various settings is to follow his own practice in taking portraits, from the early 1940s until he died in 1983. His constant rule was that the subjects needed to have a backdrop that conveyed essential qualities of their personality. The bare image of a face was never enough for Brandt; his subjects had to be 'in character', placed on a stage with the necessary props. He believed that people were defined by the surroundings that they had chosen for themselves. Often, though, the settings turn into a kind of prison, with the person in them looking like a suspect under interrogation (or already under sentence). Many portraits recall scenes from the German Expressionist films of Brandt's youth, with their sinister lighting and oppressive furniture. Their atmosphere often seems a projection of Brandt's own inner state: in the later years of his life he suffered from a persecution mania, whose main symptom was a fear of being 'found out'. Above all, to be found out as a German; yet this could not be a secret to anyone who heard him speak. Beyond the simple fact of nationality lay a deeper fear, of being caught and exposed to public view. Nothing is direct with Brandt, whether in art or in life. In the war, his three brothers took their stand openly against Germany: Walter worked in counter-propaganda at Bletchley Park, Rolf was an ambulance driver, Augustus flew with Bomber Command. Brandt chose to make images of how everyday English life had been changed by the war: London lit only by moonlight, St Paul's looming above the rubble, massed sleepers sheltering in the Tube.

Is it even fair to persist in exposing what Brandt was so desperate to conceal? Given that he is surely the greatest of British photographers, it is important to understand where his art came from. But it is not simply a matter of putting his life on record as a tribute to what he achieved with a camera. To fully appreciate his work, one needs the knowledge of why he constructed his pictures in just the way he did. Much of Brandt's success came from qualities of mood or lighting that identified at a glance a picture as his. This ability to place his 'signature' on a picture gave him public recognition; but what did the public recognise? Even the most accessible of these images – the two maids serving dinner, the girl showing off her Lambeth Walk on an East End street – have deeper layers of private significance. Over a career of more than fifty years, Brandt wrote his own life in pictures; but he wrote in code, to which he would never provide the key. Meanwhile he wrote very few letters or other texts; and even with those closest to him he was deeply unwilling to reveal his inner concerns.

Brandt achieved a commanding position in English visual culture from the 1930s onwards. Did he make himself into an authentically English observer, or was his success in representing Englishness dependent on a distinctively alien perspective?

Brandt was not alone in having the sharpness of a stranger's eye. Stefan Lorant, Kurt Hutton and Felix Man also helped to revolutionise English photographic culture in the Thirties by bringing to it techniques they had learned on the Continent. Alexander Korda and Emeric Pressburger did similar work for the cinema, Ernö Goldfinger for architecture. But of all such figures, Brandt was probably the most successful at representing Englishness from within, providing the man in the street with a shock of recognition. Part of his reward was his influence on new generations of photographers from the 1950s on. In Britain, Brandt's pictures of the North inspired Don McCullin and Philip Jones Griffiths in the 'dirty realism' that showed the underside of the new, prosperous Britain of the Macmillan era. In America, it was a more phantasmagoric Brandt who influenced Robert Frank and Diane Arbus. 'I really believe there are things which no one would see unless I photographed them,' Arbus wrote. She and Frank both created an atmosphere of emotional turmoil that saturated their pictures, which acknowledged the photo-documentary tradition while taking their photography into a dimension beyond realism. But their America was a nightmare country of excess; Brandt's England was a country of dream, made strange without being made fearsome. Wounded soul that he was, Brandt never used his camera as an instrument of cruelty; and the best use of his life must be the lesson of how, once again, sickness and pain have been transformed into art.

Bill Brandt as a young man, Budapest, about 1930, photographer unknown

1 Roots

The River Elbe flows through Hamburg just south of its centre, widening into a series of basins and canals that form one of the world's greatest ports and give the city its reason to exist. For most of its history, Hamburg was a state in its own right, proud of the trading connections that made it one of the most international cities in the world. Although it was bordered by Prussia, its identity rested on not being Prussian. Prussia, according to the old joke, was not a state that had an army, but an army that had a state. Hamburg had no army at all; it was a commercial and cosmopolitan enclave within Prussia. Even under Hitler it was considered the least Nazi-minded of German cities.

In July 1943, though, Hamburg's history of independence no longer mattered; it was part of the Third Reich, with a fate no different from any other German city. Across the North Sea, the RAF had just introduced H2S radar. By showing up features of the terrain below, especially bodies of water, it made possible much more precise navigation at night. Hamburg was already an attractive target: it was the second-largest city in Germany, and most of the approach to it was over the sea where there was no danger from flak. It was built at the junction of two rivers, where the Alster came down from the north to join the Elbe. Just above the centre of the city, the Alster opened out into a lake, which would show up on H2S like a pointer on a snooker scoreboard. If the Elbe was the ruler, the heart of the city would be exactly at the pointer's tip. On the night of 24 July, 800 heavy bombers poured their HE and incendiary bombs into the target marked for them by H2S and pathfinders' flares. The result was something new in the horrors of war: a firestorm that consumed every molecule of oxygen within its radius, suffocating thousands of the city's inhabitants.

The July raids on Hamburg killed more than 45,000 people – almost all of them civilians – and destroyed 80 per cent of the central city. Bill Brandt, the subject of this biography, had long wanted to obliterate his past; now his adopted country had done it for him. The centre of his family's life had been his grandfather's mansion at Neuen Rabenstrasse 1, one of Hamburg's finest residential streets. After the raids, only one house on the street was left standing. Scores of Brandts had lived nearby in the Rotherbaum district, on the west side of the Alster Lake. It was at the edge of the zone of complete destruction in 1943, and is now again one of the most agreeable parts of Hamburg in which to live. But the social and intellectual world in which Bill Brandt grew up is gone for ever.

The Brandts had been a leading family of bankers, shipowners and merchants in Hamburg since early in the nineteenth century. A Hamburg merchant might do business all over the world, but especially with England and Russia. Bill Brandt's grandfather, Augustus Ferdinand, had been born in Archangel in 1835, when his father was running a branch of the family firm in St Petersburg. Augustus moved to London, prospering there as a partner in the merchant bank William Brandt & Sons and living in the part of Denmark Hill that was called 'little Germany'. He had seven children, four boys and three girls, all born in London and therefore British citizens. The youngest of them was Bill's father, Ludwig Walther Brandt, born in 1875. Five years later, Augustus Ferdinand was told by his doctor that the climate of London was dangerous to his health, and he moved his family and business back to Hamburg.[1] The grain of truth in Bill Brandt's claims about his English and Russian origins was that his family traded in timber and furs between Russia, Germany and England, had established branches of their companies in all three countries and lived away from Hamburg for years at a time. But all four of Brandt's grandparents were German by language and domicile, and Lutheran by religion.

In 1888 Augustus Ferdinand Brandt acquired a splendid summer house, Villa Testorp, on the outskirts of Hamburg at Nienstedten an der Elbe. He re-named it Villa Brandt. His three elder sons, Augustus Philip, Henry and Rudolf, all went back to London after being educated in Hamburg. Two of them became partners in William Brandt & Sons. Only Ludwig Walther, Augustus's youngest, stayed in Hamburg and joined the firm of Alexander Oetling, which traded with Mexico and Argentina. He became a partner at the early age of twenty-six. Still living in his father's house on Neuen Rabenstrasse, he was ready to take a suitable wife. The one he found was Louise ('Lilli') Merck, a daughter of the Hamburg governing class. Her father, Carl Hermann Merck, was a *Syndikus*, one of the ruling elite of lawyers and bureaucrats. They usually had university degrees, and considered themselves more cultured than the commercial class to which the Brandts belonged.[2] Ludwig Walther married Lilli from his father's house on 15 November 1901. It was his twenty-sixth birthday: perhaps just chosen to bring him luck, perhaps a sign of the egocentricity that made up a large part of his character. His wedding picture certainly shows arrogance and self-possession, as he turns towards the camera and away from his submissive bride. By the law of those days, Lilli lost her German citizenship and became, like her husband, British.

Ludwig Walther and Lilli began their married life in an apartment at Moorweidenstrasse 14, two minutes across the park from Neuen Rabenstrasse. They lived in palatial rooms, with four-metre-high moulded ceilings and tall windows. Their first son, Walther, was born there a year later. Their second, who would be known eventually as Bill Brandt, followed on 2 May 1904, at 11.30 in the morning. He was christened Hermann Wilhelm Brandt. In notes for a 1976 exhibition catalogue, Brandt said that he was born in London in 1904, to parents of Russian origin.[3] Only the date was true. The Christian name he began with was Hermann, but Wilhelm – shortened to Willy – was his childhood preference. He would change his name twice more in the next thirty years, to match changes in his idea of who he was.

In the same year that Bill Brandt was born his grandfather Augustus Ferdinand died, at the age of sixty-nine. Ludwig Walther was now the head of the family in

L.W. Brandt and Lilli Merck,
Wedding Picture, November
1901, photographer unknown

Hamburg, and he bought a suitable town house at Grosse Fontenay 1 in Rotherbaum. He and Lilli had two more sons, Rolf in 1906 and Augustus in 1911. His mother kept the country house at Nienstedten until she died in 1922 and Ludwig inherited it. He expanded the house with a balcony and terrace, overlooking the huge lawn that went down to the river.

To understand the social position of the Brandts one turns to Thomas Mann, who was an exact contemporary of Bill Brandt's father. *Buddenbrooks* is Mann's great autobiographical novel about his own mercantile family in Lübeck.[4] Such families were, first of all, large; Mann was one of five siblings, and had six children of his own. Bill Brandt, so quiet and reclusive as an adult, grew up in a family of six, with at least as many servants: gardener, handyman, cook, housemaids and nanny. Around their luxurious houses the Hamburg Brandts had scores of uncles, aunts, cousins, living in a similar style – so many that a whole book has been devoted to their histories.[5] It was a life of wealth, comfort and order; of lavish food and drink; a life also of rigid hierarchies and heavy philistinism. The routine of a high bourgeois house, and the relations between masters and servants, formed Brandt's childhood world. Later, it would be one of his great photographic subjects in the England of the Thirties. The way in which those pictures were published, side by side with pictures of life in the London slums and northern industrial towns, suggested that Brandt was condemning upper-class life. The truth was more complicated, for that was the life he himself had known as a child, and still enjoyed on extended visits to his wealthy uncles and aunts. He had an eye for contrast, certainly, but the contrast did not have to be entirely antagonistic. It has been suggested that Brandt's pictures were the inspiration for the television series *Upstairs, Downstairs*, where the differences between masters and servants are less important than their shared belief in the rituals of life in the big house – and where England is imagined as the biggest house of all.

To be sure, everything in the household in Hamburg came under the rule of its centre and patriarch, L. W. Brandt. Susan Brandt, his granddaughter, knew him as an old man who enforced 'a fantastically rigid set of rules'. In her eyes, he was 'a bully and an oppressor … the kind of man who always needed to assert his power over women and children'.[6] It hardly matters whether LW's domineering ways were peculiar to him or part of the code of every German bourgeois paterfamilias; his children grew up in a world of despotism and tribal expectations. The oldest son, Walther, was the favourite, destined to succeed his father in the family business and be, as far as possible, a faithful copy of him.[7] Willy and Rolf as the middle brothers, two years apart in age, were very close; they formed an alliance to resist their father's plans and to follow a different path. They looked alike, so much so that it is often hard to tell photographs of them apart. Augustus, five years younger than Rolf, was the most cheerful and easy-going of the four, and the most handsome. He would try to be a businessman like his eldest brother, but had much less devotion to the cause of making money.

If Walther was his father's child, Willy and Rolf belonged rather to their mother; they looked like her and felt like her. Lilli Brandt's family was more cultured than her husband's; she wrote plays and poems. If it were not for Lilli, Willy and Rolf might have been simply crushed by the philistinism of the Brandt family tradition; instead, she had enough intelligence and creativity herself to see that they needed a different kind of upbringing. She realised that they had visual gifts equivalent to perfect pitch in music, which set them apart from ordinary boys. As his sister-in-law Ester Cotton would say of Willy, 'everything you could see, he saw'.[8] When he and Rolf were about twelve their mother employed a Czech drawing-master, K. E. Ort, to develop the visual talents she had seen in them. They were children of the kind described by Thomas Mann: 'it not infrequently happens that a race with sober, practical bourgeois traditions will towards the end of its days flare up in some form of art'.[9] What Lilli Brandt could not do, with her somewhat childlike temperament, was set any real limits to the overbearing nature of her husband. Her sons grew up between two worlds: on the side of the mother, Imagination; on the side of the father, Order. Yet these tensions existed within the sheltering privilege and economic security of the pre-war German bourgeoisie. The Brandt boys would never have to worry about money, and had easy access to all the resources of high culture. If Willy and Rolf rebelled against mercantile values, they did so without renouncing the material comforts they were used to. Their creativity grew from conflicts internal to bourgeois life.

The bourgeois family had another place of contradictions, the bedroom. Robert Musil, the great novelist of Vienna, said that 'every bourgeois child has two mothers'. In the nursery the Brandt boys would be cherished and coddled by their *Kinderfräulein*, often a young girl from the country who had no other outlet for her affection. Freud loved his nanny so passionately that his parents sacked her, to teach him a lesson.[10] 'You had nothing to do with your mother,' a friend of Brandt recalls, 'and everything with your nanny.'[11] Outside the nursery loomed the dictatorial father, and a mother who could not do much to protect her children from him. English boys from the same class would live at a greater distance from their parents. From the beginning they would take their meals in the nursery and receive visits from their parents at set times; then came the complete exile of being sent to boarding school, probably before the age of ten. In Germany, children were more under the eye, and the direct control, of their parents. Every day they would be pushed back and forth between the strictness of paternal rule and the consoling embrace of the nanny.

For a family of boys, this would have been an especially sharp division, between the cold world of duty presented to them by their father and the nanny's softness and warmth. Lilli Brandt does not seem to have been able to bridge this gap: people of her sons' generation found her somewhat formidable and physically austere – *Zug er Knopft* ('buttoned-up') as the saying went.[12] The children also lived in two classes at once, with the nanny creating inside the bourgeois house a little enclave of peasant ways. A boy who was happy to conform might find little conflict here; he would learn to rule like his father, and servants or nannies would be the first people on whom he could exercise power. But more sensitive boys, like Willy or Rolf, would be aware of the conflict between those who laid down the law and those who submitted. In different ways, this experience would have political consequences for both of them in adult life.

The power of the father included, finally, an element of sexual domination. The nanny might well be a pretty and submissive girl, whose affection for her charges could easily catch the eye of her master.[13] The mother might not find out what her husband was up to, or might not have enough power to drive out her rival, as in the enduring *ménage à trois* for which the household of Karl Marx was notorious. It was not unheard of for the father to arrange for his sons to be sexually initiated by one of the female servants who had also served his own needs. The father's absolute rule spawned all kinds of perversions and neuroses in those who were subject to him; this was the soil out of which psychoanalysis grew.

Some of these emotional cross-currents were present in the household of L. W. Brandt; others can be imagined from fragmentary evidence, and from obsessional themes in Bill's pictures. Rolf Brandt told his daughter that his heart was broken when he was about nine (and Willy eleven), when the nanny they both adored was suddenly sent away; Rolf wondered if it was because his father had tried to seduce her.[14] Somewhere in the bedrooms and nurseries of his home, Willy developed a florid collection of sexual fantasies. His children's books remained alive in his adult work as a photographer. One of his favourites was the English Cherry Stones, with its gallery of street types.[15] This was harmless enough; but the comically violent Struwwelpeter was a fixture in German nurseries. It has been blamed as a fountain of neurosis, with its figures like the tailor who deals with thumb-suckers by cutting off their thumbs with his giant scissors. More than the thumb was in danger, of course: the Brandt boys had their blankets pulled down tight, and had to sleep with their hands outside them.

For many upper-class boys, the 'two mothers' syndrome created, in adult life, conflicting ideas about the nature of women – the split between Madonna and Whore described in Freud's classic essay 'On the Most Prominent Form of Degradation in Erotic Life'. Brandt's solution was somewhat different: whenever he could manage it, he would be intimate with two women at the same time, and sometimes live with them under the same roof. The first of these triangular relationships was in the Thirties, with Lyena Barjansky and Eva Boros (who became Eva Brandt in 1932). From 1938 to 1948 he lived with Eva and Marjorie Beckett, until there was a crisis and Eva went off to live alone. After Marjorie died in 1971, Brandt was eager to take Noya Kernot (who became his third wife) to see Truffaut's *Two English Girls* – a film about two sisters in love with the same man. Brandt's desire to remain close to Eva played a large role in the difficulties of his marriage to Noya. However, Brandt did not conduct himself as a macho male lording it over his harem, in the style of August Sander's famous picture of Raoul Haussmann with his wife and Vera Broido. He wanted to be a more passive object of desire, and wished that the two women should be friends with each other rather than rivals for his favour.

Brandt's passivity towards women could include a positive need for submission, and even to be punished by them. A recurrent subject in Brandt's Thirties pictures was the woman in uniform. For him this does not seem to have lesbian overtones, as it did in Leontine Sagan's 1931 film *Maedchen in Uniform*. He focuses on the uniformed woman who both disciplines others and is disciplined herself: the schoolgirl in *The English at Home*, the nurses or 'Nippies' (Lyons' waitresses) that he photographed for *Picture Post* in 1939. The most important of these women in uniform was 'Pratt', who had charge of Brandt's Uncle Henry's households: a London house in Kensington and a country house in Surrey near Redhill.[16] Brandt first met her in March 1928 on his first trip to England, when he stayed with his uncles Henry and Augustus. He was both amused and fascinated by the way Pratt orchestrated the rituals of upper-middle-class domestic life, and immediately started to photograph these scenes.[17] But Pratt made such an impression on him because his imagination had already prepared a place for her. She brought together the three kinds of power that had determined his childhood: his father's stiff authoritarianism, his mother's moral regulation and his nanny's care for his feeding and physical comfort. In the German bourgeois household of the time, servants did not normally wear uniforms; visiting his English relatives, Brandt saw household roles being filled in an even more ritualised way than at home. This brought out the idea of domestic life as a performance, staged for the benefit of the family members.

Brandt was always deeply reticent about his childhood, so in understanding the roots of his character we have to make do with crumbs of evidence. What is certain is that he was a special child: one who did not really fit in comfortably, but for that very reason was acutely aware – and visually aware – of what the others in his household were thinking and feeling. He was like Mann's Tonio Kröger, who asks himself:

> Why is it I am different, why do I fight everything, why am I at odds with the masters and like a stranger among the other boys? The good scholars, and the solid majority – they don't find the masters funny, they don't write verses, their thoughts are all about things that people do think about and can talk about out loud. How regular and comfortable they must feel, knowing that everybody knows just where they stand! It must be nice! But what is the matter with me, and what will be the end of it all?[18]

Not fitting in also committed Brandt to a strategy of indirection: he expressed his ideas of family life in pictures of his English uncles and aunts, rather than of his parents in Hamburg, of whom he took few pictures for publication.[19] If he had been a more ordinary boy, perhaps he could be understood more easily within the Freudian view of such families in Hamburg or Vienna. Brandt himself would twice submit to psychoanalysis, but his family dramas did not quite run true to type; if they had, he would not have been the artist he was. And there were more dramas in store for him, in places beyond the family home.

Brandt brothers in uniform, left to right: Rolf, Augustus, Willy, Walther,
September 1914, photographer unknown

2 'Something Happened'

The outbreak of war in 1914 would change the course of Bill Brandt's life, turning him from a German into an Englishman. But at the beginning, things went the other way. Caught up in the patriotic fervour of August, L. W. Brandt dressed up his four sons as little German soldiers. Walther, the eldest, was a cavalry officer; the other boys became junior members of Hamburg's 76th infantry regiment.[1] All of Germany expected a quick victory, like their triumph over the French in 1870, and before August was out they had crushed the invading Russians at Tannenberg. L. W. Brandt had lived in Germany since he was five years old, and at first had no reason to worry about his British citizenship. He was required only to stay out of politics and report weekly to the police.

But the war did not end, and on 13 October England rounded up 30,000 German citizens for internment on the Isle of Man. Germany demanded their release, and when this was refused they interned the 5,000 British men of military age who were living in Germany – including L. W. Brandt. Starting on 15 November, they were all sent to a makeshift camp at the Ruhleben racetrack in Spandau, in the suburbs of Berlin. The horses had been taken off to war and the Englishmen were put in their place: six men shared the box, open to the weather, that had housed one horse. They had no bedding or heat, and at first very little food. Nothing daunted, they made the camp into a little England, re-naming their alleys Bond Street, Regent Street and Trafalgar Square. There they stayed until the end of the war. About a thousand of the internees were men who happened to be of English birth, but had lived for years in Germany and often spoke no English. They were loyal to Germany and had a separate section of the camp. L. W. Brandt must have been in this group, because in April 1915 he was released and allowed to return home. But he had spent a very nasty six months in the camp, and from then on the whole Brandt family became, at heart, more loyal to England than to Germany.

When L. W. Brandt returned home his autocratic temper cannot have been improved by his stay in the camp. His business had also collapsed, because the English blockade had cut off any dealings with Latin America. It may have been at this time that he got involved with Willy and Rolf's nanny; certainly his relations with Willy became more tense. Nonetheless, in the early years of the war Willy's schooldays seem to have remained reasonably happy. His preparatory schooling was at the Vorschule Bertram on the Esplanade, a few streets away from his home, where his brothers were

also pupils. This was the most exclusive private school in the city for boys up to the age of fourteen. It was specially popular with the well-to-do Jewish families who lived nearby and wanted their sons to blend in with the mainstream of German culture.[2]

Willy did well enough at the Vorschule Bertram to be admitted, in 1918, to the Heinrich-Hertz Realgymnasium on Bundesstrasse. A Realgymnasium was selective, taking about the top 10 or 15 per cent of students. It had a more demanding curriculum than the ordinary Realschule; but it ranked below the Gymnasium, which gave a rigorously classical education. The Heinrich-Hertz was a fifteen-minute walk from Brandt's home, past the University of Hamburg and into a more middle-class and commercial district. Named after the great physicist who discovered electromagnetic waves, it had a fine new neo-Gothic building and a solid intellectual reputation.[3] But this is where Willy's academic troubles began. Perhaps he suffered from being separated from Rolf; perhaps he simply disliked the emphasis on science and technology at his new school. In any case, he spent too much time daydreaming instead of buckling down to serious preparation for a profession. He may have been just 'one of those intelligent boys who do badly at school'.[4]

Brandt may have had some difficulties with being an 'English boy' at the Heinrich-Hertz, but they were probably not too serious. When the war began, his brother Walther had been called in by the headmaster of the Heinrich-Hertz and told: 'You are the enemy – but we'll keep you because you're quite good at maths.'[5] Willy dressed and spoke like everyone else, and came from an upper-class family who lived in the best part of the city. The school's atmosphere was intellectual and cosmopolitan; about 20 per cent of its students were Jewish.[6] Willy could walk to school and back with his friends. At home he lived in bourgeois comfort and had the company of his brothers. Even if he was doing poorly as a student, everything else in his life was secure, or as secure as it could be in the defeat and anarchy of Germany in 1918-19.

All this ended when L. W. Brandt decided that Willy was a lazy boy who needed a kick in the pants. After only a year at the Heinrich-Hertz, Brandt was sent away as a boarder to the Bismarckschule Realgymnasium at Elmshorn, fifty kilometres northwest of Hamburg. Ester Cotton said that it made Brandt hate his father. LW was deliberately throwing a sensitive fifteen-year-old boy to the wolves, in the belief that it would be better for him in the long run. In *Buddenbrooks*, little Hanno is a similar kind of dreamer and misfit at school; when he is eleven, his father decides 'to exert his own influence on his son, to draw him more to his side and offer manly impressions to neutralise previous feminine influences'.[7] Hanno is forced into swimming, boxing and gymnastics, where he is bullied by his more 'manly' schoolmates. But at least he can come home to his mother and play his beloved piano. Willy Brandt was sent away from everything familiar; his schoolmates would almost all be local boys, from the upper class of a very conservative community. Elmshorn, a small industrial town surrounded by farm villages, was part of Prussia – almost a different country. This brought up the issue of Willy's citizenship. In the patriarchal German system, children were registered under the head of the family until they left home or married. When Willy went to Elmshorn he was issued with a registration card identifying him as a British subject, and had to report to the police each time he came and went.

Brandt arrived at the Bismarckschule on 16 October 1919; a month later, there was a solemn assembly for the 112 old boys who had been killed in the war. Soon after his arrival, one of his masters came into the classroom and asked, 'Is there anyone here who isn't German?' Brandt didn't own up; but the master must have heard rumours about an English boy being in the school, and it cannot have taken long for everyone to find out who it was.[8] Several of Brandt's relatives had fought for England; his first cousin Willie had been badly wounded with the Sherwood Foresters and had been awarded a Military Cross. Although the war had been over for a year, civilian life in Germany had become much worse, adding to the pervasive bitterness of defeat. The country was being ravaged by the four horsemen of disease, famine, inflation and civil strife between the paramilitary forces of the left and the right.[9] Prussian schools were supposed to be democratised in 1919 and purged of hatred and intolerance. But the headmaster of the Bismarckschule was a stickler for duty; it was still a fortress of discipline that loomed up over the little white-painted houses of Elmshorn. The other boys would at least have the refuge of going home at the end of the day but Brandt was the only boarder, lodged with one of the masters.

To begin with, Brandt managed to hold his own academically. The boys were marked from one to five, with five the lowest mark; Brandt got mostly twos (ones were rarely given). He quickly rose to the rank of fifth in a class of twenty-one; but during 1920 he slipped down to the middle of the class. 1921 and 1922 brought debacle; he fell to the bottom of his class and his record was sprinkled with ominous phrases: 'promotion to the next class seems impossible … not paying attention … diligence unsatisfactory'. Mathematics gave him endless trouble, and his only good marks were in freehand and line drawing. He started out getting twos in English, but went down to three in 1921 and four in 1922 (showing that he cannot have learned much English at home).

Just to survive the rigorous curriculum at Elmshorn was an achievement. As an adult, Brandt was an intellectual and widely read; he must have owed some of this to his schooling. Still, his career at Elmshorn was one long downhill slide, with some kind of deep unhappiness and resentment responsible for it. Part of the trouble was his health: in one term of 1922 he missed eighty lessons through illness. Tuberculosis was getting a grip on him, and he also suffered from asthma (a disease with a strong psychosomatic element to it). But so long as L. W. Brandt insisted on keeping Willy at Elmshorn, sickness would have a kind of perverse attraction. It was the boy's only escape.

There is ample evidence that Brandt suffered a psychic wound in his school days, something so hurtful that it affected every area of his life afterwards. But just because the hurt was so deep, he utterly refused to explain what it was, even to those closest to him. In guessing at the nature of his trauma at Elmshorn, one thinks first of his fellow-students inflicting on him some literally unspeakable humiliation. There is a good chance that they did; but Brandt's teachers probably did their bit too. In *Buddenbrooks*, the teachers are described as more beastly than those they instruct. Almost all are grotesque types, sadistic and authoritarian; the boy Hanno effectively chooses to die of typhoid, the only way he can find peace. At the very least, the teaching staff at the Bismarckschule do not seem to have appreciated an artistic and sensitive boy like Brandt, or to have provided a refuge for him. That left him defenceless among the Elmshorn boys, for whom an alien was someone who needed and deserved to be punished.

Though Brandt himself would never speak of it, what the other boys did to him is not hard to imagine. The classic description of bullying at school in German literature is in Robert Musil's *Young Törless*, where a boy with the foreign name of Basini is tormented by two juvenile Fascists, Beineberg and Reiting. Brandt was a foreigner too; Ester Cotton adds that 'he had been ill a lot and that's not what boys like, is it?'[10] Bullies seek out the weak in every school; the ones at Elmshorn managed to inflict on Brandt a wound that he carried with him until he died. As Jean Améry (a survivor of Auschwitz) put it: 'a man who has been tortured once stays tortured'.

Elmshorn was the root of Brandt's utter repudiation of his German identity – even though, at the time he was bullied, he had never set foot in England. The kind of scenes described in *Young Törless* could just as easily have happened in an English boarding school, of course. Robert Graves was bullied to the verge of a nervous breakdown at Charterhouse because he had a German middle name, and that was before the war. But Brandt never saw what happened to him as anything but a specifically German piece of beastliness.[11] 'Of course the Nazis are in Germany,' he would say later, 'where else could they be?'[12] He rejected everything that was 'typically German'. This could mean trivial criticisms, like complaining about the 'horrible German wine' his brother Walther served at dinner, but it also required a wholesale rejection of German culture. Dislike of Wagner was general in Brandt's circle in the Twenties; but Thomas Mann was a bugbear too, in spite of his opposition to Nazism, his magisterial pictures of German bourgeois life and his sojourn on the 'magic mountain' where Brandt too served his time. Lyena Barjansky remembers having to hide a book of Mann's that she was reading while travelling with Brandt. The only author in the German language that Willy and Rolf would tolerate was Kafka, but clearly as an antidote to the poison of German *Kultur*.

Once settled in England, Brandt went to any length to try to conceal his origins, with his stories about Russian ancestry, being born in south London, and the like. As his sister-in-law put it, 'neurotic' is a boring word, but it did apply to Brandt's feelings about Germany. One reason for his reluctance to be interviewed was fear that his German accent would be apparent, and this may be why he spoke in a whisper. Nonetheless, films and tapes confirm a distinct accent.[13] In hospital near the end of his life, a doctor asked him where he was born; Brandt replied: 'What has that got to do with my illness?' There is something pathetic or even funny in these subterfuges, except that Brandt would have a nervous crisis if anyone tried to challenge him about them. He was determined to 'pass' as something other than German; and the other side of this project was his embrace of everything he considered typically English. All such behaviour grew out of the poisoned soil of his school experiences. Yet there remained a crucial respect in which he was always a German artist who happened to use English subject-matter: the one part of Germany he never left behind was its visual culture, perhaps because its effects were less obvious than German literature or politics. Scholars like Ian Jeffrey and David Mellor have traced the influence on Brandt of German illustrated children's books, of magazines like *Das Plakat* or *Der Querschnitt* and, above all, of the visual world of the German Expressionist cinema of the 1920s.[14] These gave him a repertory of types and situations, and a moody light-and-dark atmosphere, that he could transpose to great effect on to the much less sophisticated world of English photography.

Another side of the Elmshorn trauma was its effect on Brandt's sexual history. The victim in *Young Törless*, Basini, is a beautiful youth; Beineberg and Reiting first torture, then sodomise him. Basini is singled out by his tormentors because he is slender and pretty: his femininity provokes what they do and also, in their eyes, justifies it. Brandt too was a beautiful young man when he went to Elmshorn, in the high Aryan style of long blond hair and chiselled features, and it is very likely that there was a sexual element in the bullying he suffered there. His sexual interests in adult life seem to have been entirely directed towards women, but fetishism and sado-masochism were part of his sexual constitution, and became overt in his 1977-80 nudes. As with his national identity, sexuality for him was closely bound up with secrecy and a fascination with ritual; many of his nudes contain esoteric sexual meanings. Since Brandt remained at Elmshorn for three years, secretiveness may also have been his way of protecting himself from the hatefulness of his school environment. But what began as a sensible defence against real enemies became, in time, an obsession with the dangers of any kind of self-disclosure.

Brandt's fears and phantasms reflect also the troubled times in which he came to maturity. Until the age of ten, he had lived an entirely sheltered and luxurious life. From 1914 on, his life was one long series of traumas and disruptions, until he and his wife settled permanently in England in 1934. Apart from the sufferings of school, and the sanatorium that followed it, just to be German guaranteed constant hardships and insecurities. His father's internment in 1914 was a first lesson in the arbitrary power of the state, even as many of his older cousins and friends were being sent to the front. Brandt and his brothers escaped the horror of the trenches – his elder brother Walther was sixteen when the war ended – but they did not escape the social chaos of the war years and their aftermath. There was severe hunger from late 1916 on, and the rate of

TB doubled in the last two years of the war.[15] Soap disappeared completely, and the streetcars were foul with the distinctive stench of famine. The Allied blockade of Germany was maintained until six months after the Armistice: hundreds of thousands died of starvation, and diseases like influenza and tuberculosis ravaged the population. Serious food shortages affected all levels of society and lasted until 1924. Rolf Brandt would later talk of having to rummage in dustbins for food and living for a week on one loaf of bread, baked with each day's portion marked out. All his life he would gobble his meals and leave no scrap on his plate, a typical habit of people who have experienced starvation.[16] Willy did not behave in this way; it seems that by the time of the famine his mother was so fearful for his health that she kept up his strength by giving him an extra share from her own rations. However, she refused on principle to buy food on the black market, though the Brandts were well able to do so.

After the famine, inflation. The Brandts were never in such desperate straits as the 'villa proletariat' of Thomas Mann's story 'Disorder and Early Sorrow', but the security and prestige they had taken for granted before the war would have been gravely shaken. Inflation got steadily worse from the end of the war until the crisis of November 1923, when the mark was finally stabilised. The privations of the Brandt family were certainly enough to make them seriously worried about their children's health, especially Willy's; part of the reason for sending him to Elmshorn may have been that conditions would be easier in a small town than in Hamburg itself. But by the end of 1922 his lungs were so bad that he had to leave school, and would never go back.

There were ample objective reasons for Brandt to become tubercular by 1922: the hardships of war, the famine, and the spread of infection through all classes of a weakened European population. His contemporaries still believed in the mystique of a supposed psychic predisposition to TB, and psychoanalysis was already identifying a subconscious desire to escape from painful situations by falling ill. What counts most in the formation of Brandt as an artist, though, is how bullying and sickness had separated him decisively from the herd by his late teens. He became one of those named in Thomas Bernhard's memoir of his days at the Salzburg Gymnasium:

> Every school, being a community, has its victims … There was nobody who did not participate in the entertainment, for the supposedly healthy members of any society enjoy such entertainment – whether secretly or not, whether openly or behind a mask of hypocrisy – at the expense of the suffering, the crippled, the sick. In such a community, such an institution, a victim is always sought and always found, and if he is not a victim already, from the start, he will *in any case be made into one.*[17]

Yet Brandt's bourgeois upbringing had also given him the cultural and emotional resources to make something positive of his isolation. He left his school as an exceptional young man, despite his failure at conventional studies. By the end of his teens he had been singled out to be an artist, even though it would take years for his real talent to appear.

Davos, about 1926, *Lilliput* February 1948, (by Brandt?)

3   Davos: The Iron Key

At the beginning of January 1923, when he was nineteen years old, Brandt was so ill that treatment in a sanatorium seemed the only chance of saving his life. The place chosen for him was Agra, a huge mock-Renaissance complex which looked out over Lake Maggiore, not far from Lugano. Agra had opened eleven years before, one of the last TB sanatoria to be built in Europe.[1] Although it was in an Italian-speaking canton of Switzerland, Agra was essentially a German institution, with a German head of medicine, Dr Kölle, caring for German patients. It was on the southern slope of the Alps and only 550 metres up, rather than the 1,500 metres or so for mountain sanatoria. There had been opposition to Agra before it was built, from high-altitude devotees who believed that the south wind could be deadly to TB patients; others, though, claimed that the milder climate and freedom from fog at Agra were more soothing to advanced cases than the sharp air of the heights.[2] Most likely Brandt was sent to Agra as a desperate case, who might have a better chance of pulling through in a relatively soft environment.

The Ticino was a lovely corner of Europe, popular with German intellectuals like Herman Hesse, who lived near Agra. But Brandt had no chance of enjoying the countryside. He later told Tom Hopkinson that he spent 'two years in bed' when he first went to the sanatorium.[3] If the Bismarckschule had become a kind of hell for him, Agra only put him into limbo. There were no more bullying masters or students, no succession of terms and examinations; just the daily routine of the hospital, stretching ahead indefinitely. In a sanatorium, it was said, you had no past and no future. Agra put Brandt into a twilight sleep, in which he did little more than cling to life. In that sleep, almost the only reality would be the dreams and fantasies that would later be the essence of his art. Probably Brandt expected to die; he certainly lived with death, and saw many people of his own age die around him. But he gradually gained some strength, and on 17 October 1924 his mother came to transfer him from Agra to the Schweizerhof sanatorium in Davos.[4]

In 1854 Hermann Brehmer had built the first TB sanatorium at Gorbersdorf, Silesia.[5] The five pillars of his treatment were altitude, rest, sunshine, good nutrition and exposure to fresh air in evergreen forests. Many sanatoria soon followed, especially higher up in the Alps, but Davos shortly became the most famous refuge in the world for TB patients. The whole canton of Graubunden, to which Davos belonged, was a kind of time-capsule within modern Europe. Motor cars were banned there until 1925 and all local travel was by horse-drawn carriage or sled. In this remote corner of the Alps a medieval village of cattle herders and woodcutters, 1,500 metres up in an inaccessible valley, was transformed into a bizarre, cosmopolitan city of the ill. Set in its great amphitheatre of peaks, Davos drew patients from all over Europe, from America and from Russia. About half the patients could not afford to stay in a sanatorium; they lived with peasant families in the town. Wealthier clients had a wide choice of sanatoria, according to how much they could afford. The Schweizerhof, where Brandt stayed, was relatively luxurious: a private room with balcony cost about nineteen Swiss francs a day, and with extras the total cost would approach an English pound – at the time, roughly twice the daily income of a skilled worker.[6] It was run by a Swiss, Dr Staub, and of its seventy patients only a handful were German; more than one-third were from Spain, followed by Swiss, Poles, Czechs and several other European nationalities (but no Americans, English or French, who had their own favourite establishments).[7]

As the fame of Davos spread, it found itself tarred with the brush of the Traviata myth, of TB as the aphrodisiac disease. Davos was a city of the young, with an atmosphere of frivolity and sexual excitement; patients flocked to concerts and dances while their doctors looked on benignly.[8] Karl Turban, a doctor who had been tubercular himself, opened a new kind of sanatorium in Davos in 1889. He called his regime the Iron Key: a rigid daily routine, strict hygiene and moral discipline (including careful segregation of the sexes). By the time Brandt arrived in Davos, all the sanatoria had followed Turban's lead. Patients now lived in three communities at once: a resort, a hospital and a prison. For a large part of the day they lay outside on their balconies, in all weathers, segregated by sex. They were allowed to read, but not to speak. Apart from the benefits of the fresh air, this routine was meant to shield the patients from the anxieties of normal existence; but anxiety was replaced by endless hours of crushing boredom. The only relief came from frequent and lavish meals, since it was part of the cure that patients should gain as much weight as possible.[9]

There was no effective drug therapy for TB until the introduction of streptomycin in the late 1940s. In fact, no treatment of any kind was effective before then. As early as 1921, epidemiological studies were showing that more patients were cured by staying quietly at home than by going to a sanatorium.[10] But this did not deter the surgeons from plying their art on consumptive patients. In the early decades of the twentieth century, sanatoria became surgical hospitals as well as places of rest. On the Continent, about 75 per cent of all patients were subjected to the pneumothorax operation – Brandt among them. Under only a local anaesthetic, a large hollow needle was inserted between the chest wall and the diseased lung; nitrogen was then pumped into the cavity, on the theory that collapsing the lung would enable it to heal.[11] At regular intervals, more nitrogen had to be injected, to prevent the lung re-inflating. If a pneumothorax did not succeed in fully collapsing the lung, sterner measures would be used, such as cutting away adhesions that attached the lung to the chest, or crushing the phrenic nerve to immobilise the diaphragm. Shock and infection were frequent complications of these procedures.

The sanatorium regime was not much better. F. R. Walter, an eminent British specialist, defended it by saying, 'sanatorium treatment is not so much a remedy as a way of life'.[12] Living at altitude was recommended not just because of the pure air, but also because patients needed to be psychologically 'above it all'. Thomas Mann's *The Magic Mountain* opens with a description of Hans Castorp's two-day journey from the Hamburg coastal plain up to Davos. As his train makes its final climb in the Alps, he feels that 'Home and regular living … lay fathoms deep beneath him.'[13] To be so high meant even to escape from time, as the people of the world below had to struggle with it. Instead, there was the invented time of the sanatorium, where patients were tyrannised by the strict schedules of the Iron Key. Roland Barthes, who spent years in sanatoria, compared the routine to that of a monastery, where submission to an arbitrary rule is supposed to bring spiritual peace.[14] The stronger patients at Davos could claim a portion of free time for themselves, outside the sanatorium; but the many diversions that the town had to offer could never make up for the ultimate futility of being marooned indefinitely on the heights.

It was a life worse than futile since Davos was a city of fear, where patients had to see their friends dying around them, and where youth and beauty gave no protection. Davos prepared Brandt for one of the key principles of the Surrealism he would later encounter in Paris: that to be alive means also to be surrounded by things that belong to death. There were more than 5,000 patients in residence while Brandt was at Davos, and some of them would be quietly carried off for burial every day. Horse-drawn hearses took them to the cemetery; from the Schatzalp sanatorium, 300 metres above the town, those who died in winter came down in toboggans. In *The Magic Mountain*, Hans Castorp finally prefers the battlefields of the First World War to the silent carnage of Davos.

To ward off thoughts of death, the town was full of amusements: concerts, teas, dances, libraries for French, Polish, Russian and English readers. There were clubs for stamp-collecting, chess, winter sports, photography. Brandt painted, took elocution lessons and could see all the important films of the time at the two cinemas. He became a compulsive reader – except for German authors. *The Magic Mountain* was published a month after Brandt arrived at Davos. Its setting was easily recognisable as the Waldsanatorium, where Mann's wife had been a patient in 1912, and its hero was a young man of the same sort as many of Brandt's Hamburg friends. The book created a storm of gossip in the town; Brandt would have heard it discussed, but in later life he refused to say anything about Mann except that he was a worthless writer. One who did impress him was Ernest Hemingway, who published a series of poems and stories on Spain in *Der Querschnitt*, a popular German monthly.[15] Brandt had many Spaniards as fellow-patients and he learned to speak Spanish. The mystique of Spain became part of his private mythology, a country he must see if he could only escape from his city of the ill.

The most attractive diversions, for all the patients, were those they created for each other. 'Six months at most after they get here,' says Settembrini in *The Magic Mountain*, 'these young people – and they are mostly young who come – have lost every idea they had, except flirtation and temperature.' At Castorp's sanatorium they are allowed to mingle on the terrace after lunch: 'absolutely idle, over-fed on a meat and sweet diet, and without exception feverish – [they] chattered and laughed, philandered, made eyes'.[16] There is nothing intrinsically erotic about TB, whose unappealing symptoms include body odour, impotence and spitting blood; the disease has no sexual mythology in Asia, Africa or Latin America. Even in Europe, those most likely to die of TB were not poets or artists, but manual workers. But the West clung to the myth that, as Dr Behrens puts it in *The Magic Mountain*, 'phthisis and concupiscence go together'.[17] Doctors like Turban tried to control the erotomania of their patients; but in a place like Davos no one needed the supposed stimulant of the TB bacillus to seek love. What else was there to look forward to? The psychiatrist Eric Wittkower, after interviewing hundreds of consumptives, decided that the main thing they had in common was 'an inordinate need for affection'.[18] Brandt may have fallen in love with one of the señoritas at the Schweizerhof, but if so he kept quiet about it. By the time he was able to visit Spain, it was with the Hungarian woman who became his wife.

Brandt had a Kodak camera while he was at Davos, and the Schweizerhof had a darkroom for the use of its patients. There was a photography shop in the town that advertised 'everything the amateur needs'. A fine panorama of the town that appeared in *Lilliput* may be by Brandt, and a few other snaps taken at Davos survive in his friends' picture albums.[19] But the greater influence on his work came from the extraordinary visual qualities of the town, with its clear air, brilliant alpine light, and contrasts between the snowfields above and the gorges and evergreen forests below. The landscape around Davos consisted of blocks of light and dark in juxtaposition, sharply delineated. The printing style that Brandt preferred in his later years, where saturated blacks and clear whites drown out intermediate details, was a throwback to the play of light in Davos.[20] Another source of deep contrast lay in the pervasiveness of X-ray photography in sanatorium life. Martin Gasser notes that the patients carried everywhere, along with their sputum bottle, a pouch containing the latest X-ray of their lungs.[21] These plates were photographs in reverse, ghastly likenesses of the patient's inner state, where dark spots showed hidden places of infection. They were the shadows of conventional portraits that showed seemingly healthy young men and women, enjoying the pleasures of the town. The X-ray camera was an instrument of fate, predicting the future; later, Brandt would say that this was the essence of a good portrait taken with a standard camera.

There were two rival views of TB in the sanatorium world: one that it was an organic disease that could be controlled by science, the other that it was, at the deepest level, a disease of the patient's will. The idea of TB as a psychosomatic disease effectively made its victims responsible for their own misfortune. This is the complaint of a patient in *The Mermaids*, a novel about sanatorium life written by Brandt's first wife, Eva Boros:

> People no longer have any respect for our illness. Some fifty years ago we were the tragic heroes of novels and plays. Good old Freud, he put paid to that. Now we are looked upon as shirkers; parasites. It seems we *want* to be ill – I daresay the diagnosis was right, but as for the cure? How can you cure fear? It's our most powerful emotion.[22]

What was real beyond doubt was the terror, loneliness and resentment that consumptives suffered because of the conditions under which they lived, regardless of any speculation about their childhood histories or unconscious drives. Yet there was always the seductive idea that if you could cure the patient's inner conflicts, you could cure the disease. G. W. Pabst's *Secrets of a Soul* appeared in 1926, the first film to represent a psychoanalytic case history.[23] It popularised the idea of analysis as a cure for disease, and some of its scenes seem to have been filed away in Brandt's visual memory – especially its use of empty rooms as a trigger for fantasy. *The Magic Mountain* also features attempts to explain TB by the new science of psychoanalysis. 'Dr Krokowski' tells his patients that organic disease is an outlet for 'forbidden and hystericised emotions'.[24] Buried conflicts speed up the body's metabolism – the notorious Davos fever of half a degree Celsius – creating a friendly environment for the TB bacillus.

Brandt was already familiar with the idea of a psychoanalytic cure when, in the winter of 1926-7, the Viennese physician and psychoanalyst Wilhelm Stekel spent two months in Davos. He was the guest of a grateful patient who was the medical director of a sanatorium.[25] Before his conversion to Freudianism, Stekel had opposed the high-altitude regime, arguing that patients were better off being treated at home. Later, he recalled, 'I learned that the psychic component plays a formidable part in tuberculosis. Many people become ill because they are tired of life and have a wish to die. Many years later in Davos, Switzerland, a famous lung specialist said to me, "I think you should treat all my patients".'[26] Stekel was the kind of person who would call anyone who agreed with him a famous specialist. But Davos gossip took note of Stekel's presence and Brandt quietly decided that his claim to be able to cure TB by psychoanalysis was at least worth a try.

By the spring of 1927 Brandt had been at Davos for two and a half years, with nearly two years at Agra before that. His life had become more interesting as he gained strength, but his doctors could promise him only an indefinitely prolonged stay, with no chance of marrying or following a profession. If Stekel was to be believed, neither living at altitude nor submitting to the Iron Key would ever cure him; what was needed was to hack at the psychic roots of his disease, through treatment at Stekel's 'Active-Analytic Clinic' in Vienna. Brandt's brother Rolf was now living there, ready to be his guide to the great post-imperial city. Brandt's parents agreed to pay for his move and his treatment by Stekel; what he surely did not tell them was that the doctors at the Schweizerhof warned him he would be dead in a few months if he left.[27] Perhaps Brandt had seen too many friends who stayed, and died anyway; and there was always gossip that the sanatoria issued such warnings to all their patients, to keep the money flowing in.[28] It followed that the only way to escape the disease was to change those conditions: to go down from the magic mountain and take one's chances in the rough and tumble of ordinary life. Early in May, Brandt packed up and took the little mountain railway that wound down from Davos to Landquart, where one changed for Zurich and then went on to Vienna. It was a few days after his twenty-third birthday and he was determined, whatever the risk, to start a new life.[29]

Bill Brandt with Zeiss-Ikon Miroflex, Grundslee, 1929, photographer unknown

4 Vienna: The *Schwarzwaldkinder*

Wilhelm Stekel, the psychoanalyst who drew Brandt to Vienna, was born into a Jewish family at Czernowitz, Bukovina, in 1868. He took his medical degree in Vienna and was an early recruit to psychoanalysis, being analysed by Freud himself. His flamboyant personality infuriated his colleagues, and he was even accused of inventing case histories in order to have something to say at clinical conferences. Stekel left the Freudians in 1912 and set up his own psychoanalytic clinic in Vienna, but tried constantly to be re-admitted to the official body. One of his heresies was impatience with the orthodox Freudian technique of gradual self-revelation through dream analysis and free association; instead, he would quickly make up his mind about what was wrong and tell the patient what to do about it. Stekel is said to have analysed 10,000 people, and he was a walking encyclopaedia of every neurosis and perversion in Vienna. Even his enemies admitted that he was capable of rapid and brilliant insights; but he was also something of a charlatan, and an unscrupulous seducer who considered his women patients fair game. His copious writings hammered away at the idea that every disease was caused by a hidden emotional conflict; the standard joke about him was that he believed all diseases were psychosomatic, except for his own![1]

Stekel had a clinic in the centre of Vienna, but also saw patients at his home, a country villa outside the city in Salmannsdorf, one of the wine villages of the Vienna woods. In May 1927 it would have seemed a paradise of flowers and budding vineyards after the austerity of Davos, with its meadows, pine trees and crags. Stekel had arranged for Brandt to stay a kilometre from his home, at the grandly named 'Waldhotel'; in fact it was a modest two-storey winemaker's house at the edge of the woods, with a few guest rooms.[2] There were plenty of charming *Heuriger* (wine taverns) within walking distance, and the whole area was the playground of Vienna. Springtime in a wine village, full of Viennese out for a good time, would be an agreeable kind of shock therapy for a refugee from sanatorium life.

The serious business of Brandt's day would still remain: to walk along the country lane into Salmannsdorf and put himself for an hour into the hands of Dr Stekel.[3] Brandt was a classic type of Freudian patient: the 'handsome-with-problems' son of a high bourgeois family, a sensitive soul who was uncertain of his place in the world. Stekel called his method 'active-analytic' because he would not sit around while patients slowly uncovered their subconscious fantasy life. Instead, he brushed their defences aside and plunged straight into the deepest recesses of their psyche. The American author John Gunther wrote that Stekel possessed 'the most subtle, the most closely packed, the most flashingly intuitive mind I have ever had the good fortune to meet'.[4]

Apart from his active method, Stekel had a theory of symbols that helps to explain Brandt's future practice as a photographer. Stekel's 'parapathic' symbol 'manifests the attributes of a genuine symbol in magnified form'. Such symbols are produced by three psychological mechanisms. *Repression* keeps the true meaning of the symbol out of consciousness; *condensation* draws a variety of emotional drives into a single, powerful focus; and through *displacement* a strong feeling 'is deflected from some forbidden or taboo object and attached to the symbol'. The parapathic symbol fulfils a wish, but in an obscure way; it stands for a mystery to which no one has the key – 'the symbol is so continuously changed that it is finally a riddle to the fetish lover himself'.[5]

Stekel's theory suits the atmosphere of Brandt's photographs, because it assumes a more complex link between symbol and meaning than in the Freudian system. 'The fetish lover is a dreamer,' Stekel says, 'and that is why the symbolism of dreams is so closely related to fetishism.' But the fetishistic artist is like someone who dreams while awake, and can give aesthetic form to emotions that, in a dream, remain elusive and confused. He can invest objects or situations with a deep emotional significance that viewers will respond to without knowing anything about the fetishist's hidden motives. 'Brandt's art,' Ian Jeffrey says, 'looks, in many cases, very like the dreamwork of Stekel's clients, for like that dreamwork it is as fascinated by significant objects as it is neglectful of context.'[6] This gives us a clue to Brandt's elliptical relationship with the socially critical documentary photography of the 1930s and 1940s. His subjects may suffer from injustice or be recognisable social types; but they also inhabit a Brandtian world where 'they do things differently'. Brandt's documentary images thus become more deeply subversive than ones that are simply a cry for justice.

Brandt's character had been formed in three enclosed societies: his high bourgeois German family, the Bismarckschule at Elmshorn and the Schweizerhof sanatorium. All three were ritualistic and tyrannical, controlled first by Brandt's domineering father, then by the masters and boys who had tormented him, and finally by Dr Turban's Iron Key. In Stekel's consulting room, looking out into the blossoming of spring in the *Wienerwalde*, Brandt was led to understand how his conflicts produced symptoms and symbols. To do more than this, and to make his private world into one that could be communicated to others through art, would be a great leap in his development. Yet after he became an artist Brandt would remain an example of Stekel's 'fetishistic personality', for whom 'the fetish becomes the symbol of all his feeling. It represents the man's faithfulness to the objects of childhood.'[7]

Stekel believed in rapid analysis, but Brandt made it even more rapid by breaking off the sessions, after three months at most.[8] Stekel's intrusiveness may well have aroused more memories and conflicts than Brandt was willing or able to face. Stekel's view of TB was that its victims suffered from a 'wish to die'; he would quickly have got at the story of Brandt's ordeal at school, and of the mental and physical torments inflicted on him at the sanatorium. Stekel was well known as a specialist in sexual

Lyena Barjansky
reads Brandt's
palm, about 1928,
photographer unknown

deviations, having worked with Krafft-Ebing and published books on fetishism, sadism and masochism.[9] Unlike Freud, Stekel was inclined to take mistreatment of children by their parents as reality rather than fantasy. He believed that many sexual difficulties in adult life were caused by repressed hatred of authoritarian parents.

Brandt's sexual troubles were present by the time he saw Stekel, and may even have been his secret reason for choosing him. But Stekel had a ham-fisted approach to sex that soon had his patient deeply upset. Through his brother Rolf, Brandt had become friendly with a sixteen-year-old Russian schoolgirl called Lyena Barjansky.[10] She was the daughter of a Jewish businessman from Odessa, who had been imprisoned by the Reds for being a capitalist. When the Whites re-captured the city, in 1919, Barjansky got on a boat to Trieste with his wife and daughter, and went on to set up a textile business in Vienna. Despite his troubles with the Reds, Lyena's father was an open-minded man who sent her to the bohemian and mildly left-wing school for girls run by Dr Eugenie Schwarzwald.

Lyena was a tall, cheerful, outgoing young woman, with an emotionally direct manner that fits the stereotype of 'typically Russian'. She appealed to Brandt's family myth of belonging to a Russian and English family, rather than a German one. Lyena first met Brandt walking in the woods above Salmannsdorf and found him 'incredibly handsome … like Jesus Christ'. Rolf was equally good-looking and could be taken for Brandt's twin; together, they left Lyena open-mouthed. She fell head-over-heels in love with Brandt and worshipped him for the rest of his life. But at this point it was still just a teenage infatuation, by a chaste and very naive girl. Although many men fell in love with her, for a long time Lyena formed no lasting attachment, other than with Brandt.

Ester Cotton found her 'flirtatious mentally but not sexually – the least interested in sex of our group'.

When Stekel got wind of the affair, though, he decided that Lyena was some kind of sexual vampire who wanted to devour his patient. It is hard to imagine why Stekel should come up with such an idea; perhaps he thought Russian women were sexually aggressive, or imagined Brandt to be a specially passive and vulnerable young man.[11] He may have seen Lyena around the village, displaying more affection for Brandt than he thought seemly. Whatever the reason, Stekel told Brandt that he should immediately break off his affair. This came as a great shock to Lyena who, in her own words, 'was completely innocent and didn't know you kissed a man differently from your mother'. Faced with Stekel's demand that he get rid of his devouring girlfriend, Brandt, sensibly enough, decided to get rid of Stekel. He didn't want even to be seen by Stekel on the footpaths around Salmannsdorf – especially in Lyena's company – and in mid-September left the Waldhotel for good. So ended Brandt's first encounter with psychoanalysis. But he probably didn't leave because it did nothing for him; more likely, it did too much.

Rolf Brandt had also gone to see an orthodox Freudian in Vienna; he left after one session and remained hostile to psychoanalysis all his life.[12] In spite of the fiasco with Stekel, Bill Brandt kept in touch with the unconscious, especially in his art. And irresponsible as Stekel was in many ways, he delivered on his original promise to Brandt. A medical examination a few months later found Brandt to be free of active disease, and he never suffered a recurrence, despite living for some forty years with two women who were repeatedly hospitalised for TB. Within a few months, too, he had found an artistic vocation that he worked at for more than fifty years. Even if Stekel was something of a charlatan, his treatment of Brandt at least coincided with a dramatic recovery of health and purpose in his life.

In leaving Davos for Vienna, Brandt was also re-joining forces with his brother Rolf, who had succeeded in another kind of escape. Rolf had left Hamburg in 1921, when he was fifteen, to go to boarding school at Godesberg, near Bonn.[13] More outgoing and adaptable than Brandt, he was happy enough at school. But he was not very interested in the standard academic curriculum, and after four years he returned to Hamburg to do the expected thing for a young Brandt: he enrolled in a business college to learn how to be an international salesman. A younger son would not normally expect a partnership in one of the family firms; rather, he would be shunted around Europe and perhaps Latin America or Asia, until he found a berth in Germany looking after some piece of the world's trade. L. W. Brandt, to his credit, realised after a year that Rolf would never make a businessman, and agreed to send him to an academy for the history of art and theatre in Berlin. From there, Rolf went on to the Theaterschule Kalbeck in Vienna as part of an extensive training, paid for by his father, to be an actor and director.[14] He arrived early in 1927, just in time for a reunion with his elder brother. They had seen each other only intermittently for seven years, since Brandt went off to the Bismarckschule in the autumn of 1919.

Once they left psychoanalysis behind, the two brothers were drawn into a different kind of Viennese cult. Dr Eugenie Schwarzwald was one of the three leading intellectual hostesses – *Salondamen*, they were called – in the city.[15] Born Eugenie

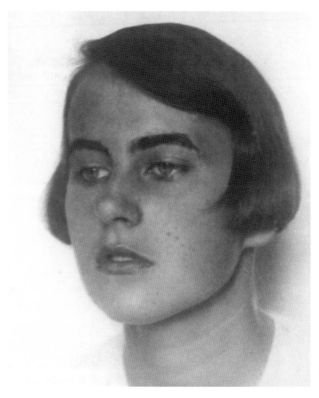

Ester Brandt, about 1929,
photographer unknown

Nussbaum in Galicia in 1872, she married a Viennese banker, Hermann
Schwarzwald. In 1900 she received one of the first Ph.D.s to be granted to a woman,
in medieval literature from the University of Zurich (at that time, the University of
Vienna would not admit women to the Ph.D). During the First World War
Schwarzwald arranged for hungry Viennese children to go and stay with families in
Denmark (the pianist Rudolf Serkin was one of these 'Wienerkinder'); in Vienna she
set up community kitchens in poor districts, with furniture designed by Adolf Loos.
After the collapse of the Budapest revolutionary government in 1919, she provided
meals and lodging for Hungarian refugee intellectuals, including Georg Lukacs;
Robert Musil was also housed by her for a while.[16]

The backing for Schwarzwald's good works came from her husband Hermann.
One of the leading financiers in Vienna, he was given credit for ending post-war
inflation by stabilising the schilling; when offered his political reward, he is said to have
replied, 'a Jew should not be the Minister of Finance'.[17] Hermann was short and
chubby, and walked with a stick due to childhood TB; he trailed amiably after his
energetic wife, who did him the favour of welcoming his mistress, Dr Mariedel Stiasny,
another progressive educator from Berlin. From her Loos-designed house at
Josefstaderstrasse 68, Eugenie Schwarzwald seemed to have a finger in everything that
went on in art, literature, theatre or music in the city. English society had no real
equivalent to Schwarzwald; one has to imagine Lady Ottoline Morrell, Beatrice Webb,
A. S. Neill and Margot Asquith, all rolled into one. It was said that every person of
talent in Vienna had ten patronesses lying in wait to catch them. As in Britain, though,
a patroness often had to suffer being parodied by those she had helped: Schwarzwald

Boys and girls at Grundlsee, 1929, photographer unknown

Rolf Brandt, top right; Bill Brandt, third from right; Helmuth von Moltke, fifth from right

Freya (Deichmann) von Moltke, third from right; Lyena Barjansky, fifth from right

became 'Hofrätin Schwarz-Gelber' in Karl Kraus's *Letzten Tage der Menschheit*, and 'Madame Tuzzi' in Robert Musil's *The Man Without Qualities*.

Eugenie Schwarzwald was domineering, slightly ridiculous and had a heart of gold. A great deal of her patronage went to help children, the poor and the unrecognised. Young protégés might, to be sure, bring her glory in the future; and the unkind hinted that Schwarzwald liked to surround herself with handsome young men. If so, this was no more than a foible. She enjoyed playing host and adviser to young people, and there were as many dazzling young ladies in her circle as there were decorative young men. She had an eye for real talent, not just a pretty exterior, and the proof is in those whom she took under her wing: they included Rudolf Serkin, the philosopher Karl Popper, the novelist Jakob Wassermann, the actress Helene Weigel, the anti-Nazi conspirator Helmuth von Moltke, and Bill Brandt himself.

Schwarzwald's main professional interest was in education, and in 1901 she founded in Vienna the Schwarzwaldschule for girls, which thrived until it was shut down after the *Anschluss* in 1938. It was a progressive school that encouraged the girls to develop all their talents, and Schwarzwald recruited many of her artistic friends to teach there, such as Kokoschka, Schoenberg and Loos. Another incubator for talent was the gathering that she ran each year at the Grundlsee, a picturesque lake in the Salzkammergut. In 1920 she and her husband bought the Villa Seeblick, a small hotel that they turned into a private summer colony. At first they ran the villa as a summer convalescent home for invalid children, but by the late 1920s Eugenie was turning more to cultural interests as the social crises provoked by the war became less acute. Grundlsee became a place where she and Hermann could relax in the company of a picked group of young people, drawn from favoured pupils at her school and young men vaguely idealistic or interested in the arts. They went to Grundlsee to sit at the Frau Doktor's feet, to swim in the lake and walk in the mountains, to hear Serkin play the piano in the evenings and to flirt with each other.[18] About twenty or thirty would be there at a time, and they paid a modest rate for their rooms and meals. Almost all of those who went to Grundlsee came from privileged backgrounds in Austria, Germany or Denmark; they had to be open-minded and progressive, but there was no strict political line.[19]

Although the Grundlsee youth spent most of the daylight hours in the open air, they scorned the *volkisch* ideology of German and Austrian youth movements – which by the late Twenties were becoming more and more influenced by the 'blood and soil' values of Nazism. Pictures of the young people of Grundlsee make them look like Aryan cult figures, with their casual dress and blond beauty; but there are no badges, peasant regalia or *Lederhosen* (in which Hitler liked to have himself photographed). Schwarzwald was an assimilated Jew who wanted to create a cadre of youth who would rise above nationality and ethnicity; 80 per cent of the students at her school were Jewish, but it was considered bad form at Grundlsee to pay any attention to who was Jewish and who not. The vision was to build what Musil had called the 'spirit of a new humanity', above the militant certainties of Communists, Nazis or Zionists.[20] Their hopes may now seem naive, but in England such groups – Bloomsbury, neo-pagans and the like – could run their natural course unmolested. Grundlsee would be destroyed in the Thirties by the barbarism gathering around it, not through any fault of its own.

Life at Grundlsee was informal but not simple, or at least not self-consciously so. Hermann Schwarzwald kept on his suit and tie, Eugenie dressed as if for a garden party; there was a stream of eminent visitors to discuss the political and financial affairs of Central Europe. The young people shared spartan rooms with iron bedsteads and plank floors, but with high ceilings and a great balcony looking down on the lake and across to the Carinthian Alps. In summer, the meadows were full of gentians. Much of the day was spent in the water; sometimes they bathed in the nude, sometimes not – but never self-consciously one or the other.[21] It was not a free-love colony, though love affairs did go on. Dr Schwarzwald had her room upstairs (Hermann and Dr Stiasny were below), where the young people would sit around her, talking far into the night. She was somewhat puritanical, and the young did not tell her everything they got up to in other places. But marriages as well as brief affairs were hatched at the Villa Seeblick.

Many of the Grundlsee visitors were friends in Vienna for the rest of the year; others came from elsewhere in Europe and it was at Grundlsee that we can see together, in scores of informal photographs, the core of friends to whom Brandt would remain attached for the rest of his life. His brother Rolf would first have come into Dr Schwarzwald's orbit through the Kalbeck Theatre School; he then brought in a school friend from Godesberg, Hans Deichmann. The Deichmanns were one of the leading banking families of Cologne, living in a mansion and running a carriage with liveried coachmen.[22] Hans, Rolf and Lyena Barjansky (though not Brandt) went to Grundlsee for the first time in 1927. In 1928 Brandt went, for the first of three years in succession; another newcomer was the sixteen-year-old Ester Bonnesen from Copenhagen, where her father was a professor of mathematics. She had been invited through Dr Schwarzwald's friendship with Karen Michaelis, a well-known feminist writer in

Dr Schwarzwald with Jowo (left) and Helmuth
von Moltke, 1929, photographer unknown

Denmark. Ester was small and dark, with a piquant, lively appearance that Brandt would take advantage of in some of his best Thirties pictures. She was introduced to the Grundlsee way of doing things when she swam out to a raft on her first day and was completely ignored by Rolf. He became less stand-offish after a while, and five years later they would marry. Ester was a fine gymnast, chosen for the Danish national team; later she became a physiotherapist who did pioneering work with brain-damaged children.

If Brandt and Rolf were a striking pair of brothers at Grundlsee, they were matched by the von Moltkes, Helmuth James and Joachim (Jowo). Three years younger than Brandt, Helmuth was more solid and imposing, with Viking looks. He belonged to Germany's most famous military dynasty, and his father still had a run-down estate in Prussia; his mother was South-African.[23] In 1929 Helmuth met Hans Deichmann's younger sister, Freya, at Grundlsee, and fell in love with her. When his father died prematurely, Helmuth abandoned his legal career; he married Freya and went back to put the family estate on its feet.

Helmuth von Moltke and Bill Brandt stood for two fundamentally opposed solutions to the problem of Germany. They came from different segments of the traditional German elite: Brandt from the Hamburg merchant bankers, Helmuth from the Prussian *Junkers*. Both were idealists and perfectionists – Brandt more in an artistic sense, Helmuth as a builder and organiser. The two young men were temperamentally so different that, despite the common ground of Grundlsee, they never became friends. Helmuth wanted to engage with the world, starting from the base of his family estate at Kreisau; Brandt was the artist and dreamer, with no interest in building in Germany anything at all. Whether or not they were Jewish, most of the Grundlsee group had become refugees from Germany by the beginning of the war; only Helmuth, Freya and Hans Deichmann tried to keep the Grundlsee idea alive inside the Nazi regime, with tragic consequences.

Eugenie Schwarzwald was above all a great teacher. Having no children of her own, she made no secret of the parental expectations that she imposed on her young followers at Grundlsee, who were jokingly called the 'Schwarzwaldkinder'. Some took her moral guidance and political principles deeply to heart; others found her intrusive and overbearing, and resisted her spell. Hans Deichmann gave Schwarzwald credit for his courageous acts of resistance to Nazism during the war, and Helmuth von Moltke's vision of Germany after Hitler owed a great deal to the liberal pacifism he absorbed from Schwarzwald's teaching and example.[24] For some, Schwarzwald's gift was a more private one, to create a charmed circle that gave young people hope in life's infinite possibilities. The darker side of her work was what Robert Musil called 'this juxtaposition of do-gooding and doing oneself good': the broad streak of egotism in even so tirelessly benevolent a person.[25]

It was precisely the over-insistent quality of Schwarzwald's idealism that caused Bill Brandt to avoid any direct participation in her causes. Her life's work was to raise and redeem German culture, while Brandt believed this was a futile task. His view of Germany was already a deeply cynical one, based on the emotional traumas of his school days. Freya von Moltke recalls him as different from his brother Rolf, who was straightforward and with an easy sense of humour; it was not that Brandt had any obvious signs of neurosis, but still 'you couldn't look into him'. It could be argued, of course, that it was Brandt who was the most sensible of the Grundlsee group, since the reality of Germany was going to become infinitely worse than even he could imagine in 1928. But mainly he was an outsider and anarchist by temperament, unwilling to commit himself to even the most idealistic design for living. He formed lifelong friendships among Schwarzwald's young followers, while refusing to be any kind of follower himself. Able to observe and appreciate what was going on around him, he could never place himself at the centre of it. But these were probably the right qualities for the vocation he now found in Vienna.

Ezra Pound, 1928

5 Becoming a Photographer

In the autumn of 1927 Brandt came down the hill to Vienna from Salmannsdorf, to avoid further contact with Stekel and to make a life for himself in the city. His new home was the Pension Cottage at Hasenauerstrasse 12, now the Hotel Park-Villa in the nineteenth district. It was an upper-middle-class neighbourhood of large villas and gardens, with the Turkenschanz park a short walk up the hill. What strikes one about the Pension Cottage, where Brandt would live for the next two and a half years, is that it is very much the kind of house in which people of his class lived in Hamburg: an impressive Jugendstil mansion from the late nineteenth century, with large rooms and a terrace where one could take meals looking out on the quiet garden at the back, with the hooded crows strutting about. At the time Brandt lived there, trams ran along the Hasenauerstrasse and reached the centre of Vienna in twenty minutes.

Among the European capitals, Vienna was the one most diminished by the war. Austria had lost nearly 90 per cent of its population in the peace settlement, a mortal blow to Vienna's economy. Its great administrative buildings and palaces contrasted with the shabby and dispirited people in the streets. History here was running backwards, as the power and vitality of the pre-1914 capital ebbed away. Vienna still had a hectic intellectual life and most of its old pleasures, even in its decadence. But Brandt was not the sort of young man to spend his day plotting in coffee houses or pursuing the legendary *süsse Madeln* of Vienna.[1] The Pension Cottage was the epitome of comfort and respectability, a place that Brandt's wealthy relatives might easily visit and approve.

Brandt encountered in Vienna the problem of nationalities, which forced him to define his own. Hamburg had an overwhelmingly Nordic population; in Vienna, all the tribes and languages of Europe filled the streets. It was a significantly Jewish city (Jews formed about 10 per cent of the population and perhaps one-third of all intellectuals), and Brandt formed many of his crucial relationships with Jews. The owner of his *pension* – to take a case typical of modern Vienna – was a woman called Melitta Kramer. In the 1938 Vienna directory she is still listed as living there, but no longer as the proprietor of the *pension*; after 1940, she disappears from the address altogether. During the war years, no one at all is listed as living at the pension. Such patterns are common in the Vienna directories, and usually have the same explanation. Four days after the *Anschluss*, on 16 March 1938, Adolf Eichmann arrived in Vienna to deal with its Jewish population.[2] In the course of that year, all Jewish property was confiscated and sold at auction for ridiculously low prices. From October 1941 onwards the Vienna Jews were deported: to the Lódz ghetto and its extermination camp at Chelmno; to Theresienstadt; or to Auschwitz. The chances are high that Melitta Kramer was one of them. Meanwhile, someone in favour with the Nazis would have taken up quarters in her *pension*. Apart from his school trauma, Brandt's bitter anti-German feelings would be fuelled by the fact that four – and probably all five – of the main figures in his early days in Vienna were Jewish: his analyst Stekel, his patron Dr Schwarzwald, his photography teacher Kolliner, his girlfriend Lyena Barjansky and his landlady Melitta Kramer. One good reason for Brandt to erase the record of his years in Vienna was that, after 1939, no one he cared for still lived there.

Vienna brought about another twist in Brandt's German identity. The German spoken in the city was so different from Hamburg as to be almost a separate language, and Vienna's mixed nationalities also brought their own languages with them. Anyone from the eastern parts of the former Empire – Czechs, Slovaks, Galicians, Hungarians, Croats, Serbs – was still free to go and live in the capital. There was also a great deal of anti-German prejudice, especially after Austria's post-war loss of power and territory. Dr Schwarzwald even suggested to Brandt that he should change his name in order to avoid being so obviously German.[3] His friends from the Vienna period all called Brandt 'Billy'; before taking Schwarzwald's advice he had gone by his second name, Wilhelm (like the ex-Kaiser, but shortened to the informal 'Willy').[4] At the sanatorium in Davos he had registered as W. Brandt. The curious aspect of this story is that Schwarzwald's husband was called Hermann, which was Brandt's first name. Perhaps his name had given him trouble, and Schwarzwald decided it was a name to get rid of if one could! In any case, the pattern of change and concealment is there: Willy in Hamburg and Davos, Billy in Vienna, and in due course Bill in London.[5]

Apart from giving Brandt a new name, Dr Schwarzwald decided that his life of drifting around Vienna and going to his sessions with Stekel would not do:

> She reproached him; he could not go on like this (psychoanalysis). If he wanted to get well he had to work. He replied in a somewhat whining tone that he did not know what he could do. Then the Fraudoktor said: 'Let me handle it.' She took the telephone and called the then top woman photographer in Vienna, [Trude] Fleischmann: 'Tomorrow I'll send you a young German friend of mine as an apprentice.' And that is how Bill Brandt became a photographer.[6]

This is Hans Deichmann's story, told some seventy years after the event and somewhat embroidered, as such stories tend to be. Rolf Brandt's version gave his brother a bit more initiative: Rolf said that Schwarzwald started ticking off possible professions on her fingers, and Billy stopped her when she came to photography. Ester, Rolf's wife, recalls that Billy had never had a camera in his hand in his life until Schwarzwald told him to pick one up: 'she had an enormous talent for telling people what they should be doing'. But Brandt had a Kodak camera in Davos, and the view of the town in the February 1948 *Lilliput* is probably by him. If so, it was his first professional photograph, taken before he ever met Schwarzwald. Brandt certainly did not want to give her credit for making him a photographer; as Ester put it, 'he was not someone who liked being recommended'. He preferred to mystify his beginnings, and in later life he stoutly maintained that he had been an apprentice in Switzerland rather than Vienna.[7]

The Schweizerhof sanatorium had its own darkroom, to cater to the craze for photography among TB patients that Mann amusingly describes in *The Magic Mountain*.[8] Brandt may even have hung around a portrait studio in the town, providing a grain of truth for his claim to have been apprenticed in Switzerland. But Schwarzwald did play a role in getting him launched, even if it was an exaggeration to say that she 'brought Billy back to life' by making him a photographer.[9] Her choice of a profession was shrewd, given Brandt's distaste for conventional education, his keen visual sense, and a medical history that ruled out any of the more strenuous ways of making a living. Nonetheless, Brandt was precisely the kind of person who would find it funny if Schwarzwald told him to do something about which he already knew a lot more than she realised.

Schwarzwald may have approached Trude Fleischmann about taking Brandt, but the photographer who actually engaged him was a more obscure figure, Grete Kolliner.[10] A former student at the Schwarzwaldschule, she was thirty-five years old in 1927; she had a studio at Frankgasse 6, near the Votivpark and the university.[11] This was a few minutes by tram from the Pension Cottage where Brandt lived. Like Fleischmann and many other female photographers in Vienna, Kolliner was Jewish, and photography was considered one of the few suitable professions for the unmarried daughters of the Jewish bourgeoisie.[12] She lived with her mother on the Peter Jordanstrasse, in the nineteenth district on the western outskirts of Vienna.[13] Brandt seems to have got on well with her, and he certainly acquired many skills in her studio.

That Brandt began his career in a studio, and in Vienna, explains a great deal about his style. After the First World War, Vienna became the capital of a country of six million instead of fifty-two million. It was an overdeveloped head on a shrunken body, with too much of everything – the most famous symbol of the post-1918 absurdity was a gigantic Marine Ministry for a country that no longer had access to the sea.[14] It had, of course, too many photography studios; photographers left for Berlin or further west, and those who remained had to scramble for a living. The bread-and-butter work for a studio would be to take portraits of the wives and children of the bourgeoisie, and the results had to be guaranteed an improvement on nature. This meant that a photographer's formal training was as much in art as in technique.

Wolfgang Suschitzky, who attended the Graphische Lehr und Versuchsanstalt in Vienna at the end of the 1920s, took classes in still life and life drawing as part of his photography training. The emphasis of the curriculum was on portraiture, and in Vienna it was taken for granted that every portrait would need to be re-touched. A standard studio camera was the size of a television set and took 16 x 21cm glass plates. Exposures were made approximately, by removing the lens cover and counting, then adjusting the results in the darkroom. But this was only the beginning: once developed, the plate would be put on a light table and the re-toucher went to work with knife, pencil, brush and the other tools of the trade. The re-toucher was a kind of portrait painter, working from the preliminary impression made by the camera. Women were often very good at this work, and a male photographer commonly married a wife who re-touched (for example, Rudolf and Anna Koppitz). Apart from such improvements as the removal of blemishes or crooked teeth, finished portraits were expected to show absolutely smooth and uniform skin texture; limbs and waists were routinely slenderised.[15] In the commercial and aesthetic context of a Vienna studio, the idea of photographic 'truth' was largely irrelevant.

Vienna studios worked hand-in-glove with theatre, dance, cabaret and popular culture. The city supported an enormous range of live performances, and each actor or dancer would go to a studio for publicity pictures. These might appear in such magazines as *Wiener Magazin*, *Die Buhne* ('The Stage') or the left-wing *Der Kuckuck*.[16] The Vienna press was remarkably uninhibited and routinely published nudes of performers, so long as no pubic hair could be seen; all kinds of kitsch erotic scenes and trick shots made up the visual world of a stroller in the city.[17] Publicity postcards for dancers and actresses, some of them nude, were sold in theatre lobbies. Kolliner did her share of this work, which might involve even more blatant artifice than portraits of bourgeois matrons. Apart from the standard tricks of lighting, re-touching and re-photographing, studio work would include a procession of performers who would pose in costume for scenes from their act. The d'Ora studio in Vienna actually had a mock stage with curtains to help with its publicity work. The Viennese studio camera was a magic box that produced fantasies, jokes, a whole world of 'hyperreality', as Moholy-Nagy called it in 1926.[18] Brandt got his start by pointing his camera towards a set where events were prepared for reproduction, rather than towards an external reality to be stalked and captured.

As Brandt began, so he continued. Even when he became a photo-journalist his approach remained that of a studio photographer, and he was scornful of those who took what he called 'snap-shots' (originally, the instant reaction of a hunter who fired without taking aim). The photography studio of 1920s Vienna still had a lot in common with the classic artist's studio, where a painting was completed through gradual re-working, and with the help of various tools. Beyond this, photography for Brandt would always be an art of composition in the traditional sense, an art he had acquired through obsessive study in picture galleries and books of reproductions. In the Kolliner studio, Brandt would have been taught how to light his subjects – all studio portraits would be artificially lit with floods – and the full range of darkroom techniques: developing, re-touching, enlarging, printing and cropping. These were all tasks that he took in hand personally throughout his career.

The only known examples of Brandt's work with Kolliner are three portraits, all probably taken in the spring of 1928 within six months of his joining the studio. Ezra Pound was in Vienna from 28 April to 15 June, to attend the premiere of an opera by George Antheil and to further the career of his mistress, the violinist Olga Rudge. Dr Schwarzwald met him and arranged for Brandt to take his portrait.[19] Brandt followed this up with a portrait of Antheil, and one of another of Schwarzwald's friends, Arnold Schoenberg. The Pound portrait set the tone for Brandt's later portraits, which were almost all of creative people – writers, artists, actors or musicians. But he was not happy with the picture, and did not allow it to be reproduced or exhibited until the very end of his life.[20] The pose is in typical Vienna studio style, with Pound's face highlighted against a plain white backdrop. In his later portraits Brandt worked very differently, placing his sitters within a context to suit their personality. He usually avoids his subjects' direct gaze, posing them looking transversely across the pictorial field, or with a meditative look that doesn't focus on where the camera is placed. The Pound portrait breaks all these rules, but gains something in doing so. Pound's tight grin, and the divergence of focus between his right eye and his left, disorganise his features, so that his expression becomes an uneasy mixture of joviality, scrutiny of the viewer, suspicion and menace. The trilby hat becomes a theatrical prop, signifying 'bohemian'; the dark underside of its brim balances the huge white wings of Pound's shirt-collar, and the lighting of the hat makes it look as if the head is turning independently underneath it. The portrait captures a desperado quality in Pound, making him into a threatening figure out of German Expressionist cinema. By Brandt's rule that a good portrait should predict its subject's future, this one indeed shows us the sociopathic Pound who would emerge over the next fifteen years.[21]

It is hard to assess Kolliner's creative influence on Brandt, when so little is known about her career.[22] Still, everything suggests that he was not a passive follower of Kolliner, and quickly started to follow his own course. The business arrangement he made with her is unknown, but it seems likely that he was not a regular employee, because he was able to spend so much time travelling away from Vienna. Probably he worked without pay, being supported by his father; he may even have paid Kolliner a student's fee. Freedom to travel also allowed him to develop his own photographic interests, which involved mainly outdoor shots, and all kinds of creative possibilities beyond the rigid conventions of the studio.

In Vienna, Brandt also considered another possible profession, architecture. He did not follow up the idea, but did maintain a passionate interest in architecture all his life; his archives contain more than 300 negatives of buildings. He took pictures of Adolf Loos's famous Moller house, a landmark of modernism and an example of Loos's maxim 'Ornament is Crime'.[23] Dr Schwarzwald was a great patron of Loos, but the connection was a dead end for Brandt in the sense that almost all his architectural pictures are of historical rather than contemporary buildings. He avoided also the *Neue Sachlichkeit* shots of spiral staircases, views looking down from high buildings, pylons, and the like. Such pictures, very fashionable at the time, were too cold and technical for Brandt's taste.

To photograph buildings and other urban subjects Brandt needed a portable camera, which he acquired probably in late 1927 or early 1928. This was a Zeiss-Ikon Miroflex which took 9 x 12cm glass plates, of good quality and large enough to be re-touched. The Miroflex, similar to the German ICA, could be used as an action camera: it had a fast focal-plane shutter and could be aimed with a pop-up wire-frame viewfinder. In this format, it suited pioneering photo-journalists like Alfred Eisenstaedt in Berlin from 1928 on. But Brandt did not use his Miroflex for such purposes. His early pictures of race meetings, for example, are notable for not having any running horses in them – though they could have been captured in the style of Lartigue's pre-First World War pictures of racing cars in motion, which were taken with an ICA.

Brandt was not interested in the horses but in the spectators, seen in variously symbolic poses, and usually in the intervals between the actual races. Such subjects were taken fairly close up and carefully composed; for this kind of shot the Miroflex could be converted into a single-lens reflex, with the photographer looking down into a bellows hood on the top of the camera. In this format there was a loud click when the viewfinder mirror swung up to allow light to strike the plate: this made it difficult to take more than one candid shot at a time, because subjects would be startled by the noise. After a few years Brandt, like Eisenstaedt, would switch to the twin-lens reflex Rolleiflex (introduced in 1927 in 6 x 6cm format). This camera had a much quieter operation and used roll film rather than glass plates.[24] It had two other great advantages for the kind of photographer Brandt was to become. One was its large and precise ground-glass viewfinder, which gave the user an excellent idea of how the actual photograph would turn out. The other was its relative unobtrusiveness for candid shots, because the photographer would take the picture while looking down at the viewfinder at waist height. Alfred Eisenstaedt has spoken of the advantage of the Rolleiflex when, in 1944, he photographed American soldiers saying farewell to their wives and sweethearts: 'I just kept motionless like a statue. They never saw me clicking away. For the kind of photography I do, one has to be very unobtrusive and to blend in with the crowd.'[25]

The 35mm Leica, which appeared two years before the Rolleiflex, gave modern photographers a choice of two paths to follow. With a Leica they held the camera up to the eye and looked directly at the subject through the rangefinder. The Leica was designed to take advantage of the fast, high-definition film that had recently been developed for movie cameras; with such a small negative, the Leica could fit in a pocket and be held steady without a tripod.[26] With its movie-camera ancestry, it was natural to think of the Leica as a tool for seizing a still picture out of a continuing stream of movement: to stop time in its flight. The similarities between a 35mm camera and a gun profoundly affected the culture of photography. The use of the term 'shoot' for taking a picture became common, along with metaphors of the shutter-release as a trigger, and of aiming, hunting, capturing and even killing. The Leica encouraged a new generation of photographers to follow their subjects into the street and fire off shots in quick succession, trying to capture what Cartier-Bresson would call 'the decisive moment'.

Brandt, however, would always think of his pictures as being composed, rather than snapped or shot.[27] His training and temperament resisted the ethos of the Leica, with its fast lens and multiple exposures: he built up his pictures until they corresponded to what his mind's eye had already envisioned. He would carefully plan each picture, sometimes even going to the scene in advance without his camera to make notes and sketches. He would gain the confidence of his subjects – rather than try to take them unawares – and gaze down meditatively into the viewfinder until he was ready to release the shutter. Once the picture had been made, he had no scruples about cropping the result, or using other manipulative techniques in the darkroom or on the re-touching table.[28] Although he used other cameras, he was formed by the Rolleiflex practice of looking at the picture rather than the subject, and never really changed his approach.[29]

Brandt's subjects first presented themselves in the spring of 1928, when he

'Family Fireside' at
Daleham Gardens,
about 1933

formed his habit of spending several months a year away from Vienna. It is notable that no Vienna street photographs by him seem to have survived: he did his work in Kolliner's studio, but appears to have confined his outdoor work to the times when he was away from the city. Perhaps this was an early indicator of his desire to separate himself from what would seem to be the obvious influence on a young photographer in his position: the thriving artistic and commercial photographic culture of the Berlin–Vienna–Budapest axis. Instead, Brandt's early independent work would be mainly inspired by London, Paris and the more remote parts of Europe.

Brandt left Vienna on 25 March 1928 for a month's holiday with Lyena. By this time they were probably lovers, of a sort, though Ester Cotton recalls that 'neither of them were very sexually organised'. Most of their time was spent in Paris, but they went to England for a long weekend: the first time Brandt had actually seen the land that was so important in his family mythology. His youngest brother Augustus, then sixteen, was living in London to learn the language; Billy and Lyena stayed with him at his boarding house, 22 Daleham Gardens, Belsize Park. The proprietor of Daleham Gardens was Sybil Knight. She had a striking daughter, whose nickname was 'Bird', and a son John. Brandt would use all the Knights as models. In his first collection, The English at Home, 'Family Fireside' shows Mrs Knight and John by the fireside. The cluttered, cosy middle-class setting caught Brandt's eye as something to which there was no real equivalent in Vienna. He also photographed both John and Bird in their school uniforms, introducing a motif that runs through his English pictures from the

Thirties.[30] Mrs Knight's house became the usual stopping place in London for younger Brandts in the Thirties, and Belsize Park was the part of London where Brandt and his brother Rolf would come back to live.

Although it was only a brief visit, Brandt was entranced by England and especially by its photographic possibilities. He went to Ascot with Lyena and Gustus, enjoying the carnival atmosphere and lively mixture of rich and poor. Both London and Paris attracted him as more interesting places to live and take photographs than Vienna. Paris gave him his first whiff of Surrealism (Buñuel's *Un Chien Andalou*, a key film for Brandt, was being made there that spring). He went to Grundlsee with Lyena for the first time in August, taking informal pictures of his friends; and at Christmas he went home to Hamburg, where he found new opportunities for street photography. In only a year he had discovered most of the subjects that would be central to his career: the Pound portrait, English life, Paris Surrealism, the Schwarzwald group at Grundlsee and staged street photography in Hamburg. Since he was also laying the technical foundation for his work in the Kolliner studio, this first year and a half in Vienna and elsewhere was an extraordinarily fertile period in Brandt's life.

In his time away from the Kolliner studio, Brandt's constant travel at his father's expense made him into a young *flâneur*, one who wanders through the great European cities, enjoying the spectacle of the streets.[31] His temperament and social position made him different from the photo-journalist whose relation to the city was a more urgent one, like a hunter stalking his prey. Brandt's eye was directed towards more static subjects or situations, to which he could take a leisurely approach. His companion and collaborator on many of these ramblings was his brother Rolf, who helped him to visualise urban incidents as little theatrical scenes.[32] One of the first of Brandt's street pictures was probably taken at Christmas 1929 or 1930. Ester Bonnesen, now Rolf's regular companion, would come down to Hamburg from Copenhagen for the holidays. She, Rolf and Billy liked to wander together in St Pauli, the red-light district of the city around the notorious Reeperbahn. Rolf had bought a Chinese mask, and Billy got Ester to pose wearing it in front of a Chinese restaurant.[33] She sits demurely on the steps next to the entrance; her dark clothing and submissive posture orientalise her, except for her mop of blonde hair that falls on either side of the mask. The poor and exotic quarters of the city were already standard locales for photo-documentary, often with a socially critical message; but Brandt's picture is not political. All it can be about is the random juxtapositions of ethnic or sexual identities that one encounters in a sea-port city. Much of Brandt's subsequent street photography would aim at creating similarly eccentric and enigmatic scenes.[34]

The late 1920s in Germany and Austria were a revolutionary time in photography, summed up in the title of Werner Gräff's book *Es Kommt der Neue Fotograf!* ('The New Photograph Arrives').[35] Under the slogan 'Der Neue Sachlichkeit' ('The New Objectivity'), this photography included 'aerial views, X-ray pictures, and police photographs, and advocated the unorthodox use of new cameras: slanted views, revealing close-ups, sharp focus, bird's- and worm's-eye perspectives, and optical distortions caused by wide-angle lenses'.[36] Brandt would put a toe into the waters of these new movements, but did not plunge in. He was probably more influenced by a show on early photography that was held at the Belvedere Palace in Vienna in the

Ester Brandt in
a Chinese mask,
Hamburg, about 1930

winter of 1928-9. Organised by the art historian Heinrich Schwarz under the title *Die Kunst in der Photographie der Frühzeit 1840-1880*, this show included English masters of early Pictorialism: David Octavius Hill, Robert Adamson, Julia Margaret Cameron and Henry Peach Robinson.[37] The show may also have included work by Oscar Rejlander, whose pictures of sweeps and street urchins in the 1860s could be considered an early form of Pictorialist photo-journalism. There was a great deal in Pictorialism to appeal to Brandt: the attempt to connect photography with the history of art, the unashamed manipulation of negatives and prints, the unapologetic use of costume and staging, the making of pictures into illustrations for a story, and the moralistic spirit that contrasted so completely with the contemporary ethic of 'new objectivity'. The unfashionable nature of Pictorialism would not deter Brandt from finding inspiration in it; and there were other elements in the show that became lifelong passions for him. One was the quality of depth that these photographs had acquired just by virtue of being old – an atmosphere of mystery, of brooding over the human condition, that became the essential quality sought by Brandt in almost all his work. The show also triggered Brandt's fetishistic absorption in the furniture and bric-à-brac of English Victorianism, objects that he would collect and use as background for his nudes and other domestic scenes in the Thirties and Forties. Finally – though this is only speculation – he may have gone to see Cameron and Robinson's soulful Victorian maidens with a new acquaintance who was herself mournful and mysterious, and who would become the most important woman in his life.

Eva Boros, about 1930

6 Eva

Brandt returned to Vienna on 2 October 1928, after two and a half months at Grundlsee and in France. While he was away, Grete Kolliner had decided to take on another assistant in the studio, perhaps because it was becoming obvious that Brandt's presence could not be relied on. This new employee would arrive in two weeks from Szeged, in Hungary; like Brandt, she was a young person of weak health who was looking for a profession. Coming from one of Hungary's minor aristocratic families, she bore the impressive name of Eva Szerena Maria von Zelenei Szikra Boros. Kolliner arranged for her to stay at the Pension Votivpark, just around the corner from the studio at Universitatstrasse 9.[1] When she arrived, on 16 October, Brandt saw a slight, fair-haired young woman with beautiful Slavic features; her manner was gay and cheerful at first sight, but her eyes had a veiled look that hinted at another side to her personality. He soon learned that, in her twenty-one years, Eva had already suffered a life's worth of illness and tragedy.[2]

Eva was the daughter of a well-to-do doctor; she had a sister, Vilma, who was two years older, and a younger brother, Josef. They had a house in Budapest and a country estate with a vineyard.[3] The children had a German governess, several servants, and every other advantage in life; but their mother suffered from tuberculosis and repeatedly left them to stay at sanatoria in Switzerland. In June 1917 she came back to die in her own country. Eva, who was ten years old, was taken to their country house to see her mother for the last time:

> I cannot remember that I experienced any particular joy or pain at seeing my mother again. Rather I felt dreadfully embarrassed for her for looking so strange, so utterly unlike herself. Her teeth seemed unnaturally large in her thin face, her smile frightened me. I examined industriously the wheels attached to the bed, the embroidery on the sheets. I was desperately glad of any trifle, any small object that would distract my attention from that face.[4]

Eva was asked to recite a poem by the Hungarian national poet, Sandor Petöfi. Halfway through, she broke down, as she realised that the poem foretold the death of the poet's mother:

I faltered. My arms, my knees, my whole body was trembling with an overwhelming desire to give up, to break into loud sobs and scream for help.

Mother's eyes, which during the whole recital never once left me, grew hard and imperative. 'You must go through with this,' they seemed to say. 'You must go through it alone. You must manage somehow. You cannot let me down.'

Eva began her fate of 'going through it alone' three days later, when her mother died at the age of thirty-four. 'She was the loveliest, gayest person,' she wrote of her mother, 'the happiest company in the world. I loved Father, I loved him perhaps more than my mother, but I was never really happy with him. I felt always so sorry for him, I didn't really know why.' In fact, Dr Boros was manic-depressive and 'gave the family a very terrible life'.[5]

Nine years later, in June 1925, Eva was learning photography in Budapest with André Kertész. She went to visit her father in Szeged, where he was now chief physician at the hospital. Dr Boros had decided to go up in a small plane to do research on the possible benefit of altitude in curing lung disease; having lost his wife, he now knew that both his daughters had consumption too. The plane crashed and he was killed in front of Eva's eyes.[6] Not long after, Vilma died. She was a strikingly beautiful and talented young woman, of whom Eva had always been jealous, and her death left Eva riddled with guilt. She spent her late teens in a sanatorium outside Budapest, terrified of sharing her sister's fate. When she arrived at the Kolliner studio, Eva was being born again into the everyday world, much as Brandt had been a year and a half before when he came down from Davos.

Everyone who knew Eva speaks of her warmth and vitality, and of her instinctive understanding of other people. 'She was a fantastically cultured person,' a niece remembers, 'that's the best way to describe her, with extraordinary tastes and in those days taste was everything.'[7] Eva loved Turgenev and Proust, and was herself something like a heroine from a nineteenth-century novel. She and Brandt fell in love at once, with her outgoing nature complementing his reclusiveness. A romantic couple, set apart from everyday life, they turned inwards and created a private mythology out of their common history. Eva both adored Brandt and wanted to take care of him; more than that, 'she was always making excuses for why he behaved as he did'.[8] But Brandt stayed within his inner castle, and some of their friends felt that he did not look after her emotionally in the way that she really needed and deserved.

Brandt had never taken a serious interest in any of the attractive German or Austrian girls who went to Grundlsee. Eva was a woman of the East, like Lyena before her: an exotic creature who could help to purge his German upbringing from Brandt's consciousness and help him imagine that he too had a Slavic soul. In *The Magic Mountain* Hans Castorp becomes infatuated with a Russian woman, Claudia Chauchat, because she is the opposite of his own stolid and respectable Hamburg background. Brandt and Eva seemed to belong together: sharing the same art, both in flight from the sanatorium, both with a similar kind of thoroughbred, almost ethereal beauty. Eva's mystique was summed up in an informal portrait Brandt took of her in Paris, around 1931. David Mellor describes it: 'Her upper body is evanescent, transfigured by an effulgence of light from below … her face is so tanned that her blonde hair

Eva at eighteen, Hungary, 1925, (André Kertész?)

appears dark by contrast. In this portrait of irradiation there is a particular pathos; physical being … seems to be on the point of dissolution.'[9] Eva's novel, *The Mermaids*, describes a picture of the heroine taken by a young man with a Rolleiflex, in a way that might fit that same picture: 'Wistful, unsmiling, with only a hint of resentment in her clear, slightly astonished eyes.'[10]

As soon as Eva appeared on the scene, Lyena saw that Brandt would fall deeply in love with this newcomer. But Lyena did not suffer from jealousy, or fight to keep Brandt for herself. She was only a schoolgirl of seventeen, while Eva was four years older. The 'Schwarzwaldkinder' still had the romantic idea that 'marriage was the end of everything' and therefore to be avoided; Lyena also assumed – naively, she came to realise – that there would be plenty of other men in her life like her Billy. She didn't know yet that he was unique. Beyond that, there was a sense in which – quite innocently – she had fallen in love with Eva herself. Eva, she recalled, was 'not the jealous type'; they often went around Vienna together, leaving Brandt to enjoy the time on his own that he always needed. Perhaps this was easier because Eva, like Lyena at this time, did not find the physical side of sex very appealing. Apart from the frailty of her health, her father had been an army officer during the war, and was temperamental and domineering at home; a young woman like her would find Brandt's gentleness reassuring. They were not a worldly pair, and Brandt was never one of those photographers, like Man Ray or George Hoyningen-Huene, who attached themselves to fashionably glamorous women. Finally, they shared a profound artistic kinship: though Eva did not persist as a professional photographer, Brandt always relied more on her judgement about his work than on anyone else's.

For all these reasons, Brandt's falling in love with Eva did not turn the pattern of either of their lives upside down. They worked together at the studio, with Eva doing mainly re-touching, but also some photography. After work, Brandt went home to his

Lyena Barjansky, Eva Boros, Ester Brandt, about 1929, photographer unknown

pension and Eva to hers, in the Josefstat. They were not formally engaged, and neither had the immediate family surveillance that, for young people of their bourgeois background, would have put pressure on them to marry. There was a Truffaut spirit of romantic intensity, while staying lighthearted about coming and going without commitments. Also, both had been solemnly warned that they should not count on living out a normal span, and should not think of having children.[11] The novel Eva wrote about her stay in the Budapest sanatorium, *The Mermaids*, describes the awful isolation and humiliation that consumptives suffered. The heroine is turned away from hotels when they see her sputum-mug; when she goes to a wedding, she recalls, 'My knives and forks were all marked with an elastic band. And a little label stuck on the bottom of my glass.'[12] Deeply as Brandt loved Eva, his reluctance to live with her may have stemmed from fear that she might re-infect him. They would be together for eight years before actually living regularly under the same roof.

Eva had some money from her father's estate, so both she and Brandt could afford to drift along together, without giving hostages to fortune. In June 1929, nine months after they had met, Brandt took Eva to Hamburg to meet his parents and attend the wedding of his elder brother. Walther was doing well at William Brandt & Sons in London, and would be made a partner in another year and a half. His bride was Dorothy Crane, an American from Belvidere, Illinois. L. W. Brandt was enthralled by Eva as soon as he met her; she became the daughter he had never had, while he in many ways replaced the father she had lost. LW was practical, generous and reliable – qualities that could be lacking in Bill, and which Eva was comforted by. Going up to Hamburg was a big step towards making Eva one of the Brandt family; but in the following month there was some kind of crisis. Brandt went off to England on 5 July, to take photographs and visit relatives; while he was away, Eva suddenly packed up and went back to Szeged. Although she seemed to live quite a free life in Vienna, in Hungary she had aunts who had put themselves into the place of her parents and exerted pressure for her to be decently settled. Perhaps they got wind of her relation with Brandt – Budapest was only two and a half hours by train from Vienna – and summoned her home to report. Two things especially would disturb them: that Eva and Brandt were intimate friends without being engaged, and that Brandt also had a history of TB. While this was being thrashed out, Brandt made a melodramatic dash across Europe and showed up unannounced at a family gathering. This was at least proof of his serious intentions towards Eva, but nothing was really settled since they still did not become formally engaged. She remained in Hungary, ending her apprenticeship with Kolliner after nine months in Vienna. Brandt returned west, spending part of August and September at Grundlsee.[13]

For Brandt's last year in Vienna, Eva remained in Hungary, though it would have been relatively easy for them to see each other. It is not known when he decided to leave; probably from the time of his first trips to London and Paris, in the spring of 1928, he would have been mulling over the possibility of moving further west.[14] Eva's friendship with Kertész could help Brandt get started in Paris, and it would be harder for Eva's Hungarian relatives to keep an eye on her there.[15] At the same time, Brandt was beginning to get some recognition in the German-speaking photographic world. In May 1929 the rising cultural importance of photography was demonstrated by the massive exhibition *Film und Foto*, organised by the Deutsches Werkbund. It opened in Stuttgart, then went on to Zurich and Vienna (20-31 March 1930). In Vienna some of Brandt's pictures were included. Which ones is not known: the original catalogue lists 977 titles, and some of these were groups of pictures.[16] As the term 'Werkbund' ('Workgroup') suggests, the show had a left-wing slant, combined with a great deal of modernist montage, formalist pictures of buildings and other expressions of *Neue Sachlichkeit*. Already Brandt's style was taking a different direction from this. The show was an excellent survey of work in the modernist style by professional photographers; but just because there was a discernible group spirit – and predominantly a German spirit – would be enough for Brandt to separate himself from it. It was an important milestone to be included in such a major show, but by the time it opened in Vienna, Brandt must have already decided that his kind of photography had a better chance in another city: Paris.

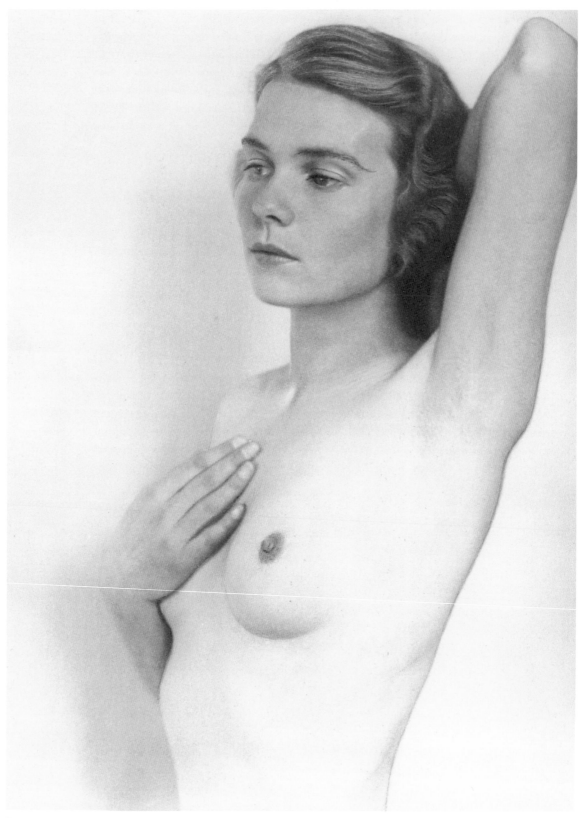

Eva, about 1930

7   Paris: With Man Ray

In later accounts of his career, Brandt left the impression that Paris was a brief interlude – a few months of apprenticeship with Man Ray – before he found his true home in England. In fact, he arrived in Paris in 1930 (not 1929, as he sometimes said) and did not take up permanent residence in England until nearly four years later. He lived as many years in Paris as in Vienna, and was a French photographer before he was an English one.[1] Brandt broadened his photographic skills and experience during his Paris years, but artistic or commercial success eluded him. Although his move to London in 1934 was partly out of disappointment with Paris, much of his eventual success with *The English at Home* and *A Night in London* was built on French foundations. Brandt was always ready to acknowledge his debt to the Surrealists, and it is fair to say that he transplanted Surrealism into English photography. But Paris fed his imagination in many other ways as well.

It was Lyena Barjansky who got the exodus to France under way. She was studying art history in Vienna, after graduating from the Schwarzwaldschule, when her father moved to Paris early in 1930 to start a business exporting textiles to South America. Lyena's real passion was for clothes, and she persuaded her father to set her up as a dressmaker in Paris. Eva soon came from Budapest to join her. Lastly, on 15 June 1930, Brandt left the Pension Cottage in Vienna and made his way to an apartment in Passy, in the sixteenth *arrondissement*.[2] The Vienna triangle of Billy, Lyena and Eva was re-established in the same non-committed way, with each living in their own place, and Eva companionably helping Lyena with her new dressmaking business. Why Eva did not live with Brandt in Paris is unclear, but the decision came from him and had to do with his love of privacy, his finicky disposition and perhaps the desire to protect his health. What was not the reason, according to Lyena, was any desire in Brandt to lead the life of a promiscuous young man in Montparnasse. As in Vienna, there was absolutely nothing bohemian about the lodgings he chose: 2 rue des Marronniers is an imposing nine-storey apartment house with an ornamental brick façade, built in about 1900; the street is quiet, and the whole area around it is the epitome of bourgeois respectability. One can be in Montparnasse in twenty minutes, but in 1930 it would be a journey to a different world.

Brandt would have taken the Métro from Passy, riding high above the boulevard de Grenelle. At Raspail he could cross the street and walk up to Man Ray's studio at

31bis rue Campagne Première. The story persists that it was Ezra Pound who arranged for Brandt to apprentice with Man Ray.[3] Pound may have claimed the credit, but Brandt did not arrive in Paris until two years after he took Pound's portrait in Vienna. By 1930, Man Ray had long given up on Pound, complaining that he was arrogant, egotistical and a wearer of 'false-bohemian getup' (the Surrealists, one should remember, favoured suits, ties and well-polished shoes).[4] Also, Pound had been living in Rapallo since 1925. That Man Ray welcomed Brandt into his studio can scarcely have been because he wanted to do Ezra Pound a favour. We can imagine two much better reasons. The first would be that Brandt (or his father) was willing to pay, since Man Ray was well known for his eagerness to get money in any way he could. Second, Brandt had now had two and a half years of training with Kolliner; he was a meticulous darkroom technician and had just had some pictures included in the *Film und Foto* exhibition in Vienna. It would be convenient for Man Ray to have a competent and self-effacing young man like Brandt around, and Man Ray had benefited earlier from taking on Berenice Abbott and Jacques-André Boiffard in a similar role.[5] In the summer of 1929 he had also made Lee Miller his assistant, from a mixture of professional motives and his infatuation with her as model and mistress.

There is some evidence that Brandt and Eva Boros came to Man Ray as a package deal, with Eva working as a re-toucher.[6] If so, the go-between for the arrangement would probably have been Kertész. While Brandt lived in Passy, Eva stayed at the Hotel Istria, a famous Surrealist haunt that was next door to Man Ray's studio (she later moved to the cheaper Hotel de Blois, on the rue des Plantes). Her transparent blonde beauty resembled Lee Miller's, and Man Ray may have had similar designs on her. But she does not seem to have posed for him; and by the time she settled in Paris Eva had given up taking pictures in her own right. Much later, she said that after she met Brandt she realised that she 'wasn't much good as a photographer'; other recollections are that he exerted some pressure on her to give it up.[7]

Man Ray (born Emanuel Radnitzky in New York in 1890) was a painter and sculptor before he became a photographer. He was welcomed to Paris in July 1921 by his friend Marcel Duchamp, and was immediately adopted by the Surrealists. Duchamp arranged for Man Ray to take over Tristan Tzara's room in a furnished hotel in Passy; when he later moved to Montparnasse the Surrealists disapproved, considering it 'too arty and bohemian a quarter'.[8] Man Ray remained close both to the original Dadaists and Surrealists, and to the various tendencies into which they fractured. A short list of the personalities with whom he worked or made friends would include André Breton, Max Ernst, Salvador Dalí, Jean Cocteau, Antonin Artaud, Tristan Tzara, Paul Eluard, René Crevel, Jean Arp and Yves Tanguy. Brandt made portraits of several of these figures after the Second World War, and it is safe to assume that he either knew them or knew about them.[9] By the time he left Paris he was saturated in the atmosphere of Surrealism and committed to developing a Surrealist vision of English streets and rooms.

Brandt said that he spent three months with Man Ray and learned very little; but when he met Man Ray again to take his portrait, in 1970, more was revealed:

'Tell me,' [Ray] asked Brandt, 'did you actually learn anything when you worked for me?' The former assistant paused for a moment and then replied: 'You went out so often that I did not learn much from you directly. But what I did was go through all the drawers and files that I would not have dared touch when you were in the studio. So I learnt a great deal when you were not there.' Man Ray was delighted.[10]

This story about Brandt's surreptitious rummaging has been smoothed over; according to Rolf Brandt, Man Ray caught Brandt doing it and sent him packing.[11] In any case, the episode is a parable for Brandt's stay in Paris, and even for his whole career. He never seems to appear in the memoirs of Thirties Paris, and this must be because he did not want to be a public personality in any of the bohemian haunts of Montparnasse. All photographers may have in them something of the voyeur, but Brandt was extreme in his desire to ferret out secrets, and to see without being seen. There is a kind of poetic justice in his spying on Man Ray, because Man Ray himself was very secretive and didn't want other photographers copying his 'Rayographs' and other inventions.

Brandt was able to keep his distance from Man Ray, yet at the same time get from him, in his own words, 'a new excitement about photography and about the world as well'.[12] Although Brandt was completely alienated from Man Ray's frenetic social ambitions, Man Ray nonetheless opened a door for him on to the spectacle of Surrealist Paris, which he fastened onto for his own artistic purposes. Man Ray's portraits of Surrealist personalities would be a precedent for Brandt's portraits of British artists and intellectuals. Then there was the example of Man Ray's hands-on approach to making a print: his autobiography is full of heroic tales of how he brought off a particular shot, in the face of unkempt or uncooperative models, incompetent helpers, blown fuses, jammed cameras, shortages of money, film, light. It all comes to a head at the *bal blanc* of the Count and Countess Pecci-Blunt in 1930. Everything starts to go wrong, as Man Ray becomes more and more jealous of Lee Miller's flamboyant behaviour; finally he decides to shoot a tableau of the guests in the garden, with inadequate light and only one plate left:

> I made my exposure; it came out well. I had never before relied on a single shot to obtain a satisfactory result and from now on I resolved to reduce the number of exposures I would make of any subject. I thus saved myself a great deal of unnecessary work. Photography need not be a hit-or-miss affair any more than painting, in which the painter limits himself to one canvas per subject. The procedure is slightly different: in photography all corrections are made in advance, whereas in painting, during and after a work in progress.[13]

Man Ray's story sheds light on Brandt's belief in photography as artifice. The core of a picture becomes the pose: first imagined by the photographer, then prepared with various technical means that will be most easily supplied in a studio. 'I seldom took a camera out of my studio,' Man Ray wrote, 'and then only for portraits.'[14] With his old-fashioned plate camera, Man Ray was at the opposite pole from the new photo-journalists like Kertész, prowling the streets with their Leicas and shooting rolls of twenty-four or more exposures.[15] Brandt, too, was economical with his shots, normally using less than a twelve-exposure roll on a given subject. Man Ray's studio was a world in itself, a storehouse of effects and symbolic objects; it was also a kind of stage, where sitters acted out roles for the photographer/director. In some of his most typical Thirties pictures, Brandt transferred the culture of the studio to the street, using walls and lamp-posts as backdrop.

Brandt borrowed other ideas from Man Ray, some of them put aside for later use. He did not, at this time, attempt to follow Man Ray's lead in making portraits of Parisian cultural figures; only in 1941 did he begin his own distinctive series of British portraits. Nor did Brandt become an experimental photographer in the sense of wanting to push the medium to its limits, as Man Ray had done with his Rayographs and solarisation.[16] Where Brandt did follow Man Ray was in a series of nudes that were close to direct copies of his work. One, of Eva, uses a typical Man Ray pose such as he used for one of his more ethereal models, Suzy Solidor. Another, a torso shot through gauze, became Brandt's first nude to appear in *Lilliput* (February 1942). It recalls Man Ray's famous pictures of Lee Miller's torso and of her exposed neck; Miller may even have been the model for Brandt's version. There are also three straightforward nudes that emphasise the play of light and shadow on the body; the composition of one of them is almost identical to Man Ray's 'Dos Blanc' (1926). Another Brandt, a semi-nude with a kimono taken some years later, follows a similar picture by Man Ray that appeared in the Surrealist magazine *Minotaure*.[17] But in spite of these formal resemblances, the atmosphere of Brandt's nudes is far cooler than Man Ray's. Only in the late 1940s did Brandt return to the nude and, this time, come closer to Man Ray's spirit. Brandt gave these later nudes a greater erotic charge and surrounded them with fetishistic props.[18] They are unmistakably English nudes, but with a Surrealist ancestry.

The personal dynamic between Man Ray and Brandt was not one of master to disciple (though later, in the 1970s, they developed a mutual liking and respect). Lyena Barjansky remembers Man Ray saying, 'You're either an artist or you're not', and at this time he seems to have put Brandt in the class of those who were not. Man Ray's real disciples and collaborators were the series of lovers he brought under his spell, especially Kiki de Montparnasse, Lee Miller and Ady, along with models like Meret Oppenheim and Nusch Eluard. His nudes of these women, in addition to their sizzling eroticism, all succeeded in making their subjects' personalities emerge from the print. Man Ray was in that sense a lyrical photographer, embodying the opposite of the enigmatic impersonality of approach that Brandt later brought to his nudes. Lyena Barjansky suggests that Man Ray, with his short and somewhat gnomish physique, resented Brandt's romantic good looks; but it does not need personal spite or jealousy to account for the distance between the two men. Despite all, though, Brandt followed in the spirit of Man Ray's central achievement: turning the camera, invented as 'the perfect machine for the reproduction of reality', into 'an instrument for surreality'.[19] Everything that happened in Man Ray's studio, and in the Surrealist movement as a whole, aimed at negating the passive acceptance of everyday things. The camera, within the Surrealist vision, was not there to record reality, but rather to transform it and make it strange. As Man Ray said, 'It's not a question of reproducing reality, but of creating it.'[20] Brandt took on this ambition in his

Semi-nude with kimono, 1930s

Paris years, and then made it bear fruit across the Channel in London.

However, Brandt learned from Man Ray while refusing to live like him. By taking Kiki de Montparnasse as his mistress in the 1920s, and having his studio in that quarter, Man Ray had made himself into a king of the bohemians. After 1930, Paris turned into a much grimmer and more political city, as the stock-market crash and the Depression forced many foreigners to return home. But enough were left to fill the Café du Dôme every night, even if they were finding it much harder to scrape by. Henry Miller came to live in Paris three months before Brandt did, and his hand-to-mouth existence became the standard picture of Montparnasse life in the Thirties. Brandt, living like a bourgeois in Passy, resisted the stock identity of the photographer who made a stir in cafés and garrets and surrounded himself with nude models.[21] Man Ray may have thought that Brandt wasn't an artist because he didn't live like one. But his aloofness from the frantic café society of Montparnasse did not prevent Brandt seeing what went on around him, and being deeply influenced by what artists believed, if not by how they lived. Here the Surrealist vision was pre-eminent, and one of Brandt's formative experiences was seeing Buñuel's *L'Age d'or*, which had its premiere on 28 October 1930.[22] The scenes in a villa garden had the most obvious effect on Brandt's later work, with formally dressed people moving among statues in a highlighted foreground, and deep blackness behind them. At the end of the film, the Sadean fantasies are disturbingly reminiscent of themes in Brandt's late nudes. But the crucial connection is always one of atmosphere, summed up in Elliot Rubinstein's comment that Buñuel was 'the man who demonstrated more clearly than any other that surrealist perspectives demanded cinematographic realism' – a judgement that could apply just as well to Brandt's art.[23]

Shop-window mannequins, Paris, about 1931

8 Paris: The Social Fantastic

As he had done in Vienna, Brandt worked in a studio in Paris but did his most interesting work outside of it, wandering the streets of the city. He took no pictures of bohemian life in Montparnasse or bourgeois life in Passy. Instead, we can imagine him, a fair-haired young foreigner with a Rolleiflex, exploring the unfashionable parts of the city: the 'real Paris' of the *petits gens*. His passport to the discovery of this world was the work of Eugène Atget, who had lived just down the street from Man Ray until his death three years before Brandt arrived.[1] For many years Atget ran a shop called 'Documents pour Artistes', with the modest aim of providing pictures of streets and interiors that painters could transmute into art. At the end of Atget's life, Man Ray had made him into a kind of godfather of Surrealist photography. Four of his pictures appeared in the magazine *La Révolution Surréaliste*, and in 1925 Man Ray bought a selection of Atget photographs, including some startling nudes.[2] Brandt may well have seen this album when rummaging through Ray's possessions. Berenice Abbott had also made friends with Atget and taken his portrait, while she was working as Man Ray's assistant.[3] The Surrealists saw Atget as an unconscious 'precursor to the vision of an epoch … He photographed the palace and the hovel with the lens of reality but also with a sense surpassing reality.'[4]

Atget had made a marvellous record of archaic and provincial France, but the Surrealists seized on a relatively small segment of his work, his pictures of contemporary Paris. Here, Atget showed the margins of the great capital rather than its monuments: he photographed small shops and street markets, the exteriors of brothels, and the 'Zone' (originally the '*Zone Militaire*', the area outside the city's fortifications that was left vacant to ensure an unobstructed field of fire). After 1870, when the walls of Paris were demolished, rag-pickers, gypsies and vagrants moved into the Zone, living in caravans and makeshift huts. Atget photographed these people as an anthropologist might; he did not bemoan their deprivation, as leftist photographers would do in the Thirties, but simply recorded their activities and the way they organised their space. Brandt was taking pictures in the spirit of Atget soon after his arrival in Paris, in an unpublished series on flea markets. These pictures ignore the human element almost entirely; they examine the borderline between shabby objects piled up for sale, and the outright rubbish surrounding them in streets and gutters. Brandt's fascination with rubbish in his Thirties pictures has usually been interpreted as social criticism. But many of the pictures he took in Paris (and later in Spain and Hungary) suggest that he was interested in waste for its own sake, as a distinctly modern phenomenon. Waste was not really a sign of oppression for him, but rather just another sign of the times, the underside of the new consumer society. The shabbiness and disorder of the back streets of Paris did more to inspire Brandt than the more regimented urbanism of Hamburg or Vienna.

Atget certainly helped to turn Brandt's eye towards such subjects as street vendors or dilapidated corners of the city. But equally important was the Surrealist theory that was inspired by Atget's work.[5] The prolific journalist and novelist Pierre Mac Orlan wrote about photography in a way that explains much about Brandt's later career, after he had moved to England. Mac Orlan supplied the preface to *Atget, Photographe de Paris* (a book that Brandt owned), and wrote a great deal of influential photographic criticism through the 1920s and 1930s.[6] He argued that photography was 'the great expressionist art of our time,' because black-and-white film and the camera lens brought out qualities that were hidden when people just looked at objects with their own eyes.[7] 'A photographic view of certain details of the world,' Mac Orlan wrote, 'quickly reveals the presence of adventure in a scene that would carefully conceal it from human eyes.'[8] Only photography can 'create sudden death and ... lend objects and people that popular mystery that gives death its romantic power'.[9] It shows things in two ways at once: objectively, and as uncanny messengers of death. In Atget's pictures Mac Orlan found a new vision of the modern city, which he called 'the social fantastic'.

The social fantastic came out especially at night, in the popular streets of the city. Small shops and street workers, not ministries or monuments, gave the real sense of a city and photography should reveal them as 'people of the shadows'. 'It is easier to make use of the night,' Mac Orlan wrote, 'to arouse public curiosity. The elements of the night are the great directors of [the] social fantastic.' In fact Atget had not done much night photography (probably for technical reasons), so Mac Orlan was opening up a new path by combining Atget's subject-matter with the idea that photography should 'use light to study shadow'.[10] The first person to put all this into practice was Brassaï, who started taking night pictures of Paris around December 1929. Brandt's *A Night in London* did not appear until 1938, but during his time in Paris, and on visits to England before 1934, he was already trying out Mac Orlan's agenda. Mac Orlan himself said that every great city is haunted by phantoms recognised by the popular imagination, and that London had them just as much as Paris.[11] Much of Brandt's English work in the Thirties involved making an inventory of those phantoms.

Following Atget and Mac Orlan, Brandt turned his back on the Paris of the boulevards and wandered the *quartiers pauvres*. His picture of two mannequins at a flea market was a homage to Atget's corset shop, with its strangely truncated female forms behind glass.[12] Such pictures expressed also the Surrealist version of 'fetichism':

> - doctrine of spirits embodied in, or attached to, or conveying influence through, certain material objects.
> - in the terminology of psychoanalysis – the transference of the libido from the whole object of affection to a part, a symbol, an article of clothing.[13]

Flea market, Paris, about 1931

Street Urchins, about 1931

The Surrealists set about making such objects (for example, Meret Oppenheim's cup and saucer lined with fur). Man Ray's first professional work as a photographer was taking pictures of art works; from there it was only a short step to creating objects specifically to be photographed. For Atget, and for Brandt too, this kind of fabricated subject would be like shooting fish in a barrel; the whole point of roaming about the seedy quarters of Paris was to find the subject ready-made, in its natural setting of rubbish and bric-à-brac. Then one could photograph it so as to reveal its Surrealist potential, the 'concrete realisation of the dream or of irrationality'.[14]

Brandt's picture of mannequins caught the eye of the Surrealist writer René Crevel. Brandt perhaps connected with Crevel as a fellow-TB patient, who had gone to Davos for treatment about three weeks after Brandt left, in May 1927.[15] One of Crevel's six novels – *Etes-vous Fous?* – was about life in a sanatorium. Like Brandt, he tried to cure himself through psychoanalysis, becoming a patient in Paris of Dr René

Allendy; and like Brandt, he quickly broke off the analysis. Crevel decided that psychoanalysis was fatal to creativity: it destroyed people's individuality by forcing them into a few stock categories.[16]

Crevel was four years older than Brandt and very different in character. He was a pretty young man with curly hair and an innocent expression, but was addicted to dangerous pleasures – drinking bouts, opium, cocaine, and rough trade from the gay underground of Paris. One of his sayings was 'No risk is fatal.' Much of his wild behaviour seems to have come out of hatred for his devouring bourgeois mother, his father having committed suicide when he was fourteen. Crevel loved Oxford and Victorian England, writing a book about the Brontës. Like Breton and other Surrealists, he looked to the French Communist Party for salvation in the 1930s, but could not be comfortable as a fellow-traveller. On 18 June 1935 he committed suicide by gassing himself, first attaching a label saying 'René Crevel' to one wrist.[17] Some said he did it out of political despair, but he also was on the brink of death from TB, in spite of a pneumothorax and ten years of sanatorium treatments.

Brandt's personal connection with Crevel remains a mystery, but they had so many interests in common that they probably were friends. All we know for certain is that Crevel admired Brandt's picture of shop-window dummies enough to write an essay about it. This was 'La Grande Mannequin Cherche et Trouve sa Peau', which appeared in the Surrealist magazine *Minotaure* three years after Crevel's death.[18] Although the Grande Mannequin evokes for Crevel the domineering female figures who populate his novels, in this essay he treats her without spite: perhaps because spite is a quality missing from Brandt's picture; indeed, from all his pictures. The crucial value of the picture, for Crevel, is its suggestiveness, which is what Brandt is struggling to achieve in his early work. His aim follows Crevel's idea of Surrealist art-making: 'surrealist objects brought back to life, *concretely*, without metaphor, the corpses of things'.[19]

Brandt, in Paris, hunts for such objects where Atget taught him to look: in the mean streets and frayed margins of the city, among pieces of waste ground and buildings half-demolished or half-built. He photographs three street urchins on a nondescript street of a nondescript suburb, St-Ouen. A shot of construction on the pont du Garigliano, with a spectral Eiffel Tower in the background, brings together symbols of the nineteenth century and the contemporary city. In later pictures taken in Spain or Hungary, Brandt also focuses on barren or disorganised spaces, but without making the obvious point of denouncing modern ugliness. Rather, waste land allows the imagination to get to work, and intensifies the effect of a single vivid figure, such as Brandt's beggar in Barcelona or pig in Hungary. A great deal of Surrealist art was influenced by the theatrical handling of space in de Chirico, where an empty street or square creates a dreamlike atmosphere. Surrealism was more than the following of a set plan, but perhaps there is a key to Brandt's idea of composition in Max Ernst's formula: 'the coupling of two realities, irreconcilable in appearance, upon a plane which apparently does not suit them'.[20] Such conflict between figure and ground was what Brandt spent his days looking for, in the back streets of Paris.

Eva as a prostitute, 1933

9   Paris: The Hungarian Table

Modernism, especially in literature, has often been defined by its hostility to the market. But for modernist photography, in Paris around 1930, nothing could be further from the truth. Photographers whose work appeared in avant-garde journals or limited-edition books could also be seen on every news-stand, in popular weeklies or pulp magazines. No photographers could make a living from being 'camera artists' alone; they survived on commissioned portraits, fashion photography, advertising and photo-journalism. Such work might then be recycled in little magazines or in the prestigious annual photography issue of *Arts et Métiers Graphiques*.[1] Major figures like Man Ray, André Kertész and Germaine Krull were not ashamed to be opportunists, while young hopefuls scrounging for commissions in editorial offices and cafés could not afford to be anything else. Brandt was unusual in having a private income that freed him from the need to scrounge; but this may also be why, in nearly four years in Paris, he never gained a secure place in the photographic world.

When Brandt arrived in Paris, French photo-journalism was enjoying a boom, following the lead of the Germans earlier in the Twenties. There was a flock of new illustrated magazines, printed in heliogravure, and catering to all tastes from the snobbish to the vulgar. They had few staff photographers and did not pay very much, but energetic and well-connected photographers could make a living from them. The best of these magazines was *Vu*, founded by Lucien Vogel in 1928, where the Russian artist Alexander Liberman was picture editor before his later career with Condé Nast; it had a circulation of about half a million.[2] *Vu* may have been the first magazine in Europe to run picture-essays, starting with its earliest issues. There was also *Voilà*, edited by Florent Fels, with suggestive stories using staged pictures like 'Diary of a Chambermaid'.[3] At the bottom end were *Détective* and *Scandale*, with their re-enactments of crimes, and the soft-porn *Paris-Magazine*.[4]

These mass-circulation magazines frequently used some of the finest work by Kertész, Krull, Brassaï, Eli Lotar and many others. The most commercially successful of these photographers was Kertész, and he must have been Brandt's best contact for breaking into magazine work. Eva Boros's brief apprenticeship to him in Budapest perhaps arose through their mutual acquaintance, the left-wing journalist Paul Ignotus; Kertész took a wistful portrait of her as an adolescent.[5] After he moved to Paris from Budapest in September 1925 he quickly made a reputation both as a commercial and an art photographer. He was a friend of Man Ray's, and held court at the 'Hungarian table' at the Café du Dôme; from 1928 to 1931 he lived just up the street, at 75 boulevard du Montparnasse. Kertész got Brassaï launched as a photographer, and acted as a general fixer for his Hungarian friends. Like Brassaï, Kertész was Jewish, but irreligious and emancipated from his roots.

Brandt's personal relationship with Kertész does not seem to have been close, and he probably used Eva as his intermediary to get leads for commercial work. To be in the know at the Hungarian table you had to speak Hungarian, and Eva could walk up there within five minutes while she was living at the Hotel Istria. Internal evidence suggests that Brandt observed Kertész's style and choice of subjects very closely, and learned from him – though, in a sense, he did not want to learn too much.[6] Kertész was a great street photographer, who took advantage of the Leica's speed and unobtrusiveness to capture the shock-effect of urban encounters.[7] In his best photographs of this kind, there is a powerful face-to-face connection between viewer and subject; but Brandt was not interested in such sudden confrontations. He preferred soft, moody textures over Kertész's polished formalism, and when he bought a new camera in Paris it was a Rolleiflex rather than a Leica.[8]

There were other Hungarian connections for Brandt in Paris. The animal photographer, Ylla, was a friend of Lyena and Eva.[9] Ernö Goldfinger, who was getting started as an architect, knew Brandt in the Thirties and bought some of his prints.[10] From Montparnasse they both went to England: one to revolutionise British architecture, the other photography. But the most important mentor for Brandt in that circle was Brassaï. Their work is so closely intertwined that they must have known each other very well; they certainly admired each other's work.[11] Brassaï's widow, Gilberte, suggests that they first met in London in 1934, when Brassaï was given a medal for *Paris After Dark*; but their paths must have crossed in Paris before that.[12] Brassaï lived on rue de la Glacière at the Hotel des Terrasses, the headquarters for Hungarian artists in Paris. His friend and collaborator Frank Dobo also lived there, as did the deaf-mute painter Lajos Tihanyi and Vincent Korda, brother of the film director. Henry Miller, who came to live in Paris three months before Brandt did, was a frequent visitor: 'for hour after hour,' Brassaï recalled, 'he pored over my nightly harvest of photographs, which were stretched out across the bed'.[13] Brassaï had started out as an abstract painter and sculptor, in Budapest and Berlin; he worked as a freelance journalist in Paris for six years before taking up photography, at Kertész's urging, in December 1929.[14] Brassaï focused on typical, indeed stereotypical French subjects. By November 1931 he had completed a book of these pictures, published in December 1932 as *Paris de Nuit*.[15]

Brassaï had a family tradition of fascination with France, a bit like the Brandt family's myth of England, and was a genius at presenting 'Frenchness' to those from other cultures. However, his popular reputation today comes mostly from the candid photographs published as *Paris Secret* in 1976, some forty-five years after they were taken. *Paris de Nuit* is a relatively mild collection of exterior shots (Brassaï took the title from the signs on buses that offered night-time tours of the city). It contains one shot of a prostitute standing under a street-lamp, and one of the façade of a brothel. At the time, Brassaï could not publish his pictures of what went on inside.[16]

Prostitute, rue Quincampoix,
1931, Brassaï

Brassaï's interior scenes are the ultimate in 'you are there' realism, satisfying everyone's fantasies about the *demi-monde* of Paris. 'I was eager to penetrate this other world,' he wrote, 'this fringe world, the secret, sinister world of mobsters, outcasts, toughs, pimps, whores, addicts, inverts.'[17] But his techniques made it impossible for his pictures to be genuine documentaries, in the sense of capturing something that exists independently of the camera that records it. The actual clients of brothels would not welcome being photographed, so for the bedroom shots Brassaï persuaded a friend to act the male role. Brassaï's bellows-type Voigtlander Bergheil camera needed very long exposures: for outdoor photography at night, he would often time his exposure by smoking a cigarette. The film was so slow that he could uncover his lens and then get into the picture himself: he is the man coming out of a *pissoir* in one plate of *Paris de Nuit*, and the bum lying on the ground in another.[18] For his interior shots of cafés and brothels (collected in *Paris Secret*), it was impossible to take pictures without the subjects' co-operation:

> Brassaï had a technique for taking pictures in which his subject knew *that* he or she was being photographed, but not exactly *when*. 'There is something like complicity … For the delicate subjects that I photographed, I had to be familiar with the people and it was difficult at that time. I didn't have a lot of money and I had to make friends and buy drinks. Technically, also, it was difficult. I couldn't become invisible … I had to invent a technique so that people … never knew when I was going to take their picture, or when they knew, I didn't take it.' Having selected a subject … he set up his camera and tripod, and placed his assistant with the flash over to one side. Such activity was unlikely to go unnoticed, and certainly not after the first picture, because Brassaï used magnesium flash powder. Magnesium explosions are brilliant, noisy, and odorous. (These offensive aspects of magnesium flash led Picasso to nickname Brassaï 'The Terrorist'.)[19]

Le premier hebdomadaire des faits-divers

5ᵉ Année - N° 207   1 FR. 50 - TOUS LES JEUDIS - 16 PAGES   13 Octobre 1932

DÉTECTIVE

Les détrousseurs

D'une auto mystérieuse, une femme est brutalement jetée sur le sol. Yvonne Desvignes fut-elle aussi victime des détrousseurs ?
(Lire, page 5, l'enquête révélatrice de notre collaborateur Luc Dornain.)

AU SOMMAIRE : "Purée de pois", par Louis Latzarus. - Les "premières" de la justice, par F. Dupin. - Le secret du ligoté, par Jacques Lombard

Cover of *Détective*, 1932

Much of Brassaï's bread-and-butter work in the Thirties went beyond documentary, into a style that puts him especially close to Brandt. Magazines for which both of them worked, such as *Scandale* and *Détective*, published re-enactments of notorious crimes and scandals.[20] The pictures might be made on the street or in indoor settings, using paid models or volunteers; they had to be melodramatic, easily understood, and convey the sordid atmosphere of criminal hangouts. A cover story in *Détective*, possibly by Brassaï, shows the body of a kidnapped maid being thrown out of a car in the Bois de Boulogne. No photographer can have been there when it actually happened, so the assignment was to re-stage the scene 'as it might have been'.[21]

Some of Brassaï's 'art photography' in *Paris de Nuit* and *Paris Secret* was excerpted from photo-sequences or other commercial stories that he did for *Détective*, *Scandale*, *Paris-Magazine*, *Vu*, *Verve* and many others. Late in life Brandt told interviewers that he had worked for *Scandale* and *Paris-Magazine*.[22] The surviving files of these magazines do not show any credited work by Brandt, so they can only have used the odd picture.[23] It is not hard to see why Brandt was relatively unsuccessful at getting such work. First, he did not really need it, whereas Brassaï was always scrambling to keep the wolf from the door. Then, he did not have the effrontery that Brassaï had, to push ahead into awkward and even physically dangerous situations. Finally, Brassaï had the kind of talent that could raise conventional subjects to the level of art, by intensifying what was typical about them. Brandt – and here he was faithful to his Surrealist vision – was always seeking to make the familiar subtly strange, so that even his apparently standard documentary pictures often have something that doesn't look quite right. Nonetheless, his familiarity with the use of staging in French commercial photography provided an essential ingredient for his English pictures later in the decade.

The intimate link between Brassaï and Brandt appears most clearly in two pictures of prostitution. Brassaï's appeared in *Paris de Nuit* and was therefore taken in 1930 or 1931, and published in December 1932.[24] Brandt decided to re-stage it in Hamburg, but using Eva as a model instead of a real prostitute.[25] The picture was probably taken around December 1932, since Brandt stopped visiting Hamburg after Hitler came to power. Its setting is the same Chinese restaurant in St Pauli where Brandt had photographed Ester Bonnesen in a mask. Eva wears a cloche hat and coat with a fur collar, which are almost identical to the prostitute's outfit in the Brassaï picture. The brightly lit sign offering standard Chinese dishes is a counterpart to the cobbled pavement on the lower right, signifying that the woman who stands on it is for sale. Two kinds of marginality are juxtaposed here: the exoticism of the Chinese quarter and the problematic figure of the prostitute, who is both a 'bad' woman and one who satisfies male desires. Ester recalls that Brandt was 'humorous rather than indignant about social exploitation', and the picture seems to be, in part, a joke at the expense of socially critical documentary. Brassaï's store sign advertising '*Fromage*' invokes modernist ideas about woman as commodity; by matching this with a sign for '*Kohlen Kartoffel*' (coal and potatoes), Brandt gives his scene an absurdist tinge.

More puzzles remain, however. Why stage a picture to replicate an 'authentic' picture taken by a friend?[26] Was this an exercise in apprenticeship, designed to amuse Brassaï, or flatter him? Was Brandt playing with the idea of documentary authenticity, since Brassaï had actually gone to live in a hotel for prostitutes to get his pictures?[27] Making pictures of prostitutes, whether in painting or photography, is central to Western art; but Brandt must be one of the first to 'postmodernise' the subject by using his wife as a model. Did Brandt make the picture as part of some erotic game with Eva, like his later picture of her in a nightgown and wearing a blonde wig?[28] The fantasy of a husband picking up his wife and treating her like a prostitute is banal enough. Visually, the picture could also come from German Expressionist cinema, with its brief, iconic scenes and stark black-and-white lighting.[29] Finally, the picture (like many of Brassaï's) could fit neatly into a photo-crime sequence: the establishing shot of the prostitute before the client approaches. This is made explicit in one of Brandt's pictures for *A Night in London*, 'Footsteps Coming Closer'. Here we are in the world of Moosbrugger, the prostitute-murderer in Musil's *The Man Without Qualities*. All these things might have been in the air at the Hungarian table of the Dôme, and we can never know exactly what games Brandt and Brassaï were playing. But there is no doubt that Brandt studied Brassaï's urban photography very closely, then went on to present scenes of his own in a much stranger light.

Beggar in Barcelona, 1932

After two years spent mostly in Paris, Brandt set off to Spain in April 1932. For the denizens of Montparnasse, Spain was both the most exotic country in Western Europe and a politically attractive place to go. The proclamation of a liberal republic in 1931 brought a ray of hope when Fascism seemed to be on the rise everywhere else. Brandt would also have personal reasons for wanting to visit Spain, having lived with so many Spaniards at the Schweizerhof in Davos. Finally, he and Eva had an invitation from one of their Vienna friends. Gyorgi Szulyovsky (nicknamed 'Djuri') had recently moved to Barcelona, where his mother had bought a *pension*. The son of a Hungarian father and an Austrian mother, Djuri had been a friend of Rolf Brandt's in Vienna, and had gone with him to join the repertory company of the Friedrichstheater in Dessau. A great admirer of both Brandt and Eva, Djuri was probably their closest friend during the 1930s, after Lyena. He often visited them in London, where he was a favourite model for Brandt's staged pictures.

Brandt's trip to Spain began a two-year period of restlessness, in which he lived more in Paris than anywhere else, but was preparing himself, consciously or not, to become English rather than French. Lyena Barjansky had started to do well in her fashion business, once she found a *midinette* who 'knew what it was about'. Eva, who was good at cutting and sewing, spent much of her time helping her. For such a business, Paris was the only place to be, and Lyena spent the entire decade there until the German invasion forced her to leave. But Brandt did his most creative work in other places, even when he was living in Paris. The whole seven years from his leaving the sanatorium in 1927 really represented a period of exploration, until he was able to strike root in England and find his true artistic home.

Brandt travelled to Barcelona in his usual unorthodox style, with both Eva and Lyena in tow. The two women stayed at Djuri's *pension* while Brandt went to a more luxurious hotel. Soon after they arrived, though, Brandt and Eva paid tribute to respectability by deciding to get married. There had been continuing pressure from Eva's aunts in Budapest for her to settle down and be respectable. Since Brandt was a Lutheran, he could not have married Eva in a Catholic wedding unless he agreed to convert. Getting married in Spain was a way of giving in, but without going through the business of a religious wedding in Hungary. On the strength of his British passport, Brandt applied to the British Consulate, and he married Eva there on 15 April, with

Lyena and Djuri as witnesses. Brandt hadn't realised that a ring was needed, so Djuri offered his signet ring, which Brandt promptly lost; having found it, he put it on Eva's wrong finger (some of this pantomime would be repeated at Brandt's third wedding). This may have been proof of Lyena's belief that Brandt was 'not the marrying kind', but married he now was. Moreover, Eva immediately became a British citizen, an excellent insurance policy when there were neo-Fascist governments in both Austria and Hungary and Hitler was less than a year from becoming Chancellor. The British Consul would have been puzzled, though, to welcome a wedding party whose only common language was German (Lyena spoke no English then), and which appeared to consist of a German, two Hungarians and a Russian!

Brandt and Eva's honeymoon was a trip to Mallorca with their two friends, to call on Robert Graves and Laura Riding – who unfortunately were not at home. Brandt got to know Graves later and took some of the best portraits of him, though one can only speculate about why he was so interested in him in 1932. Perhaps someone in Paris gave him an introduction, or he was interested in Graves as an Anglo-German (his mother was from the distinguished Ranke family of Munich). Brandt may well have heard of Graves's unusual living arrangements in 1929 at 'free-love corner' (St Peter's Square, Hammersmith). This was first triangular with his wife Nancy Nicholson and Laura Riding, then quadrilateral with the addition of Geoffrey Phibbs.[1] It would be typical of Brandt, though, to go to Deya as an observer, perhaps without any intention of discussing his own situation with Graves.

These weeks in Catalonia were also fruitful for Brandt's photography, and encouraged him to return the following March to see Madrid and Toledo. He pasted a bullfight postcard into his album of Spanish pictures, but most of what he photographed was not the archetypal Spain of, say, Hemingway, Picasso and Buñuel. He did take pictures of beggars and gypsies, as did so many photographers who went to southern Europe from Paris or Vienna. But Brandt was not interested in romantic ethnography, or in the documentation of injustice. The 'Beggar' that he photographed somewhere on the outskirts of Barcelona in April 1932 was above all a study in gesture, as stylised as a Koppitz nude. The man appears to be blind; but even if he were not, the picture makes no claim on the viewer to look at him directly, and be looked at in return. Rather, the beggar's entreaty is along the picture's vertical axis, like a figure in a Renaissance painting who implores God to fill his bowl. The arid background of road and wall suggests that the beggar is beyond any human solidarity; traditional leftist documentary might have placed him on a street corner, as a standing rebuke to the prosperous passers-by.

Two of Brandt's studies of gypsy women, taken on the same trip, are equally unorthodox. One might be a beggar, but her posture does not demand any help or understanding from the observer. In the other picture, a gypsy cooks over a brazier with her utensils spread around, not looking either pitiable or particularly exotic. Brandt also took some more predictable Spanish pictures: a family at dinner, an immemorial shepherd on a hill overlooking Toledo. Another group gives a Surrealist perspective on social roles. The night-watchman with his tightly buttoned uniform and great bunch of keys might have been one of August Sander's studies of men imprisoned in their social status, except that Brandt's subject gazes calmly at something

House in Hungary, 1932/33

outside the frame, almost like a statue of a night-watchman.[2] His companion-piece is the *porteria* (concierge), enclosed both by the door-frame and the text that identifies her role, who has withdrawn from her tenants into the fantasy world of her book. Then there is the actual statue of the industrialist in a Barcelona cemetery. With his account book and factories, he too looks off out of the frame and seems unaware of the figure of Death, who stands behind him and looks the viewer in the eye.[3]

While Brandt and Eva were in Barcelona, the liberal Alcala Zamora was trying to turn Spain into a modern, democratic state. His failure led to the tragedy of 1936; but there is little evidence of Brandt's interest in the emergence of a new Spain.[4] Brandt came to Spain as a sympathetic outsider and discovered a country of myths and extremes. Surrealism, in Paris, had been enriched by Picasso, Dalí and Buñuel demonstrating that, in Spain, nothing was 'business as usual'. Brandt's encounter with Spain also contributed to his eye for another marginal culture, that of England. Here it was a question of the eccentric rather than the extreme, but in both countries roles and rituals seemed to swallow up personality, turning people into puppets of themselves. Brassaï's Paris was rich in the humanism of comfortingly typical French figures; Brandt was more drawn to the human oddities to be found at Europe's margins, in Hungary, Spain and England.

In September 1932 Brandt and Eva returned to Hungary, now as a respectable married couple. On this trip Brandt discovered the *puszta* – the great eastern Hungarian plain – and took many pictures of the people and animals that lived there. Kertész had taken similar pictures just after the war, but Brandt's have more of an edge to them.[5] They convey a desperate, end-of-the-world quality in Hungarian life: there are drunkards waving bottles or sleeping under haystacks, beggars, gypsies and a crippled shepherd boy.[6] Leaning on his crutch, the boy is set off against one of the *puszta*'s lever-wells, which might equally well be a gallows or a crucifix. A picture of tumble-down dwellings, perhaps the home of gypsies, is the first of a series of compositions in which people are looked down on, as if they were in a prison courtyard. Near Szeged in the southeast, Brandt photographed a great pig, which wallows like an amphibian in a featureless expanse of waste land and mud. Many photographers at this time were producing cutely anthropomorphic pictures of animals, often doubled with human lookalikes; Brandt's pig offers no such cosy relationship with the viewer.[7] Brandt's Hungary is a surreal country, deliberately made to look as disconcerting as possible.

Soon after Brandt and Eva returned from Spain as husband and wife, Rolf Brandt and Ester Bonnesen also married, in Copenhagen on 30 June 1932. Ester was only nineteen, and got married on the day she finished school. The young couple set up house in Berlin, where Rolf was now working in repertory at the Schiller Theater, but the political atmosphere was so ominous that a routine career as an actor in Germany was clearly out of the question. There were constant gun battles in Berlin between Brownshirts and Communists, and on 31 July the Nazis became the largest single party in the Reichstag. In August the Nazi majority on the Dessau city council voted to shut down the Bauhaus, where Rolf had many friends from his stay in 1929-30.[8] He and Ester decided to stick it out in Berlin nonetheless, and do what little they could to support the dying Weimar Republic.

Drunkard on the *puszta*, 1932/33

Hitler became Chancellor of Prussia on 30 January 1933. Rolf was not viscerally anti-German in the way Brandt was, but he and Ester were much more politically minded, and bitterly opposed to Nazism. When Rolf was at the municipal theatre in Dessau in 1929-30, his friends there and at the Bauhaus were already being harassed by the local Nazis. The theatre put on plays they disliked, like R. C. Sherriffs's anti-war *Journey's End*, and the Bauhaus was considered a cesspit of Judaism, Bolshevism and degeneracy. Once Hitler became Chancellor, the protesters had the power of the state behind them. At the Schiller Theater in Berlin, Ester recalls, the actors were immediately required to give the Hitler salute:

> Rolf said 'I'm not going to do that, I'm just not going to do that.' That, of course, was possible for him because he had a British passport. So we decided to go away. But the others who had to say 'Heil Hitler' – what do you do when you can't go away? It's so easy to say you shouldn't.[9]

Rolf and Ester left Berlin for London on 27 February, the day of the Reichstag fire. Though they had no friends their own age in England, and no positive attraction to English life, their political views left them with no alternative. It seemed time for the Brandt family to re-group in the country they had always seen as their second home.

Brandt and Eva came to London about three months later, and stayed for the summer. It was a very fruitful visit photographically.[10] But the Brandts stayed at Sybil Knight's boarding house in Belsize Park rather than setting up on their own; and although Brandt had been saying for years that London was a most wonderful place, it took him a long time to make a final commitment to it. Around September he and Eva returned to the Continent and stayed there until April of 1934. First they went to Hungary, for another visit to Eva's relatives and more picture-taking on the *puszta*. They then spent almost all of the rest of the year in Paris, which suggests that Brandt did not feel much urgency about building on his English work, successful as it had been. He also recognised other obligations. Just before his last visit to England, Grete Kolliner had died in Vienna at the early age of forty-one, on 4 May 1933. Her heir – presumably the mother or sister who lived with her at Peter Jordanstrasse – seems to have appealed to Brandt for help in continuing the business. On 10 October he and Eva arrived from Paris at the apartment connected to the studio, Frankgasse 6, and stayed there for ten days. While there, Brandt took another of his pictures of Eva as a prostitute. She is at a rear window, peering suspiciously around a curtain, wearing a shift and a blonde wig similar to one used by Man Ray for some of his 1930 nudes.[11] Instead of the conventional figure who submits patiently to being looked over by the male, here it is the woman who gazes with hostility at the world outside her room.

Brandt and Eva returned to Paris for the rest of the year, then came back to take over the Kolliner studio on 3 January. This meant the daily grind of a Viennese commercial photographer: family portraits of the bourgeoisie interspersed with publicity shots of dancers or actors. The Brandts would have taken hundreds of plates in the early months of 1934; but all 'Jewish' businesses were wound up after

1938, and none of Kolliner's plates have been traced. It is unlikely that Brandt could have settled down to the discipline of running such a studio. His real interest now was in outdoor or domestic scenes, taken with his handheld Rolleiflex and mostly by available light. Part of his reason for leaving Man Ray had been his desire to free himself from the constraints of four walls, flood lights, plate cameras and other studio paraphernalia.

Even if Brandt found something congenial in returning to the Kolliner studio, political developments soon made it impossible for him and Eva to enjoy anything like the life they had led in Vienna in the late 1920s. The Chancellor of Austria, Engelbert Dollfuss, had dismissed the Austrian parliament in March 1933, soon after Hitler came to power. 'Red Vienna' was now an enclave surrounded by Fascist regimes (except for the equally precarious Czech Republic). Its only defence was a Social Democratic militia, the *Schutzbund*; the right had its own unofficial army, the *Heimwehr*. The hostility between Catholic rural Austria and 'Red Vienna' was boiling up to a civil war. In February 1934, the *Schutzbund* brought about a showdown by firing on the police in the provincial town of Linz. Fighting spread to Vienna, with the *Heimwehr* and the regular army moving together against the *Schutzbund*, which set up strongpoints in the workers' housing complexes that ringed central Vienna. The most famous of these was the kilometre-long Karl-Marx-Hof, which Brandt would have seen under construction when he first started coming to Vienna from Salmannsdorf in 1927. The *Schutzbund* had no heavy weapons, and within four days the army had shelled them into submission. Most of the fighting occurred in the workers' districts, but the uprising would have been a sickening and terrifying experience for anyone of even mildly progressive sympathies. The defeat of the left was followed by a cultural purge, including the suppression of *Der Kuckuck*, an illustrated magazine that was the major outlet for leftist photographers. The forces that had driven Rolf and Ester out of Berlin were now taking over Vienna. To stay there and fight against them would have required faith that the German and Austrian people could create a better society – a faith that Brandt did not have. On 2 April 1934 he and Eva left their flat and the Kolliner studio and returned directly to London. It was the end of Vienna.

It was the end of Paris too, where Brandt could have gone after leaving Vienna. Seeing actual blood in the streets might have brought home to him and Eva the danger hanging over all of continental Europe. But the main reason would have been Brandt's limited hopes for any further success in the French photographic world. He had done some odds and ends of commercial work, but he was taking more interesting pictures in foreign countries than in France. His fragmentary impressions of Spain, Hungary and England contrasted with Brassaï's speedy and single-minded completion of his book on Paris, published at the end of 1932. For Brandt now to attempt his own overview of Paris would be to follow in Brassaï's footsteps; everything he did would be, in some degree, exposed as a pastiche. By moving to London, Brandt could give his own twist to Brassaï's themes, without fear of seeming a mere copier. It is, of course, an oversimplification to say that Brandt left Paris in order to avoid competing directly with Brassaï; but it seems likely that Brandt saw great constraints in working in Paris, and great possibilities in what he could attempt in London. Paris was a crowded field for him, with not only Brassaï,

Hungarian gypsies, 1932/33

but also Man Ray, Kertész, Germaine Krull, Eli Lotar and many others in the public eye; Lyena recalls that Brandt was very conscious of how much competition there was. In Paris the 'Hungarian table' would know what he was doing almost before he had done it, and it would be difficult to be a man of mystery in such an incestuous world. The British photographic scene, on the other hand, was still quite sleepy, and there would be no need to keep looking out of the corner of one's eye to see who else might be there with a camera. Brandt was confident that many new things could be done in England; and there was also the attraction of turning himself into a new person to do them.

One-legged man at Ascot, 1933

11 In Pursuit of the English

Brandt came to London for good at the beginning of April 1934. He had a favourite route already, from Dieppe to Newhaven:

> About an hour before Newhaven the Seven Sisters appear like a fata Morgana on the horizon, brilliantly white in the afternoon sun – the sun always shines. England then looks like a small fairy tale island. It is an unforgettable experience and again and again a surprise for me.[1]

Brandt did not just choose to be in England, like his brother Rolf. He wanted to be English, and really belong to the fairy-tale island. This meant inventing a new identity for himself, as he turned thirty, but also inventing an England that would satisfy his childhood fantasies. His English elocution lessons at Davos had been a first step towards burying his German origins, and by 1934 he spoke English adequately, though with a German accent that he was never able to lose entirely, and which remained an embarrassment to him.[2] But from his first residence in England he started to construct an elaborate cover story that censored and distorted the previous twenty-nine years of his life. Erasing his three years in Vienna from the record was a simple matter of suppression. At a deeper level, Brandt's aim was to re-stage his own personality, like one of his photographic tableaux. If Rolf could play the part of an English officer in *Journey's End*, why could not Brandt play such a part permanently, in real life?

The first step on this path was to change his name again. He had been 'Billy' to his friends in Vienna and Paris, but from now on he would be 'Bill'. In May 1932 he had published a picture of a man sitting in the park, in the German magazine *Der Querschnitt*.[3] This was credited to 'Bill Brandt', so before he was even living in England he was using the name professionally. Probably he did not realise the working-class overtones of the name, which later made many readers of *Picture Post* think he belonged with the genuine article of cockney photographers, Bert Hardy.[4]

For their visit in the summer of 1933, the Brandts had lived with Sybil Knight in Daleham Gardens. They now took regular lodgings nearby but, as in Paris, not together. Brandt rented a small flat at 43 Belsize Avenue, while Eva was nearby at 24 Lyndhurst Road.[5] Belsize Park was becoming the favoured destination for Austrian Jews and other refugees from Nazism. Viennese coffee houses and bakeries started to appear, along with Viennese psychoanalysts. But this exiles' London was only part of English life for Brandt and Rolf, since they had their well-established English uncles – their father's eldest brothers, who had become partners in the family bank, William Brandt & Sons.[6] Uncles Augustus and Henry took Bill under their wing. They had large houses in South Kensington, and neighbouring country estates near Redhill: Uncle Augustus at Castle Hill, Bletchingley, and his younger brother Henry at Capenor, Nutley.

To their uncles, Brandt and Eva must have seemed a rackety young couple. They were married, at least, but not living together. Their previous existence in Paris was suspiciously bohemian, and they had no interest in merchant banking or any other kind of business. They had no shared house to which relatives could be invited, and were without visible means of support. In fact they lived on an allowance of about thirty pounds a month from L. W. Brandt (as did Rolf and Ester). One could certainly manage on that, at a time when a flat could be had for two or three pounds a week; but there must have been something extra for things like the dress clothes that Bill and Eva needed to dine at the Café Royal (or at their uncles' houses).[7] On the other hand, they knew exactly how to behave in society, and Eva was both elegant and vaguely aristocratic. They were accepted as part of the family and, what is more surprising, allowed to photograph freely within their uncles' households. Brandt did not set up a studio like the one he had just left in Vienna. For the rest of his career his photography would be done in the streets of London, the English countryside and the houses to which he had access. All he needed was a makeshift darkroom at his flat, where he would do almost all his developing and printing.[8]

Ester Brandt found it very trying to go from the savage politics of Nazi Berlin to these Alice-in-Wonderland houses of the English Brandts, where people said things like 'There isn't enough room to keep your opera hat on in the new Bentley!' When Rolf said that he had enjoyed a play by Bernard Shaw, one of his uncles said, 'Do you realise that he's a Socialist?' But Bill was less inclined to bridle at small talk, or the sheer boredom of upper-class gatherings. He wanted to experience – and to photograph – English society from top to bottom. He had scarcely left the boat in 1933 when he was off to Ascot, the Derby and the Eton versus Harrow cricket match. In Paris, foreigners were largely excluded from bourgeois social life, and Brandt saw it as a limitation of Brassaï's work that it did not reach the upper levels of society.

Within a very short time of coming to England to live, Brandt formed the basic idea of his first collection, *The English at Home*. The layout of the book would be a series of contrasts between wealth, on the left-hand pages, and poverty, on the right. On the left side he would have scenes from the life of his upper-class relatives. For the right side he would find English equivalents of the outcasts he had photographed on the Continent: beggars, gypsies and drunkards. In another sense, by showing English life in such stark oppositions, he could leave himself out of the picture: living on their seven pounds a week on the edge of Hampstead, he and Eva belonged to an undefined middle. Brandt's picture of Bloomsbury friends at an intellectual tea party, later in the Thirties, was quite unusual. When he did take pictures of his own circle, he did not show their actual lives, but had them play dramatic roles from other, more sharply defined social positions.

Ballet dancer, London, 1933

Passengers on Channel ferry, 1933

It was natural, of course, for Brandt's side-by-side pictures of rich and poor to be taken as a direct social criticism. But Lyena Barjansky doubted that Brandt was making that kind of political point. The contrast of rich and poor was something one could not help noticing in England, at an event like the Derby; and also, she thought, 'the middle is just not so interesting'.[9] This is not to say that Brandt was looking at the rich with a complacent eye; but neither was he trying to whip up dislike of upper-class manners and pastimes. There was already a tradition in European photography of making a spectacle of chaps in top hats – pinning a target on them, as it were, for the coming revolution.[10] Brandt has his own fascination with top hats, whether at Ascot, Eton or in a shop window; but his eye rests on them with bemusement rather than outrage. At Ascot, for example, he shows a plutocratic gent, dressed to the nines, studying his race-card; but he then undermines the man's privileged status by several means. He is making his way across a rubbish-strewn patch of waste ground (a staple of Brandt's racing scenes), with an advertising sign in the background. His progress is difficult because he only has one leg, having presumably lost the other in the war; but he manages with just a walking stick, and his chauffeur is not allowed to help. The chauffeur's job is to serve lunch – for which he wears an apron over his uniform – and to look after a very small monkey. What makes the whole pantomime so unmistakably English is that the master appears to be holding forth to his servant about which horse is going to win the Royal Hunt Cup, and is meeting with polite, but firm, disagreement.

This picture conveys wonderfully the distinctive body-language of social relations in Brandt's adopted country; and the disposition of bodies in public spaces seems to fascinate him from the beginning of his English documentary work. A pensive study of a ballet dancer in rehearsal is unusual for Brandt, just because of her natural gracefulness.[11] More typical is what catches his eye on the Channel ferry in June 1933, an odd mixture of formality and abandon.[12] Some passengers sit primly around a hatch cover, while others are sprawled next to them, sun-bathing or asleep. One prone woman is being used as a book-rest by her friend. Another picture shows two boys lying on the grass to watch a cricket match – in Eton suits and top hats. The obverse of these boneless figures are the silhouetted, attentive racegoers at Ascot, who seem to await a revelation. There is a tic-tac man signalling bets in a crucified pose, while others turn away from him, indifferent.[13] The upper-class types on the roof of a carriage form what will become a favourite Brandt composition: we see the responses of a group to some event, rather than the event itself.[14] Their rapt expressions recall religious paintings where God reveals himself to an awestruck collection of onlookers. Brandt's England seems to be a country full of such quasi-religious events, where people perform rituals that are hard for unbelievers to grasp.

Two other styles appear early in Brandt's English repertoire. One is the townscape of massed villas extending to the horizon: cosy little homes that become sinister when so many of them are packed together. This kind of urban vista had no real equivalent in Paris or Vienna; English intellectuals often denounced it as a lower-middle-class nightmare, the 'red rust' that defiles the landscape in E. M. Forster's *Howards End*. Brandt's 'Rainswept Roofs' owes something to *Neue Sachlichkeit* studies in urban geometry. But to fill up the whole field of view with these little boxes speaks of

Tic-tac man, Ascot, 1933

the sheer density of London – yet a density composed of individual dreams of property and privacy. In Brandt's large output of architectural pictures, there will be a similar emphasis on the singular dwelling as the English ideal, rather than on the grand vistas and monuments of the continental capitals.

Another fertile seam for Brandt appears in his 'Sailor Cox' picture from the 1933 Derby: the juxtaposition of a human figure with an intrusive script on some advertising hoarding or shop front. The bookie Sailor Cox stands in uniform like a captain on his bridge, surrounded by uncanny replications of his image. The slogan 'All the Nice Girls Bet with Sailor' gives a nudge and a wink to the obvious pun on 'Cocks'. Atget and Brassaï had already juxtaposed figures and texts to characterise the modern city, but Brandt notes how London, more than other capitals, swarms with pieces of text: on buildings, buses, news-stands and the new genre of cinema posters. Everyone in the city seems in danger of being 'plastered' with such messages. Brandt is fascinated, also, with the doubleness of these signs: as texts to be read, and as visual blocks that are part of the composition.

Brandt's compulsion to cover over his German traces, once he had arived in England, was at odds with the German influence on British photo-journalism of the 1930s. As the entire German press came under Nazi control, in the months after Hitler became Chancellor, many German journalists and photographers came to England. The impresario of the group was Stefan Lorant, a Hungarian with one Gentile and one Jewish parent. His father had run a large portrait studio in Budapest. While still in his twenties, Lorant had become editor of one of the two leading illustrated magazines in Germany, the *Münchner Illustrierte Zeitung*. When Hitler was editing a Nazi magazine in Munich in the late 1920s, Lorant got to know him as a fellow-journalist. For a while Lorant went out with Hitler's half-niece, Geli Raubal, and would see Hitler peering suspiciously from the window when he brought her home.[15] The Nazis occupied Munich on 9 March 1933, and Lorant was arrested five days later on the pretext of 'protective custody'; the real reason was that his paper had opposed their rise to power. After he had spent six months in prison, the Hungarian Foreign Minister got him released, and Lorant returned to Budapest to write a book, *I Was Hitler's Prisoner*. He tried to get it published in Paris in the spring of 1934 but failed, and went on to London, arriving on 17 April, two weeks after the Brandts came back from Vienna. In prison Lorant had learned fifty words of English a day, and he was ready to turn the torpid world of British photo-journalism on its head.

Lorant was soon followed to England by two of the best photographers who had worked for him in Munich, Hans Baumann and Kurt Hübschmann. Hübschmann was half-Jewish, Baumann was a Gentile with no particular interest in politics.[16] But, as Lorant observed, there were 'many decent people in Germany who simply didn't want to stay'. Nonetheless, having a conspicuously German name would not help anybody to succeed as a freelance photographer in England, so Baumann changed his name to 'Felix Man' and Hübschmann to 'Kurt Hutton'.[17] Two other significant figures were Edith Tudor Hart and her brother Wolfgang Suschitzky. Tudor Hart had acquired her English name through marriage to a physician; she was a Viennese Jew and fellow-traveller whose Social Realist street photography anticipated the *Picture Post* style. Her brother came to England after her, in 1934; their father, who had run the

Sailor Cox, 1933

first socialist bookstore in Vienna, stayed behind and killed himself after the workers' revolt was crushed.[18]

As Brandt was settling in England in 1934, its whole photographic culture was about to be transformed by these new arrivals from Germany, Austria and Hungary (other refugee photographers moved to Paris, New York and even to Hollywood). England was far behind the Continent in both art and commercial photography, but it had highly developed mass media that provided an excellent potential base for photo-journalism. The revolution in English photo-journalism would be of immense importance for Brandt's career over the next fifteen years, though it would take him several years to gain his rightful place in it. He was indisputably an émigré steeped in German visual culture, whether or not he wanted to be included with others of the group. Brandt never became close friends with any of them, probably because he did not want to be lumped in with them as a German refugee (which strictly speaking he wasn't, not having lived in Germany for eleven years).

Nor was Brandt interested simply in transplanting German methods to England, which is what Lorant had come over to do. Less than two months after arriving in London, and speaking only broken English, Lorant had put together a dummy of the first popular picture magazine in Britain, *Weekly Illustrated*.[19] It was based on his successful formula at the *Münchner Illustrierte Presse*: lots of pictures and very little text, and selling at a low price, thanks to new high-speed presses and rotogravure reproduction.[20] Lorant convinced Odham's Press to take on the magazine, and its first issue appeared on 7 July 1934. Its regular photographers were Kurt Hutton, Felix Man, Haywood Magee, and Jim Jarché (the son of a French photographer who had settled in London). *Weekly Illustrated* was a modest success, with a circulation of between 200,000 and 250,000 copies a week.

Lorant left *Weekly Illustrated* after six months: partly because his mother became ill in Budapest, partly because Odham's got fed up with his strong opinions and refusal to keep regular office hours. Before he left, Brandt – 'like other young photographers', as Lorant put it – came into the office to show him some pictures and ask for assignments.[21] Lorant says he gave Brandt some work, but there is nothing in the early issues of the magazine that can be positively identified as his, and no friendship developed between the two men.[22] One can imagine several reasons for this failure to connect. Their temperaments were completely different, with Brandt so retiring and Lorant a 'bumptious Hungarian' who was always peddling some new scheme.[23] Lorant would have addressed Brandt in German when he first turned up at the office, which immediately would have created a chilly atmosphere. That Lorant was Hungarian might have made Brandt even more wary, since he was in the process of being re-born as a true-blue Englishman and leaving the Hungarians of Montparnasse behind him.[24] Finally, the style of Brandt's pictures might well have struck Lorant as too static and 'arty' for a new magazine that was trying to woo a mass readership with short, punchy stories. Most of his photographers were Leica users who could do a quick job and drop off a roll of thirty-six shots; Lorant would select the ones he wanted from contact sheets, then do his own arranging and captioning.[25] He had studied the art of composition, and aimed at moving the reader's eye around the page to create a sweeping effect in the *Weekly Illustrated* format, where most stories were laid out on two very large facing pages. Brandt's painstaking production of a handful of pictures on his Rolleiflex would not have fitted in comfortably with Lorant's methods. Yet it was surely a stroke of luck for English photography that Brandt did not follow the path of Hübschmann and Baumann in 1934 and become a regular photographer for *Weekly Illustrated*. Being pinned down to weekly assignments would have been as uncongenial to Brandt as having to work year-round at Kolliner's. Instead, he was free to let his gaze wander over the infinite variety of London. When he did become a regular photo-journalist four years later, his style as an English photographer was fully formed, and by then he could accept even routine assignments without any danger of being compromised by them.

Parlourmaid and under-parlourmaid ready to serve dinner, about 1935

In August 1934 Brandt made his first excursion outside London, going to the Scilly Isles with Eva and Lyena. The Scillies appealed to him as another of the forgotten corners of Europe, like Mallorca or the Hungarian *puszta*, where curious scenes of backwardness or neglect could still be found. There, his eye fell on various ships' figureheads stranded in gardens. These uncanny bits of marine mythology, incongruously surrounded with vegetation, were just the thing for *Minotaure*, where they appeared in winter 1935. But to comb England for Surrealist oddities would leave Brandt still dawdling on the margins of his adopted society. He wanted to get closer to the centre of things, using his camera to make some kind of comprehensive statement about England, and focusing on its capital. The obvious format for such a project was a collection like Brassaï's *Paris de Nuit*, which had shown what could be done with a single place and theme. Brassaï had seized on his idea and gone from being a photographic novice to completing a landmark book in only two and a half years. Brandt would assemble a collection as significant as Brassaï's in even less time, and would cover a much wider range of subjects. His success was a measure of how right he had been to leave Paris in favour of London.

The English at Home – the book that would collect Brandt's pictures from his first years in England – combined three different kinds of photography: those of the ethnographer, the social critic and what we might call 'the director'. The work of the Ethnographer had been defined by Bronislaw Malinowski in 1922:

> In studying the conspicuous acts of tribal life, such as ceremonies, rites, festivities, etc., the details and tone of behaviour ought to be given, besides the bare outline of events … Take any example from our own culture, whether it be the pomp and pageantry of a state ceremony, or a picturesque custom kept up by street urchins, its 'outline' will not tell you whether the rite flourishes still with full vigour in the hearts of those who perform it or assist at the performance or whether they regard it as almost a dead thing, kept alive for tradition's sake. But observe and fix the data of their behaviour, and at once the degree of vitality of the act will become clear …
>
> In this type of work, it is good for the Ethnographer sometimes to put aside camera, note book and pencil, and to join in himself in what is going on. He can

take part in the natives' games, he can follow them on their visits and walks, sit down and listen and share in their conversations. I am not certain if this is equally easy for everyone – perhaps the Slavonic nature is more plastic and more naturally savage than that of Western Europeans – but though the degree of success varies, the attempt is possible for everyone.[1]

Malinowski took a camera to New Guinea, and his *Argonauts of the Western Pacific* was illustrated with sixty-five photographs. In his introduction to *The English at Home*, Raymond Mortimer notes the anthropological quality of Brandt's pictures: '[he] seems to have wandered about England with the detached curiosity of a man investigating the customs of some remote and unfamiliar tribe. And his illustrated report brings home very amusingly the variety and importance in England of clothes.'[2] Prominent among these tribal regalia are the hats that identify both status and social occasion, and one picture shows just a glass case full of opera hats. Probably Brandt was making fun of this national obsession in his picture of the Billingsgate porter, who wears a special load-bearing hat with a twenty-pound cod perched on it.

By definition, the ethnographer's insight comes from his belonging to a different culture from the one he studies. Brandt, like Malinowski (who was of Polish origin), was an outsider to the English society he photographed; but in making his pictures of the upper class he benefited from being able to pass as one of them, which Malinowski could scarcely do with the Trobriand Islanders. One can imagine Brandt and Eva dressing up in their little Belsize Park flats and then taking a taxi to Kensington to visit the uncles. If they were going to the opera, Brandt would have put on his top hat, just like all the other men there. By temperament, he was probably well suited to fit into a society where the first requirement was to follow a complex set of rules, and where conversational formulas often substituted for any real intimacy between people.

As he entered British social life, at what point did Brandt ask to bring his Rolleiflex, and what awkwardness may it have created? The upper classes expected to see photographers at formal events, and those who aspired to be fashionable would have enjoyed seeing themselves in the pages of *The Tatler*, *The Bystander* and even the popular press. But a commercial photographer in such a situation was treated as a tradesman. An obvious exception was Cecil Beaton, who had gone to Cambridge and came from a wealthy background similar to Brandt's. But Beaton did not take documentary pictures of the poor or of industrial workers, as Brandt did. *The English at Home* suggests how Brandt picked his way through the social minefield of being both a photographer and a guest. He did not include in the book any recognisable pictures of his relatives and their friends, nor did he show upper-class subjects 'at home', like the miner's wife in her bedroom. Such pictures would only appear in his second book, *A Night in London*. The three upper-class interiors in *The English at Home* focus on servants or children. One is of a nanny reading to her charge, being looked at aslant by a Surrealistic rocking-horse.[3] The other two pictures, masterpieces of Brandt's early style, are examples of ethnography with a twist. Brandt wanted to show typical English behaviour, but also to bring out some quality of strangeness in even the most conventional and privileged social occasions.

'Kensington Children's Party' is printed opposite a scene of children playing in a

Kensington children's party, about 1935

dismal East End street. It is also a picture of internal contrast. The balloons at the top of the frame are supposed to represent hilarity but, hanging up there with their dangling ribbons, they become frozen, uncanny objects. At the bottom of the frame, the children's faces are frozen too, into expressions of solemn self-control. Usually Brandt avoided having his subjects look directly at the camera, but here he seems to have *wanted* to make the children self-conscious: they appear already captive to a precocious sense of duty. The contrast between them and the street children seems to speak for itself; yet what did it mean that these solemn party-goers were Brandt's little cousins and their friends? Was he just observing English children, or judging them?

'Dinner is Served', taken at Uncle Henry's country house near Redhill, again shows people frozen into a role by uniforms and props. In socially critical documentary such a picture might be filed under 'false consciousness'; but Brandt's picture is not so easily labelled. Pictures of the oppressed typically show them united in a single condition of wretchedness, out of which they gaze reproachfully at the well-meaning outside observer. Brandt is not trying to inflict guilt and, having taken his picture, will sit down and enjoy the elaborate dinner prepared for his pleasure. Furthermore, the parlourmaid and the under-parlourmaid inhabit their roles in very different ways. The older woman is imposing discipline on the under-parlourmaid, who gazes off across the room with an expression that might spell constraint, boredom or involvement in some private fantasy. The parlourmaid suppresses her own personality entirely, in order to concentrate on the dinner table itself, as if defying any object on it to be an inch out of place. It is a role that she seems to have grown into over thirty years or more, and into which the young woman she might once have been has completely disappeared.

This parlourmaid, whose name in the family was simply 'Pratt', became an obsession for Brandt. A note found in his papers refers to his first meeting with her, on 22 March 1929: '*fortuite où nécessaire – qui sait – la rencontre avec Pratt m'était en tout cas fatale*'.[4] '*Fatale*' may mean 'fateful' or 'fatal': either a turning-point in Brandt's life, or a meeting that led to disaster. Which did Brandt have in mind? Was Pratt a woman of destiny, or a *femme fatale*?[5] We can only be sure that something momentous happened when Brandt first rang Uncle Henry's doorbell, at Capenor or the house in Queen's Gate, and found himself face to face with Pratt.

Pratt would have been about forty when Brandt met her. Ester Cotton remembers her as a very important figure in the household whom everyone adored; 'nowhere else in the world do you have anything like her'. When Brandt's five-year-old nephew Peter was asked why he liked Pratt, he replied 'because she calls me sir'. She was a hard and a soft person at the same time: she ran the house meticulously, but also made it a home. In a very English way, she both served Henry Brandt and was a member of his family. If she provided the flash of insight that led to Brandt's gallery of English types in the Thirties, there can hardly have been anything disastrous about this. Pratt may have disturbed him by re-awakening some of his childhood conflicts between nurturing figures: the strict and puritanical mother side by side with the loving nanny who provided sensual warmth. Both sides could be found in Pratt, and her uniform would make the division especially stark. She probably inspired the numerous pictures Brandt took in the Thirties of women in uniform, such as the schoolgirl in *The*

English at Home and his classic story in *Picture Post* about waitresses at Lyons Corner House: 'Nippy. The Story of her Day'.[6]

It would be far-fetched to imagine any sexual intimacy between Brandt and Pratt, though he seems to have visited her at her home to take 'A Resident of Putney' for *A Night in London*. On her day off, she looks as formidable in civilian clothes and tightly rolled umbrella as she does in uniform. The caption is an early example of Brandt's playing with private meanings: 'residents of Putney' are not familiar types, like guardsmen or fish porters, so only insiders would know the full significance of the picture. There may be a clue to Brandt's fetishising of Pratt in a game that he and Rolf played in the 1940s at Winswood, the house in Crawley, Sussex, where their parents lived after fleeing Nazi Germany. The house had a flat attached to it, rented by a Mrs Corns, who worked as a night-nurse and so was rarely seen. Bill and Rolf amused themselves with elaborate fantasies about what 'the mysterious Mrs Corns' might be up to (and when she *was* seen, she would probably be in her nurse's uniform!).[7] Brandt and his brother liked childish games, keeping the world of nursery stories alive into adulthood; Pratt was a storybook figure, yet also someone that Brandt took very seriously indeed, even if we can only guess at the deeper reasons for his fascination with her. She stood both for the typical face of English life and for the mystery of its inner workings. In Brandt's efforts to understand his new country, it seemed to him that Pratt was the best place to begin.

Ester Brandt as 'Brighton Belle', 1935

In his pictures of Pratt, Brandt cannot have been seeing her with the eyes of a social critic. Still, he was becoming more sympathetic to the left, like other young men of his sort. In the Soviet Union, the terrible years of the purges had begun, after the assassination of Kirov on 1 December 1934. But many of the Surrealists – notably Louis Aragon, Paul Eluard and René Crevel – were moving into the French Communist Party; either not knowing what Stalin was up to, or approving of it. Rolf and Ester Brandt were going in the same direction, and urging Bill to go with them. J. B. Priestley's *English Journey*, published in 1934, pointed Brandt towards the economic disaster of the industrial areas, and a trip to the south Wales collieries in 1935 yielded three memorable pictures for *The English at Home*.[1] Closer to hand were the slums of east London, such as Stepney, Whitechapel and Bethnal Green. Eva was friendly with a local priest, who helped Brandt to make contact with likely subjects.[2] She was 'not a socialist, but very compassionate and caring'; in Budapest, her friend Paul Ignotus had founded a left-wing journal called *Beautiful World*; and at the end of her life, Eva 'deeply hated Mrs Thatcher'.[3] Brandt's position was more complicated and, at the end of his life, he admired Mrs Thatcher. There was no left-wing tradition in his family, and he certainly did not feel the need to atone for past privileges by living a worker's life. In 1959 Brandt said of his documentary work, 'I was probably inspired to take these pictures because the social contrast of the Thirties was visually very exciting for me. I never intended them … for political propaganda.'[4] Brandt showed England as an eccentric society, with great gaps between its members; yet indignation at its injustices does not seem to be his primary response to it. One could even say that he was grateful to the class system for giving him so much to see.

George Orwell's *Down and Out in Paris and London* had appeared in January 1933; in November 1934 he started working in a bookstore half a mile from Brandt's flat, on the other side of Haverstock Hill.[5] He and Brandt were almost the same age, and may have met casually, but their reasons for exploring poverty in England could hardly have been more different. In January 1936 Victor Gollancz sent Orwell to investigate conditions in the northern industrial towns. *The Road to Wigan Pier* appeared a year later in Gollancz's 'Left Book Club', with an insert of agency photographs from south Wales mining districts and northern slums.[6] These pictures only documented misery; there were no pictures of the comfortable rich. Orwell was always struggling towards solidarity between his own class and the workers, while Brandt always created some strangeness or separation between observer and observed. Indeed, he aimed for a similar effect when photographing members of his own class, including his English relatives.

Titles with the word 'English' in them – like Brandt's *The English at Home* or Priestley's *English Journey* – provided a kind of justification for social hierarchy. Showing cockneys and lords rubbing shoulders at Ascot suggested that England had a place for all sorts, and could avoid the extremes of either Fascism or Communism that were engulfing continental Europe. And, moving as his pictures of the poor might be, Brandt did not contemplate them with anything like Orwell's sense of intimate discomfort and self-reproach. 'Seek and ye shall find' might be the motto of Orwell's quest for black beetles in the tripe, the better to disturb his bourgeois readers.[7] A *New Statesman* review captures the difference in Brandt's perspective: 'It is because each scene or figure has interested him purely for itself that his pictures are so good and carry such implications. He does not only set out to illustrate the contrast between rich and poor; he takes his pictures and the contrast is there. The best of them are – what can one call them? – pictorial epigrams, surprisingly, vividly, exactly, seen.'[8]

'The Home', a key picture for Brandt's book, shows a crowded bedroom with a Welsh miner's wife and her three children; it is placed opposite 'The Work', a miner at the coal face.[9] As the husband toils underground, the wife and children who depend on him wait mournfully for his return. Brandt re-used the picture for his back cover, this time as a counterpoint to the upper-class racegoers at Ascot on the front. 'The Home' seems like an obvious piece of critical photo-documentary; and in his introduction to *The English at Home* Raymond Mortimer would speak of the look of misery on the mother's face, and wonder how any English person could look at the picture 'without a deep feeling of shame'.[10] Yet one wonders if shame is the emotion Brandt set out to produce. The miner's family in their bedroom have been placed like the composition of a Renaissance devotional painting. A conventional documentary picture would have them all gazing directly at the viewer in mute appeal; but the only one who does this is the little boy – not to express suffering, but because he is curious about the camera. The other three gaze pensively out of the frame, all of them looking at different, invisible objects of interest. If the viewer's conscience is engaged, it is not by the standard eye-to-eye confrontation, and this is true of almost all Brandt's pictures of dispossession.

What Brandt achieves in 'The Home' is not so much the pathos of social criticism, but the quality he defines in his preface to *Camera in London*:

> Thus it was I found *atmosphere* to be the spell that charged the commonplace with beauty. And still I am not sure what atmosphere is. I should be hard put to define it. I only know it is a combination of elements, perhaps most simply and yet most inadequately described in technical terms of lighting and viewpoint, which reveals the subject as familiar and yet strange …
>
> When I have seen or sensed – I do not know which it is – the atmosphere of my subject, I try to convey that atmosphere by intensifying the elements that compose it. I lay emphasis on one aspect of my subject and I find that I can thus

The Home (Miner's Family), 1934/35

most effectively arrest the spectator's attention and induce in him an emotional response to the atmosphere I have tried to convey.[11]

Brandt almost always starts with the commonplace and it remains in the picture, whatever else may be added. He is not interested in pictures of, say, the heart of a cabbage (a *Neue Sachlichkeit* speciality), where you may never realise that a cabbage is what you are looking at. Nor does he set out with the aim of making the middle-class observer feel guilty. The atmospheric picture begins with a cliché, or at least an ordinary, recognisable subject, which Brandt then wants us to see in a new way. He takes what is most familiar about England in the Thirties – its styles of dress, its contrasts between high and low – and then makes it strange, moving it into what David Mellor has called the private world of his 'phantasms'.

This overriding concern with atmosphere and composition can be seen most clearly in Brandt's work as a 'director', which appears in *The English at Home* and continues to the end of the Thirties. Taking a documentary picture of someone he already knew, like Pratt, started him on this path. The next step was using his friends to construct 'English' scenes that he needed to round out his collection. If the friends he used were not, in reality, English – well, who was to know? Rolf and Ester were the handiest people to provide this service, living just up the street and somewhat at a loose end after their flight from Germany. They had been in Berlin for Max Reinhardt's great theatrical productions that sought to break down the gap between actors and audience, and for Brecht's *Dreigroschenoper* and *Mahagonny*.[12] In London, drawing-room comedy was still in vogue, and there was nothing more radical than Shaw. Rolf enrolled at RADA partly to get rid of his German accent (at which he was more successful than Bill), and partly in the hope of a British acting career, which he was not able to achieve. Meanwhile he was happy to join in Bill's photographic schemes, and could bring to them years of training in acting, directing and lighting. It might even be argued that Rolf deserves equal credit with Bill for many of the staged pictures. Ester was an important contributor too, being at home in the theatrical milieu, and from her career in gymnastics knowing how to place her body.

Only four pictures in *The English at Home* were staged with Brandt's friends; but many more were to come, and they are some of his most extraordinary pictures. Two of them show Rolf only. In one he is a young man about town, in white tie and top hat, bringing up a taxi after the opera; a study in the lights and advertising signs of the West End, the picture also contrasts the fatuous client with the imperturbable taxi-driver, a male equivalent to Pratt. The other might be a photographed *Punch* cartoon, with Rolf as a top-hatted drunk, draped around a lamp-post in the fog. 'Sunday Evening' enlists a group of five to illustrate a peculiarly English scene, the lovers who strew the ground in the great London parks. Here the story is about English respect for privacy, as each couple is left alone in their personal space, some ten yards removed from any other. The only flaw in this representation of 'The English on the Grass' is that no one there is really English: Djuri Szulyovsky is in the foreground with Eva; next come Rolf and Ester; finally Augustus Brandt by himself. No doubt courting couples would not take kindly to being posed, or photographed at all for that matter. But Brandt's use of staging is only incidentally because of the difficulties of capturing a 'genuine' picture; rather, he seems to be enjoying a private joke at the very idea of authentic or typical documentary.

The pleasure of misrepresentation seems even more plain in 'Brighton Belle'. Ester and Brandt were invited to lunch with Uncle Augustus at Castle Hill (the setting for 'Cocktails in a Surrey Garden', Brandt's great twilight-of-the-bourgeoisie picture). Expecting it to be a 'desperately boring' occasion, they sent an excuse by telegram and sloped off to Brighton, jammed with trippers for the August Bank Holiday of 1935. Here Brandt bought Ester a Union Jack and an 'I'm No Angel' hat and quickly took the picture. Her vivid figure looks almost as if it has been collaged on to the antlike masses behind her, and the smart beach-suit is not what a working girl would be wearing. But the hat and flag capture the eye and make the point: here is someone who is desperate to have a good time. That the picture shows popular fun is already unorthodox, since the working class is usually sunk in dirt and gloom in Thirties documentary. It creates two more contrasts: between Ester's limber pose and the frozen bodies of the upper class and their servants; and between the teeming beach behind her and the ominously empty landscape of 'Cocktails in a Surrey Garden'.

In 1935, Brandt and Eva enjoyed their last chance for carefree wandering on the Continent. They would no longer go to the great house on the Elbe at Nienstedten (though LW and Lilli Brandt started to visit England regularly in the late 1930s). Probably Brandt never set foot on German soil after January 1933, when Hitler came to power. But in the summer of 1935 he and Eva picked up Lyena in Paris and took her with them to Hungary; they swam in the lakes, visited Eva's aunts and took more pictures on the *puszta*. Unfortunately, Eva's health was starting to break down again, and by November she was forced to return to a sanatorium.

The King Edward VII, outside Midhurst in Sussex, had been founded by the King in 1906 to provide for 'the poorer middle classes, too proud to avail themselves of public charity'. It was an impressive neo-Gothic complex, with gardens laid out by Gertrude Jekyll. As on the Continent, the main treatment was simply rest and fresh air. But it cannot have been a happy place for someone of Eva's outgoing temperament. The superintendent, Geoffrey Todd, was a fanatical disciplinarian and perfectionist, and there was no escape from his rule. The sanatorium was buried in the country several miles outside Midhurst; this was the general policy in England, to cut patients off from the supposed burden of everyday life. Since Brandt never learned to drive, it would have been a long and awkward journey to visit Eva from north London; in addition there was his phobia about the sanatorium atmosphere. Once again Eva had to look death in the face, and to do so as a virtual prisoner for four months of winter.

A year after settling in England, Brandt had a sick wife and little encouragement for the pictures he had been taking in his uncles' houses and around London, since Stefan Lorant had not used any of his work in *Weekly Illustrated*. Around the spring of 1935, Brandt decided to try and collect his pictures into a book. Rolf by this time was studying drawing and graphic design; he helped Bill to make a dummy of the book and they took it to Anton Zwemmer in Charing Cross Road. Zwemmer, a Dutchman, ran a bookstore, gallery and publishing house from the same premises, and was a supporter of contemporary art. *The English at Home* did not please him, however: he 'dismissed the first photograph – a gull in fog over the Thames – as a fake, a collage,

Cocktails in a Surrey garden, about 1935

he said, of two separate prints. He added that the book was not "erotic" enough.'[13]

Zwemmer may have been thinking of the prostitute in Brassaï's *Paris by Night*, missing from Brandt's London; or perhaps of the art nudes by photographers like Munkacsi, Drtikol or Kertész, regularly published in Paris. The first English books of nude photography were also starting to appear, though that had little to do with Brandt's project.[14] But Zwemmer had a point in that Brandt did not represent the English with any sexual dimension to their lives, except for the 'Sunday Evening' picture of lovers in the park, and Ester as the 'Brighton Belle'. Both of these pictures were probably added after the rejection of the book, and Brandt may even have put in 'Sunday Evening' as a joke at Zwemmer's expense. Neither Brassaï-type exposés of low life, nor central European art nudes, would enter Brandt's repertoire at this time; but later in the Thirties he would produce striking pictures of staged eroticism in pubs or dark streets. All these scenes, though, used fully clothed models; Brandt would not get seriously involved with the nude for another ten years.

After Zwemmer, Chatto & Windus also rejected the dummy of Brandt's collection. But then it was shown to Brian Batsford, who was head of his own publishing firm and also a graphic artist:

> London publishers were at the time trying to emulate the huge commercial success of a series of cheap photo-books called 'Die Blauen Bücher' which were produced in Leipzig. This series covered works of art and architecture and separate towns and cities. 'We thought that *The English at Home* was the answer to it,' Batsford stated. One 'sheet' of printing paper would print 128 pages at the standard size used for a novel. This would be the size of *The English at Home*. In order to print another book simultaneously and waste almost nothing of the sheet, the quantity of plates in *The English at Home* was set at 63.[15]

In 1933 Batsford had published an English edition of Brassaï's *Paris After Dark* (which conveniently had sixty-two plates) and followed it up with a show of Brassaï's pictures at his gallery. He saw Brandt's work as a commercial proposition that could be slotted into existing categories, neither too threatening to conventional ideas about the English way of life, nor too insistently political. The title of *The English at Home* sounds like Batsford's idea, rather than Brandt's. Its implied counterpart was *The English Abroad*, and it promised to reveal to a continental audience how the English behaved when they returned from their travels. Photography itself was still considered a continental art, and the market for photography books was much larger there than in England. Europeans would get an inside look at English life: the public England of guardsmen, horse-racing and cricket would be there, but also the private England whose doors were closed to the tourist. Another book Batsford had just published, Paul Cohen-Portheim's *The Spirit of London*, was aimed at a similar market. It had a preface by Raymond Mortimer, who said that Cohen-Portheim had produced 'decidedly the best introduction to London that one could give a friend from abroad'.[16] Batsford commissioned Mortimer to do a similar introduction for Brandt.[17]

The English at Home came out in late February 1936 at the moderate price of five shillings, in a contemporary design and sans-serif type. The whole production had a nice Thirties flavour to it, and it is a sought-after rare book today. Unfortunately for Brandt, Zwemmer proved right about the book's commercial potential and it had to be remaindered. Brian Batsford deserves credit for trying to enliven British photographic culture; but his gamble on Brandt, in a short-run perspective, had failed. From Brandt's own point of view, though, the gamble *he* had taken, in making England his home and his subject, had been vindicated. He gained some positive reviews and the respect of the professional photographic community. If Valentine Cunningham is right, George Orwell took careful note of *The English at Home* (he was doing his own ethnography in Wigan when it was published).[18] Just past thirty, Brandt had claimed his place as an English photographer.

Alley off East India Dock Road, about 1937

14 A Night in London

At the end of 1935 Brandt moved to a three-room flat at 58 Hillfield Court, a couple of minutes' walk from Belsize Park Tube station. Hillfield Court was a large, just-completed block of flats, six storeys high and set back from the main road. The rent for Brandt's flat was £3.50 a week and he would hold on to it for thirty-five years, installing a makeshift darkroom in the bathroom.[1] The flats had a communal garden and smart art-deco hallways, though the rooms were quite small. But the main importance of Hillfield Court was as the Brandts' first real home in England, where they could look forward to living together once Eva was released from Midhurst.

The publication of *The English at Home* came at the end of February 1936, and Eva left Midhurst three weeks later. She and Brandt immediately went on a winter holiday to Kitzbühel, with Lyena joining them from Paris. But Eva was not really better, and may have left Midhurst simply because she could not bear the combination of the strict regime and being buried in the countryside through an English winter. Instead of returning to Hillfield Court from Kitzbühel, she went to Switzerland to stay in a convalescent hotel at Crans-sur-Sierre, in the Valais. Eva may have hoped that French-speaking Switzerland would be a more cheerful environment than Davos; and a hotel was much less rigid than a sanatorium. Nonetheless, Brandt hated going to Crans, so Eva was mostly alone there, except for when Lyena was able to visit.[2] For the next three years Eva would spend most of her time under treatment in Switzerland and France, returning to Hillfield Court for a few months with Brandt when she was well enough. But Brandt was never willing to go back into the sanatorium world to keep her company, giving up his London life and photographic career. He may have feared the psychic damage from re-entering a colony of the sick, or perhaps the immediate physical danger of re-infection. Whatever the reason, the recurrence of Eva's illness in 1935 set off a chain of events that would eventually end their marriage. It may be unfair to accuse Brandt of selfishness, since sanatoriums routinely separated their patients from their spouses, in the belief that complete tranquillity would settle their nerves and help them to get well. Still, if Brandt had been the one to suffer a recurrence, Eva would surely have clung more closely to him than he did to her.

From 1936 until the outbreak of war Brandt's work took on a steadily darker tinge, which reflects both the political disasters of the late Thirties and the shadows over his personal life. Yet these may well have been the most creative four years in his long photographic career. While Eva was in the sanatorium he lived alone at Hillfield Court, relying for company on his brothers (all three of them were now in London), on Ester Brandt and on the circle of friends that he had acquired since coming to England. Djuri Szulyovsky came regularly to London from Barcelona, and through him Brandt met an important new friend, Frances Statler. She was a young American who lived in Paris from 1934 to 1936, working as a textile designer. Towards the end of 1936 she moved to London with her eighteen-year-old brother Mark, and took up fashion drawing. She married the English novelist Chapman Mortimer; Brandt's 'Bloomsbury Party' shows her with her husband and brother.[3] Later, Frances became a professional photographer and travel writer. She remained close to Brandt and Eva all their lives and became a staunch defender of Brandt's work.[4]

Once *The English at Home* was published, Brandt decided to make another approach to *Weekly Illustrated*. It was the leading British picture magazine, and the only way for a photographer to reach a mass audience. In Paris almost all the modernist photographers were involved with photo-journalism, and Brandt was still looking for the British equivalents to *Vu* or *Verve*. Maurice Cowan was now the editor of *Weekly Illustrated*, since Lorant had left the magazine six months after it began; but the person who received Brandt's visit was a young assistant editor, Tom Hopkinson. Six years later, he recalled the occasion:

> Some time in the spring of 1936 a young man came into the office where I was working. He was tall and slim, sunburned, with golden hair brushed back. He had a rather narrow mouth with thin lips, long forehead and chin, and very clear blue eyes. He wore a grey flannel suit, had a voice as loud as a moth, and the gentlest manner to be found outside a nunnery.
>
> Altogether, he did not seem a very likely person to be given a job on a weekly picture paper. However, he carried under his arm a book, and in the book were photographs taken by himself. They were remarkable photographs, and they showed more sharply than I had ever seen before how a human eye and a piece of mechanism can combine, not so much to record the world as to impose a particular vision of the world upon it.[5]

The sunburn suggests that Brandt had just come back from his holiday in Kitzbühel, in April. He was not precisely asking for a job, but told Hopkinson he wanted to 'hang around for three weeks and study layout', and did not expect to be paid. This was characteristic of Brandt, to seek a position where he could quietly observe without having to take orders; he had had a similar relationship with Man Ray. Much later, he told Beryl McAlhone that he had 'learnt much from the work the photographers produced for the magazine'.[6]

It is unlikely that Brandt wanted to study layout in order to become a picture editor himself. What he really needed to learn was how to shoot a commercial picture-story, as opposed to making a single striking image. The pictures in *The English at Home* were of uniform size, one to each page; layout for the book required no more than deciding on the order in which the pictures would appear, and which ones would face each other. *Weekly Illustrated* had a large format and extremely complex layouts: when opened, it was nearly sixteen inches high and twenty-three inches wide.[7] The first story to which Brandt contributed, 'Derby Day', has twenty pictures altogether, spread across two pages, with much use of montage and outline figures. At least two of Brandt's are included, the blindfolded *voyante* who 'sees' the winner and, next to her, a frieze of top-hatted spectators.[8] This story used several photographers, but for the following week Hopkinson gave Brandt his first full story, on Glyndebourne. It has nine pictures, encircling a small block of text.[9] The theme is a classic one for illustrated magazines, showing 'what goes on behind the scenes' – the camera getting into places that are usually closed to the public.

Brandt had at least two more stories in *Weekly Illustrated* in 1936, one on the Eton versus Harrow cricket match and one on children playing by the Thames.[10] But he did not become a regular photographer for the magazine, probably because most of the assignments were locked up by hardened professionals like Felix Man, Kurt Hutton and Jim Jarché. From the *Weekly Illustrated* archives we can see that for Hutton's story on the herring fishery he shot at least two rolls of thirty-six each on his Leica, out of which eleven were used in the magazine.[11] He took as many as five exposures of each subject, especially when the key to a shot was facial expression. Brandt's style was to take far fewer pictures on his Rolleiflex; he aimed to get a usable picture on his first try, and to have enough variety over the roll of twelve to produce a good layout. But there was a limit to how much an assistant editor like Tom Hopkinson could do for him, and Brandt also needed more time to develop the practical skills of a working photo-journalist. Nonetheless, Hopkinson would prove to be Brandt's most loyal and powerful supporter, shaping his entire career in photo-journalism over the next fifteen years.

Another reason for Brandt to drift away from *Weekly Illustrated* was his usual unwillingness to be tied down. In the summer of 1936 he went off to Normandy to visit Georges Braque, with whom he had become friendly in his Paris years. Braque had a studio at Varengeville, a few kilometres west of Dieppe. Brandt took a portrait of him leaning over a half-door, his face shaded by a sailor's cap, and looking relaxed and confident as he surveys his domain. This was Brandt's first important portrait since he had taken Pound and Schoenberg eight years before. It set the tone for all his later portraits in showing a creative person against the background of his home, or a symbolic landscape; there would be no more studio portraits with flood lights and plain backgrounds. Nineteen years later Brandt photographed Braque again on the beach at Varengeville, still with his sailor's cap, but now with a more worn and wary look.[12] On the first trip, Djuri and his girlfriend went with Brandt; they swam and picnicked on the dramatic beaches, with their rock formations and beetling cliffs.[13] In the 1950s Brandt would return to take nudes on these beaches, at Varengeville and Vastérival.

The trip to Varengeville was the first of innumerable journeys from Britain to rural France; they would continue until the end of Brandt's life, except for the war years. Sometimes they would be made on assignment, to take a portrait or show the haunts of painters or writers; sometimes to photograph nudes; sometimes just for pleasure. In years when he was free to do so, Brandt might spend one-third or even half his time in France; he might be called a French photographer, except that he would steer clear of the traditional French subjects that were 'owned' by people like

Derby Day (*Weekly Illustrated* layout), 23 May 1936

DAY

Why trouble to go?   You can lose your money just as well at home—and here's all the fun in pictures

Keeping their minds off it.

Party—or parties—on the roof.

Service on the spot.

She can see as much of the race as most (at top). Free advice for a bobby (just above).

Gipsy children turn lunch into a cabaret.

A thoroughly legal sweepstake.

All she wants to know—except the winner.

They mean to be on—enthusiasts before the race.

Enthusiasts after the race. But they'll have found another dead cert next Derby Day.

Brassaï, Doisneau or Cartier-Bresson.

The most important consequence of Brandt's involvement with *Weekly Illustrated* was the structure of his next book, *A Night in London*. Because this has become a rare volume, few people now realise the particular shape that it gave to Brandt's work in the late Thirties. *A Night in London* is a unified picture-story, basically an extension of the *Weekly Illustrated* format to book length. It is not just a tour of familiar London sights, but a narrative that begins at dusk and finishes at first light. Five of the pictures are set at definite times, from 8.15 p.m. when 'The Curtain Rises' to 'Seven O'Clock' when the milk and newspapers arrive.[14] A similar structure had been used in Walter Ruttmann's *Berlin: Symphony of the Great City* (1927), and Brandt seems to have borrowed directly from this film's scenes of indoor sporting events, the theatre and bakers working at night. The idea of the complex but cyclical life of the city, unfolding through the night, is common in the cinema and photo-journalism of the time. It is inherently conservative rather than critical: every night, events repeat themselves to give the city its familiar character – pleasure-seekers go to the theatre, the policeman pounds his beat, fish arrives at the market, and so on to infinity.

In 1952 Brandt published an article on night photography in *The Rollei Way*, a compendium of advice for Rolleiflex users.[15] The article suggests Brandt's temperamental affinity with the night, as a time of shadows and secrets: 'Night photography can indeed be a quiet and pleasurable sort of game. But if you go after night life, it can also be an exciting one.'[16] It is also very revealing about Brandt's tricks of the trade. He was ready to exploit every kind of artifice, approaching the night-time city as if it were one big studio:

> At dusk … there is still quite a bit of light in the sky, while at the same time the lamps are already switched on. The photographic effect of that is very much more like the visual effect of a real night scene, than a straight exposure actually at night would be.
>
> So try to choose the subject and set up the camera before it is really dark. Then stand by and wait as the light fades, until the time is just right to take the picture.[17]

Brandt went to a great deal of trouble to keep the flaring effect of street lights out of his pictures; Brassaï, in *Paris de Nuit*, took flaring for granted. Brandt also used flash to supplement old-fashioned techniques: he recommended opening the shutter (with the Rollei on a tripod), then walking up to one side of the subject and setting off the flash. Rain and snow are good for atmosphere in night photography, but also technically useful because they reflect more light and so reduce exposure times.

Superficially, *A Night in London* may appear similar to *The English at Home* or Brassaï's *Paris After Dark*, as a city tour in sixty-four plates. But *The English at Home* shows a timeless country; *A Night in London* is a piece of social history belonging to one moment of the Thirties. Although there were a couple of night shots in *The English at Home*, such as 'The Homeward Way' (of a man returning from the office) and Rolf with the taxi, it was overwhelmingly a daylight collection. Brandt found a much tighter subject in the idea of narrowing England down to London and replacing day with

Footsteps coming nearer, about 1936

night. The idea for *A Night in London* may have come as a commission from the Paris publishers Arts et Métiers Graphiques, who had produced Brassai's book. Once again Brandt was following Brassaï, but in a profoundly different spirit from Brassaï's plunge into underground Paris.

Brassaï was almost a combat photographer, always wanting to get closer to the action, and even to become part of it. He felt that he was on the right track when his camera was smashed or his pocket picked by the people he was trying to photograph. Once a gangster with a knife came to his hotel room and threatened to kill him for publishing his picture in a crime magazine, where an editor had captioned it 'The Murderer'. These were knock-down proofs of the authenticity of Brassaï's work, that his pictures had exposed real underworld types in their seedy lairs. He relished the romantic notion that 'The half-dressed girl strutting along the rue des Lombards, picking up passers-by, murmurs the same "Want to come with me?" as the streetwalkers murmured to the rakes in the fourteenth century.'[18] The tremendous popularity of Brassaï's images was his reward for giving people exactly what they expected to find in Paris, even if they had never been there. His pictures are as Parisian as a dirty postcard; and many of them have become postcards.

Brandt's images in *A Night in London* are going in a different direction. *The English at Home* was full of predictable English types: the guardsman, the policeman, the schoolgirl in uniform. But *A Night in London* avoids any easy kind of recognition. The most impressive shots are elaborate staged scenes, in melodramatic settings, using a repertory company of his family and friends. 'Footsteps Coming Nearer' is a scene of prostitution, for which Eva was probably the model.[19] It derives from a straightforward journalistic sequence by Brassaï, where a man passes a prostitute in a doorway and she then comes out and takes his arm. In Brandt's version, the man's figure looms up in the left foreground, dwarfing the prostitute with her gleaming white shoes and blouse. The picture takes on the ominous quality of a scene from a German Expressionist film about the evils of the night, such as *Pandora's Box* or *M*. Brandt uses a similarly gigantesque perspective in 'Street Scene' also inspired by Brassaï.[20] But Brandt makes it into a puzzle, rather than Brassaï's standard scene of lovers shamelessly breaking the rules of how to behave in public.[21] Brandt leaves almost everything to the viewer's imagination. Ester Brandt is the model again, scarcely recognisable as the 'Brighton Belle' of *The English at Home*. The man in the shabby raincoat who whispers in her ear is Rolf; but what is he asking her to do? The huge cinema poster as backdrop suggests the cliché of the streetwalker being for sale, like other kinds of urban entertainment; but nothing in the woman's clothing, pose or closed-off expression identify her as a prostitute.

'Street Scene' lends itself to two contradictory interpretations. The man might be making some furtive sexual proposition to the woman, or even planning to kill her.[22] The magnified shadow of his trilby hat, and the area of darkness that pushes him towards her, suggest one of Brassaï's criminals, or a sinister figure from Expressionist cinema. Whatever the relationship between the man and the woman, he seems to mean her no good. Yet the picture is also an almost exact reproduction of a scene from Hitchcock's *Sabotage*, which came out just before Brandt's shot. In the film, Mrs Verloq has murdered her terrorist husband, in revenge for his having caused the death of her

Ester and Rolf Brandt in 'Street Scene', 1936

little brother. She wants to go to the police and confess; the man in the trenchcoat and trilby hat is a detective who is in love with her, and offers to help her conceal her crime. A London policeman in uniform always stands for justice and order in Brandt's pictures.[23] But the Thirties detective is a more ambiguous and untrustworthy cultural figure; the shabbiness of his raincoat in 'Street Scene' suggests that he may not even be a real detective. Brandt was now presenting stock types and situations in a way *intended* to sow confusion.

The staging of pictures in *A Night in London* challenges the idea that a documentary picture delivers an absolute truth about, say, a detective or a prostitute on the street. Brandt works with the Surrealist idea that in a city one keeps seeing little dramas, without knowing the history or the context of what is happening. The only certainty is the emotional intensity of the encounter. Atmosphere now becomes all, and the idea of documentary just a style. Frances Rice recalls that Brandt might haunt a location for weeks before taking his picture; one can imagine him wandering around the East End deep into the night, imagining scenes that might be played out in one setting or another. Sometimes he would even make preliminary sketches of how he wanted a photograph staged. 'Alley off East India Dock Road' is one of the most brilliant of these pictures.[24] Djuri Szulyovsky is the central figure with a cap; on the left is Mark Statler and on the right Chapman Mortimer. Formally, the picture depicts London as a prison-like city of brickwork and paving, with a complex composition of planes, textures and lighting. Then there are the three enigmatic figures who meet in the alley – for what purpose? The two men in raincoats, one with a trilby hat, may be detectives; and the middle figure has a cap like those worn by criminals in Brassaï's Paris pictures. Is this man offering information, or perhaps being threatened, as the hand on his shoulder suggests? The policeman with a bull's-eye lamp at his waist might be there to safeguard his colleagues, or he might have surprised a criminal rendezvous (in real life, according to Brandt, he just happened to turn up and stand conveniently still while he was included in the picture). The point of view from which the picture is taken suggests someone looking out of their window and observing a random event in the street, without being able to tell if it is mysterious or just meaningless.

Another famous picture from *A Night in London*, 'Top Floor', appears at first glance to be a conventionally erotic image, meant to inspire nudges and winks. It turns out, as always with Brandt, to be not so simple. The room was at Frances Statler's flat, and actually was on the top floor.[25] Brandt had seen a postcard from Paul Eluard's collection that was reproduced in *Minotaure* as a piece of found Surrealism, and entitled 'Le Baiser Mystérieux'.[26] He decided to re-stage it for his own purposes. By pulling the camera back from the lovers, he made room for the openly erotic props of a double bed and a bedside lamp. His models were Mark Statler and 'Bird'; she was known for her beautiful hands, and in this picture one hand and her forearms are all that we see of her. Brandt took a fetishistic interest in female hands (he had a collection of Victorian alabaster hands in his flat), which often surfaced in his later nudes.[27] In *A Night in London* the print has a sprig of mistletoe at the top of the frame, explaining the embrace. For its later publication in *Shadow of Light*, Brandt re-named it 'Soho Bedroom'; the room wasn't in Soho, but this title made the picture into a 'documentary' shot of prostitution. In this version, Brandt cropped out the mistletoe, and printed in a starker black-and-white register.

Camera in London, Brandt's next collection, would offer a rationale for his staged pictures:

> Bill Brandt's pictures of London people are not portraits; they are generalisations. He is not so much concerned about individuals as about types. It is not Mr So-and-so of So-and-so in So-and-so street he is after, but simply the sort of people who live in such streets. He tries to get the human element and the décor around it in such a way that one becomes part of the other. This means not so much catching people unaware as getting the right people against the right background – the right types in the right places. It does mean catching the spirit of London life. As opposed to the ideas of *candid* portraiture, it does not matter for his purposes that the people he is photographing may be aware of his presence or may even be *holding* it for him. Nor does this sort of posing, if it can be called that, affect the truth of his pictures. Truth is not accidental.[28]

The commentary goes on to say that 'Street Scene' shows something 'which can be glimpsed hundreds of times at hundreds of London corners'.[29] This may be so, but Brandt's idea of city life is that we glimpse many things without understanding them, since we don't know the history that has led up to whatever scenes we catch sight of.

A Night in London also includes more comprehensible scenes of Brandt's closest friends and relatives enjoying expensive pleasures: his mother is shown in a box at the opera, his father taking Eva to dinner at the Café Royal, and Djuri setting off with 'Bird' in an old-fashioned hansom cab.[30] There is little social criticism in *A Night in London*, except for the facing-page contrast where, for example, the wealthy couple at the restaurant face the tramp who scavenges in the dustbins behind it. Even there, Brandt strikes an odd note: the privileged couple are his father and Eva, and the scavenger bends over the dustbin in the same position as the waiter bends over the table.[31] It is hard to believe that these pictures were meant to stir up resentment of the upper class. Bill's support for the left was conveyed much more indirectly. The picture carefully placed at the conclusion of *A Night in London*, with the seemingly innocuous title 'Morning in Belsize Avenue', sent a private message to Rolf. It showed milk bottles on the steps of a house, one copy of the *Daily Telegraph* and one of the *News Chronicle*, folded to show the headline 'Heavy Losses in Rebel Fight for Madrid'. The date of the picture was mid-October 1936, when Franco's forces were besieging the capital.[32] The *News Chronicle* was the strongest supporter of the Spanish republic among the English daily papers, while the *Telegraph* argued that England should remain neutral.[33] Rolf and Ester lived on Belsize Avenue; presumably the *News Chronicle* was for them, the *Telegraph* for their right-wing neighbours. The political message seems clear: the morning milk is being delivered as usual in England, but the headline is telling us that it's time to wake up to the threat of Fascism. How clear is this, though? The picture might just as well say: in England (unlike Spain) neighbours can be on opposite sides but still live together in peace.

A Night in London appeared in June 1938. It was a measure of Brandt's growing international reputation that it was published in three cities: by *Country Life* in London,

Morning in Belsize Avenue, 1936

by Charles Scribner's in New York, and by Arts et Métiers Graphiques in Paris.[34] The book was provided with bilingual captions and printed in France. Arts et Métiers also put on a Brandt show at their gallery – a satisfying proof of how far Brandt had come in the three and a half years since he had lived in Paris. His career at this point, some ten years after his beginnings in Vienna, had achieved a unique blending of creation and photo-documentary. Even as he moved towards reportage in the later 1930s, he managed consistently to avoid the purely conventional shot, thanks to his dedication to the odd and the atmospheric. Some of the distinctive Brandt look came from his eye for contrasty black-and-whites. But his real achievement had more to do with composition, and the different levels of meaning that he found even in such apparently trivial subjects as children playing in the streets or regulars drinking in a pub. He had shown the British people their public faces in a way they were glad to recognise while, even in the same pictures, he expressed the phantasms of his private world.

Coal-searcher going home to Jarrow, 1936

15 Dirty Thirties

The end of the Thirties was a time when not even someone so intensely private as Brandt could escape politics. In France, the formation of a Popular Front in June 1936 was a belated and ineffectual response to the rise of Fascism. A month later, General Franco rebelled against the republic to begin the Spanish Civil War. Ester Brandt was on holiday there at the time, and took pictures of the young men in her village burning down its church; when she returned, she and Rolf decided that the best way to resist Fascism was to join the Communist Party, in which they remained for the next twenty years. This did not go down well with Rolf's uncles and his brother Walther, staunch conservatives who were shocked to hear that Rolf had been seen handing out Communist pamphlets on the street. Bill could never have gone so far, but he did not let political disagreement come between him and his brother. Much of his work in the late Thirties can be seen as a response to Rolf's commitment to the left. Bill accepted the duty to turn his camera towards scenes of injustice; though he also insisted in showing the sufferings of the Depression in his own distinctive way.

Politics, for a photographer or writer, meant making the journey to the North. Brandt had made a brief trip to south Wales in 1935, which yielded three images of miners for *The English at Home*, but that was his only foray into industrial England until the Jarrow marchers against unemployment arrived in London on 8 November 1936. They inspired Brandt to go, soon afterwards, and see the conditions that had driven them to walk 300 miles to the capital. His pictures of the North contain much more shock and indignation than his East End pictures, and are closer to the tradition of protest documentary than anything else in his work. Yet at the same time he discovered the grandeur of industrial cityscapes. Brandt's pictures of Halifax and Newcastle are really tributes to the North rather than social criticism, and they belong with his greatest formal achievements.

Brandt's documentary work outside London still has a great gap, when compared with the plan of J. B. Priestley's *English Journey* (1934). This was a book that probably influenced Brandt and suggested specific places for him to visit.[1] Priestley divided the country into three: old England, industrial England and the new England created since 1918, of motor cars, Woolworth's and the art-deco factories along the Great West Road. Priestley found this latest England quite appealing: at Southampton, where he started his journey, he found 'a fairy tale of commerce', cheerful and prosperous.[2]

Orwell saw the opposite, a lower-middle-class nightmare of tinned food and 'gas-pipe chairs'. But Brandt ignored this new way of life almost completely, except for a few pictures of suburban odds and ends, and one of semi-detached villas on the Great North Road (even here, he made the houses look like a *trompe-l'oeil* façade, with a lowering sky above).[3]

When he first had an extended opportunity to photograph British cityscapes, in the summer of 1933, Brandt presented the Bermondsey alley Shad Thames in a melodramatic style that persisted throughout his other industrial scenes. Battersea power station in *The English at Home* is a mythic night-scene of girders and a flaring chimney, straight out of Fritz Lang's *Metropolis*. Taken by night or at least in subdued light, and often in the rain, these pictures bring together three elements of composition: a textured, highlighted street or wall, a looming mass of dark buildings and a sky patterned with haze, glare and smoke. Such light as there is cannot prevail against the weight of the buildings. Orwell observed that 'At night, when you cannot see the hideous shapes of the houses and the blackness of everything, a town like Sheffield assumes a kind of sinister magnificence.'[4] The blackness and magnificence are what Brandt most relished about the North. His pictures of Halifax convey the romance of industrial civilisation, in spite of the human suffering created by the post-war Depression. They capture the historical moment when the built environment of the North is falling into ruins, but light industry and re-development have yet to appear. His industrial vistas are largely uninhabited, as if built and then abandoned. 'Halifax', 'A Snicket in Halifax' and 'Train Leaving Newcastle' are among Brandt's great achievements. It would have been difficult to enlist them in any current political cause – unlike his pictures of northern houses, which did convey indignation that people should have to live in them.[5]

Brandt's pictures of northern children may be the closest he ever came to simple polemic. In 'A Sheffield Backyard' an utterly dismal space traps the child as completely as if she were in prison. 'Children in Sheffield' also uses stonework to convey hopelessness, where other Brandt pictures are more concerned with its texture and the play of light on it.[6] The girl on the right looks like a victim of rickets, as well as of some incurable inner misery. On closer inspection, though, the message of even this picture becomes blurred. The two main figures are dressed in their Sunday best, and seem to have escaped adult control and deliberately made themselves filthy – in contrast to the dapper and self-satisfied little boy at the upper left.

When he moved on from Sheffield to the mining country around Newcastle and to pictures of adults, Brandt was still preoccupied with dirt. 'Northumbrian miner at his evening meal' has been criticised for showing a miner eating before having washed, while his wife looks on glumly. Orwell said that 'a majority of miners prefer to eat their meal first and wash afterwards, as I should do in their circumstances'.[7] Even so, Brandt certainly chose to emphasise the dirtiness of life in the North. The problem with seeing these pictures as social criticism is that none of Brandt's subjects seem to mind being dirty, and there is no positive representation of workers as the vanguard of a new society. Socialist Realism always showed workers as alert and optimistic; but the most famous of Brandt's northern pictures – 'Coal-searcher going home to Jarrow' – is a vision of defeat, where he must have asked the man to look down at the ground before

Halifax, 1937

Young housewife, Bethnal Green, 1937

he pressed the shutter. In this and its companion picture, 'Coal-searchers near Heworth, Tyneside', the barrenness of the setting confirms the hopelessness of their struggle.[8] They are perishing in an empty, indifferent landscape, which reveals nothing of the social forces that have brought them there.[9] Brandt's coal searcher is a study in bodily abjection, linked compositionally with the Barcelona beggar of 1932 (except that, here in the North of England, he never thinks of looking up to heaven for help).

J. B. Priestley said of Hebburn, near Jarrow, that it 'looked as much like an ordinary town of that size as a dust-bin looks like a drawing-room'.[10] Given the popular image of Tyneside, it is not surprising that *Picture Post* would use Brandt's 'Coal-searcher going home' as a symbol of national failure in a 1947 article on 'Where stands Britain – How did we get into this mess?'[11] It was the end of the bitter winter of 1946-7, the first major period of disillusionment with the Labour government installed in 1945, and the picture was captioned:

> The Wasted Years: The man who might have been hewing coal in tons, scratches for ounces on the slag-heaps. An unemployed Durham miner on his way home in 1936 after a day's search for coal to heat his home. He was one of an army of 1,880,000 unemployed. One miner in five was out of work. They were part of the price we paid for failing to modernise our industries and falling back on restriction, wage-cutting, price-fixing. We are paying another part of the price today in empty grates and half-time factories.

There are many examples in British popular culture of Brandt pictures being moralised in this way, and made into symbols of national decline. But Brandt himself was much less ready to put the nation on trial.

It is extraordinary that Brandt's pictures of the industrial North, which have done so much to define the Thirties in the British imagination, were all taken on a single visit of a few weeks. His pictures of deprivation in London were spread over a much longer period, when all he had to do was take the Tube from Belsize Park to Old Street and start walking eastwards with his Rolleiflex. One of the most famous of these, taken in September 1937, was captioned either 'East End Morning' or 'Young Housewife, Bethnal Green'. It struck a chord as an emblem of the Dirty Thirties and has been linked with an equally famous scene, Orwell's description of a young woman seen from a train in Wigan:

> At the back of one of the houses a young woman was kneeling on the stones, poking a stick up the leaden waste-pipe which ran from the sink inside and which I suppose was blocked. I had time to see everything about her – her sacking apron, her clumsy clogs, her arms reddened by the cold. She looked up as the train passed, and I was almost near enough to catch her eye. She had a round pale face, the usual exhausted face of the slum girl who is twenty-five and looks forty, thanks to miscarriages and drudgery; and it wore, for the second in which I saw it, the most desolate, hopeless expression I have ever seen. It struck me then that we are mistaken when we say that 'It isn't the same for them as it would be for us', and that people bred in the slums can imagine nothing but the slums. For

Train leaving Newcastle, 1936

what I saw in her face was not the ignorant suffering of an animal. She knew well enough what was happening to her – understood as well as I did how dreadful a destiny it was to be kneeling there in the bitter cold, on the slimy stones of a slum backyard, poking a stick up a foul drain-pipe.[12]

Orwell's bleak vision of 'dreadful destiny' has shaped responses to Brandt's picture of the young housewife. People tend to see it as a classic Thirties document of waste and deprivation. But what *does* the picture record? The wedding ring identifies the young woman as a householder, not an exploited skivvy. Once her husband has left for work in the morning, she puts on her pinafore and washes her front doorstep.[13] Respectability depends on the daily battle against dirt. This house-proud woman will keep her own little domain in order, by marking the line between her property and the slum street. There is nothing intrinsically futile or dreadful about doing this job, though it might appear so to middle-class observers (who would nonetheless expect their servants to keep their own doorsteps clean). The young woman of 'East End Morning' is at least working for herself. Since Brandt must have asked her permission to take the picture, she can scarcely have been ashamed of doing the job.

Many photographers of the time, Brandt included, sought out the filthiest sights they could find in the slums, telling society that such conditions needed to be swept away. In the first edition of *The Road to Wigan Pier*, for example, one of the illustrations showed the wreckage of a slum house with a modern block of flats rising behind it. Such pictures took it for granted that the existing houses – and, by extension, the way of life of those who inhabited them – were beyond repair, and could only be replaced.[14] One of the ironies of the documentary tradition is that these pictures built support for the great programmes of slum clearance after the war, which destroyed working-class communities and warehoused the poor in desolate peripheral estates. Representing the working class as dirty, pathetic victims made them fodder for social engineering whose failures, in time, became all too evident.[15]

Although Brandt's East End pictures were later enlisted in the cause of pulling down the slums, issues of staging and of his private agenda always hover in the background. In 'Family Dinner', the overturned chair and the rubbish strewn on the floor look like items that Brandt may have deliberately added to a grubby but cheerful domestic scene.[16] 'Doss-house in South London' and 'East End Bedroom' leave one wondering about the chamber pots, conspicuously placed in the foreground: were they 'just there', or was Brandt making fun of the kitchen-sink school of photo-documentary? 'Bedroom in West Ham' carries the social message of overcrowding in the slums, but the massed sleeping figures (as in 'Doss-house') point us towards a world of dreams that is a refuge from the sufferings of daylight.

Brandt's pictures of children in the East End have made a deep impression on British popular consciousness. Though childless himself, he had a wonderful rapport with children as subjects, and enjoyed working with them:

As everybody knows, they are easier to photograph than adults. They have fewer inhibitions, are less deceptive and less money-minded. They are quite willing to pose and play without mentioning model fees or asking you whether they can have a print.[17]

A classic photo-documentary treatment of children is Edith Tudor Hart's picture of a Viennese soup kitchen in 1930.[18] Against the drab backs of the adults, a girl of about twelve looks directly at Hart's camera, her face lit up with enjoyment of her soup. The other gleams of light in the picture are the face and the mug of her small brother, and his hand on the bright handle of their pram. It is a quintessential human-interest picture; after Hart emigrated to England her influence can be seen in hundreds of similar photographs in *Picture Post* and elsewhere. This picture was skilfully composed, but its main purpose was to make propaganda for the social-democratic government of Vienna.

Brandt's 'Children, South London' is far more uncomfortable for the viewer than Hart's picture. First, the geometric composition competes with the children themselves for attention: it is borrowed from a deserted streetscape by Brassaï in *Paris de Nuit*, though the grubbiness of the London street contrasts with Brassaï's formalist austerity. The children may be deprived, but they show no gratitude for adult concern. The boys are interested in the hole they have dug, the older girl looks ready to warn off adult intruders from their patch. As in most of Brandt's child pictures, we are given a glimpse into a world where the children are absorbed in their own business, rather than doing anything meant to appeal directly to the eye of an adult.[19]

In two of Brandt's most famous pictures, the children form an audience for each other: 'Street Games in Bethnal Green' (also called 'East End Fight') and 'Dancing the Lambeth Walk'. They are companion pieces, in which boys and a girl show off for their peers and are applauded for their prowess. Both pictures were taken in March 1939, just as Hitler's annexation of Czechoslovakia made war seem inevitable. Brandt took a brilliant series of pictures of children in East End streets at this time, perhaps as an escape from politics. In the boxing match, he must have persuaded the children in the audience to sit or stand where he wanted them for his composition. The boxers also seem to be holding a pre-arranged pose, though Brandt claimed that they were fighting in earnest. The post in the foreground – like the post of a boxing ring – and the frieze of roofs and chimney-pots at the top of the frame give the impression of a stage with background scenery. The whole scene is a performance, expressing the cheerfulness and vitality of slum life; there is nothing sordid or truly violent about the picture, though many photographers might have tried to bring out such qualities. Nor is it an action shot in the sense of subordinating everything to the 'decisive moment' of physical action: a punch is on its way from left to right, but it is the placement of the figures against their background that makes the picture succeed.

The same qualities, expressed even more powerfully and economically, are present in 'Dancing the Lambeth Walk'. In *Camera in London*, Brandt wrote: 'The girl in *Lambeth Walk* wanted to be a dancer. She was showing off for her companions. She graciously went on showing off for Bill Brandt.'[20] For *Picture Post*, he wrote some suggested captions on the back of a print: 'Oh Mister Wu! I'm telling you', 'Joan Whippin is the Jessie Matthews of Wolverley Street. Grab her Mr Cochran.' Wolverley Street was in Bethnal Green, and Brandt's idea was to link East End with West End, where C. B. Cochran was Britain's leading producer of comedy and revues. But the picture wasn't even

Children, South London, about 1939

In The Days Before Youth Clubs
With no club to go to, they spent their spare time
playing juvenile games in the street.

To-day, Youth Has Plenty To Do
The Girls' Training Corps gives her skilled
training, a neat uniform, and a purposeful air.

Dancing the Lambeth Walk, 1939 (*Picture Post* 1943)

published until four years later, when *Picture Post* used it in a special issue on 'Changing Britain'.[21] In small format, it was slipped inconspicuously into a story on 'Are We Planning a New Deal for Youth?' by Betty Shields-Collins, a well-meaning busybody. She predicted that, in the shining post-war Britain, state-supported youth clubs would 'become dangerous competitors to commercial entertainment, which four years ago could regard them with contempt'. Brandt's picture was given a disapproving caption: 'In the Days Before Youth Clubs. With no club to go to, they spent their spare time playing juvenile games in the street.' It was placed next to a picture of a young woman in uniform, captioned: 'To-day, Youth Has Plenty To Do. The Girls' Training Corps gives her skilled training, a neat uniform, and a purposeful air.'

In 1941 *Picture Post* had devoted a special issue to the contrast between the 'Planned' and the 'Unplanned' ways of life (in the background of such discussions were the biggest plans of all, the Soviet Five-Year Plans).[22] Brandt's great picture was enlisted into the utopian leftist crusade against the dirt, disorder and commercialism of the street. In the new planned society after the war, people would no longer be distressed by the sight of scruffy street children fighting, dancing and digging holes. The Town and Country Planning Act of 1944 gave government the power to re-build vast areas of

East London. Wolverley Street, where Joan Whippin danced the Lambeth Walk, no longer exists. On the night of 16 April 1941 it was hit by a German parachute-mine, and every house was damaged beyond repair. Only one person was killed, but the survivors were sent to a hostel and re-housed. Today, the street has become an inner courtyard of a massive council estate in Bethnal Green. The estate is fortified like a prison, and the only children to be seen are holding tight to their mothers' hands.

In a way, post-war re-development was being lamented even before it happened: the March 1946 *Picture Post* would feature 'The Doomed East End', with a Brandt cover picture of a cheerful cockney and his pint.[23] The 'Lambeth Walk' picture was used again in 1950 for 'Street Play and Play Streets': now the story was that street children had become an endangered species, and more streets should be blocked off to encourage them![24] There is a new caption, too: 'O Then She Was a Lady and This is the Way She Went. The imitation game, performed by the rising talent of the play-streets.' Brandt's own position had never changed, though: he constantly showed children creating their own world of enjoyment in the street, or wishing they could be released into it.[25]

Almost all Brandt's East End pictures, in fact, stand out for the respect they show their subjects, and for their visions of a more human London than the one we know today. His interior pictures of adults in pubs and cafés prove his diplomatic skills. How could someone so obviously upper-middle-class and foreign be allowed to bring out his Rolleiflex in such places? There are well-known 'Mass Observation' pictures taken in pubs by Humphrey Spender, where drinkers stare angrily at the cameraman. Spender used a miniature Contax for which he would set the focus through a hole in his raincoat pocket, then try to snatch his picture before anyone realised what was happening.[26] With Brandt's Rolleiflex there was no chance of a stolen shot, and he had to wait until his subjects were ready to co-operate. His friends mention his extreme quietness, patience and politeness; no doubt, as Brassaï mentions, an ability to buy drinks also helped.

In his pub pictures, Brandt seems to have made a deliberate choice between light and dark settings. The Crooked Billet on Tower Hill is the English pub of legend, with friendly barmaids and cheerful, cloth-capped patrons. Here Brandt's pictures are straightforward celebrations of working-class conviviality; some would later be used for the *Picture Post* story 'A Barmaid's Day'.[27] 'Domino Players in North London' starts to move from the real to the surreal, with its white dog as onlooker at the game. And the legendary Charlie Brown's pub in Limehouse is the scene of encounters that are uniformly eccentric, sinister or erotic. Brandt shows it as a place where different types mingle on a live-and-let-live basis, rather than a local where strangers would be unwelcome. A standard sort of colourful cockney pair share a table; but their gazes do not quite meet, the third man at the table doesn't seem to fit in, and the picture's centre of interest is the first man's filthy hand on the table. The pictures on the wall, of upper-class pastimes like horse-racing, boating or golf, don't belong at all in this kind of company.

There are other erotic pictures taken at Charlie Brown's that reinforce the idea of a place that is outside the rules.[28] A young woman emanates sex-appeal, even with her hair in rollers under a turban; but her social position is unclear – her dress is

Young woman at Charlie Brown's, 1946

perhaps a uniform – and is she pleased or sulky that her picture is being taken?[29] Another picture gives us one of Brandt's odd triangles: the bearded bohemian now embraces his girlfriend and someone else makes it a threesome compositionally, but seems wrapped up in his own thoughts.[30] For a seemingly more straightforward picture of a couple embracing, Brandt actually blacked in two of the woman's teeth in the negative, in a schoolboyish act of defacement.[31] Nothing at Charlie Brown's is allowed to meet normal expectations for going to the pub; instead, it becomes a kind of night-time fun-house where every view is distorted. Brandt's private fantasy-system also appears in such details as the picture of the clipper ship above the kissing couple: such pictures turn up again in other erotic contexts, such as a Robert Graves portrait with two women, the couple at the Blue Cockatoo coffee house, and the *Lilliput* nude called 'The Woodman's Daughter'.[32]

Just as enigmatic are Brandt's intimate pictures of his relatives in luxurious surroundings, taken at the same time as his studies of the dispossessed. 'Cocktails in a Surrey Garden' (1938) might easily be seen as an allegory of the twilight of capitalism. By the later 1930s, Brandt's camera was accepted upstairs as well as downstairs in his uncles' houses, though many of the upstairs pictures were not published until 1966 in *Shadow of Light*. In that collection, the picture of Pratt in 'Parlourmaid and underparlourmaid ready to serve dinner' now faces, across the page, her master and mistress playing bridge with their friends, as if after the dinner that Pratt had served.[33] Similarly, 'Drawing Room in Mayfair' – a younger set of Brandts playing backgammon – faces 'Late evening in the kitchen', a group of three servants in front of a giant stove, exhausted by the clearing-up.[34] All four pictures are linked by contrasts between the languid bodies and smiling faces of the upper class at play, and the tense or fatigued postures of those who wait on them. Yet these privileged persons seem guilty of complacency more than arrogance; nor does Brandt condemn the cleanliness and order of wealthy London homes. His perspective is still that of the anthropologist, making field notes on different household cultures within the same nation.

When considering the cultural impact of Brandt's critical documentary, it is important to recognise how few of these pictures were published at the time they were taken, in the late Thirties.[35] As soon as war broke out, magazines stopped publishing pictures of poverty and injustice; they were replaced by scenes of traditional English life – the ideal world that people were fighting for. When *Picture Post* started to use Brandt's critical pictures, later in the war, it was to make a contrast with the shiny new Britain promised by the planners, where squalor would no longer exist. Brandt never had the means to make an immediate appeal to Britain's social conscience, in the way American photographers like Dorothea Lange or Walker Evans were able to do in the Thirties. He was not commissioned to go to the slums, but went out of personal interest; and what he found there inspired affection as well as anger. Brandt had a social conscience, certainly, but it was that of a poet rather than a politician.

Late night coffee stall, 1939

Even with the modest success of *The English at Home* and *A Night in London*, Brandt had not found a way of connecting with a mass public in Britain. This was a difficulty for all photographers since the major journals, such as *Weekly Illustrated* and *Illustrated London News*, and daily papers generally did not credit their pictures. People might recognise a *Weekly Illustrated* house style, but only occasionally would they be able to identify Kurt Hutton or Felix Man as responsible for a particular story. Nor was *Weekly Illustrated* a major force in popular culture, thanks to its lack of editorial personality after Stefan Lorant left it.

All this began to change in the summer of 1937 when, after a couple of years in the freelance wilderness, Lorant managed to launch *Lilliput*. A year and a half earlier *Men Only* had made a successful debut, in a compact monthly format and at a price of one shilling; but it was illustrated only with cartoons and line drawings, and its editorial content was a feeble mixture of sports, financial advice and smoking-room jokes. Despite its title, it had a 'no sex, please' policy of avoiding 'doubtful innuendoes and unfunny stories'.[1] *Lilliput* was much more sophisticated and appealed to both male and female readers with its lively mixture of fiction, topical articles, art reproductions and photography. Much of its material was either translated from continental sources or produced in England by refugee writers and artists (notably the covers by Walter Trier). At 8d., *Lilliput* was also cheaper than *Men Only*, and it did very well from its first issue in June 1937.[2] No one seemed to mind that Lorant had borrowed shamelessly from the old-established German monthly *Der Querschnitt*, and from the American *Coronet*, a companion to *Esquire* whose first issue was in December 1936.[3] *Coronet* had shown that photographic nudes could be published in English-speaking countries, with careful re-touching, under the heading of 'art'. Conveniently, nudes were also very good for business. There was only one nude in the first six issues of *Lilliput*, but after that they became a fixture, once Lorant had tested the water. His magazine continued to be the only respectable periodical in England that printed photographic nudes, whether art nudes by Man Ray or Kertész, or glamour shots by middle-brow photographers like Andre de Dienes or Erwin Blumenfeld.[4]

Brandt found a role at *Lilliput* in the same way as he had with *Weekly Illustrated*: the assistant editor, Sydney Jacobson, recalled that Brandt just 'materialised in the office one day'. It must have been soon after the magazine began, because Brandt's first picture appeared in the fourth issue, September 1937: 'After the Celebration', from *The English at Home*, with Rolf as a top-hatted drunk.[5] That Brandt had to make the first approach suggests that Lorant had pigeonholed him as a photographer who lacked the common touch. Even now, Lorant did not assign him to any extended stories, but accepted a collection of individual pictures going as far back as 1929. These pictures appeared in *Lilliput* over the next seven years: in March 1938, for example, Brandt's gesticulating 'Tic-tac Men' was placed opposite Hitler waving his arms from a platform. Lorant had an extraordinary visual memory, and liked to keep shoeboxes of pictures in the office that he could raid to create juxtapositions or illustrate a topical idea. But he did not give Brandt a major sequence until June 1938, a series of pictures drawn from *A Night in London* and coinciding with its publication.[6]

In the same month Lorant sold *Lilliput*, though he stayed on as editor. He had started the magazine on £2,000, borrowed from a friend, and sold it after a year for £20,000. This allowed him to play for bigger stakes by investing in a new mass-circulation weekly: *Picture Post*.[7] The first issue appeared on 1 October 1938, published by Hulton Press. Edward Hulton had proposed that it should have a battleship on the cover; Tom Hopkinson said that it should have a girl; Lorant said, 'There will be two girls' – and got them.[8] Lorant said his ideal was 'quality with a common touch', though the common touch was more in evidence at the kick-off. The dummy he had made up to launch *Weekly Illustrated* in June 1934 had two girls jumping over a tennis net (to be trumped by five pretty girls in skin-tight shorts for the 4 August issue). Kurt Hutton's staged picture of two girls on a funfair swing, showing their garters, was the Thirties gold standard for this kind of shot; originally commissioned by Lorant for *Weekly Illustrated*, it appeared again in the second issue of *Picture Post*.[9] Brandt was capable of taking such pictures – he did one of a female ice-skater that became a *Picture Post* cover – but if he sought popularity, it was surely not by such vulgar means.[10]

Brandt's access to a mass audience through *Lilliput* and *Picture Post* came first through his talent for set-piece pictures; not until some time after the beginning of the war could he be considered a working photo-journalist who covered a whole range of popular interests. Lorant's early use of individual pictures, often of continental scenes, put Brandt into mixed company: *Lilliput* printed pictures by such major photographers as Beaton, Brassaï and Salomon, but also routine crowd-pleasers supplied by agencies. Still, it was professional work and reasonably paid. *Lilliput*'s rates at this time were about £1 for a single picture and £15 for a series of six to nine (by 1946 these rates had at least doubled). If Brandt was still getting £30 a month from his father, by the end of 1939 he could add another £15 or even £30 in a good month, with his combined work for *Lilliput* and *Picture Post*.

Brandt's first major assigned story for *Lilliput*, in May 1939, was 'Unchanging London', which recognised him as a specialist in the great city, and particularly on its dark underside. 'We asked Bill Brandt,' the caption runs, 'the well-known photographer, to follow Doré's footsteps with a camera.' Gustave Doré's *London: A Pilgrimage* had been published in 1872; the *Lilliput* story has eight Doré engravings and nine Brandt photographs.[11] This sounds like typical idea of Lorant's, constructing a whole story as a series of parallel shots. But only one of Brandt's pictures was newly taken to match a scene from Doré: a late-night coffee stall, with an outcast woman

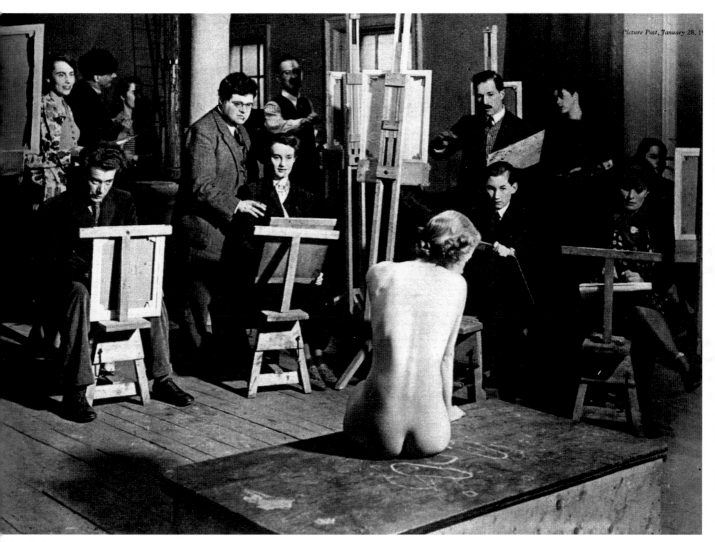

A Day in the Life of an Artist's Model, 1939

hovering at the fringes of warmth and comfort. Four of his other pictures in this story go back to *The English at Home* though one of them, 'Mist on the Thames', was printed in reverse to make a better match for its counterpart in Doré.[12] 'Alley off East India Docks Road' was cropped tighter, to fit *Lilliput*'s page size and make the policeman's bull's-eye more prominent (in Doré the lamp shines directly on three malefactors, whereas Brandt's police surveillance lurks in the background).[13] But the whole spirit of Brandt's London photography in the Thirties owes a great deal to Doré; it would even be fair to say that Brandt came to London looking for the city Doré had created – chiaroscuro, night, rainy streets, the Thames.

The text for 'Unchanging London' indicates Brandt's standing in England by the end of the Thirties:

> Bill Brandt … is a young English photographer who studied in Paris under Man Ray. Like Doré, he is deeply absorbed in the everyday life of London. He finds a depressing attraction in the endless rows of suburban houses, and in the narrow alleys between riverside warehouses. His books of photographs, 'London by Night', and 'The English at Home', are a vivid presentation of social conditions in England today. But, again like Doré, Bill Brandt has the art of infusing realism with a sense of beauty.

The idea that Brandt had a sharp eye for social conditions led to a series of *Picture Post* commissions on the theme 'A Day in the Life of . . .' Such features had become standard in German and French illustrated magazines from the 1920s on. Lorant adapted the genre for *Picture Post* with great success, though it was not used after the outbreak of war. Brandt's first *Picture Post* assignment was on the 'Buskers of London'.[14] The story was a series of portraits of buskers in action; like other *Picture Post* stories, it showed people one might rub up against in London, without knowing how they spent their day. In 1939 Brandt had six more appearances in *Picture Post*, four of them 'Day in the Life' stories on an artist's model, a Lyons' waitress, a barmaid and a parlourmaid.[15]

All of these 'Day in the Life' stories were about women employed in the service trades in London. Such women were challenging conventional female roles, and were also the kinds of readers that *Picture Post* wanted to attract. When Brandt was living in Paris, magazines like *Vu* and *Voilà* regularly ran stories about young women living independently in the city and working hard for little money. These stories were designed to titillate their readers, with frank discussions of the sexual misfortunes of chambermaids and *midinettes*.[16] *Picture Post* took an exactly opposite line from the French magazines: if you have sexual fantasies about women like these, you have got the wrong idea. The story on an artist's model shows her posing in the nude for a group of students; but the story emphasises that this is 'just a job', and the model is as decent and respectable as could be.[17] Brandt's story on the Lyons' 'Nippies' focuses on how the women are regimented by the men who are set in authority over them; personally he may have been intrigued by their uniforms, but no such fetishistic interests are hinted at in the published story.[18] The story on Alice, barmaid at the Crooked Billet, also reassures the reader that there's nothing 'fast' about her; we see her chatting politely with the regulars and reading a book with a female friend on her day off.

Alice at the Crooked Billet, 1939

Romance enters her life only as a daydream, when she looks at the poster for a Hollywood comedy, *There Goes My Heart*.[19] Any story on pubs, of course, was likely to be propaganda for an idealised 'English way of life', and Brandt was happy to cater to this need in his pictures of the Crooked Billet. His Surrealist images of pub life in Charlie Brown's came some years later.

Picture Post illustrated the daily lives of modern working women while steering clear of any difficulties they might encounter once they were on the job. When Anne Scott-James was appointed women's editor in February 1941, her first three stories were 'Make yourself a spring hat', 'My garden this summer,' and 'We adopt a hundred ABs [i.e. sailors]'.[20] Brandt's story 'The Perfect Parlourmaid' (29 July 1939) used a selection of the pictures he had taken of Pratt over the years; no one seemed to be bothered that she had been perfect at serving other people's needs. The division of labour at the Hulton Press was that *Picture Post* showed English society in a resolutely practical and progressive light; anything to do with sex or bohemianism would be left to *Lilliput*. But even there, *Lilliput* avoided political radicalism and was much less threatening to conventional morals than, say, *Playboy* in the 1960s.

In his early work for *Picture Post* and *Lilliput*, Brandt was trying to get a foothold in photo-journalism by working to order. Tom Hopkinson, his main supporter, did not become editor of the two magazines until the summer of 1940, when Stefan Lorant left for America. Brandt had to edge his way into favour, and succeeded in getting seven stories into *Picture Post* by the beginning of the war.[21] From his first approach to *Weekly Illustrated*, it had taken him three years to reach the point of being trusted with regular assignments. That he achieved this in 1939 suggests that something had given him more confidence in the constant scramble for work in photo-journalism. Most likely, that confidence came from a revolution, at this time, in his private world.

Robert Graves with Beryl Pritchard and Judy Campbell, 1941

17 Marjorie

By the spring of 1938 Brandt and Eva had been together for almost ten years. They had formed a little colony of friends and family in Belsize Park, and Brandt's second book of photographs, *A Night in London*, was about to appear. The only real threat to their happiness together seemed to be Eva's precarious health. Since the end of 1935 she had spent large parts of each year in sanatoria, first at Midhurst and then at Crans-sur-Sierre. On 28 May 1938, she entered another sanatorium at Sancellemoz, in France. It was on the Plateau d'Assy, near Chamonix, in a gentler situation than Davos: the outlook was to the south, and the altitude 300 metres lower. In fine weather there was a magnificent view of the massif of Mont Blanc. Sancellemoz was the most modern and luxurious of the sanatoria at Assy; Eva found it agreeable enough to go back for two further stays. Several members of Stravinsky's family were patients, and his daughter Mika died there in November 1938. Stravinsky himself was treated for TB in the summer of 1939, his stay overlapping with one of Eva's.[1] Sancellemoz had some of the advantages of a luxury hotel, including a fine library and many social activities; it was also an easier place for Lyena to visit from Paris. Still, the daily routine was as strict as that at Davos, including careful segregation of men and women (each had their own wing). Living in a world where sex was forbidden, Eva wondered whether it was fair to expect the same abstinence of her husband.

At one of her sanatoria or clinics, Eva became friendly with a fellow-TB patient, Marjorie Beckett.[2] She brought Marjorie to London to meet Brandt, or perhaps sent her there with an introduction. Eva's idea was that Marjorie was too shy, and needed to be drawn out socially.[3] But she also thought that if she was unable to be in London herself, then 'Billy shouldn't be alone'.[4] And if he was going to have someone else, better that it should be someone Eva already liked, and who belonged to the club of those who had suffered from TB. When Marjorie and Bill promptly fell in love it was, on some level, what Eva expected and even wanted. But she clung to the belief that she would always be the most important woman in Brandt's life, whatever happened.

Marjorie was 'very, very upper-middle class', by one report, and 'extremely pretty and well dressed' by another.[5] She had a mane of blonde hair and a slender, attractive figure. In the 1940s she became a fashion model, as well as a fashion journalist. Brandt would use her as a model for his 'Nightwalk' dream sequence, for the story 'A Day on the River,' and for one of his most beautiful nudes, 'Campden Hill, London, 1949'.[6]

Marjorie Beckett (left) in 'A Day on the River', *Picture Post*, 1941

His affair with Marjorie began in the summer of 1938, when they went on holiday together to Brittany for two weeks while Eva had just gone to Sancellemoz. The trip coincided with Brandt's first show in Paris, from 27 June to 14 July, of pictures from *A Night in London*.[7] It was a test of Brandt's and Marjorie's relationship in more senses than one, because Lyena Barjansky was invited to come from Paris and join them. That she and Marjorie should get on well was, evidently, a necessity for Brandt. Any new lover had to be compatible with his old ones; just as he calculated – rightly – that he would be able to have Marjorie without giving up Eva. He could hardly have gone on holiday to Brittany with Marjorie and Lyena without Eva either knowing in advance, or finding out soon afterwards.

To Lyena, Marjorie seemed like a 'sweet little girl' when they first met; since she was twenty-eight at the time, this must have been the effect of having a pretty face and very little to say for herself. Frances Statler, too, found Marjorie reserved to the point of having hardly any personality at all. But other evidence suggests that, behind the Dresden-doll exterior, there was more character than most people realised, including a great deal of will and persistence. Anne Scott-James considered her, with reason, 'a bit of a schemer'. Before she became ill with TB, Marjorie had decided that she wanted to have a job, despite having no qualifications and a family that considered it unseemly for girls like her to work. She found a job advertised that suited her, but it called for the ability to type; Marjorie went for the interview with her arm in a sling and was hired. By the time she had to take the sling off, she had made herself so useful that she was kept on – without having to type.

Eva came back to London from Sancellemoz at the end of August, and continued her treatment at Midhurst as an out-patient.[8] In November she had to return to Sancellemoz for another five months; when she was at Hillfield Court she lived in a *ménage à trois* with Brandt and Marjorie.[9] This created a more intimate triangle than the one between Brandt, Eva and Lyena (which had lasted ten years on an easy-come, easy-go basis), but it was not such a new or radical step for Eva to make. Marjorie's position is less clear. One view would be that Marjorie was so totally devoted to Brandt that she simply accepted that he would always need to be close to two women at once; and that, so long as jealousy did not become unmanageable, her close friendship with Eva was important to her as well. The flat at 58 Hillfield Court was pretty cramped, so they could hardly have lived there without all being on civil terms (around 1941, Brandt rented a small flat across the hall, number 60, where he set up his darkroom). The alternative view is that Marjorie was never devoted to Eva in the way Lyena was: once she fell in love with Brandt, she made an appearance of being sweet and complaisant, but was determined to get him to herself. She would tolerate Eva's presence for Brandt's sake, but her long-term strategy would be to drive Eva out. However, if this was the case, it must be explained why it took so long for Eva to go. In the early years of the relationship, at least, both women must have been reasonably content to share the man they both loved, and who wanted to love them both.

Eva's acceptance of another woman into her married life may also have been a kind of compensation for her troubled relationship with her elder sister, Vilma. In the magical thinking of childhood, Eva's jealousy of Vilma made her guilty of Vilma's early death; as an adult, Eva could herself become the 'good' elder sister to Marjorie, and repress the jealousy that most wives would have felt towards a rival. That Marjorie also suffered from TB brought out Eva's protective side, directed towards someone who was weaker rather than stronger than herself. And before becoming a rival, Marjorie had been Eva's friend; this might make Marjorie less likely to act in a merely selfish way, pushing Eva aside and taking Brandt completely away from her. Eva had never been very comfortable about sex, giving her less reason to be possessive about it. She wanted Brandt as a soulmate and companion. Between Brandt and Marjorie there was a powerful sexual passion; so at the beginning, each of the women was willing to let the other 'have the part of Billy they liked'.[10] That is to say, Eva was love; Marjorie was lust. For Brandt, of course, this created the kind of arrangement he always wanted: he enjoyed the love of two women, who nonetheless remained on friendly terms with each other.

In 1941 Brandt took a portrait of Robert Graves that is also an allegory of his own emotional and sexual life. It appeared as an illustration for a story by Graves in *Picture Post*, 'What I Believe About Ghosts'.[11] Driven from Mallorca by the Spanish Civil War, Graves had broken with Laura Riding (his Muse of the Thirties) and was living with Beryl Pritchard at Galmpton, near Brixham, Devon. His first wife, Nancy Nicholson, refused to give him a divorce, so he was not able to marry Beryl until 1950. Brandt made the long journey down to Devon and took many pictures of Graves in different settings, so he must have stayed for several days.[12] It all testified to his deep interest in Graves, going back to his attempt to visit him on Mallorca in 1932. Brandt's fine solo portrait of Graves in his study is suitably uncanny for a story on ghosts; but he also seized on the presence of a young friend, the actress Judy Campbell, to stage a triangular tableau with her, Graves and Beryl. Campbell was already famous for her performance of 'A Nightingale Sang in Berkeley Square', in the revue *New Faces* the year before. She was a friend of Graves's daughter Jenny, and was married to the war hero David Birkin. Brandt posed her as a flawless and remote classical head, gazing out of the frame; Graves contemplates her profile from across the table, while Beryl contemplates him as he looks at the 'other' woman. Beryl seems to hold him within the couple, while at the same time accepting his absorption in a second object of desire.[13]

It seems more than likely that Brandt was using this scene to express feelings about his own domestic triangle, in which he adored Marjorie while Eva adored him. Graves in 1926 had set up a notorious 'three-life' with Nancy Nicholson and Laura Riding. Later, he became the advocate for another kind of triangle, saying that the male poet needed both a wife for sustenance and a muse for inspiration. It seems typical of Brandt that he observed Graves's domestic career and used his portrait to refer covertly to their shared interests, but never made any equivalent portrait of Eva and Marjorie together.

Brandt, according to Ester Cotton, 'couldn't be alone': both in the sense of needing companionship, and needing someone to organise his everyday life. His dreamy manner inspired, in certain women, great longings to look after him. As Lyena put it, 'he didn't run after the girls, they ran after him'. Marjorie was only too happy to take on responsibility for Brandt's practical needs. She was brilliant at everything domestic, knew enough about clothes to be a successful fashion editor, modelled for

Brandt and was a shrewd business manager for his photography. The final card that Marjorie could play was her assured social position. Eva might be an aristocrat in Hungary but in England she was, at first glance, just another north London foreigner who spoke with an accent and lived in a flat. Marjorie was conspicuously well bred and well dressed; and many people agree that, in his quiet way, Brandt was a bit of a snob. It was one thing to distance himself from Germany through his affairs with Lyena and Eva, but a considerable further step to be intimate with someone as quintessentially English as Marjorie.[14] Ester Cotton recalls that Marjorie was 'a very typical upper-class Englishwoman; not a European. For some reason this very much attracted Billy.' A sexual attachment will always be the most powerful means of assimilating into another culture; if it had not been Marjorie, one suspects that Brandt would have ended up with some other Englishwoman. It may be significant, too, that Brandt never formed any close friendship with an Englishman, so that he entered the English family through the female side.

When he met Marjorie, Brandt had been a photographer for ten years without paying much attention to women as subjects. He had done some pleasing but derivative nudes in the style of Man Ray, using Eva as his model for several of them; and there were some vivid staged pictures using Ester Brandt and 'Bird'. But his fascination with Marjorie led to a much bigger project of staging pictures, probably in the winter of 1939-40. Most of Brandt's staged pictures in the Thirties had been single tableaux, but now he took multiple shots and linked them into a narrative. His brother Rolf was again an important collaborator. Dozens of pictures from this venture are preserved in the Brandt archive; seven of them were published as 'Nightwalk: A Dream Phantasy in Photographs' in the American magazine *Coronet*, in January 1941.[15] Perhaps Marjorie thought them too personal to appear in Britain, except for a single shot that came out in *Lilliput*, in September 1946, where she is unrecognisable.[16] Brandt photographed her in many strange and suggestive poses, and after taking the pictures he also put enormous effort into manipulating them in the darkroom. The sequence shows him indulging his love of special effects to the limit.

'Nightwalk', as published in *Coronet*, begins with Marjorie asleep in bed and ends with her waking up. In between is a dream sequence of five pictures where she wanders through hallways and staircases in her dressing-gown, carrying a Jack Russell terrier, and meets a sinister figure played by Rolf. She sleeps in a divan bed in the living room at Hillfield Court (the flat had only one bedroom; another picture, taken in the late Thirties, shows Eva asleep in the same bed).[17] In the darkroom, Brandt montaged into the window a full moon and a roofscape with two chimneys, as in a scene from Robert Wiene's *The Cabinet of Dr Caligari* (1920). This classic of German Expressionist cinema supplies the nightmare atmosphere, the theme of somnambulism and the threatening madman – played by Rolf in a Caligari-style stove-pipe hat. But Brandt's central idea, of female vulnerability, is only a sub-plot in *Caligari*.[18] Although the sequence is presented as a woman's fantasy, the viewer doesn't see events through her eyes. Instead, we see what a male spectator would see and, on some level, enjoy: a half-dressed woman threatened with unspeakable acts of violation. The somnambulist in *Caligari* is a man who commits crimes, including the attempted rape of the heroine; in Brandt's story, she sleepwalks in order to *become* a victim. There is nothing openly

Scenes from "Nightwalk", 1939/40

pornographic in Brandt's scenes, yet a sadistic imagination seems to be at work, one that is excited by the woman's fear.[19]

The intensity of Brandt's fantasies about Marjorie can be measured by the amount of work he did on manipulating the pictures. The first shot of 'Nightwalk' uses as background the façade of a slum house in Stepney that he had photographed in February 1939.[20] For the shot of the woman falling down the stairwell, he photographed Marjorie kneeling with her arms raised; he then inverted the picture and overlaid it on a staircase shot.[21] For the picture where Marjorie lies outdoors in a thicket, apparently with her arms and legs tied, Brandt made numerous shots of her lying on a mat in various suggestive poses. He did one more narrative sequence, 'A Simple Story About a Girl' (*Lilliput*, September 1941), but this has nothing of the obsessive quality of 'Nightwalk'. In its elaborate artifice and libidinal themes, 'Nightwalk' belongs entirely to the dream-world and the surreal, and is totally removed from the progressive aims of mainstream photo-journalism. Here, Brandt gives himself over completely to the fantasy realm that almost always co-exists with everyday reality in the rest of his work. Although he never did any further projects on the scale of 'Nightwalk', it was the prelude to his major phase of involvement with the female nude, which began later in the war. Brandt liked to say that his nudes were his most important work; if so, it was his passion for Marjorie Beckett that set him on that path.

Asleep in a sarcophagus, Christ Church, Spitalfields, 1940

Brandt's Vienna ceased to exist on 15 March 1938, when Hitler entered the city in triumph. The culture that had been so welcoming and inspiring to Brandt in 1927 was swept away within a few weeks. Trude Fleischmann, the leading studio photographer in Vienna, went to London soon after the *Anschluss*, then on to New York. She re-established her career and died in America in 1990, aged ninety-five. Eugenie Schwarzwald fled to Denmark two days after Hitler's arrival; her Schwarzwaldschule was shut down by the Nazis in September. From Denmark, she came to London to stay with Ester and Rolf; she then went on to Zurich, where her husband joined her. He was accompanied by Maria Stiastny, the third point of the Schwarzwalds' marital triangle. Robert Musil, Schwarzwald's friend and the great chronicler of Vienna in *The Man Without Qualities*, also took refuge in Zurich. Like Thomas Mann, he was both a political enemy of Nazism and married to a Jewish wife. Progressive Vienna had been mortally ill for years before this, of course, since the crushing of the Socialist forces in February 1934, and many had left between then and the *Anschluss*. Freud, with his curious reluctance to expect the worst of the Nazis, kept up his practice and his old habits to the bitter end. In June 1938 the combined efforts of his friends and the Gestapo finally convinced him to leave for London. A house had been prepared for him in Maresfield Gardens, in the midst of north London's 'Little Vienna' and a few minutes' walk from the Brandts at Hillfield Court.

Another Viennese who arrived in London was Brandt's former analyst, Wilhelm Stekel. He fled to Switzerland after the *Anschluss*, and all the books and papers he had to leave behind were burned by the Nazis (including, perhaps, his case notes on Brandt). From Berne he and his wife made their way to England, where he tried once again to heal the breach with Freud, but was rebuffed. Sick with diabetes, he led a poor and unhappy existence in London. Brandt would not have wanted to see Stekel, but neither did he want to have much to do with the refugee community in general. Having been in England for five years already, and having no worries about money or livelihood, he was not in the same plight as most of the recent arrivals. But the Free German League of Culture was established in Hampstead in 1938; there was also a Refugee Society, to which, for example, Virginia Woolf donated the manuscript of *Three Guineas* to be auctioned for their relief fund.[1] Though Brandt would have been well placed to help with relief work, his policy by this time was one of complete separation from his German background. For him, the Germans were a flawed people, beyond any potential for redemption. None of his photo-journalism covered the refugee community, as he continued his focus on typical – and native – British subjects.

Rolf Brandt, on the other hand, saw no reason to acquire protective English coloration. By the late 1930s he had given up his acting ambitions altogether; one of his frustrations was that he was regularly asked to play Nazi parts! Rolf turned to the graphic arts, studying from 1935 at Ozenfant's school in London and later with Paul Colin in Paris. He illustrated books, painted and did some teaching at the London School of Printing. But his real passion was for politics. Unlike Bill, he believed in struggling for a better Germany, proletarian and internationalist. As he and Ester saw it, Nazism was the product of a particular political situation, one that could be changed. After the German occupation of Czechoslovakia in March 1939, Rolf set off for Prague to help leftist actors whom he knew to escape. His work was backed by an organisation called the Actors' Refugee Group, probably an offshoot of International Red Aid, which had been set up by the Communist International in 1934. It was particularly active in Spain, where Tina Modotti worked for it after giving up photography. Rolf went to Germany and was questioned by the Gestapo about why he wanted to go to Prague. He was a good enough actor to persuade them that he only wanted to visit relatives. Once in Prague, he provided money and false papers to get people out; he later went back and did it again. About six or seven actors were brought to London in this way, and were then lodged with Rolf and Ester in Belsize Park Gardens to put them on their feet. Even with his British passport for protection, Rolf's actions in 1939 were heroic; but they stemmed from a political and national commitment that Bill was quite unwilling to share.

LW and Lilli Brandt had been very reluctant to leave Germany, in spite of their opposition to Hitler's regime; but at Easter 1939 their eldest son, Walther, telephoned them in Hamburg and said, 'You must come over.'[2] LW was sixty-four, and in no state to face internment again. They arrived in England and settled down in a country house, Winswood, near Crawley Down, Sussex. After the war they moved to a beautiful Queen Anne house near Micheldever, Hampshire. Both Bill and Rolf were happy to retreat to their parents' house from the danger and discomfort of wartime London, and Eva remained a special favourite with LW. The youngest son, Augustus, was working on a sheep farm in Australia when the war began; but all the other Brandts were now together in England, and Augustus would come back before long to fight for the Allies.

In the first year of the war, Brandt's major project was something typically private and off the beaten track of everyday photo-journalism. He had long been fascinated by the swarm of night-time activities in a great city; but now, London was under siege. Daytime remained relatively safe, while danger came by night. The city's first defence was to extinguish every glimmer of light, in the hope that German bombers might lose themselves in a vast, featureless expanse. The most dangerous nights were those of clear weather and a full moon, when the German raiders could orient themselves by the Thames and such great buildings as Battersea power station or St Paul's Cathedral. London then became a spectral and deserted city – vulnerable, as never before, to destruction from the air. On such nights, Brandt set out to explore

Houses in Bayswater, 1939

an urban environment that had not existed since the introduction of gas street lighting more than a hundred years before.[3]

In his post-war article 'Pictures by Night', Brandt spoke of moonlight as 'a fascinating part of night photography':

> Moonlit scenes always have a very peaceful if not desolate atmosphere. The housefronts and rows of buildings in the streets may sometimes appear almost eerily ghostlike. This deadness is what an effective moonlight picture tries to catch.
>
> Moonlight is very weak, so the exposures usually run into 30 minutes or more, even when the moon is full.[4]

Emptied of its scurrying inhabitants, Brandt's moonlit city became a place of eerie façades, seemingly with nothing and no one behind them. His own love of concealment was stimulated by the city's apparent withdrawal into secret recesses: 'The glamorous make-up of the world's largest city faded with the lights. Under the soft light of the moon the blacked-out town had a new beauty. The houses looked flat like painted scenery and the bombed ruins made strangely shaped silhouettes.'[5] London became a Surrealist tableau, as if de Chirico's visionary city had replaced the mundane reality that prevailed before the blackout.

Brandt captured the strangeness of the blackout in pictures like 'Houses in Bayswater Lit by Moonlight'. With his remarkable visual memory, Brandt seems to have reproduced the composition of a 1936 picture by Berenice Abbott, 'Fifth Avenue Houses'. Abbott's picture had the daylit sky as background; Brandt's version was dark at the top and reversed Abbott's right-to-left movement from light to shade. But the real difference is one of spirit. Abbott's picture was part of a project called 'Changing New York', which aimed to capture the paradoxical quality of the city's streetscapes: solidly there, but liable to be demolished and replaced at any time.[6] The drawing down of the blinds in the two houses on the left of Abbott's picture suggests that they are uninhabited and awaiting demolition. Brandt's Bayswater houses might also be demolished – by German bombs – but he is not trying to memorialise them. Rather, in Rupert Martin's words:

> London [appears] to be a vast, deserted necropolis. The unreality of the scene, the deserted streets and the quality of light recall the enigmatic townscapes of de Chirico. Brandt's surrealism was of the same poetic, melancholy kind as de Chirico's, and their work possesses a sense of potential drama, as if something momentous is about to happen … The light which irradiates their towns is an unearthly one and gives us a sense of timelessness.[7]

Standing by his tripod in the street for his thirty-minute exposures, with all traffic stilled, Brandt had time to ponder such dark thoughts; at the least, he saw a unique visual opportunity, and was able to capture it for London's memory.

Pictures like 'Houses in Bayswater' may give the starkest impression of wartime London, but they are not meant to inspire patriotism. The general public seized on a more iconic picture in the series, 'St Paul's Cathedral in the Moonlight'. There were

St. Paul's in moonlight, 1940

many photos of St. Paul's as a symbol of London's survival, but Brandt was not trying to bring out its monumentality; rather, his perspective gives the effect of a montage. A great heap of rubble in the foreground is photographed in *Neue Sachlichkeit* style, with loving attention to texture and the play of light and shade; against this the cathedral has no texture at all, but is just a dark silhouette. Its appearance is made unfamiliar by a camera angle that turns a damaged roofline into a cliff that looms menacingly over the church below. Instead of rising triumphantly above the chaos of bombed London – the standard approach of other war photographs – Brandt's St Paul's balances its man-made form with two powerful counter-forces: the rubble in front of it, and the ragged border of pure darkness beside it.[8] Although many responded to the picture as a great stroke of propaganda for indomitable Britain, it could also be seen as a nihilistic vision, of forces poised to bring down the temple – and, in 1939, no one could know whether or not it would survive.

The picture of St Paul's by moonlight appeared in the 'Blackout in London' series for *Lilliput*, in December 1939. This story enabled Brandt to make his first connection with a mass audience in the United States, with 'London under Blackout' for *Life* magazine.[9] The four pictures in *Life* were foggy, Dickensian views of the city, rather than the more astringent shots of moonlit façades.[10] The US was looking for pictures in the vein of 'There'll always be an England', but Brandt failed to catch on with *Life*'s London bureau. Its regular photographers, such as William Vandivert and George Rodger, were more attuned to American tastes; Brandt had two more pictures in *Life* in June, then nothing.[11] Cecil Beaton was more in favour with *Life* as a freelancer: he had a cover picture of a little girl wounded in an air-raid, followed by a major story on how 'life goes on' in a typical English village (conveniently named Churchill).[12] The same age as Brandt, and from a similar kind of wealthy merchant family, Beaton had a glossy, commercial touch that ensured he would make his way more quickly.[13] Even so, he cast a cool eye on the aristocrats and celebrities whom he photographed.

It was Brandt, though, who received one of the most important photographic commissions of the war, for the new Ministry of Information (MOI). This was housed in the Senate House of the University of London, a gigantic art-deco pile; both the style of the building and what went on inside it helped to inspire the 'Ministry of Truth' in Orwell's *Nineteen Eighty-Four*. The Minister in 1940 was Duff Cooper, a pillar of the Establishment; but in August he appointed someone much less conventional as his second-in-command. Frank Pick was the genius, or at least the monomaniac, who had driven the expansion of London Transport in the Thirties and had made it a world leader in industrial design and visual art. On 1 September 1939, he organised the evacuation of three quarters of a million women and children from London, using first the Tube and then trains from outlying stations. Having trodden on too many toes, he was re-organised out of his job in April 1940, then fell on his feet with the appointment to manage the MOI.[14]

Pick understood that London Transport was, on the Home Front, a crucial instrument of modern war. He also believed that civilian morale was the key to victory, and in December 1939 he sponsored a photographic exhibition at Charing Cross station called *Why We Are at War*, using pictures donated by agencies.[15] The show was so successful that a hundred replicas of it were made and sent to the Dominions and neutral countries; regular exhibitions at Charing Cross followed. When Pick moved to the MOI, he had a natural interest in documenting the use of the Underground system as a giant bomb shelter. Thousands of Londoners had started to spend their nights in the Tube after the first German raid on the city, on 7 September 1940. At first the government tried to discourage people from going underground; it feared that hysteria and disease would break out, or that people would abandon their jobs and stay down below indefinitely.[16] H. G. Wells's fantasies about sinister Morlocks seem to have lived on in the official mind; but before long the government recognised that the Underground was as useful for London's survival as a front-line soldier's trench was for him. Unfortunately, there were few stations in the East End (the most vulnerable part of London) or south of the Thames, so that only 5 per cent of the city's population actually sheltered in the Tube.[17]

Stations were given some rudimentary sleeping facilities and sanitation, and most of the photographic coverage followed the official line of 'business as usual', with pictures of people carrying on in typically English fashion – playing cards, chatting and drinking tea.[18] For the artist's eye, however, it was the unusual that demanded attention. Henry Moore went into the Tube one night after dinner at the Café Royal and was so fascinated that he started to fill a sketchbook with impressions.[19] He showed the book to Kenneth Clark, the director of the National Gallery, who had joined the Ministry of Information.[20] Clark commissioned Moore to make a series of shelter drawings, which he later called the most significant British art to be inspired by the war. He must have approved the parallel commission to Brandt, though the person immediately responsible was Hugh Francis, director of the Photograph Division at the ministry.[21] Brandt was told to make a comprehensive record of shelter life, and he went out every night from 4 to 12 November. He visited not only Tube shelters, but also church crypts, railway arches and private cellars. His task was a kind of reversal of the moonlight pictures of 1939: instead of standing outside in the deserted moonlit streets, he would have to work in confined and crowded spaces and be entirely dependent on artificial light.

Some lights were kept on through the night in the Tube, but Brandt also brought with him 'Kodak lamp-holders, some photoflood bulbs and enough flex to stretch the full length of Winchester Cathedral'.[22] Robert Butts, who was Brandt's assistant, recalls his obsessive concern with trying to catch everyone asleep: 'In the darker air raid shelters where it was not possible to focus with existing light I held a flashlight, which had no magnifying glass, just a small bulb, over the heads of the subjects while he focused on it.'[23] The flash unit was placed away from the camera and fired after Brandt had removed the lens cap from the open shutter of his Rollei (an archaic technique going back to Brandt's studio days in Vienna, and used again later for some of his nudes).

Brandt combined careful control of his lighting with very long exposures:

In this manner he caught the play of light and shadow on the long rows of sleeping bodies in the underground tube tunnels. The photographs display very distinct and intense contrasts, and this, though leading to loss of detail, has the concomitant effect of increasing a picture's impact.[24]

Elephant and Castle shelter, 1940

In Brandt's picture of the Elephant and Castle shelter, taken on 11 November, the platform clock shows 3.45 a.m. Other shelter photographers favoured the earlier part of the night, when people were sitting up and providing 'human interest' with their activities (and after which the photographer could go home to bed). This was not for Brandt; like Henry Moore, he was fascinated by an underworld where sleep, dreams and death came together – a world whose composition and lighting recalled Gustave Doré's illustrations for Dante's *Inferno*. Almost all the shelterers in Brandt's pictures are prone or asleep. The pictures of orthodox Jews praying, and of a Sikh family in a church crypt, are exceptions that prove the rule: they make the shelters into catacombs incubating strange sects – the kind of scene that might be dreamed by the sleepers around them. In the Elephant and Castle picture, one man was sitting up and looking directly at the camera; Brandt blanked out his face when the picture was reprinted in 1966 in *Shadow of Light*.[25]

One of Brandt's captions read, 'Deep below the ground the long alley of intermingled bodies, with the hot, smelly air and continual murmur of snores, came nearest to my pre-war idea of what an air-raid shelter would be like.'[26] Both Moore and Brandt saw the shelters as places that gave the appearance of death, even as they preserved life. In these tombs for the living, bodies were laid out like the civilian victims of bombing after a raid, something the world had first seen three and a half years earlier at Guernica. More than any other single project, Brandt's shelter pictures completed his two agendas from the Thirties: to represent his own psychic journey in symbolic form, and to make a visual inventory of his adopted country, in all its oddness and particularity. His two pictures of the coffin-sleeper in Spitalfields are good examples. The first one shows a man and a woman with a flowered bedspread and a sarcophagus, in a light strong enough to reveal the strange jumble of rubbish and personal effects in the crypt. The second version of the scene, as printed in the second edition of *Shadow of Light*, has been stripped down to a few powerful symbols. The woman sleeper has been cropped out of the frame, deep blacks have flooded out detail, and the remaining sleeper now looks like a tomb-effigy of a pilgrim or crusader (his two different poses suggest that Brandt asked him to pretend to be asleep for the second one). In this picture, as in many others, we can see Brandt deepening his themes and contrasts, making his personal style ever more distinct.

Brandt's work in the shelters was cut short on 12 November, when he fell ill with flu. He may have picked it up in the crowded conditions underground (where he also complained that the smell from the makeshift toilets was close to unbearable). Perhaps the nervous strain was more than he could cope with, coming at the end of such a disastrous year of war. But his pictures were widely reproduced, and a set was given to Roosevelt's emissary Wendell Wilkie, to help him persuade the US government to provide more aid for Britain.[27]

The shelter pictures allowed Brandt to make a direct contribution to the war effort, which surely was important to him. They also led to more official work. In 1941 the government established the National Buildings Record, to document historic buildings that might be destroyed by bombing. Its director, John Summerson, recruited Brandt as a staff photographer, probably on Kenneth

Orthodox Jews in shelter, 1940

Clark's recommendation.[28] Over the next four years Brandt took hundreds of pictures of the exteriors and interiors of historic buildings; it would have been gruelling work, under wartime conditions and combined with so many travelling assignments for *Picture Post*. The most striking pictures are of tomb effigies, where Brandt could indulge in Surrealist perspectives and bring out the grotesque side of the English cult of the dead.[29]

The Sterling Bomber, 1942

19 The Home Front and *Picture Post*

In July of 1940 Brandt took part in a group show of Modern Photography at Marx House, London. It shows his political naivety that he got drawn into such a project, presumably by Edith Tudor Hart and his brother Rolf.[1] British Communists were isolated and deeply unpopular at this time, thanks to the Nazi–Soviet Pact of August 1939, which gave both partners a free hand to attack and divide Poland. The Communist Party line in England was to hinder the war effort, on the grounds that the war was a quarrel between equally rotten capitalist states; but practically no one outside the party would swallow that argument, especially after the Soviet invasion of Finland in November 1939. The Marx House exhibition was an attempt to revive the good old days of committed art and the Popular Front, and the *New Statesman* reviewer saw Brandt's work as part of this agenda:

> Bill Brandt gets straight to the core of the reality of an industrialised world, of life on the dole, in a series of magnificent documentaries. One peers down at an angle into a slum back-yard in Jarrow where the family are huddled together in scabby confinement beneath the clothes-line, a rotting saucepan full of scum hanging on a decaying wall, a broken kitchen chair, a ruined tub … an intolerable picture of a miner's child standing in a sunken yard where nothing but the upturned rim of an enamel basin holds the light. He shows, too, a furious photograph of a Spanish beggar gesticulating against a sun-bitten building. All this is first-rate, and is, together with the work of E. T. H., photography with a vengeance, in every sense of the word.[2]

Edith Tudor Hart's career had in several ways run parallel to Brandt's up to 1940. Starting also in Vienna (she was four years younger than Brandt), she had chosen similar subjects: shop-fronts in the style of Atget, gypsies, ragamuffin children in the street and Stepney interiors. She came to Britain in 1933 and lived in Rhondda, where her husband practised medicine. Brandt arrived there in 1934 to take pictures of miners, and may have gone at her invitation.[3] Tudor Hart photographed a Welsh miner bringing home coal on his bike two years before Brandt's famous picture (taken at Jarrow). But the similarities between her pictures and Brandt's also suggest how photographs of the 'same' subject may differ fundamentally in spirit. It was reasonable for the *New Statesman* reviewer to see Brandt's pictures as critical of capitalist society, but there were other dimensions to them as well, and other ambitions. Even in the Thirties, Brandt was more interested in marginal individuals and extreme cases than in proletarians. Unlike most leftist photographers, he never took pictures of workers *en masse*.

When the Marx House show was planned, the period of the 'phoney war' had given fellow-travellers the luxury of taking a hands-off attitude to Britain's struggle, and of arguing that injustice at home was still the main issue. The fall of France in June, followed by the Battle of Britain, made it impossible to ignore where the immediate danger lay. Among Brandt's circle from Vienna days, Wilhelm Stekel killed himself in London, three days after the French surrender. He was in poor health and was terrified for his son, who was trapped in France. Eugenie Schwarzwald died of cancer in Zurich on 17 August 1940; her husband had died there a year earlier. Lyena Barjansky fled Paris on 11 June, three days before the German army entered the city, and went down to Hyères on the Mediterranean. As a Jew she knew she had to get out, but she faced endless bureaucratic hurdles. Her Austrian passport had expired and she could only renew it in person, which was impossibly dangerous; the French would only give her an 'ex-Austrian' identity card. She managed to get Swiss temporary papers, which would allow her entry into the US; but she still needed Spanish, Portuguese and US visas, and permission to leave the Vichy republic. After nine months she made the crossing from France into Spain, at about the same time as Walter Benjamin committed suicide after being turned back at the border. She reached the US by ship from Lisbon in the spring of 1941.

The Brandt family spent their second Christmas together, in 1940, at LW and Lilli's house at Crawley Down. Walter Brandt, who had anglicised his name after settling in England, joined Section X of the Special Operations Executive in Baker Street, which conducted espionage and propaganda against Germany.[4] Later he moved to Bletchley Park and spent most of the war there. After the war he refused to say what he had done, except to boast of broadcasting to Germany in 1944 that Goering was still eating butter, which drew an official denial from the German High Command! The odd man out at Crawley would have been Rolf, tarred with the party line of Nazi–Soviet friendship. It cannot have been a cheerful occasion on any account, given the Nazi triumph in the West, with Hamburg, Vienna and Paris all now under Hitler's heel. England stood virtually alone and, if it fell, all of the Brandts could expect to be victims of the Gestapo.

After the family celebrations, on 29 December Bill took the train back to London and was caught by a raid. His train was stopped just before London Bridge station, and he found himself separated from the other passengers and surrounded by burning buildings. By another account, the raid caught him as he was leaving Belsize Park Tube station (he may have been caught twice). Every time he heard the whistle of a bomb he sheltered in a doorway, but was thrown to the ground several times by the blast before getting home.[5] One wonders why he didn't stay in the Tube, but perhaps Marjorie was at home and he wanted to reach her at all costs. At Hillside Court, residents remember that he and Marjorie never came down to the communal shelter in the basement, preferring to take their chances in the corridor upstairs.

Brandt had suffered from asthma for many years, but it became much worse after this experience. A second blow soon followed, the diagnosis of diabetes. Brandt believed that the terror of the raid had brought it on.[6] At the age of thirty-six, he had now contracted a chronic illness that caused him to withdraw even further from social contact, except with the people of his trusted inner circle. As in his sanatorium years, Brandt had to submit to a strict regime in order to have any kind of a life; the difference now was that something like the Iron Key of Davos had to be imposed at home. It soon became evident that it was Marjorie, rather than Eva, who best suited the role of nurse and protector. Eva, still struggling with TB, was hardly strong enough to take responsibility for another invalid. Marjorie shielded Brandt from household worries, managed his professional affairs, and was a gifted cook who could make palatable the stringent diet that he now had to follow. Brandt was warned that his illness might make him blind; his doctor had noticed that the incidence of diabetes in Japan was very low, and told him to eliminate meat from his diet and replace it with fish.[7] To Brandt's sexual passion for Marjorie was now added his dependence on her to keep him in health and preserve his sight. By taking charge of his case, she made herself not just desirable but also indispensable; in the long run, this gave her the upper hand over Eva and ensured that, if forced to choose, Brandt would choose her.

In spite of his terrifying experience in the December 1940 raid, and his failing health afterwards, Brandt stayed at Hillfield Court with Eva and Marjorie throughout the war. To stick things out in central London, and refuse to go to the shelter, represented a quiet defiance of the Nazis. Around the end of 1941 a smaller flat across the hall, number 60, became vacant and Brandt rented it for £2.50 a week. He set up his darkroom there, and also used it as living quarters. While his marriage continued its eccentric course at Hillfield Court, his brother Rolf and Ester arrived at a parting of the ways in 1941. Ester fell in love with Bob Cotton, a writer and fellow-Communist Party member, and went off to live with and later marry him. In 1942 Rolf married a woman he had met through the party, Joyce Abraham. She was divorced and living in Hampstead with a young daughter, Ruth. Rolf had two more daughters with her, so the Brandt family now had a Jewish branch – the closest Bill would come to his fantasy of becoming Jewish himself.

Once Russia entered the war, Rolf had no reason to keep aloof, but now he became a conscientious objector and joined the ambulance service. This did not satisfy Walter, and the deep rift between them continued. The only one of the four brothers who was free to join a fighting service was the youngest, Augustus. He had been working on an Australian sheep ranch when the war broke out and had joined the Air Force there. Early in 1942 he completed his training and was posted as a navigator to 15 Squadron, 3 Group, Bomber Command. Here, as in most bomber units, airmen from Britain, Australia, New Zealand, South Africa and Canada were mixed together in each crew. 15 Squadron was based at Wyton, just outside Huntingdon, and flew Short Stirling I's: four-engined heavy bombers with a maximum speed of 255 m.p.h. When the Stirling was designed, its wingspan was set at 99 feet so that it would fit into existing hangars; this limited its ceiling to 16,500 feet, which made it horribly vulnerable to enemy fighters and flak.[8]

The commander of Augustus's plane was a young Canadian from Toronto, Thomas William Hare. When he wrecked his Stirling on landing on 25 March,

Augustus Brandt, 1910-1942, photographer unknown

Augustus was not on board, so he may not yet have arrived at the squadron. On the night of 28-9 March 1942, 3 Group took part in the war's first really successful attack on a German city, devastating the centre of Lübeck with high explosive and incendiary bombs. Lübeck was one of the historic Hanseatic towns (along with Hamburg and Bremen), the birthplace of Thomas Mann and the setting for *Buddenbrooks*.[9] But Augustus did not have much time to ponder the ironies of what he was doing. On the night of 6-7 April his Stirling took off to bomb Essen, in the Ruhr; a German night-fighter attacked the lumbering bomber and it crashed in the North Sea, killing everyone on board.[10] Alone of the crew, Augustus's body was recovered by the Germans and buried in a special section of the Kiel War Cemetery for Allied aircrew. At thirty years old, Augustus had come to rest just fifty miles north of where he had been born. Augustus was particularly close to his brother Walter, and was godfather to his son Peter. Walter was deeply upset by Augustus's death, but Bill never made any public acknowledgement of it. In December of 1942, however, he completed a *Picture Post* story on 'The Stirling Bombers', visiting a squadron like the one Augustus had flown with. The story never appeared, probably because of censorship by the Ministry of Information, and there are only a handful of pictures in the *Picture Post* file. One of them is a sinister frontal shot of the craft like that which carried Augustus to his death.

In April 1939 *Picture Post* used several of Brandt's socially critical pictures in a story called 'Enough of All This'.[11] Once war was declared any such complaints about the condition of England disappeared, though there would be many stories about the brave new world to come after victory, thanks to Socialist planning. The sick and unjust Britain exposed by the Thirties photo-journalists was now replaced by a 'bulldog Britain' of traditional images: the pub, the village, the countryside, the London street, all full of familiar, indomitable types. *Picture Post* was already successful, but the war made it a national institution, above all for its services to the Home Front.[12] For the first year and a half of the war, Brandt did surprisingly little photo-journalism of this patriotic kind. He had six stories in *Picture Post* in 1939 up to the outbreak of war, but then only a single story over the rest of the year and the whole of 1940.[13] It may be that the shock of open war with his native country caused Brandt to reconsider his journalistic ambitions for a time.

Brandt began 1941 suffering from the after-effects of being caught in the air raid; but this did not prevent him launching into an amazingly active life in photo-journalism over the next eight years. Stefan Lorant had gone to America in June 1940: partly to seek greener pastures, partly because he did not want to risk falling into Hitler's hands again, partly because he felt that the British government had treated him shabbily over his residence permit.[14] Tom Hopkinson, his successor, was willing to use Brandt's talents to the full. He edited *Lilliput* in spare moments from *Picture Post* and a hectic personal life. During the week he stayed at a pied-à-terre in London, where he had a mistress and other casual encounters. On the weekends he went back to his wife Gerti at Summer Cottage, Turville Heath (across the road from the house in which John Mortimer had grown up). Hopkinson had become involved with Gerti in 1937, while still married to the writer Antonia White, and married her in 1939 after his divorce. Gerti, whose maiden name was Deutsch, was a refugee from Vienna, the daughter of a wealthy Jewish businessman.[15] She also worked occasionally for *Picture*

Post as a photographer, and the Viennese connection may have helped to cement Brandt's relationship with Hopkinson. Perhaps his rackety journalistic existence caused him to appreciate Brandt's very different temperament (though Brandt was unconventional enough in his own way).

Hopkinson had no special training in photography, but had picked up the essentials of photo-journalism while working for Lorant at *Weekly Illustrated* in 1934. In general, his taste was for the kind of hard news photograph that could be delivered reliably by Felix Man, Kurt Hutton, Bert Hardy, Haywood Magee and, later, Leonard McCombe. But Hopkinson developed a deep admiration for Brandt, giving him both creative freedom and steady work so long as he was in control of the two magazines. Later, Hopkinson said that he would give Brandt 'very specialised series that only he could do', such as the pictures of London by moonlight.[16] But from the beginning of 1941 onwards, Hopkinson also gave Brandt commissions of every sort for *Lilliput* and *Picture Post*. Though he was effectively a staff photographer for the two magazines, Brandt's private income allowed him to keep his independence.

To appreciate Brandt's position at *Picture Post*, it helps to understand the handling of photo-stories at the magazine. Planning for an issue began with editorial conferences that photographers did not attend (nor were they credited for their work).[17] But once the story was assigned, the photographer had priority over the reporter. Anne Scott-James recalls that when they went out to interview people, her job was to keep them lively and distracted so as to make things easier for the photographer. Most of the photographers used Leicas and would shoot a hundred or more pictures per story (Lorant said that the *Picture Post* layout was planned with the Leica format in mind). *Picture Post*'s darkroom technician was Edith Kay, a Jewish refugee who had been trained by Leica in Germany and was skilled at getting a good-quality print from the Leica's small negative. Once the better pictures had been chosen from contact sheets and enlarged, the story would be laid out in Hopkinson's office: the visual element was crucial, and the reporters had to cut their text to fit and provide captions. Paper shortages kept the magazine down to about thirty-two pages during the war, so some stories would be killed at this stage for lack of space.

Instead of delivering his film to the *Picture Post* darkroom like the other photographers, Brandt would go home to Hillfield Court to do his own developing and printing. He took far fewer pictures than the Leica users, but Hopkinson recalled his 'hours of dark-room effort after which the floor would be strewn with dozens of prints hardly distinguishable from the one finally approved'.[18] Unlike Bert Hardy's, Brandt's pictures were often cropped when they appeared in the magazine – though he insisted on doing the cropping himself.[19] Taking his film home was not Brandt's only gesture of separation from the *Picture Post* community. According to Sheila Hardy, there were lots of rows over assignments, heavy drinking in a pub behind Fetter Lane, and the magazine was 'a hotbed of sex' after hours.[20] Brandt took no part in any of these goings-on. Others came into the office and asked for work; Brandt would appear and stand there silently until someone asked what they could do to help him. But with Hopkinson's patronage, assignments always came through, and with them an income of perhaps £300 a year from the two magazines.[21]

From London Brandt went on assignment all over Britain by hired car or train:

Children laughing, *Picture Post*, 1941

as far west as Devon and Wales, as far north as Edinburgh and Northumberland. This meant putting up with all the hardships of wartime travel: interrupted journeys, cold rooms, inadequate food.[22] No doubt Brandt accepted this discomfort as his contribution to the war effort; yet he also avoided many of the standard Home Front subjects, and liked to do stories on traditional British pursuits that went on more or less regardless of the war. He did the occasional war story in 1941-2, but three of them were killed before publication: 'Where Britain's Airmen are Refitted', 'Army Suitability Tests' and 'The Stirling Bombers'.[23] Other stories by Brandt were killed because of the paper shortage or for other reasons; but the Ministry of Information did censor the periodical press, and may well have considered these particular stories a threat to military security. 'Army Suitability Tests', as Ian Jeffrey has pointed out, was the opposite of the standard propaganda photography used by both sides in the war:

> Brandt must have begun the piece on Suitability Tests with some idea on a day-in-the-life of a recruit because, at one point, a grocer is seen selling butter before going on to a chest examination. The tests themselves, carried out under elaborate, improvised apparatus, owed more to Heath Robinson than to a modern army, and might have brought about the collapse of national morale had they been published. At first sight it might look as if Brandt, with his inflexible hieratic style, had simply made an awful mistake in this gimcrack camp with its farcical cast. Yet its lampooning of the everyday is consistent with much of what follows.[24]

By February 1942 the British public had been saturated with stories about the machine-like efficiency of the *Wehrmacht*, and Brandt's story could only have confirmed the fear that the British Army was no match for it. The picture of an officer taking a shower would be unprintable for its nudity alone; but the shower itself is a truly appalling display of misplaced effort, complete with a batman who is using a hand-pump to raise hot water out of a jerry-can. In his Thirties pictures of slum life, Brandt had often focused on scenes of disorder or squalor, and even intensified them by staging turned-over chairs or full chamber pots. The 'Army Suitability Tests' pictures suggest that Brandt couldn't help including an edge of oddness or subversion, as if, even in the desperate struggle against Fascism, he could not shake off his old irony towards the English way of doing things.[25]

Brandt's health was never good enough for him to serve as a combat photographer, but his treatment of war in his Home Front stories suggests that he mostly wanted to push it into the background and to show, as much as he could, the continuity with English life in the years of peace. These stories make the case that every success in keeping up pre-war pleasures is a small victory in itself, and they celebrate the *un*-warlike nature of the British people. Typical examples are 'This was the War-time Derby' (5 July 1941); 'A Day on the River' (12 July 1941); 'Saving Britain's Plum Crop' (12 September 1942); and 'Spring in the Park' (10 May 1941). The running headline for this last story is 'Spring in the Park … just the same in 1941'. Brandt includes pictures of salvaged bathtubs and bomb debris, but only to show that there are more important and timeless things to be seen in London's parks: nesting

Army Suitability Tests, 1942

ducks, recumbent lovers, an unruly crowd at Speakers' Corner, and a peaceful flock of sheep. The text for 'The War-time Derby' complains about the undemocratic arrangements at Newmarket, but the pictures all celebrate 'business as usual', except for the uniformed Guards officers sprinkled through the crowd.[26]

Another feature of Brandt's Home Front stories for *Picture Post* was an emphasis on wartime as woman's time. 'A Day on the River' shows women relaxing, including a languorous blonde Marjorie Beckett, paired with a brunette friend rather than the conventional male half of the couple. 'Saving Britain's Plum Crop' celebrates cockney women going to the Kent countryside to pick fruit, as they had done for decades. A *Lilliput* story, 'Backstage at the Windmill', shows another kind of women's work: taking off their clothes to entertain the warriors (as usual, the emphasis is on the Windmill as a great British tradition, rather than on sex for its own sake).[27] Tom Hopkinson's radicalism did not extend to imagining new roles for women, except as auxiliaries to the war effort. The magazine also avoided the most sensitive issue of all: that the war had given women a lot of new sexual opportunities. Overall, *Picture Post* offered a highly stylised view of British women, with a great deal left unsaid (these were also terms that quite suited Brandt's photographic agenda). Perhaps the most subversive representations of women in the mass media were the Brandt nudes that began to appear in *Lilliput* in 1944.

In 1943, Brandt took on another major commission that looked beyond the war. The Bournville Trust in Birmingham had been founded by George Cadbury at the turn of the century to provide housing for industrial workers in a pleasant garden city setting. They wanted pictures from Brandt that would show how ordinary people could hope to live after the war, this time in a land that was truly 'fit for heroes'.[28] Brandt's mandate was to show the contrast between Bournville housing and the slums of central Birmingham. A standard feature of these stories was to show children at play in model houses and parks; some of those who posed for him still remember the excitement of riding in his big hired car and being bought treats. They represented a sunny future for Britain, where planning would ensure that all children would be clean and happy, not the scruffy urchins that Brandt had photographed in Sheffield and Stepney. The old Birmingham was indeed destroyed in pursuit of this cause, and Brandt had done his bit to make it happen. Ernö Goldfinger and E. J. Carter were pursuing the same agenda when they published a popular version of the official 'County of London Plan' in 1945. Brandt contributed several pictures to this volume, drawing from *Picture Post* stories he had worked on.[29] Most of his pictures were of typical Thirties scenes and had little to do with the modernist vision of London's future. When it came to plans for changing the English way of life, Brandt's sympathies would always be with the old rather than the new.

Dylan Thomas, 1941

In December 1941, *Lilliput* turned Brandt's career in a new direction by publishing 'Young Poets of Democracy', a series of eight portraits he had taken over the previous year and a half. The propagandistic title was probably not of Brandt's choosing; several of the poets were left-wing, but he was surely not interested in them for that reason. Brandt had started with portraits in the Vienna studio style: close-up head shots with stark lighting and a plain background. He must have done hundreds of these as routine commissions while working for Grete Kolliner in the late Twenties, keeping negatives only of the important ones: Ezra Pound, George Antheil and Arnold Schoenberg (all from about 1928) and, a bit later, his brother Rolf. But the roots of his mature work as a portraitist lay in the various social types he had presented in *The English at Home*, such as the schoolgirl, the policeman, the Cambridge don, the guardsman. It was no coincidence that so many of these figures were placed in the English social order by wearing a uniform: the uniform was what they had instead of an individual name and personality.

In his Vienna portraits, Brandt had been hemmed in by strict conventions. Pose, make-up, lighting and re-touching were all designed to make the subject look like 'someone special'. This was what the client expected the studio to deliver. Once in England, and free from commercial restrictions, Brandt was drawn to subjects who were given dignity by their place in the world, rather than by individual force of character. He did not have the grand ambitions for social documentation of the incomparable August Sander, but pictures like 'Northumbrian miner at his evening meal' (1937) or the cheerful drinker in 'The Doomed East End' (1946) managed to be both individual and typical portraits at the same time. Brandt's Thirties portraits avoided a full-face presentation, and instead placed the subject in relation to iconic objects – a set table, a glass of beer – or to other figures in the frame. Personality was not conveyed directly, but through connection with a distinctive setting. The staged pictures that used his family and friends as models were a special case, where the models were acting out an imaginary role. The 'I'm No Angel' picture of Ester on Brighton beach was a likeness of its subject, but she was playing up to the camera and would never have presented herself in this way of her own accord. Almost the only named portrait by Brandt in the Thirties was of the painter Georges Braque, taken at his country home in Normandy in 1936.[1]

Brandt's lack of interest in portraiture during the Thirties may have been part of his flight from the Vienna studio; or it may show that he found English types more intriguing than English individuals. The *Lilliput* commission on 'Young Poets' re-awakened his interest, and from then on he took portraits regularly for the next forty years (there are more than 400 in his archive). Part of the reason for doing them was economic, since there was a steady market for this work, not just in *Lilliput*, but also in American and British editions of *Harper's Bazaar*, and later in the *New York Times Magazine*. However, Brandt would only accept commissions to take people who were in some way creative: writers, musicians, painters, actors and film directors had the qualities of difference, of a visible gift of imagination, that he required. The inaugural series of poets for *Lilliput* reveals a characteristic Brandtian quality of remoteness – often tinged with melancholy – in these sitters. They seem to be surrounded by a glass bell, impervious to any gaze from outside. His portraits of continental artists, effective as they may be as likenesses, lack the cumulative effect of the parade of English culture-heroes who passed before his lens. These appear as members of a distinct national family, yet each also seems set apart in lonely self-containment.

This aloneness infuses Brandt's great 1941 portrait of Dylan Thomas in the Salisbury pub. There is a brilliant play of textures here, between the shiny, dimpled upholstery and Thomas's suit (which merges into the pattern of foam on the glasses of beer). But the real impact of the portrait comes from the contrast between the manic self-assertiveness of Thomas's checked jacket, shirt and tie, and the dreamy introversion of the face above it. Equally haunting is the portrait of Robert Graves, in a subdued light and domestic setting that contrast with the bright public lighting of Thomas's Salisbury. Of the eight portraits in Brandt's *Lilliput* portfolio he chose five, forty years later, when his portraits were collected in book form.[2] That he was so successful in his first portrait essay suggests that for some time he had thought carefully about what he wanted to achieve in the genre. Brandt explained his aims in a caption for his 1948 portrait of the actress Josephine Stuart:

> I found that there was a sadness in Josephine Stuart's eyes which seemed to me more revealing than the obvious charm of the girlish smile. André Breton once said that a portrait should not only be an image but an oracle one questions, and that the photographer's aim should be a profound likeness, which physically and morally predicts the subject's entire future. Snapshots show only the likeness of a certain moment and are never good portraits. The photographer has to wait until something between dreaming and action occurs in the expression of a face.[3]

Brandt's interest in prophecy appears in his second portrait of Dylan Thomas, three years later. He and his wife Caitlin are in their Chelsea studio. Already Thomas seems tarnished by the signs of domestic decay, and by his wife's glum presence in the background. The trajectory can be imagined from the earlier portrait, to this, then to death from alcohol poisoning ten years ahead in New York. When Brandt collected his portraits into a book in 1982 he made good some of his predictions by including seven people photographed in youth and age, with up to forty years between the pictures.[4] All these pictures seem to emphasise the sternness and melancholy of age, rather than

Josephine Stuart, 1948

Alun Lewis, 1941

any achievement of tranquillity. In a letter to his wife, the poet Alun Lewis gave a glimpse of Brandt at work in the autumn of 1941. Lewis had just joined the army, and was in camp near Heysham, Lancashire:

> I went to Lancaster to find rooms for Bill Brandt, the *Lilliput* photographer, and a woman journalist who was travelling with him. Then I called in the Co-op and got fixed up for a uniform – the whole transaction lasting five minutes! – and then met the London train with my camera man and his tripod on it. We had some fun taking the photographs – me leaning against a dirty wall reading your letter, sitting on a pile of demolished wall lighting my pipe, etc., etc. … I had had no tea, so at seven we tried to get a meal – all cafés closed! And so I left them looking very hollow-cheeked and hurried back to camp.[5]

In the portrait used by *Lilliput*, Lewis's troubled gaze is at odds with the battledress he wears. The picture can be considered another of Brandt's prophecies since Lewis died three years later in Burma, probably by his own hand.

Brandt began to publish portraits of a more conventional and commercial kind in the London edition of *Harper's Bazaar* from September 1943 onwards, along with his pictures of English gardens and country houses. *Harper's Bazaar* was a Hearst publication, modelled on the New York *Harper's Bazaar*, but distinct from it. The New York editor was Carmel Snow, who was also the dominant personality in the entire Hearst magazine empire. Marjorie Beckett got a job with the London edition in the early 1940s, and soon became a favourite of Snow's; through this connection, Brandt was taken on as a regular contributor to both magazines. Snow's Irish-American background made her hostile to England, but passionately devoted to France; so Brandt's portrait of Françoise Rosay, his first to be published in *Harper's Bazaar*, may have sealed his favour with Snow. The caption ran:

> In this remarkable picture of the famous French actress, Bill Brandt has captured something of the spirit of her unhappy country. Françoise Rosay looks out from a London window, after her escape from France. Defying the Germans to the last, she refused to return to Paris to make films for them.[6]

Compared with *Lilliput*, London *Harper's Bazaar* had the advantage of being in a larger format and on better paper; but it lacked a strong editorial direction (it had no single editor) and treated culture somewhat snobbishly, as an adjunct to gracious living. All this was far removed from Brandt's incisive pictures of street life and slums in the 1930s. Two of the best things he did for *Harper's Bazaar* were the portraits of Sir Kenneth and Lady Clark, and of T. S. Eliot – both slightly quizzical treatments of persons at the centre of Establishment cultural life.[7] Brandt's handling of these commissions may have reflected his general unhappiness with the terms he had to accept for such work:

> Photography can be singularly frustrating. It was after the war, when I was busy photographing London celebrities for English and American magazines, that I

Francis Bacon, 1963

began to feel irritated by the limitations imposed by such jobs. I was taking portraits of politicians, artists, writers, actors in their own surrounding, but there was never enough time for me to do what I wanted. My sitters were always in a hurry. Their rooms were rarely inspiring backgrounds, and I felt I needed exciting backgrounds to make pictures of the portraits. I wanted more say in the pictures; I wanted rooms of my own choice.[8]

In the Thirties, pursuing his own projects, Brandt might spend hours or even days in setting up a shot, and would be relentless in drilling his models. When working for *Harper's Bazaar*, his plebeian first name and self-effacing manner made him the victim of snobbishness or condescension from some of his sitters. Vanessa Redgrave, for example, had treated him in an offhand way before she realised who he was.[9] The 'exciting backgrounds' that he preferred could sometimes be an instrument of revenge, by reducing his subjects' faces to a mere detail in the composition – as in his pictures of Graham Sutherland peering out of a fig tree, or Laurie Lee looking over a wall.[10]

All through the Sixties and Seventies, the one constant in Brandt's photography was his taking of commissioned portraits, especially for the New York *Harper's Bazaar*. A portrait could be done in a single sitting, and gave Brandt the opportunity to meet almost every leading British cultural figure of his time.[11] From 1952 to 1955 all of Brandt's work for the magazine consisted of portraits. The forerunner of this series – not published in *Harper's Bazaar* – was one of an epicene Kenneth Tynan, sitting primly on a couch, with 'I love Ken' written in lipstick on the mirror above him.[12] Carmel Snow commissioned Tynan to do profiles of British writers and theatrical people, with an accompanying portrait by Brandt. The first, of Alec Guinness, appeared in April 1952; it was followed by John Gielgud, Terence Rattigan, Cecil Beaton, Cyril Connolly and Peter Brook.[13] In April 1955 Brandt contributed a bizarre portrait of Agatha Christie with her face deliberately out of focus; this may have caused him to lose favour at *Harper's*, for his work disappeared from the magazine for several years.[14]

In the late Fifties, Brandt switched from using his Rolleiflex or Deardorff cameras for portraits to a Supreme Wide Angle Hasselblad with a Zeiss 4.5 Biogon lens:

> The 90° angle of the lens was exactly right for Brandt's portrait interiors. For outdoor pictures it allowed Brandt to calculate the composition of his three-quarter length study of Francis Bacon and to include the sweeping lamp-lit perspective of Primrose Hill in Camden Town, London. The high-energy vanishing lines and the high-contrast printing style Brandt then adopted gave the later portraits an abrasive edge dissimilar to the earlier portraits and highly typical of the 60's.[15]

Cyril Connolly, in his introduction to Brandt's collection *Shadow of Light*, called the Bacon portrait 'a symbol of the despair of his generation'. It is certainly a quintessential Brandt portrait, with Bacon's haunted look matched by what he does not see behind him: the ominous trees on the skyline, the path in an impossible perspective, the leaning lamp-post seemingly transported to a London park from a German

Peter Sellers, 1963

Expressionist film. Does it matter that Bacon himself hated the picture? In *Shadow of Light* the Bacon portrait is offset, on the facing page, by the quiet resignation of an eighty-year-old Man Ray among tropical foliage.

In the same year as the Bacon portrait (1963), Brandt took another striking portrait in the paranoid style, of Peter Sellers. The background looks like a studio set, perhaps for the second Inspector Clouseau film, *A Shot in the Dark*, which Sellers was making at the time. Sellers stares out from behind the Establishment newspaper, *The Times*, looking like a man whose split personality is ready to disintegrate altogether. He had done his three Dr Strangelove roles between the first and second Clouseau films, and was three months away from a heart attack triggered by his use of amyl nitrate as a sexual stimulant. The sticking-plaster on Sellers's forehead Brandt must have seized on as a gift, showing Sellers as both vulnerable and held together by artificial means.[16]

John Berger has argued that Brandt's portraits of artists and writers 'are highly mannered and … romanticise all the sitters in the name of art, establishing the superiority of the private reality'.[17] They also might be criticised for their unrelieved melodrama, as if everyone is as trapped and frightened as Donald Pleasance, photographed 'in character' on the set of the film of Pinter's *The Caretaker*.[18] Many use low-angle shots in the *Citizen Kane* style, turning their subjects into looming, ominous figures.[19] David Mellor commented that everyone in Brandt's portraits looked as if they had been sentenced to death.[20] Susan Brandt recalls seeing her uncle laughing and joking at the opening of his London show at the Marlborough Gallery in 1976; then someone asked to take his picture, and he put on a solemn expression. When asked why he did it, he replied, 'When you take someone smiling, they look stupid.' Yet for Brandt's artists, writers or actors, solemn expressions are not just a cliché: repeatedly he captures the depressive element in them, showing the despair that always stalks the perfectionist. There is often, also, a perfect fit between the mood of the sitter and the setting Brandt has chosen for them; the portrait volume extends this with its facing-page encounters between, say, the brooding Nicol Williamson and a jaunty Ralph Richardson in his garden. Brandt's portraits do not pander to the cult of celebrity, in which a famous face is made into an icon – a mask all too recognisable and larger than life. Brandt zeroes in on the contradictions in his subjects' achievement, the sadness and fallibility written on their features. His English artists, actors and writers make up a gallery of types from the Fifties and Sixties who are as consistent, in their demeanour, as the policemen or schoolchildren of *The English at Home.*

Near Bodkin Top, 1945

21 The Land

Before 1940, Brandt rarely took pictures of landscapes for their own sake. His pictures of statues in parks and gardens followed the Surrealist idea of using nature as a backdrop for queer artefacts. The views of the Hungarian plain were equally theatrical, visions of desperate people in desperate places. Brandt was overwhelmingly a photographer of cities, of social encounters within man-made streets and domestic interiors. Like many English people, he became more connected with the countryside as a result of the war. The fall of France and the Battle of Britain roused a primal emotion: to defend the land from being invaded and desecrated by Nazism. The land became a spiritual resource and the foundation for national identity. A threatened land was more valued and needed, even by people who in peacetime might have taken little interest in it.

John Piper, an artist, photographer and critic, became a key figure in English visual culture during the war. In *English Romantic Artists* he called on artists to turn away from continental movements like post-Impressionism or Surrealism, in favour of the native landscape tradition of Blake, Turner and Samuel Palmer.[1] Other painters and critics were happy to follow Piper's lead. The idea that the English landscape was a mystical source of national unity was very attractive in wartime, and love of the land went deeper than just the practical need to defend built-up areas and factories.[2] Many people, also, were fleeing the cities to escape the bombing, as they had earlier fled the plague. On arrival, they found a landscape that had gone back to its state of a century before, thanks to the disappearance of private cars and holiday trippers. Given a respite from the modern world, the countryside could easily be seen as the haunt of Merlin or the 'precious stone set in a silver sea' of *Henry V*.

This wartime mood inspired Brandt to give his English patriotism deeper roots in English nature, and John Piper was one of his tutors. Piper lived during the war at Fawley Bottom, near Tom Hopkinson's country home at Turville Heath. Brandt took Piper's portrait outside his flint cottage in 1945, and knew him socially before that. The illustrations in Piper's *English Romantic Artists* surely influenced Brandt's landscape photography, which began in the year after it was published.[3] Piper's section on 'Sublime Landscape' begins with James Ward's 1815 painting of Gordale Scar, Yorkshire, which Piper then painted himself. L. W. Brandt bought the picture, and Bill was inspired by it in photographing Gordale Scar in the 1940s.[4]

In his pre-war journeys to northern cities blighted by the slump, Brandt rarely turned his camera on the countryside between one city and another. His grim picture of the coal-searcher returning home to Jarrow showed the landscape around him as utterly desolate, without any trace of beauty or hope. The war put the relationship between town and country in a new light. Northern cities were again humming with industry, so that Brandt was no longer being assigned to places of desperation. He did picture stories on Bath and Edinburgh, beautiful and historic cities that were now threatened by German bombers.[5] In his first major landscape story, 'The Threat to the Great Roman Wall', the danger came from another quarter: neglect.[6] Hadrian's Wall was a spectacular achievement in stone; its aim – to keep out the barbarians – had an obvious relevance to England's contemporary struggle against the Nazis. It was also an example of people interacting with the land, re-working the natural setting to achieve some human purpose; this set the tone for much of Brandt's landscape photography thereafter.[7]

Another way of humanising landscape appeared in Brandt's painterly approach to composition. People scavenging for coal on Tyneside captured his eye through their resemblance to Millet's 'The Gleaners'.[8] Flax harvesters in Wiltshire were photographed in the style of a nineteenth-century genre painting.[9] Brandt saw the land with an eye shaped by his studies in art history and his reading of English literary classics. The modernist masters of landscape photography, especially Ansel Adams and Edward Weston, focused on the sheer otherness of nature, its inhuman, uninhabited beauty. Brandt preferred nature at second hand, in partnership with human cultivation and history.

This does not mean that Brandt had an entirely pastoral view of the natural world. If rocks and mountains are the skeleton of landscape, and cultivated land the flesh, then most of Brandt's landscape pictures of the 1940s are more attuned to stone than to soil. He often aimed at an atmosphere of grandeur that required peaks and expanses of water; his masterpiece in this style was of the Skye mountains rising up out of the sea.[10] 'Near Bodkin Top' gives a lovely interplay between fields and their enclosing stone walls (this was an offshoot of Brandt's assignment to Brontë country for *Lilliput*).

Brandt's treatment of scenery showed his continuing debt to the nineteenth-century Pictorialists. In his landscapes, a brooding atmosphere dominated the physical structures of the composition. He approached his subjects as a kind of portraitist, wanting to capture a particular expression on the face of the land. This called for just the right state of light or weather, and Brandt was fanatically insistent on getting the conditions he had in mind. He waited for hours at Gordale Scar until the cliffs were free of climbers; Stonehenge was set aside until the deep winter of 1946-7 put it under snow. Sometimes Brandt would make a preliminary visit, then come back months later for the right combination of moon, cloud or tide. His sublime picture of the meanders of the Cuckmere River, under a lowering sky, was taken in 1963 near Seaford, the location for most of his English outdoor nudes. It was another reward for Brandt's fanatical persistence in waiting for the exact weather and time of year to get the result he had in mind.[11]

Brandt was specially fond of skies filled with a turbulent mass of clouds, to make

Cuckmere River, about 1949

Isle of Skye, 1947

a truly romantic vista. His picture of Top Withens – the supposed home of Heathcliff, on the moors above the Brontë parsonage – showed the lengths to which he was willing to go in search of atmosphere. Brandt collaged in the sky from a different picture, creating an inconsistency between the state of the sky and the angle of light falling on the snowy moor. He was trying to project his own moods on to his landscapes, giving them a painterly quality as distinctive as a Claude Lorrain or a Turner. The pictures by other photographers that he chose for *The Land*, a 1975 exhibition at the Victoria and Albert Museum, all have this quality of radiating spiritual force.[12] There could be a gentler side to Brandt's landscapes, as in the heritage-style stories on 'The Thames' or 'The Hardy Country' that he did for New York *Harper's Bazaar* after the war.[13] But in his best landscape pictures, romantic intensity was his principal aim.

Part of that intensity came from Brandt's removal of human figures from his landscapes (something he was also doing with his city pictures in the later 1940s). In his pictures of writers' houses or writers' country, to be collected in *Literary Britain*, the contemporary inhabitants have disappeared; occasional sheep or cattle only emphasise the loneliness of the scene. An exception was Brandt's picture of Aldeburgh beach, for his story on the poet George Crabbe: there, he waited patiently for a solitary fisherman to come by and provide a centre for his composition. But *Literary Britain* is a tribute to the landscape haunted by the ghosts of the great departed writers who made each part of England their own.[14]

When Brandt spoke in *Camera in London* of regaining a 'sense of wonder' in seeing the world, he might well have been thinking of his work on writers' landscapes, and how their imagination can infuse our sight. The revival of reading during the war years filled in the time left vacant by the loss of pre-war amusements, but also met a need to connect with an enduring England, preserved in the pages of authors like Austen, Dickens and Trollope. In a sense, English literature was mobilised for the struggle against Fascism. Brandt read obsessively, and by the end of the war had a solid acquaintance with the English classics. He began to draw on this knowledge in the spring of 1945, with his sequence on 'The Brontë Country', eight haunting images of the Brontë house in Haworth, the churchyard and the moors.[15] This was followed by three more literary stories: 'Thomas Hardy's Wessex', 'The Borough' (on Aldeburgh and the poetry of Crabbe), and 'The Poet's Crib' (a miscellany of poets' houses).[16] A hundred photographs were included in *Literary Britain*; only nine of these were of London, so the book was the product of Brandt's travels all over the British Isles. These were heroic journeys for a man suffering from diabetes, burdened with equipment and harassed by post-war delays and shortages.

Literary Britain was, when published, by far the most comprehensive photographic record of Britain's literary heritage. Brandt set out to capture the atmosphere of each writer and succeeded brilliantly, especially in the sequences on the Brontës, Hardy and Dickens. Beyond its technical achievements, *Literary Britain* was also a further advance in Brandt's campaign to anglicise himself and make his mark as an indigenous cultural figure. Cassell produced the book with fine printing and paper quality, at the stiff price (for 1951) of forty-five shillings. But there was much more to *Literary Britain* than a routine coffee-table book. Its introduction and literary notes were by John Hayward, an Establishment figure who shared a flat with T. S. Eliot; and everything about it

Stonehenge, 1947

suggested that Brandt had now fully 'arrived' as a figure in contemporary culture. It contrasted with the appearance of *Camera in London* three years before; this was produced by a lesser publisher specialising in photography, in a small and somewhat scruffy format, with commentary by the relatively unknown Norah Wilson.[17] From *Literary Britain* on, Brandt's books would arrive with weighty critical or scholarly endorsements. Both personally and professionally, by 1951 Brandt had gained his share of renown.

Brandt's Englishness was reinforced, in the 1940s, by his commitment to English literature, and by his greatly expanded knowledge of English provincial town and country. This was evident in *Literary Britain*, but appears also in his many portraits of contemporary writers and even, I would argue, in some of his nudes. The human presence that disappears in Brandt's literary landscapes re-emerges in his outdoor nudes of the 1950s. His pictures of the moors and mountains of northern Britain suggest that our deepest pleasure in landscape comes from the way it evokes the contours of the maternal body, the first place in life where one encounters such valleys and hills. Brandt remained a Freudian in looking at the land with a sexual eye and accepting the intimacy, in Western visual culture, between landscape and the female nude.[18]

Brandt's turning to landscape in the 1940s can also be seen as part of a broader plan: to make himself into a complete and indispensable English artist. In the Thirties he focused on London, a city where the frantic vitality of everyday life would always dominate the historical past. London's mightiness created the need to find a balance for it in the English countryside, a place for contemplation rather than action. Perhaps that was why Brandt's landscapes had no people in them: to compensate for the city, where people could never be avoided.[19] The keystone of his landscapes was Stonehenge under snow in 1947. By eliminating every trace of present occupation, Brandt showed Stonehenge as the ancient capital of another Britain. This mystical realm could be imagined as what had guaranteed the survival of modern Britain in the ordeal it had just endured.

Nude, August 1944

As the war neared its end, Brandt took up the work for which he most wanted to be remembered: his studies of the female nude. Shortly before he died, he told Stephen Dwoskin that the nudes were his great love and everything else in his work was commercial.[1] If so, it is curious that Brandt waited nearly twenty years to come to the nude; but when he did, his interests went much deeper than the standard elements of texture, lighting and composition. The nudes he did in the Man Ray period were really a false start, perhaps because Man Ray's own nudes had set such a fearsome standard. The work from that time of Brassaï, Weston, Drtikol, Koppitz, Munkácsy or Kertész would be scarcely less intimidating. English photographers contributed little to the genre, in part because there were so few legitimate outlets for their work. Almost all the photographic nudes seen in England would be imported in continental books or magazines (including the German nudist magazines that were suppressed by Hitler in 1933). The most powerful English nudes of the Thirties were by Rosalind Maingot, but few people saw them at the time. That left the tepid efforts of John Everard and a few others. It was not even clear what an English nude would look like.[2] Brandt, almost single-handed, created a place for the photographic nude in English visual culture.

The originality of Brandt's nudes begins with his passion for technical innovation, almost for its own sake. Nudity itself often seems less important to him than the formal possibilities of photographing a figure in a room. Brandt's inspiration here did not come from earlier masters of nude photography, but from the many inventions of the most important film in his life, Orson Welles's *Citizen Kane*. After its New York premiere on 1 May 1941, *Kane* was seen in London in October of the same year.[3] Brandt went to see it many times. *Kane* was an immensely original American film in many ways; but its paramount innovation, for Brandt, was simply the way it looked. Most of this look should be credited to the cameraman, Gregg Toland, rather than to Welles.[4] Welles brought to his first film his training in the theatre, including some knowledge of stage lighting, and there was a continuity between directing a play and shooting *Kane* under artificial light in a studio (where almost all the film was made). But lighting and photographing a film were vastly more complex than for a stage production. On the first day of shooting, Welles set up the lights himself; he did not even know that on a film set this job belonged to the director of photography. To his credit, he soon realised that Toland should be given a free hand, and Welles made the

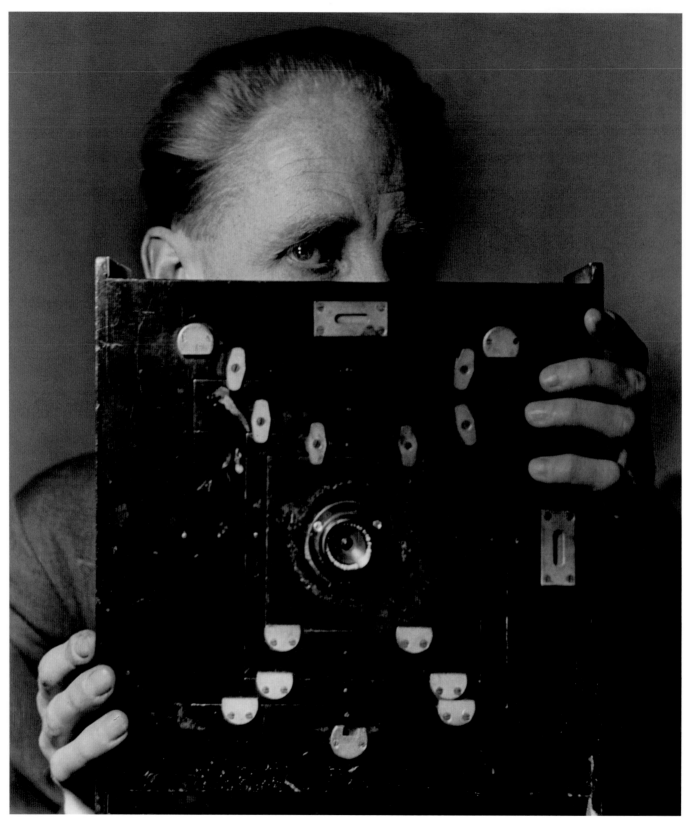

Brandt with police camera, 1945, Laelia Goehr

extraordinary gesture of giving Toland equal billing in the final credits with himself as director. David Thomson describes Toland's distinctive visual style:

> Toland used *Kane* as a test case for many cinematic developments in the late Thirties. The first was unusually wide-angle lenses that allowed a greater depth of focus than was common. Such lenses risked distortion: the image easily began to warp or curve at its edges. They also made for a dramatic but rather queasy stretching of space. Nor were they well suited to close-up photography, that staple of movie factory glamour. In the classic close-up, the face feels natural and is lifted out of a blurred backdrop by backlighting. So we are helped to fix on and feel for the lovely emotions in the face. A close-up from a wide-angle lens can quickly make the face seem bloated and rubbery, and it gives you the background as sharp as the face, which may detract from the romantic emphasis of the standard close-up …
>
> Super XX film had become available, four times faster than prior stocks – thus more susceptible to depth of field . . .
>
> In concert, these opportunities permitted a kind of deep-focus cinematography in which everything seems in focus (and thus relevant), no matter that the overall image might contain a great deal of shadow and darkness. Simultaneously, Toland could deliver a new degree of realism allied to all those brooding feelings that accompany low-key, or very contrasty, photography. He could do something that was unique to *Kane* in 1941 – make us believe we are seeing the entire world while feeling the anxieties and hopes of the inner mind.[5]

The technique perfected by Toland in *Citizen Kane* rendered all the elements of the shot – background, middle ground and foreground – in sharp focus (as in 'Gull's nest on Skye').[6] The viewer then has to survey the whole composition to decide what is most worth looking at, and different viewers will find different meanings in the same shot. Everything in three dimensions can be equally important: for example, the interplay between the human figures of *Kane* and the cluttered Victorian objects that fill their rooms. Deep focus distorts the relative size of people; they loom like giants in the foreground or become lilliputian if they are at the back of the shot.

Another feature of *Kane* was its frank acceptance of photography as artifice. 'Roughly eighty per cent of the film,' Pauline Kael notes, 'was not merely printed but reprinted, in order to add trick effects and blend in painted sets and bits of stock footage.'[7] Many of these effects had first been developed in still photography and then transferred to motion pictures. Brandt already knew a good deal about special effects from his studio training; he also had help from three *Picture Post* stories he did on film sets in the early 1940s, and from Rolf's stint with the Emelka film company in Berlin in 1931.[8] He had never shied away from staging his pictures, but *Kane* suggested a more radically theatrical approach to photography. Instead of the camera as witness to truth, it could be an instrument for playing on the viewer's emotions.

The lighting, the brooding atmosphere, the distortions of the human figure in *Kane* combined to make it a *German* Hollywood film. Gregg Toland had previously photographed *Mad Love* (1935), a Hollywood re-make of a German film by Robert

Wiene.[9] The director of *Mad Love* was the German émigré Karl Freund, who had been head cinematographer at UFA in Berlin and the cameraman for Fritz Lang's *Metropolis*. *Kane* was thus a lineal descendant of the Expressionist films that Brandt had soaked up at Davos when he was a patient there in 1924-7. But Welles's genius, and Toland's camera work, created a new synthesis that helped to set the agenda for much of Brandt's camera work after the war. The visual world of *Kane* could be summed up as '*Alice in Wonderland* meets German Expressionist cinema'. For someone with Brandt's interests, there could hardly be a more seductive combination.

Apart from his fifteen years of experience in photography, and what he had learned of theatre from Rolf, Brandt had an extraordinary grasp of complex visual images. In a documentary made at the end of his life, he summed up *Kane*'s impact:

> When *Citizen Kane* was first shown I'd never seen a film in which real rooms were used and you could see everything, the ceiling, and terrific perspective, it was all there. It was quite revolutionary, *Citizen Kane*, and I was very much inspired by it and I thought: 'I must take photographs like that.'[10]

Brandt was able to absorb the look of *Kane*, and reproduce it, in the way that someone with a perfect ear can pick up a foreign tongue. *Kane* was a confirmation of long-established elements in Brandt's style: the love of deep contrasts, the haunted look of pictures like 'Cocktails in a Surrey Garden', the stagey grouping of figures and the search for 'atmosphere' as the key quality of a picture. But *Kane* encouraged him to go further along these lines of development, while leaving behind the conventions of Thirties social documentary.

To exploit fully the possibilities of deep focus, Brandt had to take a step backwards in camera technology:

> I was working with a marvellous old camera, which I found while searching for a lens with a sufficiently wide angle, to enable me to take nudes in enclosed space. Such lenses hardly existed in England in those days, and it was thanks to Peter Rose Pulham, the painter and former *Harper's Bazaar* photographer, that I discovered one in a second-hand shop near Covent Garden. It was a beautiful old wooden Kodak, old enough for a museum. It had a fixed focus, no shutter, and could take a complete panorama of a room with a single exposure. I learned that the camera had been used at the beginning of the century by auctioneers, for photographic inventories, and by Scotland Yard for police records.
>
> My first try-outs were hardly nudes; I called them experimental interiors. It was fascinating to watch the effect of the lens which created a great illusion of space, and an unrealistically steep perspective, and soon I discovered that it could produce fantastic anatomical images which I had never seen before.[11]

It was in the spring of 1944 that Brandt found this camera in Covent Garden and bought it for £5. It looked like an antique, with its wood frame and absence of controls, but Brandt was mistaken about its age. In fact, it had been introduced as recently as 1931, under the name of the 'Kodak Wide Angle':

Gull's nest on Skye, 1947

Micheldever Nude, 1948

It was in use by the New York Police Department and others during the 30's, and it required no skill to operate. The camera had a fixed lens which covered a 110° angle. Anything four feet or more from the camera was in focus. A frame at the front guided the operator. Any point in the room which could be seen inside this frame would be included in the picture.[12]

Brandt no doubt thought that a piece of Victorian technology would be the right instrument for taking pictures of Victorian rooms, his favoured setting for both portraits and nudes. As his interests shifted away from the recent past – how England had looked when he arrived there in the early Thirties – nineteenth-century interiors and façades became central to his vision. This was the distorted, chiaroscuro world of artists like John Tenniel or Gustave Doré.[13] The London policeman was a Victorian invention too, and Brandt's obsession with such sentinel-like figures made him the butt of Bert Hardy's jokes. The idea of a 'police camera' would be irresistible to Brandt; he may also have noticed Weegee's recent pictures of New York crime scenes, with their goldfish-bowl perspectives and sinister flat details.[14]

Brandt was also intrigued to find that the police camera had a very inadequate viewfinder. This meant that he could never be sure how a picture would turn out until he developed the film, when his model would be long gone. One of his first police-camera nudes dates from August 1944. The model appears to be Mary Pulham, who also modelled for her husband Peter Rose Pulham.[15] Behind her figure, the composition recedes to the window frame in trademark *Citizen Kane* style; the desk in the window looks like doll's house furniture in relation to the woman who fills the foreground. An even more extreme use of recession appears in the so-called 'Micheldever Nude' of 1948, taken at Brandt's father's house in Hampshire. The symbolism of this picture remains enigmatic, but its troubling quality is reinforced by the strange proportions, where the space from the model's eyes to her nipples is exactly equal to the size of the doorway in the background. Brandt probably set up the picture by placing the police camera on the table in front of the model, and then asking her to extend her hand towards it.[16] Some of the picture's atmosphere derives from the ominous visuals of *Kane*. But *Kane* was not particularly a film about sexual anxiety; Brandt himself supplied that, as he used the look of the film to serve his own long-standing sexual obsessions.

The Policeman's Daughter, Hampstead, 1945

Stefan Lorant's *Lilliput* had shown how a formula of humorous bohemianism could gain a place for photographic nudes in the English mass market. *Der Querschnitt* had done this earlier, in the 1920s, helped by the easier acceptance of nudity in Germany. Nudes could be seen in German film (most notoriously, Hedy Lamarr in *Ecstasy*), in popular journalism and in real life through the fresh-air cult of the body.[1] In the United States, the fourth issue of *Coronet* (February 1937) included soft-focus nudes, which appeared in every issue from then on. Lorant brought out the first issue of *Lilliput* four months later. Most of the early *Lilliput* nudes had a dreamy, idealised quality and came from either Paris or Budapest. Erwin Blumenfeld, Berko and Andre de Dienes were the most reliable producers of them. Distributed in hundreds of thousands of copies each month, these 'art nudes' gave the English public a more sophisticated appreciation of the female form. The sophistication probably should not be exaggerated, though: *Lilliput* titillated its male readers as no other British magazine did, and its nudes were a large part of its commercial success.

Brandt's first published nude appeared in *Lilliput* in February 1942. It was completely unadventurous, using the ultimate art-nude cliché of a gauze veil obscuring the figure, and had been taken some ten years before in Paris.[2] In May there was 'She sells sea shells', a semi-nude on a beach modelled by Lyena Barjansky, perhaps on the trip to Barcelona in 1932.[3] Both of these pictures were typical *Lilliput* nudes, re-touched to remove anything disturbingly sexual, and placing the body in a bare studio or on a beach. What made Brandt's Forties nudes distinctive was that he decided to make the bohemian atmosphere of *Lilliput* an intrinsic part of his pictures, by putting his models into settings more suggestive and closer to everyday life than the formal lighting and bare walls of the photographic studio.

In 1961, Brandt spoke of this shift as a product of his frustration at making portraits of celebrities in their home settings:

> I wanted more say in the pictures; I wanted rooms of my own choice. And so I came to nudes. Nudes, at that time, were photographed in studios. I thought of photographing them in real rooms, and suggested the idea to Leonard Russell, the founder and, at that time, editor of a very successful annual, the 'Saturday Book'. The idea pleased him, and he asked me to do a feature of sixteen pictures.[4]

The Saturday Book, published annually from 1941, was a snobbish, milk-and-water version of *Lilliput*, with a mixture of stories, articles and photographs. A 'purity campaign' by Russell's publisher, Hutchinson, kept Brandt's nudes out of *The Saturday Book*, but he went on with them regardless. It may seem whimsical for Brandt to hanker after rooms of his own choice, as if the women in them were just an afterthought, but he wanted to get beyond the basic elements of form and light in nude photography. What did it mean to enclose a nude body in a room furnished in the style of a hundred years before? Victorianism meant the repression of the body; nudity in England typically existed 'behind closed doors', unlike the free-spirited outdoor nudes by continental photographers. The English tradition belonged to the dark rather than the light, with its images of women cloistered or restrained, like Samuel Richardson's Clarissa or Charlotte Brontë's madwoman in the attic.[5]

In finding a way for his indoor nudes, Brandt was greatly influenced by Peter Rose Pulham, the man who had told him about the 'police camera'. Pulham, who was six years younger than Brandt, was a son of the Norfolk gentry, and became a successful fashion photographer in the Thirties. He moved to Paris to paint at the end of the decade, influenced by Surrealism and friendly with such figures as Balthus, Max Ernst and Salvador Dalí. While holding court in a café he met Theodora Rosling, an Irish actress and model. They narrowly escaped the Germans in 1940 and then lived in rackety wartime style in Chelsea, with friends like Dylan and Caitlin Thomas, the critic John Davenport and the art editor of *Lilliput*, Mechtild Naviasky. Brandt did a picture story on Chelsea for *Lilliput* in August 1944, for which Dylan Thomas wrote the captions (including one for his own portrait with Caitlin).[6] For a while Brandt seems to have become a Chelsea bohemian himself, hanging around studios and pubs. For the *Lilliput* story, Marjorie Beckett and Mechtild Naviasky posed with John Davenport outside the Black Lion (another of Brandt's scenes of one man with two women).

While in Paris in the Thirties, Pulham took a series of portraits of Surrealist artists, which were published in *Lilliput* for October 1943.[7] His style was to front-light the subjects so that they looked almost like cut-outs in front of a shadowy, cluttered studio background. This look had a great influence on Brandt's portraits and nudes. Around 1941, Maitland Pendock of the Ministry of Information gave Pulham a Rolleiflex and he took up photography again, in addition to his painting. Pulham's ideas about photography were very close to Brandt's. 'He always developed and printed his own negatives,' Theodora Rosling recalled, '(he would tease Cecil Beaton by calling him an amateur when he sent his rolls of film to be processed) for he said that any fool could click a shutter but the true art was in the dark-room.'[8] In 1942 he made two nudes of Theodora in rear view: one standing next to his artist's easel, one sitting on a painting by Max Ernst.[9] A year or two later he made nudes of his new wife, Mary Pulham, and of other models. Some of these were reproduced in *Lilliput* from March 1944 on. By 1942 he and Brandt were working closely together, and Brandt took a portrait of Pulham in his studio for the Chelsea story. This was also the period of Brandt's portraits of Dylan and Caitlin Thomas, and of Dylan supplying verse captions for Brandt pictures.[10] There can be no doubt that Pulham contributed to Brandt's new style of deep-focus nudes in raffish interior settings. In something of a

'The Blue Cockatoo', 1944

Drawing for *Wuthering Heights*, Balthus

private joke, he and Theodora posed for a pastiche of Degas's 'The Absinthe Drinkers' at the Blue Cockatoo, a Chelsea restaurant popular with artists.[11]

All these influences, from *Citizen Kane* to Chelsea, came together in Brandt's first great success in the genre, the so-called 'Hampstead Nude' of 1945. For some reason it was held back from *Lilliput* and first appeared in *Perspective of Nudes* (1961). The picture was taken on VE Day, 8 May – a typically eccentric way for Brandt to celebrate the peace.[12] Frances Rice says that the setting was a house on Church Row, Hampstead (one of Brandt's favourite streets); but whose house she is unwilling to say.[13] The 'Hampstead Nude' became one of Brandt's signature pictures, though few people were aware that it was an obsessional work, thick with secret meanings. Only Brandt's intimates knew that he had a private name for the nude, 'The Policeman's Daughter'.[14] This may have been a joke about Brandt's 'police camera', but that was just the beginning.

Brandt's pictures of the Scilly Isles had appeared in *Minotaure* 6 (December 1934), and many images in that magazine find reflections in his work. In the next issue of *Minotaure* (June 1935), the critic Georges Lafourcade discussed an unpublished erotic novel by Swinburne, *La Fille du Policeman*. It had been written in French around 1860, when Swinburne was a young man living in Paris.[15] Set in London, the novel is a feeble burlesque of Sade and other French revolutionary writers. 'John Whitestick', Bishop of London, is the leader of the forces of reaction and a secret atheist. He rapes and tortures Nelli, daughter of a virtuous policeman, Williams Hervey. The people try to rise up against Whitestick, but Hervey is killed, his daughter dies and the revolution fails. *La Fille du Policeman* is not a work to be taken seriously in any way, except as evidence for Swinburne's well-known interest in sado-masochism. That could have been the interest for Brandt too. He had long been fascinated by the authority figure of the policeman; in the Swinburne novel, it is a policeman who is unable to protect his daughter or revenge her death.[16]

Minotaure placed two pages of Balthus's illustrations for *Wuthering Heights* just before the Lafourcade article. *Wuthering Heights* was a cult novel for the Surrealists; with *Alice in*

'Reflection', *Lilliput*, March 1949

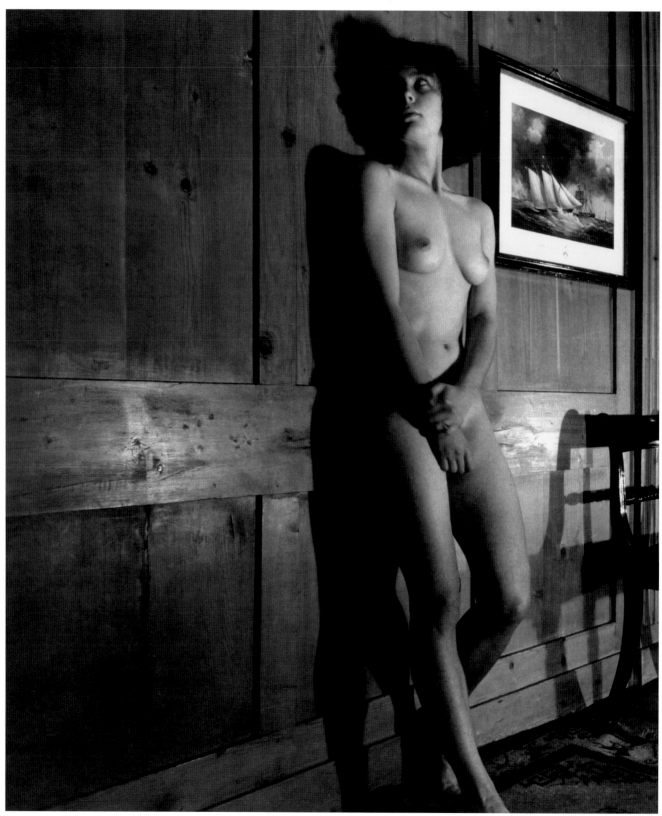

'The Woodman's Daughter', *Lilliput* 1948

'The Woodman's Daughter', 1851, J. B. Millais

Wonderland, it became evidence for the idea that Victorian England was the closest thing there had been to a Surrealist civilisation.[17] One of the Balthus illustrations shows Cathy Earnshaw climbing over a window-sill in a pose very similar to Brandt's nude.[18] The Lafourcade article is also illustrated by a Man Ray semi-nude, with one breast exposed and the rest of her body swathed in a Victorian-looking shawl.[19]

Somewhere in this hall of mirrors was a sexual fantasy that Brandt was satisfying by calling his nude 'The Policeman's Daughter'. Bert Hardy told David Mellor that Brandt hired prostitutes to pose for some of the nudes of this period, and that they also 'took care of him'.[20] If so, Brandt was probably still trying to cope with some scene of shame or humiliation from his childhood, or from the torments inflicted on him at school. Being mistreated by a woman in adult life can be a compensation for childhood pain. The same model appears in two other nudes, unpublished at the time, where she sits at a table with food and wine.[21] In one of the pictures an umbrella points at her (Rolf Brandt uses one to threaten Marjorie Beckett in some of the out-takes from 'The Nightwalk'). Both were probably taken with the police camera.[22] These are characters from some sexual drama or from one of Stekel's case histories; but what they are doing can only be seen in glimpses. Perhaps Brandt was after something that Artaud and Balthus had talked about, the idea of the 'cruel nude'.

Apart from 'The Policeman's Daughter', there are several *Lilliput* nudes from the Forties that Brandt did not re-publish in the 1961 *Perspective of Nudes*. Ian Jeffrey calls them 'Hitchcockian', but these women don't seem dangerous in any *film noir* way. Rather, they are acting in private dramas, where Brandt teases the viewer with captions or props that hint at hidden meanings. The nude captioned 'Reflection' uses 'The Policeman's Daughter' model again; the title refers both to her pensive expression and to the way her figure 'reflects' the spoon-backed Victorian chair on which she sits.[23] This chair keeps appearing in Brandt's nudes and elsewhere, as in the 1948 'Eaton Place Still Life'.[24]

Another puzzle picture and counterpart to 'The Policeman's Daughter' is the 'Woodman's Daughter', which appeared in *Lilliput* .[25] Here Brandt borrows from one of the most famous Victorian narrative paintings, John Millais's 'The Woodman's Daughter' (1851). The painting shows the woodman with his axe; his young daughter; and the young son of the estate-owner, to whom the girl is offering strawberries in her cupped hands. The boy is flicking his whip against his riding boot; the implied story is that when they grow up he will rob the girl of her virginity, use the whip on her, then be murdered by her father in revenge.[26] The theme of the painting – a girl of the people seduced and mistreated by an aristocrat – is similar to Swinburne's *La Fille du Policeman*. Why did Brandt borrow Millais's title for his nude 'Woodman's Daughter'? As with his staged scenes of the Thirties, he was making a conventional image, and also hiding his own agenda behind it. In the Millais painting the girl's cupped hands, stretched out towards the squire's son, symbolise her genitals; in Brandt the model shields herself with her hands as she looks warily out of the frame – perhaps at a man advancing towards her. The Victorian chair and picture of the sailing ship are stock items from Brandt's erotic inventory. Such ships also appear, for example, in the staged picture of lovers embracing at Charlie Brown's pub, and in the portrait of Robert Graves with Beryl Pritchard and Judy Campbell.[27] If we take our cue from Millais, Brandt's picture becomes a coded expression of sado-masochistic interests that are openly revealed in his nudes of the late 1970s.

In many of these Forties nudes the model locks eyes with the observer, but her gaze is hard to read. Her mood may be sullen or even threatening; what she never conveys is seductiveness. Perhaps tired or dissatisfied, she always wants to keep herself emotionally at a distance from the one to whom she is physically exposed. Two of the traditional qualities of the female nude are lacking: sexual availability, and beauty displayed as a male possession. Eroticism and individual personality can often be combined in a nude portrait, but in such cases there always seems to be a tension between actual possession and the possibility of loss or estrangement. In these nudes of Brandt's, however, the model is too enigmatic and self-controlled to come within the range of male desire.

Another way of approaching Brandt's *Lilliput* nudes is through the models he used. Frances Rice, when asked if Brandt used his friends as nude models, replied, 'the way he made them suffer, he wouldn't have had a friend left'.[28] By this she meant simply that he insisted on very long and demanding sessions; but he also used different models for different purposes. Bert Hardy's claim that he used prostitutes may well have been true for several of the Forties nudes. But Brandt also used three other classes of models. There were professional figure models, who might be art students or anyone else just doing it for a fee (in 1939, Brandt had done a story for *Picture Post* on 'A Day in the Life of an Artist's Model'). Occasionally Brandt did nudes of fashion models that he met either through his commercial photography for Rima gowns in 1945-8 or through Marjorie Beckett's work as fashion editor of *Picture Post*. Brandt produced a routine story for *Picture Post* on 'Fashion in Bras', then took a semi-nude picture of the

Campden Hill Nude, 1949

model (which obviously could not be included in the story as printed).[29] Finally, there were friends and relatives. Marjorie Beckett posed for many nudes, especially when she and Brandt went on holiday together to France. Another important model in the Fifties was Ruth Goodall, Rolf Brandt's step-daughter by his second marriage.[30]

Brandt's Forties nudes are a series of inspired experiments, growing out of his friendship with Peter Rose Pulham and his fascination with *Citizen Kane*. Some of them are vehicles for his private sexual agenda, containing fetishistic themes or props. The end of this phase is marked by his uxorious 'Campden Hill' nude of Marjorie Beckett, taken in 1949. Like 'The Policeman's Daughter' it has a single bed in the background; but Marjorie's eyes are averted, and the picture's atmosphere is gentle rather than challenging. The composition of the picture owes something to the famous nude by Ingres in the Louvre, but it might also be a typical shot from *Citizen Kane*: the model is seen from behind in the right foreground, with a ceiling pressing down on her.[31] In the background, a lamp in deep focus seems to provide back-lighting for the figure. In spite of the erotic symbolism of lamp and bed, there is great tenderness in the soft texture of Marjorie's flesh, and the way her body dwarfs the furnishings set in the background suggests that she herself is more important than the conventional boudoir setting. The picture was taken a few months after the break-up of the *ménage à trois* at Hillfield Court, when Brandt and Marjorie had moved to a new flat at Airlie Gardens. After this, Brandt's nudes start to move from cloistered rooms into the open air, as if to leave behind the dark broodings that hang over the *Lilliput* nudes of the Forties.

The Night Watch on Crime, 1948

In 'A Photographer's London' (1948), Brandt's introduction to *Camera in London*, he took a curiously detached view of his commitment to his work:

> As a matter of fact I am able to forget photography almost completely when I am not working and never carry a camera except on an assignment … It is not that I do not get pleasure from the actual taking of photographs, but rather that the necessity of fulfilling a contract – the sheer having to do a job – supplies an incentive, without which the taking of photographs just for fun seems to leave the fun rather flat.[1]

There is a good deal of exaggeration here. For the first ten years or so of his career – until he started to publish regularly in *Lilliput* and *Picture Post* in 1939 – Brandt had few commercial assignments, and most of his pictures were published (if at all) only years after they had been taken.[2] In the Thirties Brandt took pictures mainly to please himself, and only worried later about getting them seen. Few, if any, of the pictures in *The English at Home* had been commissioned, though it was on the strength of that book that Brandt got his start as a photo-journalist at *Weekly Illustrated*. The period in which he worked regularly on photo-stories was from the late 1930s to about 1948, a small fraction of his total career of fifty-six years.[3] To keep up his photographic activity for so long, and in so many different genres, was proof of a dedication beyond any merely commercial persistence; and a very large part of his work was done as an independent artist, supported by family wealth. Nonetheless, the kernel of truth in Brandt's comment was that he did take more pictures during the 1940s, when he was most active as a photo-journalist, than in any of the decades before or since.

Why did Brandt drift away from photo-journalism, where he had done so much wonderful work and made himself a national figure?:

> Towards the end of the war … I gradually lost my enthusiasm for reportage. Documentary photography had become fashionable. Everybody was doing it. Besides, my main theme of the past few years had disappeared; England was no longer a country of marked social contrast. Whatever the reason, the poetic trend of photography, which had already excited me in my early Paris days, began to

fascinate me again. It seemed to me that there were wide fields still unexplored. I began to photograph nudes, portraits, and landscapes.[4]

By ending unemployment and extreme poverty, the war had made England into one nation rather than two; and the contrast between two ways of life had always been Brandt's English subject. He had never been simply an advocate for the oppressed, nor a satirist of the rich, but rather someone who focused on the incongruities between two worlds in co-existence. In the more 'poetic' work after 1945, the principle of contrast remains, in formal oppositions within the subjects he chooses. But political contrast, as expressed in the juxtaposition of images of rich and poor, fades away.

Brandt continued to work occasionally for *Picture Post* after 1945, but his stories took on a gloomy tinge, as if he now wanted to focus only on the disappointments of post-war life and the Labour regime. His alienation from social documentary became clear in his abortive assignment on the slum-dwellers of the Gorbals, in January 1948.[5] Bert Hardy took a sardonic view of this affair:

> Knowing Bill Brandt's feeling for atmosphere, Tom [Hopkinson] had sent him up to get a set of pictures of the slum. Bill returned with his usual contrasty pictures of the backs of policemen standing at the ends of streets, but nothing which really showed the human side of poverty. Tom decided to send me with Bert Lloyd, to see if we could do any better.[6]

Brandt's pictures of massive tenement façades showed the Gorbals as one of de Chirico's sinister abandoned cities. But they also showed a kind of magnificence in the Victorian streetscapes, whereas the spirit of the time was to show slums as festering places that should simply be cleared away. After using Brandt's pictures for the first page of the story, *Picture Post* switched to Hardy's. The Gorbals reminded Hardy of his own ragamuffin upbringing in Blackfriars and he concentrated on the children, including the favourite picture of his career, of two boys jostling each other in the street. Spotting the boys, he set the focus on his Leica to twelve feet, then walked towards them and tripped the shutter at the right moment without taking aim. This was the kind of populist action-photography that Brandt was unable or unwilling to produce.

As the Labour regime took hold, a new agenda for photo-documentary started to appear. The government was responding to the Thirties cry of 'Pull Down the Slums', but already people were feeling the misgivings expressed in Brandt's pictures for 'The Doomed East End'.[7] The text of the story followed the *Picture Post* line of building a bigger and better modernist utopia; Brandt's pictures were an elegy for the everyday lives of the people who were going to be swept away with the rubble, and for the warmth and disorder of Charlie Brown's pub. The packs of 'deprived' children that Hardy photographed playing on the Glasgow streets (and even in a graveyard) would no longer be a cause for liberal concern, because slum clearance would remove them from public sight. Once they were gone, of course, people would start to lament their absence – dirty faces, ragged clothes, and all. Much of what Thirties photography decried ended up as what people in the Fifties and Sixties wished had

Street in the Gorbals, 1948

been kept; and it is in Brandt's books that its memory may best be preserved.

In 1947, *Picture Post* stories on 'The Day that Never Broke' and 'Where Stands Britain?' showed a fog-bound, freezing country that had lost faith in its own greatness and was enjoying none of the fruits of victory.[8] 'The Night Watch on Crime', in the following year, returned to Brandt's obsession with policemen watching over the city by night.[9] At this time, films like Basil Dearden's *The Blue Lamp* (1950) responded to the fear that British morals were collapsing in the post-war era. Symbolically, the policeman was the Freudian superego who kept the dream-world of the city under control; Brandt's imagination swung between the authority of the policeman's uniform and the nakedness of the policeman's daughter. But 'The Night Watch' was Brandt's last story for *Picture Post*, and after 1948 the policeman disappears from his work altogether. The Labour utopia of slum clearance and free milk for schoolchildren put an end to the phantasmic underworld that Brandt had seen in the city street.

Misgivings about the Labour agenda also appeared in the *Picture Post* story, 'Street Play and Play Streets'.[10] This was shot by Haywood Magee, but Brandt's 'Lambeth Walk' picture was now re-used to argue that more streets should be closed so that children could play safely. People were complaining that the streets had become sterile, as the children who used to run and shout in every street had somehow disappeared. Many other sights that Brandt had photographed in the Thirties had disappeared too. Some kinds of poverty really had been relieved by the Socialism of 'Fair Shares for All', but others were just being moved out of sight, to the new housing estates of the urban fringe. In such places, workers were also getting a taste of the new consumer society; but neither their gains nor their losses provided much inspiration for documentary photographers. The poor were no longer a handy source of images for well-meaning reformers and the documentary pictures of the Thirties were starting to be looked at with nostalgia, as the indignations of that time started to fade.

The late Forties also marked a watershed in the way Brandt's work would be presented to the public. He was losing favour at *Lilliput* and *Picture Post*, and the magazines themselves were losing their readers. The main outlet for Brandt's work again became the book collection, rather than the magazine story. *Camera in London*, published by Focal Press in the spring of 1948, was Brandt's third study of English ethnography, following *The English at Home* and *A Night in London*. All three books were collections of the various English types, showing them in their distinctive environments – whether it be lovers in Hyde Park or coal miners in the North. But Brandt's project assumed that the whole society shared a core of Englishness; after the war, such a belief was more difficult to hold on to. The introduction to *Camera in London* shows Brandt moving away from the kind of unified social vision that had inspired his English photography in the Thirties:

> I believe this power of seeing the world as fresh and strange lies hidden in every human being. In most of us it is dormant. Yet it is there, even if it is no more than a vague desire, an unsatisfied appetite that cannot discover its own nourishment. I believe it is this that makes the public so eager for pictures. Its conscious wish may be simply to get information. But I think the matter goes deeper than that. Vicariously, through another person's eyes, men and women can see the world

anew. It is shown to them as something interesting and exciting. There is given to them again a sense of wonder.

This should be the photographer's aim, for this is the purpose that pictures fulfil in the world as it is to-day. To meet a need that people cannot or will not meet for themselves. We are most of us too busy, too worried, too intent on proving ourselves right, too obsessed with ideas, to stand and stare. We look at a thing and believe we have seen it. And yet what we see is often only what our prejudices tell us to expect to see, or what our past experiences tell us should be seen, or what our desires want to see. Very rarely are we able to free our minds of thoughts and emotions and just see for the simple pleasure of seeing. And so long as we fail to do this, so long will the essence of things be hidden from us.[11]

These principles seem to exclude two kinds of photography: social documentary, aimed at exposing evils and changing the world into a better place to live, and the staged scenes that Brandt favoured in the Thirties. Many of the pictures in *The English at Home* gave people precisely 'what they wanted to see': all those recognisable English types, like the guardsman on duty or the schoolgirl in her uniform. The section called 'The People' in *Camera in London* makes an excellent case for the staged work of the Thirties:

Bill Brandt's pictures of London people are not portraits; they are generalisations. He is not so much concerned about individuals as about types … As opposed to the idea of *Candid* portraiture, it does not matter for his purposes that the people he is photographing may be aware of his presence or may even be *holding it* for him. Nor does this sort of posing, if it can be called that, affect the truth of his pictures. Truth is not accidental. Sometimes you may get a glimpse of it by a quick glance. But the showy thing that catches the light at the wayside is rarely a diamond. Like the diamond, truth only emerges for everybody to see in all its purity after polishing. The realistic novel or play or film – do they not all owe their over-sized truth to life to deliberate planning and selection, to deliberate art?[12]

Norah Wilson's remarks here seem to echo Brandt's justification for his work, and to refute Cartier-Bresson's theory of the 'decisive moment'. But most of the pictures of people in *Camera in London* date from the Thirties. Brandt's desire to show the world as 'fresh and strange' points him towards landscapes and cityscapes where actual people appear only as occasional symbolic figures like policemen or shepherds. After the war, the personal encounter largely disappears from his photographic world, perhaps because of his growing reclusiveness. Even his portraits and nudes go out of their way to avoid the intimacy that one would normally expect from such pictures.

Brandt did his last story for *Lilliput* in December 1950, a series of show-business portraits.[13] His last appearance in *Picture Post* was on 5 May 1951, a story on the Festival of Britain.[14] Since the beginning of 1949 most of Brandt's work for *Picture Post* had been fashion illustration, thanks to Marjorie's position as the magazine's fashion editor.[15] But Marjorie was under threat too: Edward Hulton's wife took Tom

Hopkinson to lunch and told him that she wanted him to give her an office so that she could be the fashion editor of *Picture Post*. Hopkinson's reply – that he already had a perfectly good one – did not go down well.

In October 1950 James Cameron and Bert Hardy filed a story for *Picture Post* about the mistreatment of North Korean prisoners by United Nations forces; Hulton, once he saw the story, stopped the presses and had the issue reprinted without it. Hopkinson refused to tone down his coverage of the Korean War and was fired. Marjorie Beckett chose to go with him, and that put the final nail into Brandt's distinguished career with *Picture Post*. Bert Hardy stayed on, but the magazine steadily declined in editorial quality and circulation until it ceased publication in June 1957.[16] Its importance had always been bound up with its support for the 'New Britain' agenda of the reforming left; that phase of British history ended in February 1950, when the general election reduced the Labour government to a majority of five.[17] The era of 'Fair Shares for All' was on its way out. When the Tories came to power in October 1951, Labour's New Jerusalem gave way to the Conservative programme of building a prosperous consumer society, largely on the American model. It was no accident that Harold Macmillan's slogan, 'You Never Had It So Good', was in American English.[18] But even if *Picture Post* had still been able to present a convincing social agenda, British photo-journalism had been dealt a body-blow by the new age of television. The circulation of *Picture Post* and *Weekly Illustrated* fell relentlessly as the number of television sets in use went up.[19] There were no other significant outlets for photo-journalists, and Bert Hardy became an advertising photographer before giving up photography altogether to become a farmer.

In 1962 British photo-journalism was re-born when the Sunday newspapers began to publish colour supplements.[20] Colour made its greatest impact on the advertisements, while many of the documentary stories remained in traditional black-and-white. These supplements revived the tradition of socially critical photography, but for subjects outside the affluent West. Thirties documentary had an inherently positive agenda, concerned to vindicate the poor and portray them with dignity. The new photo-journalism would be both more extreme and more nihilistic, defined by what John Berger called 'pictures of agony'.[21] Such pictures came from wars, famines and genocides. Photographers would now seek out deprivation and tragedy in the Third World, as well as in the slums or dustbowls of the West. The new work was epitomised by Don McCullin's coverage of wars in Cyprus, Biafra, Vietnam and Lebanon. Shock and atrocity, as well as compassion, defined this photo-journalism, and the photographers themselves became part of the action: more than 130 were killed in Vietnam, including such legendary figures as Robert Capa and Larry Burrows.[22] This was not the kind of photography in which Brandt could have any part, either in its front-line ethos or its technical equipment (multiple 35mm cameras, often with motor drives). Although the Sunday magazines accorded him respect as a classic photographer, he did no stories for them on assignment; effectively, his career as a British photo-journalist ended at the same time as Tom Hopkinson's.[23]

Eaton Place Still Life, around 1948

25 Farewell to Eva

During the war years the lives of Eva and Marjorie Beckett went in different directions, except for their shared devotion to Brandt. After her return to the sanatorium world in 1935, Eva had no interest in pursuing a career, other than through supporting her husband's work. She was still one of the people to whom he turned for judgement on which of his pictures should be released for publication, and still at the centre of their social circle in north London. But being so devoted to Brandt and her friends also made her vulnerable, as she failed to develop any life outside her personal relationships. She must have become quite reclusive at this time, since other tenants at Hillfield Court have little memory of her. Perhaps her fragile health made her feel that the most important thing was to find security in the company of those she loved; at this point she could not foresee that she would live to be eighty-one, two years older than Brandt's age at his death. But as she moved into her thirties Eva could only hold on tighter to what she had and, in the long run, this was not the best strategy for keeping it.

Marjorie, meanwhile, was quickly making up for the time she had lost to illness before the war. During the war she became fashion editor of London *Harper's Bazaar*, as well as doing fashion modelling herself. Beauty helped her career along, but she also had solid journalistic talents. As a rising figure in the British magazine world, Marjorie was well placed to further Brandt's social and professional ambitions. Through her, he could get commissions from *Harper's*, and acquire more social cachet than Hulton Press could offer. Marjorie might have been responsible for drawing Brandt away from social documentary, towards more complacent, or commercial, or simply private kinds of photography. But if she was instrumental in Brandt's absorption into the English Establishment, it was surely an acceptance that he himself desired.

During the war, London *Harper's Bazaar* had no editor-in-chief and was run in haphazard fashion – 'an absolute shambles', in Anne Scott-James's view.[1] The Hearst headquarters in New York was in no position to exercise day-to-day control. Carmel Snow managed to cross the Atlantic towards the end of 1944, to visit liberated France and help with the revival of the French fashion industry. She also came to England to review the Hearst publications, and may have encouraged Marjorie to think that the editorship of London *Harper's* was within her grasp. In the summer of 1945 Snow brought Marjorie over to America, including a trip to Hearst Castle at San Simeon.

But when Frances McFadden (the head of Hearst publications in England) finally appointed an editor for *Harper's*, she did not pick Marjorie. Instead, Anne Scott-James came in from her position as women's editor at *Picture Post*. She had been a successful journalist for twelve years, starting with British *Vogue*; but she was three years younger than Marjorie, and Marjorie could not accept working under her. 'I would have liked to get on better with Marjorie,' Scott-James recalls, 'but if you advanced a friendly hand, she could be implacable.' Marjorie left *Harper's Bazaar* to work in a different division of Hearst; and Brandt evidently went with her, since he did nothing for the magazine after October 1945.[2] Instead, he shifted his allegiance to the New York edition of *Harper's Bazaar*, of which Carmel Snow was still editor. The art director was Alexei Brodovitch, who was an important patron for modernist photographers. Brandt's first appearance in New York *Harper's* had been in December 1943, with the same portrait of Françoise Rosay used by London *Harper's* in September. A few small portraits followed, but in 1945 Brandt started to get much more prominent treatment, second only to Beaton among British photographers.

In July 1945, New York *Harper's* ran a special section on England to celebrate Victory in Europe. It began with Brandt's 'London at Dawn on V-E Day', which had already been featured in the 'Victory Special' issue of *Picture Post*.[3] The picture showed the Thames and Waterloo Bridge, with the dome of St Paul's rising in the background – a triumphal counterpart to Brandt's earlier picture of a beleaguered St Paul's by night. *Harper's* chose to show an eternal, heritage England. There were Cartier-Bresson pictures of the English countryside and Speakers' Corner in Hyde Park, Brandt pictures of Charlie Brown's pub and English cultural heroes. Over the next year *Harper's* used Brandt repeatedly to show a grandiose England rising up from the damage of war, while Cartier-Bresson and Brassaï took up similar themes for France. This was the Europe cherished by upper-class, would-be cosmopolitan Americans, without such awkward realities as rationing, bomb damage or the struggle between the Communists and the right in France.

When Hopkinson resigned from *Picture Post* in 1950 there was no strong figure in England who could direct and promote Brandt's work; but Carmel Snow came forward to play this role in the United States. By the first half of the 1950s, Snow had become the dominant influence on Brandt's commercial work. She knew what she wanted, and she paid generously for it.[4] Between 1945 and the summer of 1951 Snow commissioned several major stories by Brandt in *Harper's Bazaar*, such as 'An Irish Itinerary', 'The British Export Drive' and '*The Queen Elizabeth*'.[5] Brandt supplied portraits of the Sitwells, Lord Berners and Augustus John; he did stories on Salisbury Cathedral, the Thames, 'The Hardy Country' and 'England's Stately Homes'. Pictures like these might not lend themselves easily to his search for mystery or atmosphere, but they were a way of continuing his passion for England, in a different style from the political Thirties. A good deal of this work for *Harper's Bazaar* would end up in Brandt's *Literary Britain*, published in 1951.

It was largely thanks to Marjorie that Brandt finally gained a transatlantic reputation (before 1945 he had only scattered pictures in *Harper's Bazaar*, *Coronet* and *Life*). Apart from the income it provided, New York *Harper's Bazaar* had an oversize, glossy format that gave Brandt's work more aesthetic appeal than the way it appeared in *Lilliput* or *Picture Post*. His ghostly picture of the park at Chiswick House, London, could now be spread dramatically over two full facing pages in *Harper's Bazaar*. The price of this exposure, though, was that Brandt's work lost most of its social relevance when it was drawn into the orbit of the American cultural market place. Like Brassaï and Cartier-Bresson, Brandt was now one of the artists asked to represent Europe to America, rather than to itself; and America, inevitably, already knew which Europe it wanted to see.

Brandt's shift to the American market meant that, in the Fifties, English people never saw much of his best work. His fine portrait of Moira Shearer at practice, or the Surrealist fashion shot on the *Queen Elizabeth*, appeared only in New York. Nor did *Harper's Bazaar* have any social or political agenda that mattered in Britain. It did take an obsessive interest in European high culture, but its aim was to distinguish the East Coast from the philistine masses of the American heartland. The uncanny side of Brandt's work – as opposed to his socially critical documentary – fitted in neatly with this agenda. He was expected to present the British people whose portraits he took for *Harper's Bazaar* as exotic figures, persons of talent apart from the herd. Brandt was himself becoming one of those post-war intellectuals who were no longer part of the communal effort, as they had been during the war. Fulfilment now lay in the private sphere, and Brandt was no exception. His picture of a gull's nest on Skye (1947) is seen by John Berger as the turning-point of his career: 'here for the first time everything has been sacrificed to Brandt's private purpose'.[6] Berger argues that the documentary work of the 1930s and early 1940s is the best of Brandt; from Brandt's own point of view, private interests had much stronger claims than the disappointing public face of Britain after 1945.

In 1947 Lyena Barjansky (now Lyena Dodge, having married Roger Pryor Dodge, the jazz dancer and critic) came to London to visit the Brandts. She found herself in an unhappy family, with Eva crying all the time, and Marjorie also coming to Lyena in tears to lament the break-up of the shared household. Not having seen Marjorie for seven years, Lyena was amazed by the change in her. Instead of the 'sweet little girl' Lyena had first met in 1938, Marjorie was now a sophisticated and successful fashion journalist. To Lyena, this showed Brandt's great power to 'develop' people; but if so, he had developed Marjorie to the point where he was willing to sacrifice Eva to keep her. He told Lyena that Marjorie was the ideal wife for him, and that she was making all the business arrangements for his work.

Around the end of 1947 Brandt bought a bookshop near his flat, on Haverstock Hill. This may have reflected his passion for literature, since he was busy assembling the pictures for *Literary Britain*. A more likely motive, though, was to provide an occupation for Eva. But the bookshop project did not help and, around the autumn of 1948, the triangle at Hillfield Court was broken by Eva's decision to leave. L. W. Brandt was as devoted to Eva as ever; he took her away on a trip to Hamburg, and provided her with a regular income by settling some shares on her. In the winter of 1948-9 Eva went to New York, to get away from her troubles in London; she stayed with Lyena and with Lyena's Hungarian friend Ylla, best known as a photographer of animals. When she came back, Eva moved to a flat in Eaton Place, Belgravia, that LW bought for her. She would go down to Micheldever to stay with LW every second

Chiswick House gardens, 1944

weekend, with Brandt going on the other.[7]

Bill's farewell present to Eva was the 'Eaton Place Still Life', with its spoon-backed chair, opera glasses and music to recall pre-war evenings at Covent Garden.[8] 'In all his other pictures of this moment,' David Mellor writes, 'the great Victorian spoon-back chairs – the chairs that bear Alice in *Through the Looking Glass* (1872) – carry the nudes, the woman's body and the mother's body, lost and refound.'[9] If the chair does stand for the mother, perhaps Brandt was also thinking of his actual mother Lilli, who died in early 1949. What is certain is that the music book makes the farewell a conditional one, because it is open to a song whose refrain is 'We still will cling to friends of other days'. Before long, Eva started coming to meet Brandt at a park near where he lived, and Marjorie found them there and 'made a terrible scandal'.[10] Scandal or not, a complete break with Eva would have required Brandt to give up the connection with his old life in Vienna and Paris; more than that, he would have had to deny his need to be in some relation with two women at once. Nor did Eva fall in love with anyone for years after she left Brandt. She no longer lived with him, but neither had she entirely given him up.

Quite soon after the separation, in late 1948 or early 1949, Brandt and Marjorie moved to a new flat in Airlie Gardens, off Campden Hill in Kensington. In the preface to *Camera in London* (1948), Brandt had written: 'The casual visitor may never discover the real beauty of London unless he finds the surprising backwaters and small towns hidden behind the noisy main streets … the quiet streets of Campden Hill where over the tops of the chestnut trees of a Victorian garden one can see all London and beyond as far as the Surrey downs.'[11] This was the view from Brandt and Marjorie's first flat at Airlie Gardens; later he bought a larger flat in the same block. With L. W. Brandt providing financially for Eva, Brandt and Marjorie could now afford something a step up from Hillfield Court. Both were making substantial professional incomes, and there may have been more money from Marjorie's family or from the death of Brandt's mother.

Airlie Gardens, with its dark entranceways and hidden gardens at the back, is a place secluded from the great city swarming outside. Its atmosphere fitted in with Brandt's move to an even more enclosed life. He stayed at Airlie Gardens until his death and took many pictures there, especially of nudes. His widow, Noya, still lives there. It is an imposing late-Victorian apartment block, with high-ceilinged rooms looking out on to a large shared garden at the rear. This was a much better setting than Hillfield Court in which to display Brandt's growing collection of Victorian furniture and knick-knacks.[12] During the war years and after, Brandt sometimes used the even more impressive rooms of Frances Rice's flat in Ennismore Gardens (the portraits of Franco Zeffirelli and Nicol Williamson were taken there). Such rooms, apart from the Victorian atmosphere that Brandt loved, also provided longer vistas for his experiments in deep-focus photography.

The move to Campden Hill from Belsize Park also reflected London's complicated local hierarchies. Belsize Park meant 'little Vienna', psychoanalysts, writers, artists and refugees. Campden Hill was less fashionable than Belgravia, but still more Marjorie's London than Brandt's, though he was now quite happy to make it his own. He was moving away from the first fifteen years of his London life; except that, characteristically, he maintained a kind of geographical division of allegiance by keeping on one of the Hillfield Court flats. This would have made good sense financially: with protection for sitting tenants, a pre-war rent of £2.50 a week was a mere trifle by 1949. Brandt kept his darkroom there for some time, and also used the living space occasionally, as one sees from the 1962 portrait of him there by Roger Hill.[13] Hillfield Court allowed him to keep a pied-à-terre in his old neighbourhood (where Rolf and Ester still lived), and not feel entirely enclosed by his new, monogamous home with Marjorie.

The end of his work for *Lilliput* and *Picture Post* helped to make the 1950s the quietest part of Brandt's career. Some of this may have been due to sheer fatigue, after his labours during the war years; part may also have been due to the intensity of his concentration on a single kind of photography, the nude; part, finally, a psychic crisis after his separation from Eva that led him to re-enter psychoanalysis towards the end of the decade. Once he had settled down with Marjorie alone, there would have been the temptation to live a more sequestered and cosseted life. Judith Brandt, Rolf's youngest daughter, remembers them as a shy, rather prim couple, sensitive and turned in on themselves. They were always together and had few friends; Brandt did little for himself and was happy to let Marjorie take care of things. She became a regular writer on food for the *Scotsman*; at home, she produced delicious meals and ensured every other kind of comfort for Brandt. By this time, also, Brandt had enough money to make it less urgent for him to take on assignments just to help pay the bills.

Another priority of the 1950s was to catch up on the foreign travel that had been difficult or impossible during the previous decade. Brandt and Marjorie were both eager to escape British austerity and, in the winter, the British climate. Almost all of their travel would be to France or Spain.[14] Germany and Austria remained off limits, and Brandt never went to the US.[15] He went to Italy in 1950, but said he could not 'recognise' what he was seeing because he hadn't read Italian literature.[16] His first escape from England to France after the war came in 1948, when he went to Provence for a *Lilliput* story on places associated with Van Gogh. Travelling on assignment would avoid the rigid control of foreign currency for pleasure travel that was imposed by the Labour government. In the 1950s, Brandt also did portrait commissions in France of Braque, Gordon Craig and Picasso.[17] He never lived in Paris again, but spent more and more time in the French countryside. Giving up photo-journalism seemed to correspond to Brandt's declining interest in the visual possibilities of everyday English life, and his return to the more experimental work he had done in Paris in the early Thirties. It also meant the effective disappearance of political concerns from his work. Portraits, nudes and landscapes were all subjects removed from history; which, it would seem, is where Brandt himself wanted to be.

Living at Airlie Gardens and travelling constantly in France also helped to turn Brandt inwards to domestic life with Marjorie, and away from both his old continental friends and the journalistic world. There is a fragmentary diary of Marjorie's for 1949 to 1951, which shows her absorption in the squabbles and chit-chat of the Airlie Gardens community: the tenants who secretly fed the wild cats, the woman who set her kitchen on fire.[18] Some of the entries are little sketches that Marjorie may have hoped to revise for publication in magazines; Eva had started writing such pieces, and perhaps Marjorie thought she could do so as well.[19] The diary says little about relations between Marjorie and Brandt; but one episode reveals a lot about Marjorie's character. In January 1950 she went to the X-ray department of Brompton Hospital for a check-up. Waiting in the corridor, she gradually realised that all the other patients had been in sanatoria and had come to have their pneumothoraxes re-filled:

> Every body looked at me curiously. They knew I didn't belong and then I had one of my awful coughing attacks & they looked again & of course they guessed and accepted me. I became more and more depressed looking at the patiently waiting red tents & the old man next to me – & when I realised that they were all more or less admitting me to their club membership when they heard my cough, I suddenly got furious – what the hell was I doing among such people again – wasn't I a fool to be in such a state again after having escaped so completely – All my depression went – I was just angry and determined whatever happened not to get ill again – Even the operation which had seemed almost a relief from the awful endless coughing seemed to be something that I had to avoid at all costs – anything rather than again become a chatty ex-patient living entirely in a TB world bounded by rest-hours & part-time work & positives & negatives & refills & other patients' symptoms – all that awful club membership world of Tubercle – or worse still one of poor patient resigned creatures under the red tents, or sitting on benches – not people any more – just battered bodies treated like imbeciles or children by any one on the hospital staff [20]

Later in 1950 Marjorie had to be hospitalised again, returning home at the beginning of July; she may have gone in for the pneumothorax operation, or for a course of streptomycin treatment. But after that her determination was rewarded: she kept out of the sanatoria, and lived past sixty. One can see that she would bring similar determination to keeping Brandt's illness at bay and allowing him to lead a productive life.

Seated Nude, 1954

Between 1944 and 1950 almost all of Brandt's nudes had been taken indoors, in a style that made the rooms almost as important as the model herself. The rooms were sets, and each picture was like a scene from Brandt's private *film noir*. This began to change in June 1951 when he and Marjorie went to France. The main purpose of their trip was to photograph houses and landscapes associated with Flaubert, Maupassant, Gide and Proust.[1] But towards the end they became fascinated by the dramatic cliffs and beaches around Etretat. After an agreeable lunch at Bruneval they stayed late on the beach and, Marjorie wrote in her diary, 'Bill had the idea of taking a nude there.' The next morning they came back: 'there was a strong wind and a high sea and I posed for a nude – it was horribly uncomfortable and very cold and I was very bad tempered. But the tide was coming in so we had to be fairly quick & thank goodness.'[2]

The pictures from Bruneval did not turn out well enough to be published, but the idea of taking nudes on the beach became a passion for Brandt over the next nine years.[3] In none of them does the sea itself count for much: the conventional glamour shots of women rising from the surf had no interest for Brandt. Nor does he make use of sand, as in Weston's classic nudes of Charis Wilson on the Oceano dunes. Brandt places his nude figures against rocky shores and cliffs. Sometimes rounded boulders on the beach echo the roundness of the female form; more often, the softness of the model's body contrasts with the jaggedness of the rocks.[4] The first nude in this series to be included in the collection *Perspective of Nudes* was taken later in 1951 at St-Cyprien, a seaside resort near Perpignan on the Mediterranean. It shows the model's legs only, raised and crossed in the foreground; most likely Marjorie posed for it, since she and Brandt were there on holiday and he would have had difficulty finding a local model. He continued to take these holiday nudes of Marjorie at Taxo d'Aval near Perpignan (1954, 1957, 1958) and at Baie des Anges, Nice (1958, 1959). All these pictures show a partial figure – sometimes only a hand or a shoulder – and exclude any sense of the model as a personality, unlike the tender 'Campden Hill' nude of 1949. Marjorie was in her early forties by the time Brandt started taking these outdoor nudes, and she may have been shy about pictures that were too revealing (especially in natural light), or in which she could be recognised. But impersonality was now central to Brandt's explorations of the nude. In none of the outdoor studies does the model return the viewer's gaze, unlike such basilisk nudes as 'The Policeman's Daughter' or the 'Micheldever nude' of 1948.

The outdoor nudes of the 1950s are Brandt's most important work of that decade, conceivably of his entire career; yet he preserved only a small harvest from nine years of effort. Twenty-three of these pictures appear in *Perspective of Nudes* and in the later volume, *Nudes 1945-1980*.[5] A group of three from 1958 belong to a favourite rocky beach on the East Sussex coast near Seaford; Brandt's account of how he took these nudes could hardly be more enigmatic:

> Over the years, I learned much from the old Kodak [police camera]. I learned even how to use modern cameras in an unorthodox way and, for the last section of 'Perspective of Nudes', photographed on the beaches of East Sussex, Normandy and southern France, I discarded the Kodak altogether.
>
> But I continued to let the lenses discover images for me. It is difficult to explain how I took the last photographs. They were perhaps chance pictures; unexpected combinations of shapes and landscapes. I watched them appear on the ground glass and exposed. It was as simple as that.[6]

It is as if the viewfinder is in charge, not Brandt himself or the person who inspires his images. Although Marjorie provided a model who was both beautiful and conveniently to hand, she did not dominate Brandt's nudes of the Fifties. In 'The Nightwalk' of 1940, Brandt had surrendered to his sexual obsession with Marjorie, like Alfred Stieglitz with Georgia O'Keeffe, Edward Weston with Tina Modotti and Charis Wilson, Raoul Haussmann with Vera Broido. But these photographers used outdoor settings to reveal the female body as intrinsically erotic and beyond morality. Brandt's outdoor nudes went in the opposite direction, seeking an escape from the menacing female sexuality in many of his indoor nudes.

Brandt had other models, besides Marjorie, for his outdoor pictures. For the ones taken in Sussex he often used Rolf Brandt's step-daughter, Ruth Goodall, who was eighteen when she started posing for Brandt. His best-known picture of her is the 'Ear on the Beach', taken at Seaford in 1957. She recalls that Brandt was too shy to ask her directly to model for him, but made his approach through Rolf.[7] They were all on holiday in Provence at the time, and the Eygalières nude of 1953 was among the first that Brandt took of her.[8] Goodall was a student at the Guildhall School of Music and she recommended to Brandt a fellow-student, Diana, who needed the money and was willing to pose. One of Diana's pictures was the head-and-shoulders nude of 1953, where the model's right arm rises up to obscure her face; a nude of the year before gives a side view of a similar pose, using a different model.[9] They are two of Brandt's most beautiful nudes; in both the upraised arm seems to ward off intruders.

Brandt's table of contents for *Nudes 1945-1980*, his later collection, divides the pictures into distinct groups. In the first two sections each nude is labelled with a specific part of London where it was taken, such as Hampstead or Campden Hill. The third section is all outdoor nudes from Sussex or France; the fourth section names only 'London' as the setting.[10] In the first two sections the nudes are set in recognisable rooms that are intrinsic to the composition; in section three bodies are placed in a context from the natural world; the nudes of section four are close-ups

Nude, 1952

where the setting does not count and all the complexity lies inside the boundaries of the female body.

Brandt's aims for his indoor nudes of the Fifties can be seen most clearly in the four that were taken in 'Belgravia' – that is, the Eaton Place flat that Eva moved to after she left Hillfield Court. His first Eaton Place nude (1951) shows a woman's crossed legs – they may be Marjorie's – seen from the head; in the same year he took an outdoor nude of Marjorie at St-Cyprien with a similar composition. The Eaton Place nude belongs with two other pictures that feature the French doors of the flat, opening on to a balcony, and a Victorian spoon-backed chair. One is the 'Eaton Place Still Life' that had been Brandt's farewell present to Eva in 1948, the other is the 'Portrait of a Young Girl' of 1955, for which Rolf's ten-year-old daughter Judith was the model. In all three pictures, the chair seems to be a surrogate for Eva herself, absent from her flat while Brandt does his work. In the Eaton Place nude, the chair stands sentinel over the woman who has displaced her sexually and is again in her house. The deep-focus portrait of Judith makes her into an uncanny, Alice-like figure – perhaps the ghost of the child that Eva and Bill could never have.[11] These three pictures show how Brandt made rooms into equal partners in the human dramas that they enclose.

Apart from the formal effects that Brandt was seeking in his Fifties nudes, he was also a male photographer trying to come to terms with the female body. The whole genre of the female nude is now politically suspect, as an indulgence of the conquering 'male gaze'. This may well be true of pornography, whether hard or soft, and even of many art nudes; but 'the gaze' is not enough to explain Brandt's work. The corresponding French term, '*le regard*', has overtones of control or supervision; Brandt's nude figures are not subordinated in any such way. Rather, they express female giantism, with partial views of the model's body dominating the visual frame. One precedent for such pictures was the series of 200 glass-plate pictures of nudes that Kertész did in 1933 for the humour magazine *Le Sourire*.[12] These were taken in a studio, using two fun-house mirrors to distort the model's body. Brandt must have known Kertész's work, but did not want such radical distortions. He sometimes used mirrors for his nudes, but only plain ones.

In Brandt's overwhelming frontal nude of June 1954, the torso is guarded off by the strength of the crossed arms and the dome of the knee. The model exposes herself, but also projects a massive self-sufficiency that blocks and belittles any attempted male scrutiny.[13] The camera's perspective is precisely that of an infant standing in front of its mother and being denied access to her lap: the lap of the goddess, one might say. Brandt's friend Chapman Mortimer developed this idea as a key to the outdoor nudes, in his introduction to *Perspective of Nudes*:

> And now we are really seeing, unhampered by bad habits and truly outwards from ourselves. We have ceased to doubt what seems strange and think it strange only that we should have been till now so unobservant.
>
> We are seeing, in fact, with the infant's eye or the lover's; with the unembarrassed eyes of reality. We are marvelling that it has never occurred to us before, looking aghast at a Picasso eye jumped out of place behind a Picasso nose, that that was how we saw eyes we knew and even a nose we knew when we had

Portrait of a young girl, Eaton Place, 1955

Eaton Place Nude, 1951

finished kissing. We are wondering, very probably, at our conventional conception of what is monstrous, at our polite distance-keeping.

For most of us it is impossible to remember how we saw when consciousness meant warmth and milk, and when our measure of the world was its closeness. Yet is it not likely that our notions of what may be beautiful are based on the experience of that time? And is it not with love that we see most strongly and best?[14]

When he wrote this introduction, Mortimer had been a close friend of Brandt for twenty years; Brandt probably suggested him for the commission, and would not have accepted an introduction that he fundamentally disagreed with.[15] Mortimer's comments suggest that Brandt's Fifties nudes came out of a psychic crisis involving the primal realm of infantile sexuality. The sexual concerns of his childhood, never well integrated into his adult life, were again demanding attention. Most critics have assumed that after his brief analysis by Stekel, Brandt shifted his allegiance to Surrealist symbolism – an open-ended series of associations between reality and fantasy – and left behind the more rigid and codified psychoanalytic system. The Surrealists created a wild variety of combinations, drawing on the artefacts of the modern world as well as natural objects; the Freudians linked all symbolism to the pre-social unconscious. No one could deny the profound influence of Surrealism on Brandt's photography; but it seems equally important that, thirty years after breaking with Stekel, Brandt returned to an orthodox Freudian analysis in London.

Brandt posed for a portrait by Laelia Goehr in 1945 holding a book called *The Living Thoughts of Freud*.[16] His analyst was Barbara Lantos, who in the 1950s practised from her home at 100 Fellows Road, NW3 (a postal code that was something of a joke for its concentration of psychoanalysts). She was born Barbara Ripper in Budapest in 1894, of Jewish parentage, and graduated in medicine from the university. Her first husband, Albert Lantos, fled to the Soviet Union after the collapse of Béla Kun's Communist regime in July 1919. Barbara Lantos went to the West, first to Vienna and then Leipzig. By 1924 she had joined a group of young leftist analysts in Berlin, the 'political Freudians'.[17] Their leader was Otto Fenichel, a Viennese who had been one of Freud's most brilliant disciples. Fenichel tried to combine psychoanalysis with revolutionary politics. Members of his group made pilgrimages to the Soviet Union during the 1930s, where Fenichel was impressed by the 'constructive spirit' of the Soviet prison system. But when the Nazis moved against German psychoanalysis, Fenichel went to New York rather than Moscow. Barbara Lantos made a marriage of convenience to a businessman named Georg Schneider and left for Paris, where she lived for a year and a half and gave birth to a son in 1934. She then went on to London, and entered the British Psychoanalytical Institute in 1938. She had little money when she arrived, but managed to buy a house and make it a haven for refugees from Nazism.

In the 1940s and 1950s British psychoanalysis was riven by the great feud between Anna Freud and Melanie Klein over infantile sexuality.[18] Lantos was firmly on Anna Freud's side in this battle. She wrote about the emotional importance of work, and how people who lost their professions might regress to childlike helplessness (no doubt she had observed such symptoms among the refugee colony in north

London). Elsewhere she discussed the 'Sublimation of Genitality into Creativeness' – arguing, in classic Freudian style, that 'in human beings, sexuality pervades every other activity'.[19] Painting, writing and scientific enquiry are all sublimations, so that 'the truly creative element in them is derived from the genital sexual impulse'.

To say this of a man whose creativity takes the form of nude photography would be to shoot fish in a barrel; it is surely more interesting, in Brandt's case, to look at the elements in his art that go beyond standard genital fantasies. Susan Brandt mentions two possible reasons for Brandt to enter analysis with Lantos: the 'spectre of his childhood', and guilt over leaving Eva for Marjorie.[20] The childhood trauma had two main consequences for Brandt's adult life: his extreme remoteness from other people (combined with secretiveness and suspicion), and his fetishistic sexual interests. Both of these traits persisted, and even intensified, until the end of his life. If psychoanalysis provided some relief from neuroses, it cannot have effected any definite cure. Guilt about Eva came closer to resolution, though at a cost to Brandt's two subsequent marriages. By the time he began treatment with Lantos, in the late 1950s, his mother Lilli had been dead for about ten years; Eva had been very close to her, and in some ways had taken her place in Brandt's life, as an ever-reliable and nurturing figure. For Brandt to choose a Hungarian woman as his analyst suggests a desire to build a bridge to his past life with Eva. What actually was said on the couch is lost for ever; but analysis means a return to the past, all the way to infancy, and for Brandt this may have reflected some uneasiness about the new life he had created with Marjorie over the previous ten years. Psychoanalysis may also have blunted his creative urges. He stopped taking nudes in 1960, soon after his analysis began, and most of his pictures for the seventeen years after that were commissioned portraits – for him, the easiest kind of work to undertake.

Brandt's relationship with Barbara Lantos also took an oddly incestuous turn. Normally a psychoanalyst would consider it unethical to treat a husband and wife simultaneously, but Lantos took Eva as a patient also, believing that her divorce made her sufficiently independent of Brandt. Once again Brandt had managed to construct an intimate and secretive triangle, between himself, Lantos and Eva. As if this were not enough, Lantos turned out to have triangular projects of her own. She was now married to Sandor Rakos, a dentist who was a prominent figure in the Hungarian exile community. When she was diagnosed with cancer, around 1960, she told her husband that after she died he should marry Eva, as they were well suited to each other. Lantos died in September 1962, and Rakos and Eva did indeed marry, living in the same house where Eva had previously come for her analysis. Ironically, Brandt's triangle was now inverted, since Eva had two men vying for her attention. Not surprisingly, they soon became jealous of each other.

Where Marjorie stood in all this is not clear, except that she did her best to keep aloof from the goings-on in NW3. Her diary entry about the TB clinic at Brompton Hospital suggests that her way of dealing with painful episodes in the past was simply to leave them behind; Eva, by contrast, wanted to remember them and work through them. The story that she published in *Harper's Bazaar* about her mother's death was part of long-drawn-out attempts to write her autobiography, which she was never able to complete and publish.[21] But in 1956 Rupert Hart-Davis published her novel *The*

Mermaids, about the love-affair of a young woman in a Budapest sanatorium. The heroine, Lalla, is a flighty, doll-like creature, quite different from Eva herself, but surely based on a fellow-patient for whom Eva felt deep affection.[22] *The Mermaids* is a delicate study of the sanatorium world that shows Eva's real talent for fiction. It was also published in New York and Eva went there for the occasion, staying with Lyena. Unfortunately, after this novel she was unable to publish anything further. Her psychoanalysis and subsequent marriage may have helped her to come to terms with her unhappy past, so that she no longer felt the same need to write about it. Rakos, at least, provided an anchor for her: apart from being a fellow-Hungarian, he was an outgoing, highly masculine type, the opposite of Brandt in personality; and possibly all the better for Eva because of this.

Harold Pinter, 1951

It was in the 1950s that Brandt gained his place in the top rank of English photographers. This recognition may have come, paradoxically, because of his withdrawal from active photo-journalism: he was less tainted with commercialism, and more likely to be categorised as an 'art photographer'. Brandt had not had a gallery show since the one at Marx House in 1940, but in 1955 he was featured in the most successful photography exhibition ever: *The Family of Man* at the Museum of Modern Art in New York. This was the landmark show that made photography widely popular (or widely vulgarised, in the view of its critics). Edward Steichen, the show's curator, selected 503 pictures from two million submissions; sixty-eight countries and 273 photographers were represented. The show's central theme was 'The Ages of Man', from birth to death. Steichen proclaimed that the photographs he had chosen were 'concerned with the religious rather than religions. With basic human consciousness rather than social consciousness.'[1] His emphasis on the similarity of human experience, regardless of race, class, culture or the Cold War, provoked hostility from intellectuals of both right and left. The show ended the era of socially critical documentary photography, as even classic protest pictures were absorbed into Steichen's prevailing spirit of woolly-minded universalism. The harsh realities of poverty and oppression were reduced, by the title and the ideology of the show, to family squabbles that were minor blemishes on the solidarity of the human race.[2]

The photographer who had the most pictures in the show, and who epitomised the spirit of the whole project, was Henri Cartier-Bresson. Brandt made a respectable showing with four pictures, matched only by Beaton among English photographers. Two of Brandt's pictures were fairly routine: a small picture of gravestones in the section on death, and one of Salisbury Cathedral in the section on religion. His picture of the Bethnal Green housewife washing her steps appeared in the section on work, where the caption 'Bless thee in all the work of thy hand which thou doest' was an epitaph for social-protest photography. Most important, though, for Brandt's image was the full-page reproduction of another of his East End pictures, 'Dancing the Lambeth Walk'. To someone unfamiliar with its history, the 'Lambeth Walk' was just a brilliant point-and-shoot street picture, one that could equally well have been taken by Cartier-Bresson. It made Brandt famous for representing the eternal joyfulness of children; what fell away was the actual history of the East End, including the disappearance of Wolverley Street where Joan Whippin had played in 1939. By the time of *The Family of Man* the well-intentioned work of post-war modernism was in full swing, filling in the bomb sites and sweeping away everything that seemed old and shabby. But as the London street became a more tidy and predictable place, Brandt found less of interest in it to photograph. After the early 1950s, only one of his pictures stands out as a street photograph, his portrait of the young Harold Pinter in 1961. The Battersea street is a seedy dead-end, with the deep black of a railway arch looming over it, and a solitary, gigantic Pinter in the foreground (the composition makes it look like a still from *Citizen Kane*). Both Brandt and Pinter might be wondering, as they look at this corner of London: 'Where has everybody gone?'

In the Sixties Brandt consolidated his fame, but took fewer and fewer pictures. He continued with the portraits that magazines wanted from him and were happy to pay for. Yet surely other commissions would have come if he had made the effort to find them – above all, on the great subject that had first made his name:

> Often I am asked if I do not feel that I have come to an end of the possibilities of photographing London – I have been photographing it for several years now and surely the subject must be exhausted. Happily, I have never had to ask myself that question. Even if London did not change, my own outlook on life does. And that means that for me photography changes too.[3]

This was written in 1948 and London did come into Brandt's photography indirectly during the Fifties and Sixties, as façades seen from rooms where he took portraits, or the parks where he placed Francis Bacon or Dorothy Tutin. But street life, or the urban prospects that had become his trademark in the Forties (the Thames, St Paul's, terraces in the West End), no longer drew Brandt out of his home. His increasing reclusiveness in his personal life seemed to carry over into a preference for cloistered photographic subjects: portraits as attempts to penetrate the subject's inner life, nudes as a necessarily private encounter with the model. Externally, also, the new London of modernist brutalism had no appeal for Brandt. One sees this in his portraits of the architects Robin Seifert and Denys Lasdun, each of them overshadowed by modernist buildings they designed.[4] London would always change, but not necessarily in a way that would attract Brandt's interest. Certainly the 'swinging London' of the Sixties, which had its own photographic chroniclers (mainly in colour), was not a natural subject for Brandt in the way Thirties London had been. His portraits of Sixties personalities – Peter Brook, Kenneth Tynan, Harold Pinter, Jonathan Miller, Nicol Williamson – all have a shut-down, cornered look that is at odds with the explosive happenings of the decade. From 1962 to 1964 Brandt experimented with colour photographs on beaches in Normandy and Sussex; eight of these pictures appeared in the first edition of *Shadow of Light*, but he cut them from the second edition and they remain a brief diversion from his modernist dedication to black-and-white.

Brandt's commitment to England was much reduced after about 1960, when he and Marjorie bought a flat at the Résidences Séréna, a post-war development within walking distance of the medieval town of Vence, above Nice. It was a modest two-bedroom flat, but with a balcony overlooking the Baie des Anges where Brandt loved to sit for hours reading. Vence was still a quiet provincial town where Renoir, Matisse, Chagall and many others had come to paint. In 1964 the Fondation Maeght opened its gallery of modern art and magnificent sculpture gardens. Lartigue and Brassaï also had houses in the neighbourhood and became close friends of Brandt. From now until the end of his life, he would spend half the year at Vence, arriving in September after stopping over at the Hotel le Royal in Paris and staying until spring. It was not just that Brandt enjoyed the climate and the pleasures of French provincial life; Vence was also a relief from the strain of being a public figure in London, and all the intrusions that came with it. In 1962 Brandt took a picture of the prehistoric stones at St-Barnabé, in the hills above Vence; but that seems to have been one of very few taken during his French visits. When David and Peggy Godfrey met him in Vence as neighbours in 1982, he no longer even brought a camera with him when he came south.

Apart from the pull of lazy days in Vence, Brandt had little need to seek out commissions after 1965, when his father died at the age of eighty-nine. L. W. Brandt had been a widower for sixteen years; he had not been active in business since he came to England in 1939, but had lived the life of a country gentleman, managing investments that extended from tannin plantations in Argentina to a small housing estate in Hamburg. His sons, and Eva too, came regularly to stay with him at Micheldever; he still presided over the collective fortune of the family and was intensely proud of Bill's success. The funeral was a small family affair in Micheldever church. Eva came, always devoted to the man who had come closest to replacing the real father she had lost when she was eighteen; Marjorie made all the funeral arrangements; Susan Brandt was told to look after her uncle Bill, and found him in shock that he had actually outlived his father. At the reception, she remembers an awkward moment when a noisy aunt who had come over from Hamburg cornered Bill and addressed him in German. He gave her a blank look, and finally replied in English.

L. W. Brandt had given money steadily to his sons and to Eva during his lifetime, but there was still plenty left. His will divided the estate into four equal parts, each worth about £150,000 (equivalent to about £1,900,000 in 2003).[5] Because LW had put up the capital for his eldest son to become a partner in the London firm, Walther's share skipped a generation and went to his sons, Peter and Dennis. The three remaining parts went to Bill, to Rolf and to Eva. It was probably soon after this that Bill and Marjorie moved from their first flat in Airlie Gardens to the larger one at number 4, where Bill had room to move his darkroom equipment from Hillfield Court. Eva, for her part, married Sandor Rakos soon afterwards. LW had met Rakos and approved of him; but, with his old-fashioned views, he might not have provided so generously for Eva if she had a husband.[6]

With some of his friends Brandt had a reputation for being mean; but, three years after his father's death, he gave £30,000 to each of his five nieces and nephews. He may have wanted to escape death duties, for which he would have had to survive for seven years after the gift. But it was an extremely generous act – so generous that one wonders if Marjorie had also inherited money on which she and Brandt could rely. Certainly by this time Brandt only accepted work he wasn't already inclined to do. The portraits, mainly for American magazines, could be done quickly and easily, and they brought him into contact with most of Britain's creative elite.[7] Meanwhile his health was gradually failing, and he may have feared that it would be hard to match the brilliance of his earlier work. Much of his energy over the last twenty years of his life would be devoted to the work of retrospection, the collecting and publishing of his pictures in a definitive form. There was also the duty, strenuous enough in itself, of harvesting the tributes brought to him by age and distinction.

Chapman Mortimer observed in 1961 that 'For long periods [Brandt] has been content to remain out of sight.'[8] Mortimer would have been thinking especially of the previous decade, when Brandt was concentrating either on his nudes or on work that was published only in the United States. In the Sixties, though, Brandt published two collections that gave him a visibility he never afterwards lost. The first book, *Perspective of Nudes*, was published in 1961 in three countries and two languages: by the Bodley Head in London, Amphoto in New York and Le Bélier-Prisma in Paris. *Literary Britain*, ten years before, had made only a limited impression, thanks to its high price and highbrow content. *Perspective of Nudes* was without precedent in English photography, and was bound to draw attention for its subject-matter alone. But to appear at all it had to fit clearly into the category of the art nude, and this may well have been Brandt's reason for excluding his staged *Lilliput* nudes from the 1940s.[9] These pictures, with their models who looked as if they had walked in off the street, and with their fetishistic overtones, belonged to a distinctly shady English milieu. *Perspective of Nudes* was a different kind of cultural event: the belated arrival in England of the high-modernist nude, enhanced by the finely textured heliogravure of the Swiss printers.[10] Lawrence Durrell's preface also set a tone of continental sophistication, as if to disarm any lurking Mrs Grundies:

> 'Celui-là, c'est un maître!'
>   We were sitting in front of an olive-wood fire, Brassaï, the child and I, talking photographs. All around us, spread on the floor, were Brassaï illustrations to a book on Paris. But the remark he made was about an English photographer who is easily his peer – Bill Brandt.[11]

Chapman Mortimer also sprinkled his introduction with French phrases, including his readers in the cosy circle of those who are culturally in the know. Given that most of Brandt's work for *Weekly Illustrated* and *Picture Post* had been uncredited, the appearance of *Perspective of Nudes* both raised Brandt in the British cultural hierarchy and re-positioned him. He had been recognised for his nudes and other credited work in *Lilliput*, certainly; but that was a shilling monthly with a somewhat raffish reputation. By 1961 *Lilliput* was dying and *Picture Post* was gone. *Perspective of Nudes* placed Brandt firmly in the camp of art photography and black-and-white high modernism. The art nude had been established internationally since the turn of the century – with the work of Stieglitz, Weston and Man Ray – so Brandt's book belatedly added the British nude to the tradition. But from now on he would be defined as an artist rather than a journeyman, a fundamentally different photographer from colleagues like Bert Hardy.

At the age of fifty-seven, Brandt had now gained an unrivalled reputation in England – which he then, in most ways, spent the rest of his life running away from.

His career had gone through many phases, and he had been a notably restless photographer. When Tom Hopkinson asked him if he planned to follow up the success of *Perspectives of Nudes*, Brandt replied:

Probably not. Once I've worked out a theme I very seldom go back. And in this case there's another reason – the terrible effect my distortions had on other people's work. For months afterwards I couldn't pick up a magazine without seeing distortions. The worst were the fashion pictures and advertising, in which there was often distortion for distortion's sake with no thought of composition.[12]

In photography, more than most other arts, any professional can make plausible copies of a distinctive style. Brandt feared being turned into a cliché, and worked almost desperately to avoid it. He had three means of keeping critics, imitators and image-makers at a distance: to change repeatedly his subject-matter, to withdraw into a shell where no one could follow him and, where these two failed, to promote a deeply deceptive account of his life and career.

There had been a number of articles on Brandt in photographic journals during the Fifties; Tom Hopkinson led the way in building Brandt's reputation, but all the critics were at least respectful.[13] Ansel Adams praised Brandt in *Photography*.[14] Younger photographers, such as Robert Frank, Diane Arbus and Duane Michals, were heavily influenced by Brandt. Frank took pictures of England in 1952 that were tributes to Brandt's Thirties work; Arbus moved Brandt's uncanny qualities into the realm of the grotesque. All this attention had the unfortunate result, for Brandt, of arousing curiosity about his personal history. The first biographical note seems to have been by Roméo Martinez in 1961, in his luxurious magazine *Caméra*:

Bill Brandt, 55 years old, the greatest contemporary British photographer, began his apprenticeship in a Swiss portrait studio. Around 1929/30 he went to Paris, lived there for some years and worked for a while with Man Ray. Back in London, where his work was much in demand by the major English reviews and magazines, he worked as a photo-journalist.[15]

When Brandt was in the sanatorium at Davos he may have hung around the photo shop that advertised 'everything the amateur wants'; but his apprenticeship in a portrait studio was undoubtedly with Kolliner in Vienna. Once he started to deceive, by erasing Vienna and Hamburg from the record, he was caught in the trap of having not just to repeat his lies, but also to embroider them. Fear of being challenged gradually became a mania with him. In England he must often have been asked where he was from, and managed to turn aside the question; but to appear in the public record under false colours was a more serious, and more dangerous, decision. Perhaps Brandt slipped into deception through being asked if he was connected to Willy Brandt, then a rising politician who became mayor of Berlin in 1957: when Bill was a child, 'Willy Brandt' was probably what his schoolmates called him.[16] His entry in *Who's Who* gave no place of birth, but said 'parents of Russian descent; British by birth'. The 1966 profile by David Bruxner in *The British Journal of Photography* said,

'Born … in London of partly Russian parents, he was brought up mainly in Germany'; an obituary would have him 'Born in south London … to prosperous parents of mixed Russian, German and English descent'.[17] Indeed, Brandt's father had been born in south London; and *his* father was listed on the birth certificate as a 'Russia Merchant' (not a Russian one!). Brandt's evasiveness even led some to suspect – wrongly, of course – that he was Jewish. He was indeed philo-semitic, but the closest he came to Judaism was taking pictures of orthodox Jews at prayer in his shelter series, and having Jewish nieces and nephews by way of Rolf's second marriage.

From at least the publication of *Perspective of Nudes* in 1961, Brandt could be considered famous; this made him uneasy, but there was no way for him to escape scrutiny. Unfortunately, he did not have the kind of temperament that might have allowed him to ration out information while preserving his essential privacy. His mystifications only whetted the appetite of those who wanted to make Brandt a monument of English photography, on a level with the great figures of the Continent and the United States. Critics like David Bruxner, for example, compared Brandt's early pictures to those of Cartier-Bresson:

> One may detect in these unposed photographs of people an affinity with the photographs of Cartier-Bresson who has since gained so many followers, but Brandt does not think that his own work was greatly influenced by his French contemporary.
>
> 'Perhaps I was influenced a little [Brandt replied]. I thought he was a very good photographer, but mine were not the same kind of pictures as his. He took and still takes anecdotal photographs, while I tried to take photographs that were symbolical of the time. I also set out to photograph London, whereas he never photographed a place systematically and never took pictures of people at home. He just walked around and snapped everything. I think I always thought more of Brassaï, who was much more varied. Brassaï photographed Paris more as I photographed London, although he concentrated on the architecture and hardly photographed the life of the upper classes.'[18]

Bruxner did not seem to realise how much planning had gone into Brandt's street scenes from the Thirties, so he saw just the superficial resemblance in *The Family of Man* between, say, Brandt's 'Lambeth Walk' and Cartier-Bresson's pictures. In April 1954 Cartier-Bresson had published his essay 'The Moment of Truth' in *Caméra*; point by point, this essay showed the fundamental incompatibility between his idea of photography and Brandt's. 'The elements which, together, can strike sparks out of a subject,' Cartier-Bresson wrote, 'are often scattered – either in terms of space or time – and bringing them together by force is "stage management", and, I feel, cheating.'[19] The French term for stage management is '*mise-en-scène*', and when questioned about this issue in an interview Brandt replied: 'My photos required what you call a "mise-en-scène". I don't reject the term, on the contrary.'[20]

The title of Cartier-Bresson's essay comes from the kill in bull-fighting: something alive is to be frozen in time by a sudden intervention, which cannot be planned in advance. 'Our task,' he said, 'is to perceive reality, almost simultaneously recording it in the sketchbook which is our camera. We must neither try to manipulate reality while we are shooting, nor must we manipulate the results in a darkroom.' Nor, in Cartier-Bresson's view, should the moment be modified by anything done after the shutter has fired:

> If you start cutting or cropping a good photograph, it means death to the geometrically correct interplay of proportions. Besides, it very rarely happens that a photograph which was feebly composed can be saved by reconstruction of its composition under the darkroom's enlarger; the integrity of vision is no longer there.[21]

Brandt, however, told his interviewer that 'he tried to make his pictures better by cropping'. To the question 'At what moment in your work is your creative gift most evident?' he replied, 'When I pull a proof in the darkroom (a very long operation).'[22]

Brandt told Bill Jay of meeting Cartier-Bresson at his Paris exhibition of 1966: 'He said to me "Of course we are on opposite sides." I laughed. I believe there are no rules in photography. A photographer is allowed to do anything, in order to improve his picture.'[23] Cartier-Bresson's aim was to capture the truth as it flies; before that moment the photographer should lie in wait, making himself as unobtrusive as possible.[24] Brandt's pictures could never be the product of a single moment: they began with his years studying composition in the great picture galleries; then came his visits to the site without a camera, the *mise-en-scène*, the exposure, the hours of work in the darkroom. Finally, as we have seen, especially with 'The Lambeth Walk', there was the after-life of a picture as a document of social history. But the two approaches to photography are so different that it is not really a question of choosing between them; great pictures have come from each camp, and the ideas behind them matter more to the photographers who took them than to the public who need only enjoy the results.

It was only with the publication of *Shadow of Light* in 1966 that a selection of Brandt's best pictures in all genres were gathered together in an impressive and accessible format. But from then on Brandt was acknowledged to be the dean of English photographers, as the full scope and richness of his work, over a span of nearly forty years, became clear. *Shadow of Light* (the title was Marjorie Beckett's idea) was published in England by the Bodley Head, in America by Viking and in France by Prisma.[25] That Cyril Connolly was commissioned to write the introduction was a good marker of Brandt's arrival as a cultural figure. Connolly's piece was marred by social complacency, and by his compulsion to puff himself up, flourishing his learning instead of truly paying attention to his subject. Nonetheless, he performed a service by placing Brandt so firmly as a *European* photographer:

> Soon after [the Paris of the Twenties] the main stream was to divide into what might be called the reflective school, the photographers who allowed the poetry to predominate and who used distortion and fragmentation like abstract painters, and the moment-of-truth school who concentrated on the historical view, of whom the leader was Cartier-Bresson. As violence increased so these went from strength to strength and violence sometimes caught up with them as

with the combat photographer Robert Capa.[26]

Connolly suggests 1942 as 'the date when Brandt decided definitely to remain a poet rather than a reporter'.[27] But we can see Connolly also turning his own experience of the Thirties into poetry, looking back at it with a touch of wistfulness: 'Brandt recorded all groups and grasped the fact that in a class-ridden society all groups could still be happy – the middle classes through their possessions, the workers through their capacity for enjoyment.' This verges on the sentimentality of *The Family of Man* project; yet Connolly sensed that the critical stance of the Thirties was bound to transform itself, as society changed, into a softer view of the exemplary sights of the decade:

> We need to look at pictures like these to realise how classless we have now become, how the general gain in comfort, cleanliness and freedom from want has diminished a certain picturesque tenacity and resolute cheerfulness which made us, up to around nineteen-fifty, a nation of cruder, warmer, shabbier individuals. One day the first half of the twentieth century will seem as different, sociologically, as the first half of the nineteenth does from the second, as Dickens and Thackeray do from Yeats and Wilde.

Crucial to that transition, and coming just at mid-century, was the arrival of the television age. It destroyed, with amazing speed and completeness, social structures that Brandt had documented so lovingly, on the street or in Charlie Brown's pub. The decline or death of illustrated magazines in both Britain and the United States was not just the result of competition for advertising from commercial television. Television modified the entire visual environment: the rhythm of seeing and the expectations of visual stimulation shifted into a higher gear. Black-and-white still photography could not hold the attention of eyes attuned to the new medium; it was pushed out of the mass media, into a suburb of the city of art.[28] Connolly's introduction to *Shadow of Light* argued that, even in his photo-journalism, Brandt had been fundamentally an artist.

Brandt's ties to the world of art had always been close: through his painting in the sanatorium, his finding inspiration in art galleries, his many portraits of artists and sculptors. Around 1968, he decided to become a practising artist himself. Man Ray had always combined the two careers; Brassaï and Cartier-Bresson had trained as artists, and Cartier-Bresson has returned to painting in his old age. Brandt's chosen medium was three-dimensional assemblages that he called collages. They were not made by building up flat layers, like Cubist collages, but by gluing found objects to a painted board, then enclosing the whole in a shallow perspex box. Twenty-one of these assemblages were exhibited in London in 1974, and Brandt was furious that the art establishment did not take his work seriously.[29] Yet he kept making assemblages for the rest of his life. During the portion of the year that he spent in France, they became the only artistic work that he did.

Whatever the success of the assemblages as art works, their first importance is as products of the eye of a great photographer. They may have attracted Brandt as a way to experiment freely, whereas if he had turned to painting he would always be in the shadow of the masters he had photographed – Braque, Picasso, Miró, and the rest.

Two of Brandt's passions came together in the assemblages: his love of Victorian knick-knacks, and his fascination with the sea-wrack on his favourite beaches.[30] Rolf Brandt's second wife, Joyce, was an antique dealer who helped Brandt find pieces, especially fish-shaped artefacts. Victorian bell-jars, wreaths, hair-lockets, shell boxes, alabaster hands were things Brandt cherished; many people would find them sinister, but Brandt seems to have relished their associations with death and dismemberment. The assemblages used the sort of objects that could be gathered at the tide-line: weathered wood or pebbles, bits of toys, carcasses of birds. Peter Brandt observed, half-seriously, that being restricted to a fish diet gave Brandt lots of fish-skeletons for his collages. This work leaves two impressions: one is of a feathery lightness of texture – almost a wispiness – and the other is of a preoccupation with a world after death, what remains when spirit and flesh have withered. Yet the fastidiousness of Brandt's constructions also suggests an attempt to compensate for the horror of death by putting the evidence of it so carefully in order, and by insisting on the desiccation of all these bodily remnants.

At the end of the Sixties, Brandt received the kind of exhibition that matched the importance of the book *Shadow of Light* with recognition in the museum world. *Bill Brandt: Photographs* opened at the Museum of Modern Art, New York, on 16 September 1969; Brandt himself would not go to New York for the opening, fearful of intrusive questioning by journalists. The show then moved to the Hayward Gallery, London, on 30 April 1970, and for a year after that travelled to twelve provincial museums in Britain. The exhibit included 123 prints, chosen by the American critic John Szarkowski. This was the first photography show in Britain to be sponsored by the Arts Council, and Brandt was the obvious choice to convince a general audience that photography deserved respect as an art (even if that respect came later in Britain than in most other countries). The show was also the occasion for tributes to Brandt from other masters, such as Walker Evans and Robert Frank.[31] Taken with earlier testimonials by Cartier-Bresson, Doisneau, Adams, Renger-Patzsch and others, Brandt was both the leading British photographer and someone with the special status of a 'photographer's photographer'.[32]

Brandt's only rival in Britain was Cecil Beaton, who certainly had greater commercial and social success than Brandt but, perhaps for that reason, was not taken so seriously by the critics.[33] Beaton recalled that during the Thirties and Forties he and Brandt had sometimes photographed the same events. At that time, Beaton had no hesitation about placing himself at centre stage, and he saw Brandt as a retiring and even a negligible presence. By the Seventies, Beaton was saying to Gail Buckland, 'How wrong I was [in my judgement of Brandt].' When the two men had a long session of reminiscence in the spring of 1973, Beaton said directly to Brandt, 'I consider you the greatest living English photographer.' He left with Buckland and, as they got into the hired car, Beaton suddenly said to her, 'I apologise to you and all your people.' This was a gesture of repentance for his anti-semitic prejudices during the Thirties. That he chose that moment to apologise makes one wonder if Beaton, like many others, had jumped to the conclusion that Brandt was Jewish and, because of that, thought less of him.[34]

Noya Brandt, about 1972

Brandt was sixty-five when his show opened at the Museum of Modern Art. Given his fragile health – he had now been diabetic for nearly twenty years – he might look forward to further honours and a peaceful semi-retirement, musing on his balcony in Vence. He was less inclined than ever to go out into society, but could be very generous to those he thought worth helping. Gail Buckland was a nineteen-year-old American exchange student in 1968; she got Brandt's number from the phone book and said to him, 'I'm a young photographer, will you look at my work?' He invited her down from Manchester and spent hours discussing her pictures and explaining how his own had been taken. A year later, Derry Moore contacted Brandt and asked if he could be his assistant (as Brandt had approached Man Ray forty years before).[1] Brandt declined, but offered to give Moore lessons; he also looked at the work of a Chilean photographer in London, Marco de Valdivia, and became friendly with him.[2] Moore bought a Supreme Wide Angle Hasselblad at Brandt's insistence, accompanied him to portrait sessions and took nudes under his direction.[3] Brandt struck Moore as 'the most fastidious man he ever met', with a melancholy temperament lightened by a wonderful sense of humour. Portraits should be taken in the subject's environment, Brandt told him; and nowhere else.

In Brandt's private life, his father's death created a new equilibrium in his circle. Eva was now comfortably off financially, and her marriage to Sandor Rakos 'brought her back to life' after her fifteen years of pining for the loss of Bill.[4] Rakos, a hearty and generous man, wanted Eva and Bill to be reconciled; and this seemed possible on the basis that a square – with two couples facing each other – was an intrinsically more stable configuration than a triangle. Relations did become more friendly for a while; but Eva could not give up her hero-worshipping attitude to Brandt, while he could not set aside his need to enjoy the devotion of two women at once. Only two of the four – Eva and Bill – were really satisfied, while both Sandor and Marjorie felt jealous that their spouses had such an intense outside attachment. So Eva's marriage did not really cure the tensions of the Brandt/Eva/Marjorie triangle; it just created new tensions around Sandor's presence in the group. And Eva, like Brandt, always felt the pull of her friends from Vienna: every Saturday in the Sixties and Seventies she would meet up in Belsize Park with Ester Cotton and Rolf Brandt to gossip about old times and new developments. Bill also came whenever he could manage it and the four of them, all living with someone else, made up a kind of permanent conspiracy – even if it was not a conspiracy to do anything in particular.

In a characteristic evasion of commitment, Bill had divorced Eva when their marriage failed in 1948, but then refused the second step of marrying Marjorie (she contributed the notes to *Shadow of Light* as Marjorie Beckett).[5] This left him in limbo between the two women, even if Marjorie held the stronger cards. By the end of the Sixties, however, her health was failing. Derry Moore found her quite frail when he first met Brandt in 1970. Streptomycin had brought her TB under control for some twenty years, but it could not repair all the early damage, and Marjorie was left with only one functioning lung. It was not until 1971, though, that Brandt finally agreed to marry Marjorie and gave her his name, when it became clear that she was dying of lung cancer. She spent the last months of her life in France, and Eva travelled down to Nice to see her, just a few days before she died. The visit closed a circle that had begun thirty-three years before when they were TB patients together. Eva had been thirty-one then, and Marjorie twenty-nine; they had lived together with Bill for ten years, then gone through two decades of alienation. In another hospital, at Nice, they were now reconciled. The impetus must have come from Marjorie, because Eva always wanted to be close to Bill at all costs, even if the price was acceptance of another woman in his life. For Marjorie the need was to be absolved from her guilt over displacing Eva in 1948. She, Eva and Bill were all tenacious of their pasts: little was ever left behind, so that for Marjorie and Eva to exchange forgiveness was also a way of preserving the memory of their early days together at Hillfield Court.

Derry Moore came to Vence to work with Brandt in the spring of 1971, and was told that he could not see him because Marjorie was so ill. Moore bought 'masses of flowers' and took them to the Hôpital Pasteur in Nice, where Marjorie was staying in a little bungalow in the grounds. He was not allowed to see her, but Brandt told him later that the flowers arrived at the exact moment she died on 8 April – 'a Surrealist scene', in Moore's words. Marjorie was sixty-two, and had lived with Brandt for thirty-two years. His English marriage was over, and he faced a new life, one hard to imagine without Marjorie's endless devotion to buoy him up.

Brandt's friends and family gathered for Marjorie's burial in the cemetery at Vence, then considered how best to look after him. He was sixty-seven years old, an unstable insulin-dependent diabetic and psychologically fragile. Rolf thought he should go to a convalescent home, a suggestion that horrified Eva – though, now that she was married to Rakos, she was not in any position to look after Brandt herself. In any case, her own health was not strong enough to provide the twenty-four-hour supervision that Brandt needed. It was finally agreed that he should go back to London, and Marjorie's younger sister Barbara offered to drive him. She was quite a different personality from Marjorie, practical and horsey rather than conventionally feminine. Regardless, Brandt proposed to her along the way. Barbara had always been fond of him, he was in a highly vulnerable state, and he saw her as the most comforting person to help him survive his loss. She gently refused, but did agree to look after Brandt until he got settled: she came to stay at Airlie Gardens as a platonic companion, and Brandt paid her a salary for her help. She was a soothing presence, and every evening they decorously went out to a restaurant together.

Keeping Brandt stable, which Marjorie had managed for so long, turned out to be no small task. Barbara found herself having to wake him every morning at four to check his sugar levels; if anything went wrong, she might find him unconscious. When Brandt went to stay overnight with Eva, to give Barbara a rest, Eva would get up not once in the night, but twice. Eva's own health was not up to the strain, and finally Rakos put his foot down and said Brandt could not come to stay any more. Barbara also was becoming impatient and wanted to get on with her life (she later married). She took Brandt down to her bungalow in Sussex and left him there for the weekend while she went off to visit friends. Brandt was cold and frightened by being left alone, even for a day or two – understandably, since he could so easily slip into a coma. The only solution was to hire a professional nurse-housekeeper, and a Mrs Eve Goldstein took on the job. She had previously been married to the Hungarian playboy Count Zichy, and seems to have kept a fondness for Hungarians since she found Sandor Rakos highly attractive. Eve had gone to school at Roedean and came into the household as a social equal. Brandt complained that she was 'brassy and vulgar', with a 'tarty' taste in interior decoration.[6] But by the summer of 1972, a year after Marjorie's death, he was completely dependent on her for his daily routine.

In the early summer of 1972 Noya Kernot was told by an acquaintance that 'an artist was looking for somebody to look after him'. Noya was fifty-six years old, an elegant woman with a background that Brandt was sure to find intriguing. She had been born Dorothy Anne Lezlover in Heliopolis, Egypt; her parents, Ivan and Rosine, were originally from Odessa. Ivan was a ship's chandler, who served in a camel corps of the British Army during the war. Noya was strictly educated at French convents in Egypt, a proper child who always wore white gloves. She married a British civil servant called Kernot with whom she had two sons, Peter and Cecil. When she met Brandt, Noya had been divorced for many years. There had been enough money to send one of her sons to Cambridge, but her life had often been difficult and insecure. She had been brought up to marry and have children, not to take her chances in the world of work.

Noya went to Airlie Gardens to meet Brandt and Barbara Beckett. He was dissatisfied with Eve Goldstein, and immediately charmed by Noya. With his legend that the Brandts were more a Russian than a German family, he was delighted with Noya's pleasing accent and manners. In fact, she didn't speak Russian, because her parents only spoke it to each other. Her childhood languages were English, French and Italian. But Brandt wasn't paying much attention to Noya as a person with her own history and concerns. Ill, lonely and afraid of the future, he was looking for a saviour. Brandt spun a web of fantasy around Noya, as he always did with the women in his life. Though she responded to his excitement, she kept her feet on the ground and saw the problems involved in looking after someone in Brandt's condition. She had wanted to be a companion rather than a nurse or housekeeper, but Brandt's needs went far beyond mere company.

In his first letter to Noya, Brandt signed himself 'Love, Billy'.[7] He persuaded her to come and stay at Airlie Gardens for the month of July; at the end of the visit, when Noya went off to stay with friends at Eze, on the far side of Nice, he was completely in love: 'I shall have to live on Valium until I hear from you. Sweet Noya darling please write at once. Billy.'[8] Brandt had been going out occasionally with a woman who worked in publishing, and who wanted to pursue the relationship; but once Noya appeared, he dropped her. He half-realised, at the same time, that in his relation to Noya he was being carried away by his own imagination. 'Everything about you is so mysterious,' he wrote to her, '. . . you are sometimes a little too mysterious even for me, though Eva says that's what I like.'[9] Brandt had a highly suspicious temperament but, like many suspicious people, he also tended to idealise those who took his fancy. A stranger might appear either threatening or wonderful, without much reason for either judgement. On closer acquaintance, too, his feelings might be reversed. Another of his fantasies, already obvious in his proposal to Barbara Beckett, was the belief that life could repeat itself. After Lyena Dodge visited him from New York, in August, this was his report to Noya:

> when I showed her your photograph she said 'how pretty, she looks so much like Marjorie.'
>
> Sweetest Noya, can you understand how excited I was when you first came to see me – I had secretly always been hoping for another Marjorie ... I don't know how often Barbara told me 'you will never find another Marjorie. Why don't you just take anybody.'[10]

Not only Lyena, but Eva too was drawn into Brandt's fantasy. When Noya came to stay at Airlie Gardens, Brandt went off at the end of the week to have Sunday lunch with Eva and Sandor Rakos at Fellows Road. 'I told Eva,' he reported, 'that these had been the happiest four days of my life.' And I remember how she laughed and said "Oh Billy, I know you would come out with such a marvellous statement."'[11] Barbara Beckett had tried to get Brandt to see things in a sensible way; but Eva's and Lyena's hero-worshipping attitude only encouraged him to plunge in more deeply. Eva also wrote to Noya directly, to welcome her into the magic circle of Brandt-worshippers:

> Darling Noya,
> Having met you only once I suppose it's rather absurd to address you like this, but your sweet letter, and Billy's long one about you, makes one feel quite extravagantly affectionate.[12]

On the face of it, this was a warm and generous gesture by Eva; unfortunately, her habit was to make up to Billy's women in order to safeguard her own place – as close to him as possible. This meant that anyone who married Billy would find herself in a crowd of three.

In September 1972 Brandt set off for his apartment at Vence as usual, this time with Eve Goldstein to look after him. Noya, staying again at Eze, was writing affectionately; but she was certainly not infatuated in the way Brandt was. Having made a life of her own, in London and France, she was far from sure that it would be wise to give it up; and she had misgivings about taking responsibility for someone in such frail health, and so emotionally demanding. At Eze, she was also looking after her eleven-year-old grandson, John-Paul Kernot. His parents had divorced when he was a year old, and Noya had taken the place of the mother he had not seen since the divorce. Brandt came over to Eze to press his suit, and finally they all returned to London: Brandt and Eve Goldstein, Noya and John-Paul. What Brandt wanted was to give Eve notice and have Noya take her place; by this time he was exasperated with Eve, especially because she accused Noya of deliberately losing a bracelet so that Brandt would buy her another one.

In London, Noya was persuaded to take over at Airlie Gardens, on the understanding that John-Paul would come there for his school holidays. Eve's parting shot was 'you'll be carrying a very heavy cross'. Noya observed to Frances Rice that Marjorie must have been an angel to do so much for Brandt; Frances replied, 'She was a martyr.'[13] Angel or martyr, Brandt needed a woman to provide what, given his background and temperament, he had never been able to provide for himself. Noya wavered about stepping into the role, but finally agreed, and they were married on 21 December 1972 at the Chelsea Register Office. A few days before the ceremony, she asked Brandt if he had the ring, and found that he hadn't realised it was necessary. At Barcelona forty years before, when he married Eva, he had managed to lose the ring before the ceremony. He certainly wanted to marry Noya in 1972, but at some level, as Lyena put it, 'he was not the marrying kind'.[14] Or perhaps he just had a different idea of marriage. When he married Eva, Lyena was there as a witness; this time, it was Eva's turn to look on and sign the register.

So Brandt's third marriage was launched. It was happy enough at first, but with a budding conflict between Brandt's manic enthusiasm and Noya's misgivings. Brandt's circle of friends was happy to see him taken in hand by the very capable Noya, who made sure he was well turned out, wrote his letters, made his appointments, drove him everywhere and, above all, kept his diabetes under control. Brandt continued to take portraits, and to give lessons to Derry Moore and others. But in two areas the marriage had an unfortunate lack of common ground: Noya felt no sexual attraction to her new husband and, in her own words, she 'knew nothing about photography and was too old to learn'.[15] With two strong-willed personalities who had few shared interests, there was likely to be stormy weather ahead.

Another area of friction lay in Noya's concern that Brandt should husband his energy, faced with increasing demands on him by students, scholars and curators. From the outside, it might seem that his wife had put Brandt under guard; from Noya's perspective, Brandt was in constant danger of overtiring himself and slipping into insulin shock. Noya might see him continuing to nod his head and smile at a visitor, when she could tell from his eyes that he was having a reaction; people did not always realise that they had stayed too long. Sometimes Brandt just needed to take a couple of glucose tablets, but even if they were put into his hand he often just sat there and fiddled with them. Noya felt obliged to get up at four o'clock every morning to test Brandt's blood sugar, and his doctor warned her that her own health might fail under the strain. Diabetics often act recklessly or forgetfully in reaction against the constant burden of living with the disease, and such behaviour can be very difficult for their family and carers to cope with. In addition, impotence, irritability and depression would be common symptoms for someone with Brandt's condition. Both physically and psychologically, he could only go downhill.

John le Carré, 1974

One way for Noya to step into Marjorie's shoes was by helping Brandt with his portrait assignments. In 1974 she went with him to photograph John le Carré for the *New York Times* in Cornwall. The occasion was the publication of le Carré's *Tinker, Tailor, Soldier, Spy* (a very Brandtian title!). Le Carré's memories deserve to be quoted at length:

He came out to the cliff in Cornwall where we live … it is a completely barren piece of landscape. It's the wilderness. It's tremendously spectacular. And we stood out in the garden – I thought this must be the greatest photo opportunity a man could look for – and he peered around and said 'Certainly, ja, but a face like this with no trees, how can I photograph a face like this with no trees.' And I said, 'Well, we haven't got any trees, they were all cut down by impoverished labourers during the great slump' … And he said, 'Now you must find me trees, there is no good here. And with such a face.'

I drove him and the elegant lady he brought with him to Sancreed churchyard where I knew there were very sad yew trees.

First I had to look out of the yew tree and he didn't like it. Then I peered around it and he didn't like it. Then I think I looked over the top, and he was certainly happy.

And he had an old Rollei camera, and had very shaky hands and he was peering down into it. And I was thinking, how on earth can you take photographs when your hands tremble so much? And he was going 'Nah, nah don't make faces, no faces please.' And he wound himself up and as he did so his hands grew steady. And the camera was suddenly locked solid, and I should think he took three or four frames and that was it.

I wondered what baggage he brought to the table, what he was trying to achieve, and I was left with the impression that it was an inductive kind of photography where he had a preconditioned notion of the picture he wanted to take. He wanted a bit of gloom, a bit of enigma … and of course the gloomy yew tree, and the very stark lighting to which he exposed my face, getting those heavy shadows and the sad look … I think he came to confirm what he had in his mind and to take the photograph that underlined the existing image …

I've lived in Hamburg for a while and it used to be said that when British bombs were raining down, the Hamburg people said 'well thank God at least they are British bombs.' … So Brandt brought to England – I'm sure – a kind of sentimental attachment to Britain. And perhaps he also brought that romantic vision of 'ein perfect gentleman'. Which endures in German and indeed in French culture, long after the perfect gentleman has somewhat expired from the British scene.[16]

Motorcycle Girl, about 1977

As he entered his seventies, two years after marrying Noya, Brandt suffered from deepening fear, anxiety and depression. These troubles coincided with an artistic shift in the reproduction of his work; but it would be simplistic to understand his 'late' or 'dark' printing style as a direct result of his personal unhappiness. As his fame increased, Brandt's books had become rare and expensive; the first step in keeping his work available was to provide a new edition of *Shadow of Light*. This would be the definitive collection of the work by which he wanted to be remembered. He added several portraits from the Sixties, but only a handful of other pictures. All were studies of nature, such as a statuary garden near Paris that recalls Brandt's Scilly Isles pictures from thirty years before, and a *trompe l'oeil* butterfly in a bush at Taxo d'Aval, south of Perpignan.[1] Brandt also revised the layout, and removed the colour pictures he had included in 1966. But by far the most important change was in the way he wanted his pictures to look on the page. *Lilliput* and *Picture Post* were printed in photogravure, with brownish-sepia tones and soft and continuous textures.[2] The first editions of *Perspective of Nudes* (1963) and *Shadow of Light* (1966) had a similar patinated, sensuous quality. For the second edition of *Shadow of Light* in 1977 the publishers, Gordon Fraser, shifted to a more modern process, photolithography, on glossy rather than matt paper. Brandt saw an opportunity to give his work a more stark and melodramatic appearance. It is impossible to say whether he would have chosen this look for the books he published in the Thirties if it had been technically possible; but his earlier 'soft' style was the one on which he built his reputation.

John Parfitt, who supervised the printing of five of Brandt's later books by Westerham Press, found that in the late seventies Brandt wanted 'strong blacks' above all, and 'hated grey'.[3] He was willing to sacrifice shadow detail, sometimes completely, for 'weight of colour' – that is, intensity of black. At the other end of the spectrum, Brandt would apply blocking-out fluid to his negatives with a brush, to get areas of stark white.[4] However, Brandt arrived at this extreme look in stages, as one can see by looking at the printing history of 'A Snicket in Halifax'. The original *Lilliput* version (February 1948) shows window frames and even individual bricks on the façade of the warehouse at top left, and the background sky is clear. In the first edition of *Shadow of Light* (1966), the façade is much darker (though some window frames are still visible), and smoke now drifts from the top right corner of the building: Brandt has both darkened the print and brushed in the smoke.[5] The print for the second edition of *Shadow of Light* makes the warehouse no more than a black geometric shape against a darkening sky. In this version the smoke has been re-done, to make it look as if it is coming from the factory chimney on the facing page.[6]

John Parfitt developed great respect for Brandt in printing his later books, but found him 'a very difficult person to deal with – what he wanted sometimes wasn't in the picture'.[7] Strong blacks were everything, and the book was printed in two blacks, for long and short range (one picked up the details, one the highlights). When Brandt saw the first proofs of *Shadow of Light* he got very upset that they weren't dark enough, and took a taxi down to Westerham in Kent to remonstrate; he only calmed down when he saw the kinds of changes the press could make to meet his requirements. Once, Parfitt recalls, the proof sheets were double-printed by mistake; Brandt found them 'wonderful', with the blacks really 'standing up' from the page. He asked for the book to be printed like that, and was disappointed when told that the sheets would stick together! But the overwhelming impression that Brandt left on Parfitt was one of sheer meticulousness. Parfitt might spend an entire day with Brandt, as he took up to an hour to pass the proofs for one picture. When Gordon Fraser balked at the cost of doing another complete set of proofs, Brandt offered to pay for them himself. In his mind, evidently, the three major Gordon Fraser books, *Shadow of Light*, *Nudes* and *Portraits*, were his legacy: they allowed his major work to appear in the hard, contrasty style by which he wanted to be remembered.[8]

Against the idea that Brandt's dark prints in the 1970s were a direct result of his dark mood, it is important to remember that he had started to produce exhibition prints in this style in the early 1950s.[9] Prints with too much contrast did not reproduce well in the photogravure used for *Picture Post* and *Lilliput*, so Brandt was constrained by that in his photo-journalism work.[10] In his 1970 'Statement' he wrote, 'Photography is still a very new medium and everything is allowed and everything should be tried. And there are certainly no rules about the printing of a picture. Before 1951, I liked my prints dark and muddy. Now I prefer the very contrasting black-and-white effect. It looks crisper, more dramatic and very different from colour photographs.'[11] By this account, the later style did not arise from personal gloom, but rather from Brandt's having the chance to be more innovative after he left *Lilliput* and *Picture Post* in 1950.[12]

David Mellor reports that the change came after *The Family of Man* exhibition, when the Museum of Modern Art requested four Brandt prints and Edward Steichen rejected them as 'too grey'.[13] Nigel Warburton suggests that Brandt wanted to emphasise 'form at the expense of detail', but that he was also responding to a market imperative: 'With his growing stature and popularity among photographic collectors, he was now [in the 1970s] forced to define a style. It is with the harsh later style that he made his biggest impact on the art world … with this printing style … he declared himself a photographic artist.'[14] Yet it is not just a question of opposing the photograph as document to the photograph as an exercise in form. The photogravure version of a female torso in *Perspective of Nudes* is both warmly tactile and monumental; in the second edition of *Shadow of Light* the flesh has a smoky texture and we are much more aware of the sharp demarcations between elements of the composition.[15] Brandt himself had varying preferences, but remained sceptical about any single, definitive

A Snicket in Halifax,
1948 print

process of reproduction. Faithful to his beginnings in the Kolliner studio, he saw the negative as no more than a potential picture that could change drastically as he worked on it in the darkroom.

Beyond Brandt's personal preference for softer or harder prints there is, finally, the difference in social context that can make the 'same' picture into a different cultural object. In *Lilliput* and *Picture Post*, Brandt pictures might have appeared with other pictures on the page (sometimes by different photographers), with the text of accompanying articles or captions, with margins around the picture. From the late Seventies on, the pictures were seen in art books, usually one picture to a page, without captions and sometimes filling the entire page. During the war, Brandt pictures could be bought for one shilling in *Lilliput*, for 3d. or 4d. in *Picture Post*. They now belong in the more expensive realm of art-book publishing. In *Picture Post* Brandt was rarely even credited for his work. The presentation of photographers like Brassaï and Kertész, who started as photo-journalists, has gone through a similar transformation. The difference in social context between their earlier and later careers is at least as radical as their geographical migrations from one country to another.[16]

There is one body of work that belongs completely to the world of art: Brandt's late nudes of 1977-80. They were exhibited in Paris and at the Marlborough Gallery, New York, in 1980 and 1981, and were published as part of *Nudes 1945-1980*, a successor volume to *Perspective of Nudes*. These nudes are the most controversial part of all Brandt's work, and many of his friends and admirers wish they had never been published. Noya, Eva and Rolf all had their doubts about them, but didn't want to confront Brandt when he was so determined to press ahead with the pictures. Some of them surely harmed his reputation; yet, to a biographer, they open a window into Brandt's lifelong obsessions with suffering and constraint.

Brandt's major nudes had been taken between 1945 and 1960: in London, on the Sussex coast and in France. Once they were published in *Perspective of Nudes* (1961) he claimed that he would have nothing more to do with the genre, out of disgust with the way other photographers had turned his techniques into clichés. For seventeen years, therefore, most of the photography he did consisted of portraits. In 1977 the publication of the second edition of *Shadow of Light* seemed to give his career its final shape; he was seventy-three, and nothing very new or startling was to be expected. That he should suddenly take up nudes again, producing nearly fifty of them over the next three years, was one of the most surprising turns in Brandt's career.[17]

Though they were presented as art, these pictures have more in common with the *Lilliput* nudes of the late 1940s, where story-telling and fetishism are more important than the female form in itself. Brandt also went back to his practice in *Lilliput* of using props for shock effect.[18] Apart from his personal quirks and obsessions, Brandt's nudes also belong with a long misogynistic tradition in Western art: many others before him had shown faceless bodies or dismembered torsos.[19] The Surrealists, in particular, routinely indulged in sadistic fantasies about women. *Minotaure* published work of this kind by Georges Bataille, Balthus and his brother Pierre Klossowski (Peter Rose Pulham was one of the links between this group and Brandt). Surrealist photographers who created such images included Man Ray, Jacques-André Boiffard, Raoul Ubac and Hans Bellmer.[20] Many were more outrageous than anything done by Brandt. His late nudes are a revival of the Surrealist agenda he had promoted fifty years before. One aim was to disrupt everyday reality by throwing into it the erotic and antisocial female body. Another was to bring the unconscious world into view, in scenes that showed women not as they were, but as they might appear in dreams.

In the 1970s there were actual incidents of terror and chaos that could pass for Surrealist nightmares, and Brandt may have been influenced by them.[21] But why express that terror through bound and vulnerable female nudes? That Brandt made this the major project of the last decade of his life, suggests that he suffered from compulsions that he could not manage in any other way. In a letter to Noya before they were married, Brandt apologised for his anxious and obsessive behaviour:

> Please let's be happy, even in Vence. Don't make things difficult for me. You must remember that I really suffer from persecution mania. From your letters I seem to have discovered, Noya, that you suffer from the same mania. You misunderstand my letters so often …
>
> By the way your husband must have suffered from the same illness. His unjustified jealousy must have been a manifestation of a deep rooted persecution mania. Poor man.[22]

There is no reason to think, of course, that Noya and her first husband suffered from paranoia; rather, it was a symptom of Brandt's illness that he thought those around him had it too. Brandt was tormented by anxiety and suspicion in the Seventies,

A Snicket in Halifax, 1977 print

Bound Nude, 1977/80

worrying especially about the secrets of his German birth and his residence in Vienna. He used Valium regularly to keep his fears under control. But how did his distress connect with the artistic aims of his late nudes?

The 'Micheldever Nude' of 1948, taken at his parents' house in Hampshire, is an early example of an uncanny nude who inspires fear rather than desire. The model stretches out her hand like a ghost who is going to take you to some sinister place.[23] Thanks to the distortion of the deep-focus lens, the hand becomes an intrusive, threatening object; it suggests a link with Brandt's hobby of collecting Victorian alabaster hands. His armless torso of 1977 follows a similar picture by Man Ray, but also seems to be a counterpart to the Micheldever nude: one woman has a disproportionate, invasive hand, the other no hands at all.[24] Brandt's frequent use of the model's hair or arms to cover her face is less extreme than mutilation, but still a denial of the model's integrity. Sometimes this gives the freakish impression that the head has been rotated a half-turn, so that one simultaneously sees the back of the woman's head and the front of her body. This is an old playground joke, of course; but in these nudes the effect is more sinister, as if Brandt wants to show the sexualised torso, but not the face that goes with it.[25] In earlier nudes, pubic hair was either obscured or removed by re-touching, a standard feature of the art nude. Several of Brandt's late nudes show the pubic region full on, but fill it in to a deep, solid black – one critic suggests that this was done with a Magic Marker.[26] As with the covering of the face, this seems to be an obliteration, Brandt's desire to remove both face and genitals from the woman he sees in front of him.

Noya Brandt recalls that the models for these nudes were not professionals, but young women with some connection to the art world, or just in need of the £10 that Brandt paid per session. Noya disliked the whole project, understandably enough, and Derry Moore recalls that Brandt worried about upsetting her: once the model had left, he carefully replaced every piece of furniture in its exact previous position. Particularly disturbing was a young woman whom Noya remembered as 'very photogenic'. She was a motorcycle courier who arrived on her noisy machine and blithely dumped her clothes on the floor. Most of the more extreme pictures are of her: the armless torso, the woman touching her hand on a mirror, and the women gagged, sitting at a table wearing rubber gloves, and bound with twine.[27] Another rear-view seated nude seems innocuous enough, but an unpublished version has a huge toy spider on the towel next to her.[28]

That all these pictures should be of the same model suggests that her looks or personality provided a focus for Brandt's obsessions. The model for 'The Policeman's Daughter' played a similar role around 1945. The pictures of the 1977-80 model recall Brandt's story nudes for *Lilliput* in the late 1940s, combined, according to Derry Moore, with the influence of contemporary advertising photography. It is easy to imagine them being captioned 'Little Miss Muffett' for the nude with the spider, 'The Collector' for the hooded nude.[29] Brandt in these pictures seems to be toying with his audience: they are conventional nudes, up to a point, but also private stories.[30]

The nudes seem to express the accumulated neuroses of Brandt's life, going back all the way to childhood. At the same time, they are provocative examples of what feminist critics would denounce in the whole Western tradition of the female nude in art. The impulses behind these pictures are deeply conflicted: hostility towards women is combined with using women to convey Brandt's own feelings of victimisation. There is a mixture of projection – 'women are to blame for my suffering' – with identification, 'I am suffering in the same way as the women in my pictures.' Freud claimed that sadism and masochism always go together. In Brandt's images sometimes women are being frightened, sometimes they are frightening. There were misogynistic subtexts in Brandt's *Lilliput* nudes of the late 1940s, but in the late nudes this hostility is expressed in a much more open and extreme way. The pictures certainly form part of the psychic crisis that began with Marjorie's death in 1971 and continued until Brandt himself died in 1983. Yet they are also a typical provocation in the Surrealist style. As with all the Surrealists, it is impossible to say whether Brandt was deliberately exploiting images from the subconscious, or just releasing them.[31]

Noya and Bill Brandt, Cornel Lucas, 1982

The troublesome late nudes are all indoor pictures, from the secret part of Brandt's life that was haunted by dark forces of sickness and paranoia. At the same time, Brandt now enjoyed great respect and recognition as a public figure. Part of his status was the traditional English reward for durability, as he kept producing new work while his peers left the scene: Man Ray died in 1976, Lee Miller in 1977 and Cecil Beaton in 1980. Old rivalries faded, too, as the photographers of Brandt's generation now celebrated what they had in common: their contributions to the heroic age of modernist photography, on which the curtain had fallen at the time of Vietnam. At *The Land*, the Victoria and Albert Museum's exhibition of landscape photography in 1975, Brandt, Brassaï and Ansel Adams posed amiably together on a bench outside the museum, each pleased to be in the others' company. When Manuel Alvarez Bravo came over for a London show, he and Brandt got on famously and spent hours in conversation at Brandt's flat.[1]

In 1975 Barbara Lloyd made contact with Brandt through Norman Hall, who was her photography teacher. She was the daughter of Frank Lloyd, one of the founders of the Marlborough Gallery in London and New York. He was a Hungarian, born Franz Levai, who had lived in Vienna and fled to England shortly before the war. By the mid-Seventies, the Marlborough Gallery was the pre-eminent dealer in modern painting and sculpture. Barbara Lloyd became friendly with Brandt and arranged for him to be represented exclusively by Marlborough. He and Brassaï, who came to Marlborough at the same time, were the first photographers to be taken on by such a major gallery. Marlborough mounted Brandt shows in both New York and London in 1976.[2] Brandt's prices shot up, and he was kept busy supplying 200 or more prints for sale each year.[3]

Three young critics began to work closely with Brandt in the 1970s, bringing into view the magnitude of his achievement and some parts at least of his personal background. These were Mark Haworth-Booth, David Mellor and Ian Jeffrey.[4] Mellor and Jeffrey first met Brandt in 1973, when they were organising a show on British photography called *The Real Thing*. They were Young Turks who wanted to combat what they saw as an American agenda to make photography into one of the fine arts. As Mellor recalls, 'We went straight for dirty realism' – Victorian engineering photographs and the like.[5] A crucial part of their project was to 'rescue Brandt from Steichen': that is, to remove him from the sentimental and formalist agenda of *The*

Family of Man. The natural focus for Mellor and Jeffrey's re-evaluation would be Brandt's pictures of London slums and northern industrial towns; but a funny thing happened on their way to reclaiming Brandt for dirty realism. Talking to him at length (and to his friends and relatives), they came to understand the importance of Brandt's continental background, of psychoanalysis and Surrealism; and they learned how many of Brandt's 'documentary' pictures of the Thirties had been deliberately staged.[6]

As Mellor and Jeffrey studied Brandt's work, it revealed layer upon layer of motives and influences. Perhaps Brandt was neither a formalist nor a realist, but a successor to Pictorialism – at that time a discredited movement, damned for imitating studio painting and producing only kitsch. Most importantly, Brandt's career was now seen as possibly the most complex of any major photographer. The formalist nudes of the 1950s, for example, contrasted with the socially conscious documentary pictures of the Thirties; but even within such categories, Brandt was full of further contradictions. Is 'A Snicket in Halifax' a piece of social criticism, a study in urban forms or a Surrealist allegory (the answer also depends on whether one is looking at an early or late print of the picture)? If the Fifties nudes are in the spirit of high modernism, then why are they *preceded* by the 'postmodernist' Forties nudes, with their hidden narratives? Rather like James Joyce's strategy of stuffing his work with riddles to keep the scholars busy, Brandt's eclecticism and secretiveness have provoked endless commentary by historians of photography.

Mellor, Jeffrey and Haworth-Booth's dedication to Brandt produced a stream of books and exhibitions from the Seventies on. Haworth-Booth also encouraged Brandt to make the selection of photographers for the 1975 exhibition *The Land*.[7] Exhibitions of Brandt's own work followed: not just in England, but in the US, France, Germany, Sweden and Austria.[8] Yet in all this collaboration with Brandt, they could only touch obliquely on the main events of his life. It was understood that Brandt did not want interest in his work to extend to his private history, and that no one should challenge, for example, the way his entry in *Who's Who* blacked out his German and Austrian past. David Mellor recalls that Sarah Kent wrote a piece in *Time Out* that said Brandt was German; there was great concern to make sure he didn't see it, in case it provoked a nervous collapse. Brandt did see an article by Roy Strong in June 1982 that called him a 'mid-European intellectual', and this set off a fit of rage:

> I read your piece in *Creative Camera* & was surprised to see that you think I am a foreigner looking at the inhabitants of his adopted country. I am actually British by birth. My family comes from South London & I have no connections with mid-European intellectuals.[9]

Strong wrote back saying that he was hurt by Brandt's letter and had only followed the entry in *Who's Who* (of which he enclosed a copy). Brandt's draft reply was heavily scored through: 'I am terribly sorry to have hurt you by my letter. Please forgive me. It is just that I dislike being a mid-European intellectual … I don't know who wrote the entry in Who's Who. I did not.'[10]

Brandt's slip of the pen – 'being a mid-European intellectual' for 'being called a mid-European intellectual' – indicates precisely his problem: that his identity was too deeply rooted to be changed just by what was said about it, or known about it by outsiders. Further, Mellor and others were starting to talk to the key figures from Brandt's 'mid-European' background: Rolf Brandt and his ex-wife Ester Cotton, Eva Rakos and Lyena Dodge, who had all shared Brandt's formative years in Vienna. The influence of Man Ray in Paris, Brandt was willing to acknowledge, but not, in the same city, the equally important influence of Brassaï and Kertész (more 'mid-Europeans'!). Brandt was good friends with Brassaï and his wife Gilberte in Provence from the 1960s onward (where J. F. Lartigue and his wife Florette were also in their circle); but he remained secretive about his acquaintance with Brassaï in the early Thirties.[11] The more Mellor and Haworth-Booth kept delving into Brandt's background, the more they realised that he could not tolerate anything but a highly selective account of his life being published.

Another young admirer of Brandt was David Hockney, who in 1982 made a composite Polaroid of himself, Brandt and Noya. After Brandt's death, though, Hockney criticised Brandt's 'Top Withens'. He thought at first that the hillside in the foreground was lit by flash, since its brightness was inconsistent with the cloudy sky; later he realised that it had been patched together from two different exposures. Hockney, who had grown up a few miles from Haworth, denounced the picture as virtually a fake:

> There's nothing wrong with collage at all, but it should be quite clear that one thing is stuck on top of another. This photograph was not like that and so people would assume that it had been made from a single image. When you can tell that the sky is from another day and yet you pretend that it's not, then I think you can talk about Stalinist photography.[12]

The best justification for what Brandt did – in all his landscape photography, really – can be found in Wordsworth's 'Elegiac Stanzas'. Brandt, with his wide reading in English literature, probably knew the verses:

> Ah! *then*, if mine had been the Painter's hand,
> To express what then I saw; and add the gleam,
> The light that never was, on sea or land,
> The consecration, and the Poet's dream;

Behind the brute reality of a landscape lay the potential for a higher truth. Brandt was seeking to express the romantic essence of Top Withens, which had inspired Emily Brontë in *Wuthering Heights*. In this case, Hockney took a puritanical view of photography that Brandt never felt himself bound by; the picture of Top Withens may be 'unnatural', but it works. Given his lifelong affinity with the world of art, it was fitting that Brandt should receive an honorary degree in 1977 from the Royal College of Art.[13]

Despite Brandt's invalidism in the 1970s, his productivity as a portraitist continued to be remarkable. In 1980 alone he produced nineteen portraits – as always,

Top Withens, 1945

placing his subjects in a setting that showed how they had chosen to live.[14] Unlike the fashionable head-on style of portraiture in the Seventies and Eighties, in which the celebrity's face is typically the only object of interest, Brandt's portraits showed an interplay between three elements: the 'props' of the sitter's habitat, the perspective of the shot (usually with some Surrealist oddness about it) and a melancholy or haunted inwardness of expression. No one in his portraits, it would seem, looks like a *happy* person. That might make Samuel Beckett an ideal subject (and Cecil Beaton had called Brandt 'the Samuel Beckett of photographers'). But Brandt's commission in 1979 to do a portrait of him led to a somewhat comical clash of wills.[15] Brandt wanted to take the picture in Beckett's Paris apartment, but Beckett resolutely barred the door to strangers. In any case, Beckett said he preferred to be taken against a plain background – which Brandt scorned as a 'passport photo'. Then Brandt suggested posing Beckett against the grim wall of the Santé prison on boulevard Arago (which Brassaï had photographed for *Paris de Nuit*). Beckett loathed the prison: he could see into its cells from his apartment, and even hear the despairing cries of its inmates. Both men stood by their own ideas, and the portrait was never taken.

Roy Strong was more co-operative. His diary describes Brandt's visit to his house in Herefordshire in 1980:

> Bill Brandt came to photograph me. At 12.30 p.m. they arrived with Mrs B at the wheel. He is an old man with wispy white hair and marvellous eyes. I opened the car door. 'Oh' he said, 'I've lost two buttons from my overcoat.' I said, 'That doesn't matter. Do you want to take the photo before or after lunch?' 'Now', he replied and paced round the exterior of the house. I walked him to a garden vista. No good. Then he alighted en passant on the embowered bay window in the hall. It was curious. The camera stuck. The plug at the end of a light bulb in a metal helmet was old-fashioned and only fitted into the chandelier. He also had no camera to fall back on and both film and camera rattled around loose in an attaché case. She stood by and held the primitive light under his direction. He snapped and it didn't work and he couldn't understand why. It took ages. It was surreal …
>
> In the end reel after reel of film was taken and the result is me placed off centre to the right against a clambering climbing network of geraniums with a curtain acting as a strong vertical to the left. Day light perforates through the window forming a lacy aureole around my head. The artificial light has been made to fall on the right side of my face casting heavy black shadows from my nose and losing virtually the whole of the left side of the face. No attempt has been made to avoid the bounding light or shadows cast by my glasses. The overall image is soft focus but no one could argue that Brandt ever uses this device to flatter as Cecil Beaton would have done. The image is posed but not arranged, as again was the essence of Beaton. I don't know but I suspect that he had decided long before what he was after and what he wanted to say. And the sitter is the last person to comment on the result.[16]

From Strong's memoir, we can guess at the strain on Brandt in taking so many pictures on location when he was past seventy-five, and how his lighting and focus might sometimes be out of kilter. But Brandt's style had never relied on technical virtuosity to get a distinctive result. Moreover, his apparently aimless fiddling around had always been part of his strategy in taking portraits, so that ideally the subject did not even realise that the crucial shot had already been taken. Brandt's late portraits are an amazing gallery of creative individuals; with time, they are also becoming a precious record of what English intellectuals looked like in the later twentieth century. They show, finally, how, in spite of sickness and personal unhappiness, Brandt could continue to be a witness to Englishness some fifty years after he had first stepped off the Channel ferry.

Portraits was the last book published in Brandt's lifetime, in 1982. It contained six pictures, from 1981, that were nearly the last of his career. Two of them, of Michael Tippett and Harold Pinter, were repeat sittings; Brandt could show, through them, both the continuity of personality and the results of age.[17] The publication of his book of portraits coincided with their exhibition at the National Portrait Gallery from May to August. However, the review by Roy Strong in *Creative Camera* set off the nervous crisis over his status as a 'mid-European intellectual'.[18] In March 1982, Brandt was honoured with a show at the Israel Museum, which had been arranged by his friend and admirer Dorothy Bohm. He was not well enough to go, though he was pleased with recognition by the Jewish state, as part of his lifelong quarrel with Germany. The final show of his lifetime was the collective *Atelier Man Ray* at the Pompidou Centre in December 1982, re-uniting the work of Brandt, Berenice Abbott, Jacques-André Boiffard and Lee Miller.

In marrying Noya, Brandt also took her ten-year-old grandson, John-Paul Kernot, into his family. Brandt encouraged John-Paul to read L. P. Hartley, and their relationship brings to mind the friendship between the twelve-year-old boy who narrates *The Go-Between*, and Lord Trimingham.[19] At first, Brandt doted on John-Paul, and perhaps saw him as an ally with whom to indulge his love of intrigue. To John-Paul, Brandt seemed 'the perfect British gent', someone who read the *Daily Telegraph* and was a staunch supporter of Mrs Thatcher. Brandt liked to read the mainstream English authors: in addition to Hartley, his favourites were George Orwell, Graham Greene, Anthony Powell, C. P. Snow, Iris Murdoch and Lawrence Durrell (he took portraits of all of these except Orwell and Snow). He had no TV, but liked going to films, preferably by himself.

Brandt was proud of John-Paul going to Eton and liked to dress up for parental days there. 'In a nice way,' John-Paul recalls, 'he was a bit of a snob.'[20] His photography in the Thirties had satirised the upper class, but also showed fascination with their rituals; and he had, of course, dressed for dinner and the opera like the rest of his English relatives. When he went to Eton in the Seventies, one imagines Brandt both pleased to be there and conscious of himself as an artist and masquerader. The Brandt who was impressed, on meeting Noya, to hear that she had a son at Trinity College, Cambridge, was also the Brandt who told John-Paul that 'people in the City were all crooks'. This was a statement with various barbs on it: that his brother Walther had gone into the City and become rich, which Bill and Rolf had not; that artists were superior to money-grubbers; that there were cheats and conspiracies that most people never knew about. Perhaps the only vicious picture that Brandt took was his reptilian portrait of John Paul Getty.

John-Paul found Brandt 'childlike – he loved an air of mystery or strangeness'. His darkroom was a mystery in itself, and John-Paul only managed to see inside it once. It had an enormous, old-fashioned Kodak enlarger, eight feet tall. Brandt was always anxious about it, since replacement bulbs were no longer made. He could have afforded to have an assistant, but insisted on doing everything himself, including mixing his own chemicals with tap water. The results were predictably erratic: spotted or uneven negatives, blurred prints, amateurish re-touching. John-Paul had to beg to go with Brandt on an assignment, and was finally taken to the Lartigue portrait in France in 1974.[21] Seven years later, at a time when John-Paul's ambition was to become a film director, he was allowed to come to John Schlesinger's house for a portrait session, though 'only if you stay out of the way'. Brandt ran off three rolls in his Hasselblad in half an hour, and it looked to John-Paul as if the session couldn't produce anything worthwhile; but it did. These were almost the last pictures Brandt took.

When John-Paul had the schoolboy ambition of becoming an architect, Brandt was delighted and eager to help him get started. Later in the Seventies, though, relations between them became strained. As his health declined, Brandt became very depressed; John-Paul remembers days when Brandt said he was 'bloody low', and had lost confidence in the value of his work as a photographer. He would sit for hours staring out of the window, or retreat into his studio and shut the door.[22] John-Paul became argumentative as an adolescent, and there was a crisis when Brandt sent him out for an evening paper and then accused him of being a thief, because he had forgotten to return the change. Brandt had become suspicious of those around him, but hated any kind of rudeness or confrontation. His solution was to slip away to confide in trusted members of his old circle like Eva, Rolf or Frances Rice. They could be relied on to take his complaints at face value, but this inevitably made Noya more exasperated and suspicious in return. She once went looking for Brandt in Holland Park and saw Eva trying to hide behind a tree. It was a bitter pill that Brandt's ties to Eva seemed more important to him than his present marriage.

Brandt's unpredictability appears in a bizarre story by Martin Breese, who in the early 1970s was a professional photographer. He ordered a print of 'Top Withens' at a cost of £14, and asked Brandt if he could take his portrait when he came to Airlie Gardens to pick up the print. Brandt agreed, and Breese arrived at the flat with his Mamiyaflex, tripod and reflector. After two months, Brandt wrote to say he liked the portrait and wanted to use it for the 1975 exhibition, *The Land* at the V&A. Some years later, a family tragedy forced Breese to give up photography and find other employment. He contacted Brandt again and asked him if he would sign the 'Top Withens' print and a copy of *Shadow of Light*. Brandt invited him over, and when Breese arrived asked him, 'How is photography?' Breese replied that he had had to give it up. Brandt looked at him and said flatly, 'Get out of my house.' Breese had to flee, with no chance of explaining himself.[23]

Brandt's reclusiveness was surely his own preference, rather than Noya's keeping people away from him. Few of the many who did try to visit were admitted, except for the students from the Royal College of Art whose work he had agreed to look at.

Anyone who wanted to interview Brandt had to be checked for hidden tape-recorders (perhaps because of his phobia about his German accent). Brandt was much more relaxed in France, where David and Peggy Godfrey got along well with him by taking him on his own terms. They rented the flat next to the Brandts at the Résidences Séréna in Vence, and arrived on a cold and miserable evening in October 1982. Brandt immediately made them welcome and helped them to settle in, though he was evidently quite frail and ill. David Godfrey was an amateur photographer, and Brandt was happy to make suggestions (as he had done for Mr Fry, a neighbour of his at Hillfield Court). The Brandts and the Godfreys became friends. Brandt and Noya were living very quietly, seeing few people but enjoying going to their neighbours on Sunday nights to watch English television. Noya was meticulous about keeping Brandt's sugar levels stable, and the Godfreys would help by checking on him when Noya was out shopping. Brandt took them one day to see the megaliths he had photographed twenty years before at St-Barnabé; though, when they arrived, he was too weak to get out of the car. A sudden pea-souper fog came in, and they could only find their way back to the car by Brandt's constant blowing of the horn.

Both of the Godfreys had a background in British Intelligence, and it seems clear that one reason they got on well with Brandt was because they avoided unnecessary questions and accepted his reluctance to say anything about his past. At Vence, Brandt and Noya seem to have been secure and fundamentally in harmony. Their unhappy differences arose when they were in London, partly because of outside pressures that Brandt could not easily resist, partly because of the provocation of his work on the late nudes. Noya felt that she was 'walking on eggshells' in criticising the project, but the fact that Brandt was making such disturbing images was itself a sign of his inner crisis. There were problems also with money, on which Noya found it impossible to get straightforward answers from Brandt. She had an apartment in Chelsea of which she was very fond, but which she was not allowed to sub-let. She and Brandt went to stay there from time to time until the lease came up for renewal, when Noya let it expire. In the light of troubles to come, this was not a prudent move.

In 1981 Brandt went on a last journey to Normandy, with Rolf and his daughter Judith. Brandt took a picture of Judith's clasped hands on the beach near Dieppe, like the one he had taken of Marjorie's hands thirty years before. The trip was a brief escape from troubles at home. Brandt's memory had been failing for some years and he had difficulty in grasping business matters, especially when his blood sugar was low. This was good reason for Noya to be present when he had to meet outsiders; but his old friends resented what they saw as Noya's control over his everyday life. About a year before his death, Brandt took drastic action. He and Noya had mirror-wills, in which whoever died first left the bulk of their estate to the survivor, but Brandt did not honour this agreement. His tangled web unravelled when he died. The conflicts present in the years leading up to his death intensified, when it was revealed that a series of comical and clandestine meetings had led him to change his will at the last minute. He created an ill advised and unworkable trust, opening a rift that took two years to resolve, after much family conflict and expense.[24] To secretly deprive Noya of a wife's rightful share in his estate was, for Brandt, a characteristic way to resolve a conflict that he could not deal with in any more direct manner. But he also needed the co-operation and encouragement of his circle of friends to do this as, in the usual dismal sequence, Noya's suspicions of her husband led him to practise more deception.

Stephen Dwoskin, a friend of Rolf Brandt's from the London College of Printing, arranged to make a documentary film of Brandt in the spring and summer of 1983. Part of the film was shot at Rolf's house, and part at Eva's on Fellows Road. Dwoskin recalls that some of the prints Brandt supplied for the film had little poems to Eva on the back, which he didn't want Noya to see.[25] Dwoskin was intrigued by Brandt's cavalier treatment of his prints: each one was different because he worked on them by hand, scratching at them or laying on photographer's white. He took some pictures of Dwoskin with his Hasselblad and the negatives came out very scratched; this did not bother Brandt, as he took it for granted that they could be fixed up by retouching. Dwoskin found Brandt like a little boy who enjoyed jokes and was fascinated by the mechanics of making a film; but he was also suspicious and fearful of going out. Sometimes there seemed to be a fine line between paranoia and liking to have people on: Brandt bought an old screen with photographs on it in the Portobello Road, then claimed that they were pictures of his family!

It seems fitting that Brandt's last dealings with the camera involved playing the part of himself in Dwoskin's dark and moody film, while a nude model wandered around his flat. He had an extended stay in hospital in 1982, and became very fragile. On 11 December 1983, he had a minor heart attack at Airlie Gardens and was taken to St Stephen's Hospital on the Fulham Road, a forbidding Victorian edifice.[26] He had always disliked hospitals, and was still plagued by the tensions between his wife of eleven years and those who had known him since Vienna. Noya was indignant to arrive one day and find Eva discussing Brandt's case with the doctors. Friends and relatives wanted to come to make their farewells, while Noya wanted to preserve Brandt's peace and keep away visitors who came without her permission. Rolf, his daughter Susan and Frances Rice were able to see him, at least. Even on his deathbed, Brandt was still withdrawn into his fortress, while outside others struggled to claim possession of him.

Noya kept a notebook during Brandt's last illness. 'For the past two years,' she wrote, '[Bill] deceived me regarding his movements when it was vital that I should know where he was just in case he was taken ill … But there were many times that he would feel remorse especially after a bad fall or severe reaction. When he would say Noya Noya you saved my life once again.'[27] In St Stephen's, lying in a gloomy public ward, he wanted to make peace in his marriage:

> 'I'm so sorry Noya. Put your hand in mine. I'm going to put a stop to all this anti Noya business.'
> I said, 'It's too late the damage has been done.'
> 'When I leave this awful place Noya Noya I'm going to change everything. Put your hand in mine, I'll do anything for you.'[28]

Brandt did not have the will power or the time to revise his will. He was hoping to go home for Christmas, but in the early morning of 20 December he died. There was a small, private funeral at Putney, followed by cremation. Brandt took with him the answers to the many riddles of his life, leaving us with no more than clues – and the open secret of his work.

Afterword

I came to Brandt in search of the Forties of my childhood, and of an England that had been obliterated by the great newness of the Sixties. For Brandt, the Sixties did not come as any kind of personal liberation; rather, they marked the collapse of the project he had worked on since he had come to England thirty years before. The publication of *Shadow of Light* in 1966 set the seal on his reputation; but 1966 was also the year of Antonioni's *Blow-Up*, a tribute to the new photographic scene of 'swinging London'. *Blow-Up* might have been scenes from the life of David Bailey, whom Antonioni asked to play himself in the film. Brandt's separation from such a life and the photography it produced may seem complete. But David Bailey had begun his career doing moody black-and-white street scenes in the Brandt idiom. These streets were in the East End where Bailey had grown up, and where he had been one of the ragamuffin street kids whom Brandt had enjoyed photographing in his *Picture Post* days. Bailey was happy to pay his debt to Brandt by coming to Campden Hill to take his portrait in 1967 and again in 1982.

Brandt was in partial eclipse from the late Sixties until his death, taking mostly portraits and excluded from the fashionable photo-journalism of the Sunday supplements. But it was better for him to make no move towards re-inventing himself for the frenetic pursuits of swinging London. The hippies who mobbed Stonehenge at the summer solstice were a universe away from Brandt's lonely symbol of a nation besieged, 'Stonehenge Under Snow'. Only after the Sixties scene had dissipated could one see clearly the foundations of Brandt's contribution to British photography, not to mention his influence on the cinema and even the novel.[1] Apart from his nudes and landscapes, the centre of gravity of his work lay in the Thirties, his formative years behind the camera. One side of his work drew on German Expressionist film (an obsession during his years in Davos and Vienna) and on the visual world of Surrealism. The other side belonged to British street photography and photo-journalism, full of the spirit of social protest. Brandt fused these borrowings into a style of his own.

Surrealism went in for shock effects: furry teacups, ink-stained nudes, uncanny dummies in shop windows. Brandt started out in Paris by taking pictures along similar lines. His temperament, though, was less destructive, without the Surrealist ambition to infect everyday life with irrationality. In his Paris days Brandt remained a milk-and-water Surrealist, taking pictures that were whimsical rather than explosive. Surrealism drew on a long French tradition of contempt for the bourgeoisie. Brandt was content to be thoroughly bourgeois in his personal life and sexual attachments, and had no agenda of disrupting the French social order. He had moved to Paris from Vienna out of affection for the French way of life – an affection that remained constant for fifty years – not because Paris was the rallying point for those who wanted to shock or defeat the bourgeoisie.

When Brandt moved to England in 1934 he became even more detached from the avant-garde. Long before he settled there, England had his profound loyalty; and in London, unlike Paris, he could share the comfortable life of his rich uncles. When Brandt used Surrealist techniques to represent English gestures, clothing or symbols, he was not aiming to mock or undermine them. Rather, it seemed that the English were amateur Surrealists already: why parody them, when they were already happy to parody themselves? Nor did Brandt sign on for the leftist onslaught against the British class system. His brother Rolf, who joined the Communist Party not long after arriving, would have liked to enlist Brandt too; but Brandt never joined anything in his life. His documentary pictures might look like standard social-protest photography, with their dark streets, dosshouses, and ragged children. These were the expected sights of the English 'dirty Thirties', but Brandt never delivered them in quite the expected way. He got results that no one else could reproduce.

Brandt died in London fifty years after Hitler came to power. That death was another marker in the dwindling away of the generation of 1930s émigrés, who had done so much for British intellectual and creative life. The arrival of the émigrés transplanted the culture of Weimar Germany on to British soil; for photography and film, that meant above all the dark mythologies of Expressionist cinema. Brandt could show London in a German light (or half-light) and be believed. Across the Atlantic, other émigrés helped to create the imaginary America of *film noir*. But such visions could not outlive their first makers, who had the actual experience of flight from a criminal state. Brandt might continue to inspire the dark style of representing England, but his special angle of vision no one could share.

Brandt was an unusual émigré in that he was free from the traditional afflictions of nostalgia and loss of roots. For him, there was no feeling of self-division. He never returned to Germany after 1933, and refused to speak his native language. The English public also took his adopted first name at face value and assumed that such definitive pictures of London had been taken by a cockney Bill. The thirty-odd years that he lived with Marjorie Beckett were further proof that he was wedded to England in the most literal sense. Yet Brandt's childlessness could be taken as a symbol of his failure to establish himself as a true native Englishman. With his inveterate wariness of social connection, later deepening into paranoia, he could never become the English gentleman he would have liked to be. And for all his protective coloration, the origins of his paranoia lay in his German youth. He could not be at home in England so long as his deepest needs and fears were still connected to Hamburg. He brought his neurosis with him to England in 1934 and it continued to possess him, in spite of his physical removal from the place that had spawned it.

By the time Brandt died it no longer mattered to English photography and film that Germans and Hungarians had revolutionised those arts, decades before. For most people, the visual world relevant to them was provided by Hollywood and by television. Black-and-white photography of Brandt's era now belonged to the coffee-table book and the museum. The women I spoke to in writing this biography, who had known Brandt in his youth, had the femininity of another era; how charming, but also how distant! Yet something can overcome that distance: the photographic image that instantly connects the woman in her eighties, who sits across from you, to the same woman laughing on a beach, sixty years before. Even ordinary photographs have a touch of this power, but it is the great photographers who can truly and fully summon up the past. This was George Santayana's case for the importance of photography:

> It happens that the body's memory is better than the mind's … The upper strata of the brain … would seem to be of an inconceivably subtle texture, and the thousand vibrations that constantly sweep through that gossamer web, tear and tangle the threads into a mesh, from which it is hard to pull out anything whole. Nothing can be repeated with exactness in the fancy, nothing accepted with literalness, nothing retained without accretion … The greater part of the experiences which fill a life are lost irretrievably … photography has come to help us in the weakest part of our endowment, to rescue from oblivion the most fleeting portion of our experience – the momentary vision, the irrevocable mental image.

Some things can be preserved by being taken out of their time altogether, such as Brandt's landscapes and formal nudes. But for most of his pictures, the time of their taking is of the essence; and they can deliver that time to us today. 'The real world,' Santayana says, 'and that natural beauty which photography reproduces have always been, are now, and ever will be the ultimate object of human interest.'[2] Still, not just any photographer can do this. Brandt's pictures of the Thirties arose from his special perspective: London as seen from Paris and Vienna. But as time did its sifting, they became everybody's Thirties, just as it is August Sander's Weimar that everyone now sees. Over and over again, the history of art shows how the extraordinary vision of a culture ends up being the typical one.

So it is that Brandt and Cecil Beaton, born three months apart, divide between them the accepted image of England in the middle years of the twentieth century. No other photographers have been able to impose such comprehensive views of English life, from the highest to the lowest. Once the public has become convinced that this is how some part of the past *should* look, the artist or photographer who made it look that way becomes an imperial eye. Paris in the Thirties has to be Brassaï, America in the Depression has to be Dorothea Lange or Walker Evans. There may be a kind of visual laziness in this, a slide towards the stereotype; but it pleases people to have this means of being transported into the past. In the ruthlessness of present time, the past becomes the slave of present purposes, reduced to the kind of past we want and need. Bill Brandt, with his great store of images, will surely continue to do England that service.

Notes

Introduction

1   Ester Cotton, interview with Aysha Rafaele.

2   *Hearing Secret Harmonies* (London: Heinemann, 1975), p. 84.

3   Hopkinson, radio interview, 1984.

4   Pierre Borhan (ed.), *André Kertész: His Life and Work* (Boston: Little, Brown, 1994), p. 43.

1 Roots

1   The danger would be from tuberculosis; but it was Bill who would fall victim to it, and in Hamburg.

2   After completing high school, young men of Brandt's class were sent for business training, which included working in various foreign countries. No one in Brandt's immediate family went to university.

3   *'Né en 1904 à Londres, de parents d'origine russe'*: exhibition catalogue, Galerie Municipale de Toulouse, 1976.

4   Lübeck is only sixty kilometres from Hamburg, but its port lies on the Baltic rather than the North Sea.

5   Eric Amburger, *Die Familie Brandt: Hamburg – Archangel – St Petersburg – London* (Groitzsch: G. Reichardt, 1937). There is a copy in the British Library.

6   Susan Brandt, interview with the author, March 1997.

7   He later anglicised his name to Walter.

8   Ester Cotton, interview with Aysha Rafaele.

9   Thomas Mann, 'Tristan', in *Death in Venice and Seven Other Stories* (New York: Vintage, 1954), p. 335.

10   Paul Roazen, *How Freud Worked: First-Hand Accounts of Patients* (Northvale, NJ: Jason Aronson, 1995), p. 223.

11   Freya von Moltke, interview with the author.

12   Ibid.

13   Freya von Moltke recalls a flirtation between her father and her mother's maid, which ended with the maid being sent home.

14   Susan Brandt, interview with the author.

15   See the discussion in David Mellor's seminal essay, 'Brandt's Phantasms', in Mark Haworth-Booth, *Bill Brandt Behind the Camera* (Oxford: Phaidon, 1995), pp. 71-97.

16   The country house was called Capenor, at Nutley. Pratt also kept a flat in Putney. Most of the famous Pratt pictures were taken at Capenor.

17   Though most of Brandt's pictures of Pratt were not published until later. There was one picture of her in *The English at Home* (1936), captioned 'Dinner is Served'; his photo-story on her, 'The Perfect Parlourmaid', appeared in *Picture Post* of 29 July 1939.

18   *Death in Venice*, p. 80. Ester Cotton suggested the resemblance between Brandt and Kröger.

19   In *A Night in London* Brandt did include pictures of his parents' visits to London in the late Thirties, but in public settings such as restaurants or the opera.

2 'Something Happened'

1   The uniforms are of high quality and must have been expensive. Walther has an Uhlan tunic; Willy and Rolf wear the imperial *Pickelhaube*, Augustus a field cap. I am indebted to Ralph Reiley for this information.

2   When Brandt was at the Bertram about 10-15 per cent of the pupils were Jewish; some of them attended the classes on Christian doctrine. The school was closed by the Nazis in 1939. See Andreas Hoffmann, *Schule und Akkulturation: Geschlechtsdifferente Erziehung von Knaben und Maedchen der Hamburger Judisch-liberalen Oberschicht 1848-1942* (Munster and New York: Waxmann, 2001).

3   Oswald Spengler, author of *The Decline of the West*, had been a student-teacher there before the war.

4   Ester Cotton, interview with the author.

5   Dennis Brandt, interview with the author.

6   The school was re-named in the Nazi period because of Hertz's origins: his father was a Jew who had converted to Christianity and married a Gentile. Hertz himself was buried in the Jewish cemetery at Hamburg.

7   Thomas Mann, *Buddenbrooks: The Decline of a Family*, tr. John E. Woods (New York: Knopf, 1993), pp. 536-7.

8   Noya Brandt, interview with the author.

9   On the right-wing *Freikorps*, see Klaus Theweleit, *Male Fantasies*, tr. Stephen Conway (Minneapolis: University of Minnesota Press, 1987). As a study in the pathology of sexuality and violence, this book may shed light on the mentality of Brandt's tormentors at school.

10   Ester Cotton, interview with Aysha Rafaele.

11   Brandt seems to have found Eton and Harrow merely quaint when he photographed them in the Thirties; later, he was proud that his step-grandson John-Paul Kernot was at Eton, and enjoyed visiting the school.

12   Ester Cotton, interview with the author.

13   While a patient at Davos, Brandt took elocution lessons in English; but for most people an accent is almost impossible to eliminate, unless they are immersed in a language before the age of twelve.

14   See Ian Jeffrey, *Bill Brandt: Photographs 1928-1983* (London: Thames & Hudson, 1993), and David Mellor's 'Brandt's Phantasms', in *Bill Brandt Behind the Camera*.

15   C. Paul Vincent, *The Politics of Hunger: The Allied Blockade of Germany, 1915-19* (Athens: Ohio University Press, 1985), p. 50.

16   Susan Brandt, interview with the author.

17   Thomas Bernhard, *Gathering Evidence* (New York: Knopf, 1985), p. 137.

3 Davos: The Iron Key

1   Agra was closed in 1967.

2   It is now believed that altitude has no discernible effect, positive or negative, on the progress of TB. In any case, Agra was twinned with another German institution, the high-altitude Wolfgang sanatorium in Davos, so that patients could be shuttled back and forth between them to get the benefits of first one altitude, then the other.

3   Tom Hopkinson, 'Bill Brandt – Photographer', *Creative Camera* 211 (July/August 1982), p. 600.

4   She was accompanied by 'Herr Augustus Brandt' – who could have been Brandt's eleven-year-old brother, but was most likely his uncle Augustus from London, his father's eldest brother. Augustus's nephew Hans Goverts had died at Davos in 1917, at the age of twenty-three.

5   Brehmer was a botany student who believed that his TB had been cured by a stay in the Himalayas.

6   The Swiss franc was about twenty-four to the pound in the early Twenties.

7   Before the First World War there had been 3,000 Russian patients at Davos, and they figure prominently in *The Magic Mountain*; after the revolution, however, only a handful remained.

8   See F. B. Smith, *The Retreat of Tuberculosis 1850-1950* (London: Croom Helm, 1988), pp. 99-101.

9   This was the routine in 1935 for the Sancellemoz sanatorium in France, where Brandt's first wife Eva was a patient: 7.15, rectal temperature; 7.30, body rub; 8.00, breakfast, one-hour rest; 9.30-10.30, gentle walking; 10.30-12.00, outdoor rest; 12.00, lunch; 1.30-4.00, absolute rest outdoors: horizontal, isolation, silence, no reading; 4.00, food; 4.30-5.30, chaise-longue outside; 5.30-7.00, walk or quiet conversation; 7.00, dinner; 8.30-9.30, chaise-longue outside; 9.30, bed, no reading.

10   Ernest Ward found that 54 per cent of stage-1 patients who stayed at home were cured after four years, compared with 31 per cent of those who stayed at sanatoria; for more advanced cases the cure rates were 10 and 7 per cent (Smith, p. 166). Surgical treatment of TB is discussed in Smith, pp. 139-47.

11   George Orwell was given a pneumothorax as late as 1948, though it did not prolong his life.

12   Smith, p. 167.

13   Thomas Mann, *The Magic Mountain*

(New York: Knopf, 1944), p. 4.

14   Roland Barthes, *The Grain of the Voice: Interviews 1962-1980*, tr. Linda Coverdale (New York: Hill & Wang, 1985), pp. 259-60.

15   From autumn 1924 on, *Der Querschnitt* ran a series of bitter and scatological poems by Hemingway, such as 'The Soul of Spain' and 'The Undefeated', a story about an ageing bull-fighter, illustrated with photographs. See David Mellor in *Bill Brandt Behind the Camera*, p. 89.

16   *The Magic Mountain*, pp. 198, 231.

17   Ibid., p. 417.

18   Quoted in Smith, p. 224.

19   *Lilliput*, February 1948.

20   Martin Gasser suggests that Brandt may have known the work in this style by Ernst Kirchner, the Expressionist artist and photographer who was living in Davos until shortly before Brandt's arrival. 'Bill Brandt in Switzerland and Austria: Shadows of Life', *History of Photography* 21, no. 4 (Winter 1997), p. 4.

21   Gasser, p. 5.

22   Eva Boros, *The Mermaids* (London: Rupert Hart-Davis, 1956), p. 53. The novel is set in the mid-Twenties in Budapest; Boros published it under her maiden name after she had divorced Brandt.

23   Karl Abraham, a prominent Freudian, collaborated with Pabst on the film, but Freud repudiated it.

24   *The Magic Mountain*, p. 654.

25   W. Stekel, *The Autobiography of Wilhelm Stekel* (New York: Liveright, 1950), p. 230. Stekel says that he completed *Zwang und Zweifel* ('Compulsion and Doubt') during his stay; Part One of this work appeared in 1927, Part Two in 1928.

26   *Autobiography*, pp. 92-3.

27   Gasser, p. 5.

28   Lyena Dodge, interview with the author. After the First World War, Davos had trouble keeping its beds occupied, thanks to the loss of its Russian customers and the general economic turmoil.

29   Brandt's name disappears from the weekly register of those staying at Davos after 6 May 1927. He was not registered as a resident in Vienna until 24 May, so it is possible that from Davos he went first to Hamburg, to gain his parents' support for the move to Vienna.

4 Vienna: The *Schwarzwaldkinder*

1   By the 1920s Stekel suffered from diabetes and other ailments.

2   The Waldhotel is now a private home, at Salmannsdorfer Str 92. In Vienna, 'Hotel' usually means any self-contained building that lets rooms; 'Pension' a hotel that occupies one floor of an apartment house.

3   At this time Freud was paid twenty US dollars an hour by his patients; Stekel's fees were probably around ten dollars an hour.

4   Quoted in Wilhelm Stekel, *Autobiography*, p. 283.

5   Wilhelm Stekel, *Sexual Aberrations: The Phenomena of Fetishism in Relation to Sex* (London: Vision Press, 1953), p. 332.

6   Ian Jeffrey, *Bill Brandt: Photographs 1928-1983*, p. 18.

7   *Sexual Aberrations*, p. 333.

8   Brandt arrived at Salmannsdorf on 24 May 1927, and left Vienna for a month-long holiday in Italy and Hamburg on 14 September; he must have broken with Stekel before then.

9   The German original of *Sexual Aberrations* was published in 1923 as *Sadismus und Masochismus: Für Ärzte und Kriminalogen Dargestellt* (Berlin: Urban & Schwarzenberg, 1925). Stekel also wrote on impotence, frigidity and homosexuality.

10   Lyena Dodge, interviews with the author, September 1995, April and December 1996.

11   Freud supposedly forbade his female patients to have sexual relations at the beginning of their analyses, and Stekel may have wanted Brandt to be celibate as part of his treatment. Paul Roazen, *How Freud Worked: First-Hand Accounts of Patients*, p. 109.

12   Savita Brandt, interview with the author, August 2002.

13   He went first to the Paedagogium Godesberg, then to the Deutschen Kolleg.

14   Rolf still had a strong interest in art, but for the moment this could be satisfied with work on costume and stage design.

15   The other two were Alma Mahler-Werfel and Berta Zuckerkandl.

16   Schwarzwald also financed a meal service, the 'Schloss Kuche', which fed university professors and students in Vienna from the famine years until 1927.

17   Freya von Moltke, interview with the author.

18   Although Serkin was only a year older than Brandt he was already famous, having made his debut with the Vienna Philharmonic at the age of twelve.

19　Freud spent two months at the Grundlsee in the summer of 1930; he took a house just below the Villa Seeblick, and his entourage rented four others nearby. But both sides kept their distance. The Freudians had their own school in Vienna, and Schwarzwald had a much more outward-looking idea of education than they did. At the 'Burlingham-Rosenfeld School', which operated in Vienna from 1927 to 1931, almost all of the children and staff were in analysis. On the Grundlsee milieu, see also Anna Freud, *Anna Freud's Letters to Eva Rosenfeld*, ed. Peter Heller (Madison, Conn.: International Universities Press, 1992).

20　Robert Musil, *Briefe 1901-1942* (Hamburg: Rowohlt, 1981). When satirising Dr Schwarzwald and her husband in *The Man Without Qualities*, Musil did not identify them as Jewish.

21　Ester Cotton recalls that when she went as a young woman to learn English at Cambridge, her academic hosts made a point of bathing nude; so she kept her costume on, to protest at making such a fuss about it.

22　Hans passionately admired Dr Schwarzwald and has preserved her memory in several memoirs. See J. Sachs, *The New Yorker*, 4 June 1990; also Deichmann's autobiography, *Objects: A Chronicle of Subversion in Nazi Germany and Fascist Italy* (New York: Marsilio, 1997).

23　The most famous member of the dynasty was Helmuth von Moltke, who commanded the German forces in the Franco-Prussian War; he was Helmuth James's grand-uncle.

24　However, von Moltke's radical Christianity, movingly expressed in his prison letters, was a post-Grundlsee development. See Helmuth von Moltke, *Letters to Freya* (New York: Knopf, 1990).

25　'*dieses Nebeneinander von Wohltun und Sichwohltun*': Robert Musil, *Tagebücher I* (Hamburg: Rowohlt, 1983), p. 631. It has to be said, though, that Musil's monetary dependence on Schwarzwald after the First World War had rankled; he had the kind of temperament that could never forgive a favour.

5　Becoming a Photographer

1　The *süsse Madeln* were the easygoing shopgirls and seamstresses of Vienna. Arthur Koestler, who was a year younger than Brandt, describes student life at the University of Vienna at this time in his autobiography, *Arrow in the Blue* (New York: Macmillan, 1961).

2　Eichmann was born in Germany but moved to Linz, Austria, as a child of eight; he joined the Austrian Nazi Party in 1932 and fled to Germany in 1933.

3　Lyena Barjansky, interview with the author.

4　To the end of his life, Brandt signed himself 'Billy' in letters to his family and old friends.

5　At the time of his death, however, his London bank account was still in the name of Hermann Wilhelm Brandt.

6　Hans Deichmann, quoted in Martin Gasser, 'Shadows of Life', p. 6.

7　Ester Cotton reported Brandt's reluctance to credit Schwarzwald; Lyena Dodge that he tried to keep his apprenticeship secret.

8　*The Magic Mountain*, pp. 45, 627-8.

9　Freya von Moltke, interview with the author.

10　For Fleischmann's work, see Anna Auer, *Trude Fleischmann, Fotografien 1918-1938* (Vienna: Galerie Faber, 1988).

11　M. Haworth-Booth provides the information about the Schwarzwaldschule, though without naming Kolliner: *Bill Brandt Behind the Camera*, p. 7.

12　For information about Viennese photography in the 1920s I am greatly indebted to Monika Faber of the Albertina Museum, Vienna.

13　Or perhaps with her sister; two women named Kolliner lived there, the other a teacher.

14　Pola, the base for the Austrian Imperial Navy, was annexed by Italy in 1919.

15　In Koppitz's famous nude 'Bewegung', the entire left foot of the dancer was drawn in by the re-toucher.

16　*Der Kuckuck* was also an outlet for 'workers' paradise' shots of outings and sports, Soviet agency photos, and pictures by 'worker-photographers'.

17　For a survey of this world, see Monika Faber, *Divas and Lovers: Photographic Fantasies from Vienna Between the Wars* (London: Thames & Hudson, 1998).

18　László Moholy-Nagy, *Malerei, Fotografie, Film*, quoted in Faber, *Divas*, p. 103.

19　In the catalogue for his National Portrait Gallery exhibition of 1982, Brandt said that the portrait was taken in Paris, but this was almost certainly part of his phobia about concealing his residence in Vienna. Lyena Dodge remembers meeting Pound at Schwarzwald's salon.

20　See R. B. Kitaj, 'R B Kitaj and Two Faces

of Ezra Pound', *Creative Camera* 210 (June 1982), p. 536.

21 On portraits as prophecies, see p. 188 below.

22 The Dora Kallmus studio in Vienna (Atelier d'Ora) made about 70,000 exposures between 1907 and 1927 (equivalent to about ten a day). Of these 3,000 were preserved and sold to the National Library in the 1960s (Faber, interview with the author). Unfortunately, only a few prints have survived that can be attributed to the Kolliner studio. Monika Faber reports that in 1945, when most of the windows in Vienna were broken, photographic plates were sometimes cleaned of their emulsion and used as replacement panes!

23 Brandt's picture has not been preserved. David Mellor discusses Loos's influence on Brandt's use of domestic space in *Bill Brandt Behind the Camera*, p. 75.

24 The early rolls held six exposures; in 1932 a twelve-exposure model was introduced.

25 Quoted in an essay by Ray Zone, *http://artscenecal.com/ArticlesFile/Archive/Articles1997/Articles0397/AEisenstaedt.html*. Robert Doisneau confirms this view: 'The Rollei is really useful because it's not aggressive at all. When you photographed people on the street, you weren't looking at them so nakedly as with a 35mm camera … I loved the Rollei because there was a certain politeness inherent in the gesture of looking down into the viewfinder.' Quoted in Peter Hamilton, *Robert Doisneau: A Photographer's Life* (New York: Abbeville Press, 1995), p. 362.

26 In early model Leicas the film had to be hand-loaded by cutting off lengths of movie film. The Leica negative was 24 x 35mm, less than a quarter the size of the 6 x 6cm Rolleiflex; skilled darkroom work was needed to achieve professional print quality.

27 Of war photography, Brandt commented, 'A camera looks like a weapon under those circumstances. As you're holding it up to your eye, someone could easily think you're about to fire at them.' Quoted in Dave Saunders, 'Bill Brandt: Not Resting on his Laurels', *Hot Shots* 15 (1981).

28 In illustrated magazines of the time, one can roughly distinguish between a rectangular 35mm print and a square Rolleiflex one, unless the picture has been cropped.

29 Brandt's main other cameras were an American Deardorff for portraits, a 'police camera' for nudes, and a Hasselblad Supreme Wide Angle for some of his later portraits and nudes.

30 Plate 19 of *London by Night*, 'Children are sent upstairs to bed', shows John Knight again. He was killed in the Second World War.

31 The classic discussion of the *flâneur* is by Walter Benjamin; for example, in his essay 'On Some Motifs in Baudelaire'. For photographic aspects, see Colin Westerbeck and Joel Meyerowitz, *Bystander: A History of Street Photography* (Boston: Little, Brown, 1994).

32 Rolf left Vienna in the spring of 1928 to study voice projection at the Sprachbildners Muller, Berlin; a year later he joined a repertory company at the Friedrichsteater, Dessau. However, the brothers continued to meet regularly at Grundlsee, for family Christmases in Hamburg, and elsewhere.

33 Brandt returned to this restaurant to take a photo of Eva; see p. 79 below.

34 Stephen Spender, in *World Within World* (London: Readers Union, 1953), mentions the flagrant gay sex scene on the Reeperbahn; but Brandt never documented this.

35 Berlin: Reckendorf, 1929.

36 Martin Gasser, 'Shadows of Life', p. 6. The New Objectivity was a broad cultural movement that extended beyond photography; the originator of the term, Gustav Hartlaub, said, 'Cynicism and resignation are the negative side of the *Neue Sachlichkeit*; the positive side expressed itself in the enthusiasm for the immediate reality as a result of the desire to take things entirely objectively on a material basis without immediately investing them with ideal implications.' Quoted in Peter Gay, *Weimar Culture: The Outsider as Insider* (Harmondsworth: Penguin, 1974), p. 128.

37 See also Nigel Warburton, 'Bill Brandt: Pictorialist', in N. Warburton, ed., *Bill Brandt: Selected Texts and Bibliography* (New York: G. K. Hall, 1993).

6 Eva

1 After a week at the *pension*, Eva moved to more permanent quarters at Hamerlingplatz 8, then in the tenth district.

2 Later, Eva would take some years off her age; but the Vienna municipal records have her date of birth as 10 April 1907.

3 In what follows, I am assuming that Eva's memoir, 'The End of the Poem' (*Harper's Bazaar*, New York, April 1950), is substantially true to life. In it, she uses the actual names of her sister and brother, and other details can be confirmed.

4   'The End of the Poem', p. 197.

5   Interview with Jim Marsh, who married Eva's step-daughter.

6   *The Times*, 3 June 1925.

7   Susan Brandt, interview with Aysha Rafaele.

8   Ibid.

9   David Mellor, *Bill Brandt Behind the Camera*, pp. 74-5.

10 Eva Boros, *The Mermaids*, p. 146.

11 Such warnings to people with TB were a vague mixture of misgivings: that the woman might not be strong enough to bear a child or look after it, that it was not fair to children to have parents who might die, and that 'weak lungs' might be passed on to offspring. Thomas Mann's story 'Tristan' develops the mythology of a consumptive woman who is 'killed' by having a child. In *The Mermaids* the heroine, Lalla, says, 'it takes a lot of calcium to make a child … I need the calcium myself with this illness' (p. 51).

12 *The Mermaids*, p. 143. In 'The End of the Poem,' Eva writes, 'I noticed Mother's handkerchief lying on the floor, but when I moved to pick it up Father grabbed my arm.'

13 Eva was not there for any of Brandt's three summer visits to Grundlsee.

14 Brandt also visited London, stopping at Paris, in July and October 1929.

15 Kertész had moved to Paris in September 1925.

16 See Beaumont Newhall (ed.), *Photography: Essays and Images* (New York: Museum of Modern Art, 1980), pp. 243-9.

7 Paris: With Man Ray

1   Though none of the three photographers who most influenced Brandt when he lived in Paris was French: Man Ray was American, Kertész and Brassaï were Hungarian (Brassaï was born in Transylvania, part of Romania, but with a population mainly of Hungarian descent).

2   Municipal records place Brandt firmly in Vienna in 1929, though he did visit England in July and again in October. Man Ray went off to Biarritz in July 1929 with Lee Miller. It is just possible that Brandt was with Man Ray in September, but much more likely that Brandt said he was in Paris in 1929 to conceal his presence in Vienna.

3   Pound was said to be a family friend of the Brandts; if so, it must have been some connection with Brandt's uncles before the First World War,

when they lived near Pound in Kensington.

4   Man Ray, *Self Portrait* (Boston: Little, Brown, 1963), pp. 185-6, 149.

5   Man Ray trained Abbott and Boiffard more or less from scratch in 1923 and 1924. See Centre Georges Pompidou, *Atelier Man Ray: Berenice Abbott, Jacques-André Boiffard, Bill Brandt, Lee Miller, 1920-1935* (Paris: Philippe Sers, 1982).

6   Paul Ignotus, interview with the author. Ignotus lived with Eva after his mother died when he was a child.

7   Paul Ignotus, interview with the author; 'pressure on her to give it up'; Lyena Dodge, interview with the author.

8   Man Ray, *Self Portrait*, p. 118.

9   Brandt did portraits of Man Ray, Ernst, de Chirico, Arp, Dalí, Magritte and Giacometti.

10 Ian Fraser, 'Bill Brandt in Camera', *The World of Interiors*, London, February 1983, p. 80.

11 Stephen Dwoskin, interview with the author.

12 Quoted in *Current Biography*, 1981.

13 Man Ray, *Self Portrait*, pp. 170-1.

14 Ibid.

15 Oskar Barnack said that he invented the Leica because he was tired of having to carry a heavy camera and auxiliary equipment on his hiking expeditions.

16 Rayographs were made by placing objects directly on to photographic paper and exposing to light, thus producing photographs without using a camera. Solarisation, which Ray used especially for his nudes, involved the deliberate exposure of negatives or prints to light during the developing process, to achieve haloing or contrasting effects.

17 *Minotaure* 7 (June 1935), p. 65.

18 Brandt's last nudes (1977-80) again picked up motifs of bondage and dismemberment that Man Ray was exploiting around 1930; see Chapter 29.

19 Julien Levy, *Surrealism* (New York: Arno / Worldwide, 1968), p. 21. First edition 1936.

20 Quoted in Patrick Roegiers, *Bill Brandt* (Paris: Pierre Belfond, 1990), p. 23.

21 Brandt left Passy eventually, but moved to rue Rochechouart, across the river from Montparnasse in the ninth *arrondissement*.

22 At the beginning of December, a right-wing mob disrupted the showing, and the film had to be withdrawn from circulation.

23 Elliot Rubinstein in *The International Dictionary*

of Films and Filmmakers: Volume II: Directors /Filmmakers (New York: Perigee, 1984), p. 74.

8 Paris: The Social Fantastic

1   Atget (1856-1927) had lived at 17 rue Campagne Première.

2   The photos are now at the Eastman Museum, Rochester, New York.

3   After Atget's death, Abbott and Julien Levy arranged for his collection to be acquired by the Museum of Modern Art, New York.

4   Julien Levy, *Surrealism*, p. 59.

5   Rosalind Krauss and Jane Livingston, *L'Amour Fou: Photography & Surrealism* (New York: Abbeville Press, 1985).

6   Eugène Atget, *Atget, Photographe de Paris* (Paris: H. Jonquières, 1930); the *Dépôt Légal* was dated March 1931. It contained ninety-six plates. There was also a German edition, published in Leipzig. Brandt's purchase of a copy is mentioned in David Mellor, *Bill Brandt Behind the Camera*, p. 96.

7   Pierre Mac Orlan, preface to André Kertész, *Paris Vu Par André Kertész* (Paris: Plon, 1934).

8   Pierre Mac Orlan, preface to *Atget, Photographe de Paris*, p. 4; *'une vision photographique de certains détails du monde ne tarde pas à montrer la présence de l'aventure dans un paysage qui la gardait soigneusement cachée pour des yeux humains'*.

9   Ibid., p. 6. *'La puissance de la photographie c'est de créer la mort subite et de prêter aux objets et aux êtres ce mystère populaire qui donne à la mort son pouvoir romanesque'*.

10   Preface to *Atget*, pp. 17, 18.

11   Preface to *Paris Vu Par André Kertész*.

12   John Szarkowski, Maria Morris Hambourg, *The Work of Atget. Volume IV: Modern Times* (New York: Museum of Modern Art, 1981). Shop-window dummies had also been a feature of Ruttman's 1927 'city symphony' film, *Die Symphonie der Grosse Stadt Berlin*.

13   Levy, pp. 98-9.

14   Ibid., p. 102.

15   He went back to Davos in November 1931.

16   François Buot, *René Crevel: Biographie* (Paris: Grasset, 1991), p. 166.

17   An alternative version claimed that the label said: 'Please cremate me. Disgust.'

18   'The Big Mannequin Looks For and Finds Her Skin', *Minotaure* 5 (1938).

19   *'les objets surréalistes ont ranimé*, concrètement, *sans métaphor, les cadavres des choses'*. René Crevel, *L'Esprit Contre la Raison* (Paris: Pauvert, 1986), p. 301. The formula was quoted in the first issue of *Minotaure*.

20   Tim Martin, *Essential Surrealists* (London: Dempsey Parr, 1999), p. 99.

9 Paris: The Hungarian Table

1   This first appeared in March 1930 under the title *Photographie*. It continued through the Thirties, and Brandt became a contributor, though not until after he had left Paris.

2   Lucien Vogel (1886-1954) was a Franco-German businessman and photographer who came to Paris from Berlin. He was a fellow-traveller and printed in *Vu* the first photographs of German concentration camps. He fled Paris in 1940 and spent the rest of the war in the US. See Kim Sichel, *Germaine Krull: Photographer of Modernity* (Cambridge, Mass.: MIT Press, 1999), pp. 98-108.

3   *Voilà*, 1933.

4   *Scandale* and *Paris-Magazine* had the same publisher; the latter featured soft-focus nudes from Atelier D'Ora and Manassé, photographers who had come to Paris from Vienna.

5   Jim Marsh, interview with the author.

6   In the 1950s Brandt's nudes drew inspiration from Kertész's brilliant distorted nudes of the 1920s and 1930s.

7   Kertész continued to shoot more static subjects with a 9 x 12cm plate camera. In Hungary he took one of the earliest staged street photographs in 1914, using his brother as a model. Pierre Borhan, *André Kertész: His Life and Work*, p. 43.

8   The Rolleiflex then cost 1,500-1,700 francs, about £15-17.

9   Ylla (1911-55), whose real name was Camilla Koffler, was born in Vienna to a Yugoslav mother and a Hungarian father. She worked as a re-toucher in Paris for Ergy Landau, then set up her own studio.

10   Goldfinger had presentation copies of Brandt's *The English at Home* and *A Night in London*.

11   See Anne Tucker, *Brassaï: The Eye of Paris* (Houston: Museum of Fine Arts, 1999), pp. 61-3.

12   Alain Sayag and Annick Lionel-Marie (eds), *Brassaï: The Monograph* (Boston: Little, Brown, 2000), p. 303. Gilberte married Brassaï in 1948, and did not know him in the Thirties.

13   Brassaï, *Henry Miller: The Paris Years* (New York: Arcade, 1995), p. 3.

14   In later life the two men disagreed radically about how much Brassaï owed to Kertész.

15   Published by Arts et Métiers Graphiques.

16   A collection of these pictures was published in 1934 by a pornographic bookstore, under the title *Voluptés de Paris*. This was a shabby, semi-clandestine production that Brassaï himself disowned.

17   Brassaï, *The Secret Paris of the 30's*, tr. Richard Miller (London: Thames & Hudson, 1976).

18   Pl. 11, 47; see Tucker, p. 43.

19   Tucker, p. 39.

20   *Détective* began weekly publication in 1928 and continued into the Thirties. In Germany, Wilhelm Goldmann published *Das Kriminal-Magazin* along similar lines, from 1929. The first issue of *Scandale*, billed as a 'Revue Mensuelle de Criminalogie (sic)', appeared in August 1933.

21   The story includes a picture of a Peugeot sedan belonging to the actual suspects, which is a different model from the Peugeot used for the re-enactment.

22   For *Scandale* see Westerbeck, p. 184; Brandt mentions *Paris-Magazine* in the chronology published in the catalogue of his National Portrait Gallery show of 1982.

23   *Paris-Magazine* for October 1932 has 'Comédie Sentimentale', an uncredited five-picture sequence of a pick-up on a park bench. This might be by Brandt, as he did a similar sequence for *Lilliput* in September 1941, 'A Simple Story about a Girl'.

24   Brandt may have seen the picture before it was published.

25   There are two versions of the Brassaï picture: a darkly atmospheric one in *Paris de Nuit* (followed by Brandt), and a more brightly lit one in *Paris Sécret*. Brandt must have been the follower, because how could Brassaï have induced a prostitute to dress up as Eva?

26   Brandt also re-shot Brassaï's picture of lovers under a railway bridge (*Paris de Nuit*, pl. 44); see p. 126.

27   Around February or March 1932.

28   See *Bill Brandt Behind the Camera*, p. 8. That picture is usually dated Vienna, 1933; but Frances Rice thinks it was taken in Paris.

29   Brassaï worked as a still photographer on a film by Alexander Korda in 1932, and Rolf

Brandt worked for the Emelka film company in Berlin in 1931.

10   Wanderings

1   The affair was widely publicised; the inside story may have reached Paris via Gertrude Stein, in whom Graves confided at the time.

2   Sander travelled to Sardinia in 1927 to photograph people and landscapes. The first book of his pictures was published in 1929, and Brandt may well have known Sander's work by the time he went to Spain.

3   The negative of this picture has been re-touched to remove the industrialist's name and replace it with an ellipsis and question marks. On Brandt's fascination with effigies, see Nigel Warburton in *History of Photography* 17, no. 3 (Autumn 1993).

4   He has one picture of a great modernist building going up on the outskirts of Madrid (*Bill Brandt Behind the Camera*, p. 90), but it is made insignificant by the expanse of waste land in the foreground of the picture.

5   For the Kertész pictures, see Pierre Borhan, *André Kertész: His Life and Work*, pp. 35-81.

6   Brandt's picture of a village drunkard appeared in the French annual *Photographie 1933-34*, and again in the March 1938 *Lilliput*.

7   Stefan Lorant claimed credit for the animal/human layout on facing pages, a staple of *Lilliput* and other magazines.

8   The Bauhaus had been subsidised by the municipal government; by October 1932 it had moved to Berlin and re-opened as a private institution. In July 1933, with Hitler in power, the faculty voted to close the Bauhaus permanently.

9   Ester Cotton, interview with the author, December 1995.

10   The pictures of this time are discussed in Chapter 11.

11   See Man Ray, *Man Ray 1890-1976* (New York: H. W. Abrams, 1994), p. 58, and other nudes in the Man Ray archive of 'Natacha'. Frances Rice believes that the picture may have been taken in Paris rather than Vienna, in which case it may even have been the same wig.

11   In Pursuit of the English

1   Letter to Noya Brandt, 21 August 1972, Brandt Archives.

2   His nephew Peter Brandt recalls that Brandt

had a distinctly Hamburg accent.

3   Reproduced in Martin Gasser, 'Shadows of Life', p. 6.

4   Perhaps Brandt was also making a joke about the English version of Kaiser Wilhelm during the war – 'Kaiser Bill'.

5   Electoral register, October 1935.

6   Billy and Rolf's elder brother, Walther, was now a partner too.

7   Rolf is fully dressed for the opera in white tie, tails and top hat in *The English at Home*, pl. 7.

8   The *Ilford Manual of Photography* (first published in 1942) has directions for converting a standard bathroom into a darkroom; and this is what Brandt did.

9   Lyena Dodge, interview with the author, 1995.

10   See, for example, Humphrey Spender's loathsome upper-class types in 'Eights Week, Cambridge, 1938'. *Humphrey Spender's Humanist Landscapes* (New Haven: Yale Center for British Art, 1997), pl. 57.

11   The picture appeared in the Paris annual *Photographie* for 1939, captioned 'London 1933'. The dancer is unidentified, though the set suggests 1933 productions of either *Petrouchka* or *Coppelia*.

12   The picture, previously unpublished, is in Brandt's 'London 1933' photo album.

13   Brandt's album has a related group of tic-tac men, wearing caps rather than trilby hats.

14   The picture is used twice in *The English at Home*: on the cover it is cropped to give a vertical composition; on p. 28 the view widens to include a uniformed chauffeur, who is the only one not in a worshipful pose.

15   Geli Raubal committed suicide in 1931 under suspicious circumstances; she lived with Hitler, who was thought to have an incestuous passion for her. Stefan Lorant, interview with the author, April 1996.

16   Lorant said Baumann was 'a Baumannite', that is, interested only in bullying others into doing what he wanted.

17   For background on the German influx in British photo-journalism, see *Creative Camera* 211 (July/August 1982).

18   Suschitzky succeeded in getting his mother to England from Vienna in 1939. There is a survey of his career in *Visual Art*, no. 97 (Spring 1977).

19   The dummy, dated 9 June 1934, was preserved by Stefan Lorant in his papers, now at the Getty Library. Tom Hopkinson, '*Weekly Illustrated*: Photojournalism's Forgotten Pioneer', *Creative Camera* 211, p. 580.

20   The *Illustrated London News* had installed rotogravure presses in 1912, but its cover price of one shilling limited its circulation. *Weekly Illustrated* cost 2d., one-sixth the price of the *Illustrated London News*.

21   Stefan Lorant, interview with the author.

22   Ian Jeffrey (*Bill Brandt: Photographs 1928-83*, p. 176) credits 'Fog Comes to London' to Brandt (*Weekly Illustrated*, 1 December 1934); but Lorant thought it was by Jim Jarché.

23   The phrase is Lyena Barjansky's; she didn't know Lorant personally, so she may have been repeating Brandt's own judgement.

24   Kertész had been a regular contributor to Lorant's German magazines.

25   Stefan Lorant, interview with the author. Sometimes the photographers would make their own selection of the best, and deliver 8 x 10-inch prints. For Lorant's layout methods, see *Creative Camera* 211 and p. 120 below.

12 The English at Home: The Ethnographer

1   Bronislaw Malinowski, *Argonauts of the Western Pacific* (New York: Dutton, 1961; first published 1922), pp. 20-1. On the application of ethnology to social observation in 1930s Britain, see James Buzard, 'Mass-Observation, Modernism, and Auto-Ethnography', *MODERNISM/modernity* 4, no. 3 (September 1997), pp. 93-122.

2   *The English at Home* (London: Batsford, 1936), introduction, p. 4.

3   The little girl is Elizabeth Money, granddaughter of Augustus Brandt, and the nursery is at his country house near Bletchingley.

4   'Random or determined – who knows – the meeting with Pratt was in any case a fatal one for me.' The date given in Brandt's note cannot be right, since the Viennese residency records place him at the Pension Cottage on that day. The year before (1928), he left Vienna for his first visit to England on 25 March, and it seems most likely that he met Pratt then, though a few days after the 22nd.

5   In 1933 André Breton and Paul Eluard sent out a survey to 300 people that asked two questions: 'Can you say what was the most important encounter of your life? To what extent did or does this encounter give you the impression of happening by chance? Or by necessity?'

Minotaure 3-4 (December 1933). Brassaï's reply, printed in the magazine, was: '*fortuite où nécessaire – qui sait – la rencontre avec Goethe m'était fatale.*' Brandt's note is another example of his shadowing Brassaï, in this case by following his phrasing. But Goethe and Pratt are rather different as instruments of fate!

6   *Picture Post*, 4 March 1939. His *Picture Post* story on Pratt was 'The Perfect Parlourmaid', 29 July 1939. Brandt would certainly be familiar with Leontine Sagan's film *Maedchen in Uniform* (1933), though its main theme was a lesbian crush between a student and her teacher.

7   Peter Brandt, interview with the author, December 1999.

13 The English at Home: The Critic and the Director

1   *The English at Home*, pp. 15, 55, 56. Brandt may have been alerted to the possibilities of such pictures by a story in *Weekly Illustrated* (6 October 1934) by Jim Jarché: 'Coal and the Men Who Get It'. Valentine Cunningham's *British Writers of the Thirties* records Brandt's interest in Priestley's book.

2   David Mellor, *Bill Brandt Behind the Camera*, p. 83.

3   Paul Ignotus junior, interview.

4   'Bill Brandt Today … and Yesterday', *Photography* 14, no. 6 (June 1959), p. 21.

5   Orwell lived over the 'Booklover's Corner' shop, in Warwick Mansions on Pond Street.

6   Brandt told Mark Haworth-Booth that 'When Orwell saw the finished book he was very upset about the pictures and insisted that they should be taken out of all later editions.' Brandt / Mark Haworth-Booth, 14 November 1975, Victoria and Albert Museum.

7   A Wigan Communist, Jim Hammond, reproached Orwell for taking a masochistic approach to his inquiry: 'He could have gone to any of a thousand respectable working-class houses and lodged with them or stayed right where he was. But he doesn't do that. He goes to a doss-house, just like he's down and out in Paris still. You see, when they've left the upper class, they've got to go right down into muck and start muckraking … Did he have a taste for that sort of thing?' Quoted in Bernard Crick, *George Orwell* (Harmondsworth: Penguin, 1982), p. 281.

8   G. W. Stonier in *New Statesman*, 29 February 1936.

9   The picture was taken on Brandt's first trip out of London to photograph the 'distressed areas', to south Wales in 1935. The oldest of the children is incongruously well dressed and wearing a string of pearls, for a reason unknown.

10   *The English at Home*, p. 7. Mortimer was literary editor of the *New Statesman* at the time he wrote the introduction.

11   *Camera in London* (London: Focal Press, 1948), pp. 11-12.

12   Reinhardt, an Austrian whose real name was Max Goldman, left Germany for the US in 1933; Brecht left in the same year for Scandinavia.

13   Mark Haworth-Booth, *Bill Brandt Behind the Camera*, p. 12. On whether it *is* a collage, opinions differ.

14   Routledge published in 1934 *The Beauty of the Female Form*, edited by Bertram Park and Yvonne Gregory.

15   *Bill Brandt Behind the Camera*, p. 12. Presumably some of Brandt's pictures had to be excluded to meet the quota.

16   Paul Cohen-Portheim, *The Spirit of London* (London: Batsford, 1935) Cohen-Portheim was a German who died just before the book was published. He had been interned in Britain during the First World War and wrote a book about it. He also published *England, die Unbekannte Insel* in 1931 (England, the Unknown Island).

17   Reviewing *The English at Home* in the *New Statesman*, G. W. Stonier mentioned the 'excellent photographs' in Cohen-Portheim's book: 'snapshots of people lying idly in the park or marching in phalanxes to the station, of elderly men in pubs and clubs, children playing rounders, Gracie Fields on the stage of the Holborn Empire – all those *lieux communs* of London life which the essayist and the gossip-writer contrive to miss'. *New Statesman*, 29 February 1936.

18   Valentine Cunningham, *British Writers of the Thirties* (Oxford: Oxford University Press, 1988), p. 83.

14 A Night in London

1   Prices are given in current style; in 1935 this was £3.10s.

2   Lyena Dodge, interview with the author.

3   See *A Night in London* p. 27. The participants are, from left to right: a friend of Frances Mortimer called Mariel, Chapman Mortimer, Mark Statler, Frances Statler, unknown, Mariel's husband.

4   After the death of Chapman Mortimer, she became Frances Rice.

5   *Lilliput*, November 1942; repr. *Creative Camera* 211, p. 600.

6   Brandt / Beryl McAlhone, 7 September 1978.

7   *Picture Post* was considerably smaller; its page size was 13^1/4 inches high by 10^1/4 wide.

8   *Weekly Illustrated*, 23 May 1936. The spectators are cropped from a picture reproduced in Ian Jeffrey, *Bill Brandt: Photographs 1928-1983*, p. 56. That picture is wrongly attributed to *The English at Home*, and is printed reversed from the *Weekly Illustrated* version.

9   'Opera in a Country House', *Weekly Illustrated*, 30 May 1936. Brandt also sold other Glyndebourne pictures to *The Bystander* ('Prelude to Glyndebourne', 8 June).

10   'Topper versus Boater', 11 July, and 'These little kids stayed at home', 8 August. In *Bill Brandt: Photographs 1928-1983*, Appendix A, Ian Jeffrey speculates that many other stories in *Weekly Illustrated* might be by Brandt, but there is no confirmation of this.

11   *Weekly Illustrated*, 10 November 1934; see *Creative Camera* 211, pp. 587-9.

12   Brandt's scrapbook also contains unpublished pictures of Braque at work in his studio, and a set-up picture that shows both Braque and Brandt as a shadowy figure at his tripod camera.

13   The woman with Djuri bears some resemblance to 'Bird', who posed as a schoolgirl in *The English at Home*; but the identification is uncertain.

14   The other timed pictures are '10.30, Mr and Mrs Smith Prepare for Bed'; 'The Thames Towards Bermondsey at Two O'Clock in the Morning'; '6.00 A.M. at Billingsgate'. Brassaï's *Paris After Dark* (London: Batsford, 1933) has some timed pictures, but includes mainly static shots of exteriors; it does not follow closely the sequence of what people are doing at various times of the night. However, Paul Morand's introduction to *Paris After Dark* does follow this format, and may have influenced Brandt.

15   'Pictures by Night', in L. A. Mannheim (ed.), *The Rollei Way* (London: Focal Press, 1952); reprinted in Nigel Warburton, *Bill Brandt*.

16   Warburton, p. 41.

17   Ibid., pp. 42-3.

18   *Secret Paris*, introduction.

19   *A Night in London* (London: Country Life, 1938) has bilingual captions; the one for 'Footsteps Coming Nearer' is more explicit in French: '*A l'affût du client*' ('On the lookout for a customer').

20   'Passageway in the Metro'; Brassaï, *Brassaï: The Monograph*, p. 63.

21   'Street Scene' was the caption in *A Night in London*; later it was captioned 'Couple, Peckham'.

22   His dirty raincoat and stance suggest another English cliché, the exhibitionist.

23   Compare the shot at the end of *The Thirty-Nine Steps* (one of Brandt's favourite films), where the shadow of a policeman's helmet looms up in a doorway as a sign of the villain's doom.

24   It was later captioned 'Off India Docks Road'.

25   Frances Rice, interview with the author.

26   *Minotaure* 3/4 (1933).

27   The composition makes it appear that the hand and forearms are severed from their owner's body; compare plate 68 of *Bill Brandt: Nudes 1945-80* (London: Gordon Fraser, 1980), a torso whose hands and forearms have been severed. Such fragmented female bodies were a common Surrealist motif. See also Hans Bellmer's photographs of clasped hands in *Minotaure*.

28   *Camera in London*, p. 43. This commentary is credited to Norah Wilson, but she obviously followed Brandt's direction.

29   Ibid., p. 44.

30   *Shadow of Light* (London: Gordon Fraser, 1977), pl. 176 and 266. *Bill Brandt: London in the Thirties* (London: Gorden Fraser, 1983), p. 90; pl. 176.

31   *A Night in London*, pp. 42, 43. The scavenger's pose also follows Brassaï: *Brassaï: The Monograph*, p. 53.

32   Another headline reports the arrival in New Zealand of the aviator Jean Batten, on 16 October.

33   *The Chronicle* also tended to follow the Communist line on Spain, for which it is criticised in Orwell's *Homage to Catalonia*.

34   Scribner's had also published a US edition of *The English at Home*.

15 Dirty Thirties

1   See Valentine Cunningham, *British Writers of the Thirties*, p. 239.

2   J. B. Priestley, *English Journey* (London:

Heinemann, 1968), p. 13.

3   *London in the Thirties*, p. 42.

4   George Orwell, *The Road to Wigan Pier*, p. 107.

5   See, for example, 'Coal-miners' houses without windows to the street', *Shadow of Light* (London: Bodley Head, 1966), pl. 46. John Taylor has a useful discussion of Brandt's politics in *A Dream of England: Landscape, Photography and the Tourist's Imagination* (Manchester: Manchester University Press, 1994), pp. 171-81.

6   *Shadow of Light*, 44c, 45.

7   *The Road to Wigan Pier*, pp. 36-7.

8   For 'Coal-searchers near Heworth' Brandt was probably inspired by Millet's 'The Gleaners', with its three figures at a similar task.

9   This separates Brandt from Mass Observation's desire to turn poverty to political use: 'The men down here [in South Wales], in fact all the people down here, have grown very, very sensitive about the enormous number of people who come down here from London and Oxford and Cambridge, making enquiries, inspecting places, descending underground, questioning women about their cooking, asking men strings of questions about this and that and the other … they object to all these people coming down and asking questions. That's all. They're not animals in a zoo. That's what it is.' Report by James Hanley, quoted in D. Frizzell (ed.), *Humphrey Spender*, p. 33.

10   *English Journey*, p. 314.

11   *Picture Post*, 19 April 1947.

12   *The Road to Wigan Pier*, p. 18. Valentine Cunningham (*British Writers*, p. 240) suggests that Orwell may have been thinking of Brandt's 'East End Morning'; but the picture was not taken until six months after *Wigan Pier* was published.

13   The ritual is also documented in one of Humphrey Spender's Bolton pictures for Mass Observation: *Humphrey Spender's Humanist Landscapes*, pl. 24.

14   Orwell's text, however, was prophetic about the social disruption caused by slum clearance.

15   See, in this context, Humphrey Spender's 'City Architect, Anxious Tenants, Tyneside 1939', *Humanist Landscapes*, pl. 81.

16   In *Camera in London*, Brandt claims that the room was that way before he arrived.

17   Brandt, *Camera in London*, p. 60. See ch. 19, n. 25 below for Bert Hardy's complaints about Brandt's tightness with money.

18   Hart was a twenty-two-year-old student at the Bauhaus when she took the picture. Her work is collected in *The Eye of Conscience* (London: Nishen, 1987).

19   'Window in Osborn Street' is a partial exception (*London in the Thirties*, p. 7), but these troglodytic creatures are not conventional objects of compassion.

20   *Camera in London*, p. 60.

21   *Picture Post*, 2 January 1943. The cover was also by Brandt, a winsome three-year-old girl in an unusually straightforward full-face image.

22   'A Plan for Britain', 4 January 1941.

23   *Picture Post*, 9 March 1946.

24   *Picture Post*, 8 April 1950.

25   For the latter, see 'Window in Osborn Street' and 'Attic Room in Shoreditch', *London in the Thirties*, pp. 7, 13.

26   In available light Spender needed exposures of up to a second, which was bound to attract attention. *Humphrey Spender's Humanist Landscapes*, pl. 22, 72.

27   *Picture Post*, 8 April 1939.

28   The proprietor of Charlie Brown's pub was charged with encouraging prostitution at one time, but was acquitted. Pierre Mac Orlan visited the pub in 1925, escorted by a policeman, and saw it as a place of adventure: *La Lanterne Sourde* (Paris: Gallimard, 1982), p. 149.

29   In the second edition of *Shadow of Light* (London: Gordon Fraser, 1977) she gets a much lighter print, making her jacket grey instead of black. *London in the Thirties*, completed just before Brandt's death in 1983, carries the note: 'Bill Brandt personally supervised the reproduction of the prints in this book, and gave his full approval to the final appearance of the collection.'

30   *London in the Thirties*, p. 23.

31   Ruth Goodall, Brandt's step-niece, recalls that he and Rolf used to amuse themselves by defacing Christmas cards – drawing turds falling from robins, and the like.

32   *Lilliput*, July 1948. See p. 220 below.

33   *Shadow of Light* (1966), pl. 18, 19.

34   *Shadow of Light*, pl. 24, 25.

35   The main exception was the special issue of *Picture Post* on poverty, 'Enough of All This', 1 April 1939.

16 Becoming a Photo-Journalist

1   *Men Only*, February 1936, p. 6.

2   In 1941, *Lilliput*'s price went up to one shilling.

3   Both *Coronet* and *Esquire* were edited by Arnold Gingrich.

4   André de Dienes was a Transylvanian, like Brassaï; he moved to the US from Paris in 1938.

5   In *Lilliput*, Lord Iveagh was on the left page, with the caption 'Chairman of Guinness … Is Good for You'.

6   One of the *Lilliput* pictures, of dancing in Mayfair, was not included in *A Night in London*.

7   Maxwell Raison says that *Lilliput* was purchased for £30,000, but perhaps there were other shareholders besides Lorant who had to be bought out. The total cost of launching *Picture Post* was £250,000. *Creative Camera* 211, p. 571.

8   Gavin Weightman, *Picture Post Britain* (London: Collins & Brown, 1991), p. 8.

9   See Kurt Hutton, *Speaking Likeness* (London: Focal Press, 1947), p. 72.

10   *Picture Post*, 14 January 1939.

11   Gustave Doré and Blanchard Jerrold, *London: A Pilgrimage* (London: Grant & Co., 1872). The book had fifty-two plates by Doré.

12   The others from *The English at Home* were shots of London Bridge, a traffic policeman and lovers in the park.

13   An alternative title for this picture is 'Dark Alleyway'.

14   3 December 1938.

15   28 January, 4 March, 8 April, 29 July 1939.

16   See, for example, 'Carnet d'une Femme de Chambre', *Voilà*, July/August 1933. Under the pretext of social concern, this story is full of semi-pornographic sexual adventures, illustrated with staged pictures of life in a fictional hotel.

17   In another picture the model, Freda Walker, poses for a poster being drawn by Rolf Brandt.

18   Urban folklore also had it that Nippies were often former prostitutes, but *Picture Post* never raised such issues.

19   Several pictures from this story are reproduced in Ian Jeffrey, *Bill Brandt: Photographs 1928-1983*, pp. 80-1; the cinema picture is in Weightman, p. 21.

20   Scott-James had worked at English *Vogue* since 1933, after graduating from Oxford. In June 1944 she married her colleague at *Picture Post*, Macdonald Hastings; later she married the cartoonist Osbert Lancaster. She wrote constantly on women's topics; some of her stories were mildly controversial, such as 'Should women wear trousers?' (1 November 1941) and 'Why women don't have babies' (13 November 1943).

21   In *Lilliput* he had thirteen individual pictures, plus the story on Doré's London in May 1939.

17 Marjorie

1   Stravinsky worked on the second movement of his Symphony in C at Sancellemoz, using a piano in the dentist's waiting room.

2   Lyena Dodge thought that Eva met Marjorie in Midhurst, but there is no record of her being there as a patient; nor is there at Sancellemoz. She may have been at another sanatorium in Assy, or was perhaps at Crans-sur-Sierre.

3   Frances Rice, interview with the author.

4   Lyena Dodge, interview with the author.

5   Ester Cotton, Anne Scott-James, interviews with the author. Marjorie's father was Henry James Beckett, with the family wealth based on coal.

6   *Coronet*, January 1941; *Picture Post*, 12 July 1941.

7   The exhibition was sponsored by his French publishers, Arts et Métiers Graphiques.

8   A year later she became a patient of Dr Andrew Morland in Harley Street, an eminent TB specialist who also treated D. H. Lawrence, the painter Mark Gertler and George Orwell.

9   Eva was listed on the electoral register at Hillfield Court, and other friends have mentioned this living arrangement. However, Mrs Sally Fry, a neighbour at Hillfield Court during the war, can only remember seeing Marjorie in the halls.

10   Paul Ignotus, interview with the author.

11   *Picture Post*, 27 December 1941.

12   The unpublished pictures exist in the Brandt archive.

13   There is another shot in the archive, without the cat and lacking the play of gazes across the table.

14   The standard Freudian explanation for attraction to foreign women is incest phobia: '"neurotic exogamy" … occurs where a man experiences an insuperable aversion to any close relationship with a woman of his own people or nation. Or, to put it more correctly, of his mother's people. This is an indication of special

measures taken to avoid the possibility of incest.' Karl Abraham, 'On Neurotic Exogamy', *Clinical Papers and Essays on Psychoanalysis* (London: Hogarth Press, 1955), pp. 48-9. By this logic, the foreign woman is really a permissible substitute for the mother.

15   Reproduced in Ian Jeffrey, *Bill Brandt: Photographs 1928-1983*, pp. 16-17.

16   It shows a woman disappearing through a door with a dog under her arm; the caption was 'But Soft ….'

17   This picture was published by *Lilliput*, July 1941, as 'The Sleeper'; Brandt filled in the window with a pattern of searchlight beams to make it look like a war picture.

18   The little dog that she carries under her arm was perhaps borrowed from Dorothy's Toto in *The Wizard of Oz*.

19   The sexual or murderous threat posed by the Caligari figure is more explicit in some of Brandt's out-takes.

20   See Jeffrey, p. 87.

21   Some of the pictures were taken at Hillfield Court, others at different settings – perhaps at Rolf's flat.

18   Blackouts and Shelters

1   Virginia Woolf, *Letters VI* (London: Chatto & Windus, 1983), p. 319; this was in February 1939.

2   Peter Brandt, interview with the author. Easter 1939 was on 9 April; Hitler had occupied Czechoslovakia on 15 March.

3   Gas lights intrigued Brandt. His 'Lamplighter, Kensington' is in *Bill Brandt: London in the Thirties*, p. 85; and compare Brassaï's 'Lighting the Lamps at Dusk on the Place de la Concorde' in Anne Tucker, *Brassaï: The Eye of Paris*, pl. 12. Gas lighting was introduced in London in 1807, in Paris in 1820.

4   'Pictures by Night' (1952) in Nigel Warburton, *Bill Brandt*, p. 46.

5   Bill Brandt, 'A Photographer's London', in *Camera in London* (Warburton, p. 48).

6   As Abbott put it, 'The tempo of the metropolis is not of eternity, nor even time, but of the vanishing instant.' *Berenice Abbott* (New York: Aperture, 1988), p. 7.

7   Rupert Martin, 'War Work', in Warburton, p. 48.

8   Brandt also made a more conventional image of the cathedral, 'St Paul's and the Thames'.

9   *Life*, 1 January 1940.

10   The *Lilliput* pictures used by *Life* were 'Moon Over London's Chimney Pots', 'Houses of Parliament and Westminster Abbey', 'St Paul's Cathedral and the Thames' and 'Adelphi September 1939'. In *Life*, the last picture was printed reversed and re-titled 'Extinguished Street Lamp and Waning Moon'.

11   *Life*, 3 June 1940, pp. 112-13. The pictures were of riding in Rotten Row and of lovers in Hyde Park. For Rodger's pictures of this period, see *The Blitz: The Photography of George Rodger* (London: Bloomsbury Books, 1994).

12   *Life*, 23 September and 18 November 1940.

13   He had featured in a special issue on England in *Der Querschnitt* as early as January 1930. Beaton had also done better than Brandt at *Coronet*, where Brandt's only contribution before the war was a picture of a greyhound running on a beach (August 1937).

14   Pick was notoriously dogmatic and inflexible; after he lectured Churchill on why the ministry should never tell anything but the exact truth, Churchill is said to have given orders that the 'sanctimonious bus conductor' should never be allowed to see him again. Christian Barman, *The Man Who Built London Transport: A Biography of Frank Pick* (Newton Abbot: David & Charles, 1979).

15   Assembled by Christian Barman, with captions by Christopher Hobhouse.

16   See Tom Harrisson, *Living Through the Blitz* (London: Collins, 1976).

17   The peak for one night was 177,000 on 27 September 1940. Harrisson, p. 112.

18   See, for example, the shelter pictures in *Life*, 14 October 1940.

19   However, Moore considered it an intrusion actually to draw people in the Tube: he made regular visits to observe, but only drew after he got home. Lee Miller's well-known picture of Moore shows him taking notes rather than sketching; it was staged for a propaganda film. Anthony Penrose, *The Lives of Lee Miller* (London: Thames & Hudson, 1985), p. 111.

20   Clark's job was in suspension while the National Gallery was closed and its collection stored underground in Wales. He also chaired the War Artists' Committee, which provided support for artists, since the private market for art had collapsed.

21   See Joanne Buggins, in Warburton, p. 51.

22   *Camera in London*, p. 89.

23 Robert Butts, 'Bill Brandt at Work', in Warburton, p. 57.

24 Joanne Buggins, in Warburton, p. 54.

25 The picture of a jolly couple under their quilt, taken in circumstances described in Butts's article, is so untypical of Brandt's shelter pictures that I suspect he included it as a joke, to show that he could also take popular pictures like his *Picture Post* colleague Bert Hardy.

26 *Lilliput*, December 1942.

27 The pictures were appended to Wilkie's report on the British war effort, and were also shown, along with Moore's drawings, in the 'Britain at War' exhibition in the Museum of Modern Art, 1941. Two shelter pictures and two of London by moonlight appeared in *Horizon*, February 1942, incongruously sandwiched into Orwell's essay on Kipling.

28 Summerson, who was the same age as Brandt, was a distinguished architectural historian.

29 See Nigel Warburton, 'Bill Brandt's Cathedral Interiors: Rochester and Canterbury', *History of Photography* 17, no. 3 (Autumn 1993), pp. 263-76.

19 The Home Front and *Picture Post*

1 Tudor Hart was known only as a fellow-traveller, but in his memoirs Kim Philby claimed that she recruited him to work for Soviet intelligence, and she has also been named as a go-between for the other Cambridge spies.

2 *New Statesman*, 27 July 1940, p. 87.

3 Tudor Hart was photographing gypsies in Monfalcone, Italy, in June 1932, just about the time that Brandt was photographing gypsies and beggars in Catalonia. She also used mainly a 6 x 6cm Rolleiflex, like Brandt. Tudor Hart divorced her husband in 1939, after his return from the Spanish Civil War, and took fewer pictures from the 1940s onwards.

4 In 1944 it organised a plot to kill Hitler, which was cancelled on the grounds that he might be replaced with a more effective military leadership.

5 Peter Brandt, interview with the author. Frances Rice said it was Victoria station (Patrick Roegiers, *Bill Brandt*, p. 94).

6 Anne Scott-James notes that her father developed diabetes after being blown out of bed by a bomb. However, such episodes probably uncovered a diabetes that was already present but not recognised. Fear causes a 'fight or flight' response that floods the body with glucose – which a diabetic cannot properly metabolise.

7 Roegiers, p. 94.

8 The Lancaster I had a top speed of 286 m.p.h. and could reach 24,600 feet.

9 The attack on Lübeck provoked the 'Baedeker Raids' in retaliation, on historic towns like Bath and Canterbury. Brandt photographed the results of the raid on Bath for *Picture Post*, 4 July 1942.

10 W. R. Chorley, *Royal Air Force Bomber Command Losses of the Second World War. Vol. 3: 1942* (Leicester: Midland Counties, 1994); RAAF records.

11 *Picture Post*, 1 April 1939.

12 Nonetheless, *Picture Post* was regarded with suspicion by the Ministry of Information and was not allowed to circulate in the US.

13 'A Plea for Mothers', *Picture Post*, 30 March 1940.

14 In New York, Lorant did some work for Henry Luce, but did not become editor of any magazine and spent the rest of his long life as a freelance author. He died in 1998, at the age of ninety-seven.

15 See Lyndall Passerini Hopkinson, *Nothing to Forgive: A Daughter's Story of Antonia White* (London: Chatto & Windus, 1988), Antonia White, *Diaries 1926-1957* (London: Constable, 1991).

16 Tom Hopkinson interview, *Kaleidoscope*, BBC Radio, 23 May 1975.

17 Legend had it that this was because so many had German names; but Man and Hutton had anglicised their names long before the magazine was founded, and there were several native English photographers.

18 Tom Hopkinson, obituary of Brandt, December 1983.

19 Hardy believed that if the picture was taken properly, it should not need to be cropped.

20 Sheila Hardy, interview with the author.

21 The rate for a longer story at *Lilliput* was £15 in 1942, and Brandt did six of them. *Picture Post* paid £8 for the first page of photos, then £6, £4 and £2 for subsequent ones. Tom Hopkinson gave Bert Hardy a guarantee of one page a week in 1942, or about £400 a year minimum (Sheila Hardy, interview with the author).

22 The April 1943 *Lilliput* has a picture by

Brandt of Anne Scott-James trying to sleep on a station bench.

23 July 1941, February 1942, December 1942.

24 Ian Jeffrey, *Bill Brandt: Photographs 1928-1983*, p. 30. Heath Robinson was a cartoonist who drew ludicrously complex pieces of machinery.

25 The nude male in 'Army Suitability Tests' is almost unique in Brandt's work. In 1942 Brandt asked Bert Hardy, who was then in the army, to find him a tall, muscular male model. Hardy sent Bill Wooldridge, a fellow-army photographer, who met the specifications, and Brandt used him for a story on 'Colonel Blimp' in *Picture Post* (19 December 1942). Hardy recalls having to use pressure to get Brandt to pay his model – 'He was a tight bugger.' Bert Hardy, *My Life* (London: Gordon Fraser, 1985), and Sheila Hardy, interview with the author.

26 The race was covered collaboratively by Brandt and Bert Hardy, with Macdonald Hastings supplying the text.

27 *Lilliput*, October 1942.

28 The Bournville pictures are now in the Birmingham Public Library, which put them on exhibition in 1996.

29 The pictures were not individually credited; Edith Tudor Hart and others also contributed.

20 Portraits

1 There was also an informal portrait of Max Ernst with Roland Penrose, taken at the London Surrealist Exhibition of 1936.

2 *Bill Brandt: Portraits* (London: Gordon Fraser, 1982).

3 'Five Photographers in Search of a Portrait', *Lilliput*, November 1948. The occasion for Brandt's comment was five portraits of Stuart, who played Oliver's mother in David Lean's *Great Expectations*. Brandt's point is reinforced by the portrait that follows his, a 'girl next door' glamour shot by Angus McBean.

4 The subjects are Georges Braque, 1936 and 1955; Harold Pinter, 1961 and 1981; Henry Moore, 1946 and 1972; J. B. Priestley, 1941 and 1969; Robert Graves, 1941 and 1978; Michael Tippett, 1946 and 1981; William Empson, 1940 and 1980. The Pinter portraits are not printed together. Brandt included a beaky Sir Kenneth Clark in old age, but not the chipper young administrator that he took for British *Harper's Bazaar* (December 1944).

5 Alun Lewis, *Alun Lewis: Letters to my Wife* (Bridgend: Seren Books, 1989), p. 165.

6 *Harper's Bazaar* (London), September 1943, p. 40. Brandt also photographed two other exiles for *Harper's Bazaar*, Iya Lady Abdy (January-February 1944) and the Countess Karolyi (July-August 1944). For *Lilliput* (July 1944) he did the anonymous portrait 'The girl from occupied Europe'.

7 *Harper's Bazaar*, December 1944, June 1945.

8 Brandt in Nigel Warburton, *Bill Brandt*, p. 121, written 1961.

9 Letter from Bill to Rolf Brandt, October 1971, Brandt archives.

10 Compare the more informal and accessible portrait of Lee from his earlier sitting for *Lilliput* in 1941.

11 In conversation with Mark Haworth-Booth, Brandt lamented one of the few English culture heroes he could not connect with: 'Ah, Hitchcock, I would love to have photographed him. It could never be arranged. I had even chosen the exact spot. It was to have been at Charing Cross Underground Station. There is an amazingly long empty corridor that looks as if it goes right under the river. That is where I wanted to photograph him.' Warburton, p. 113.

12 Included in Brandt's *Portraits*; it was taken in 1951.

13 *Harper's Bazaar*, August 1952, November 1952, October 1953, March 1954, April 1954. The essays on Guinness, Gielgud, Connolly and Brook are reprinted in Kenneth Tynan's *Profiles* (London: Nick Hern Books, 1989), without Brandt's portraits.

14 In the Seventies, Brandt again became a regular contributor of portraits to *Harper's Bazaar*.

15 Mark Haworth-Booth, in Warburton, p. 113.

16 Three years later, Brandt photographed René Magritte holding up a print of one of his paintings as a kind of shield, like *The Times* in the Sellers portrait. Brandt told Stephen Dwoskin a curious story about the sitting: there was an apple on the floor in front of Magritte, and Brandt was not sure if it was there on purpose. Magritte saw it, and kicked it out of the way. But the print he held up was the self-portrait in which he has an apple instead of a face! (Stephen Dwoskin, interview with the author).

17 Warburton, p. 128.

18 The Bacon, Sellers and Pleasance portraits were all taken in the same year, 1963. It is easy

to imagine that Brandt was passing through a personal crisis of anxiety and suspicion at around this time.

19 Dennis Laywell comments: 'In the great portraits Brandt later produced, from the 1940s through the 1960s, we have some of the finest examples of Surrealist portraiture in any medium by any Surrealist artist. Here the full panoply of Surrealist techniques comes masterfully into play: the vast stage-like space; the wild disparity of scale between the subject and the objects around him; and the dizzying shifts of perspective that confound foreground with background.' Introduction to *Surrealist Photographic Portraits 1920-1980* (New York: Marlborough Gallery, 1981). Quoted in Warburton, p. 161.

20 David Mellor, interview with Aysha Rafaele, 2001.

21 The Land

1 John Piper, *English Romantic Artists* (London: Collins, 1942).

2 In John Betjeman's poem, they weren't even worth defending: 'Come friendly bombs and fall on Slough! / It isn't fit for humans now …' Betjeman was a close friend of Piper.

3 Brandt's main period of interest in landscape ran from 'The Threat to the Great Roman Wall' (*Picture Post*, 23 October 1943) to 'History in Rocks' (*Lilliput*, August 1948).

4 *Brandt: The Photography of Bill Brandt* (New York: Abrams, 1999), p. 308. 'Brandt said that when he photographed Gordale Scar he had John Piper's painting of it in mind, and had to wait until the sun was out and there were no climbers.' Peter and Elizabeth Brandt, interview with the author, December 1999.

5 'Bath: What the Germans Mean by a Baedeker Raid' (*Picture Post*, 4 July 1942); 'The Northern Capital in Winter' (*Lilliput*, February 1942).

6 It has been pointed out that Brandt's pictures followed closely the composition of standard postcard views of the wall. This could be justified by his constant concern to show familiar subjects in an unexpected light.

7 The revival of interest in landscape during the war is discussed further in Robert Hewison, *Under Siege: Literary Life in London 1939–45* (New York: Oxford University Press, 1977), pp. 148–53. For a detailed treatment of the modern landscape, see David Matless, *Landscape and Englishness* (London: Reaktion Books, 1998).

8 *Shadow of Light* (1977), pl. 38.

9 Illustration for H. T. Massingham, 'The Wiltshire Flax-Mill', in *Geographical Magazine* XVI (1943–4).

10 'Over the Sea to Skye', *Lilliput*, November 1947.

11 'For his picture of Chichester Harbour [in 'The Vanished Ports of England', *Picture Post*, 24 September 1949] he wanted a precise conjunction of light and tide, and would have had to wait another three months if he missed his chance.' Peter and Elizabeth Brandt, interview with the author.

12 Mark Haworth-Booth (ed.), *The Land: Twentieth Century Landscape Photographs Selected by Bill Brandt* (New York: Da Capo Press, 1976).

13 *Harper's Bazaar*, February, March 1946.

14 As might be expected, Brandt took an interest in ghosts; see his illustrations for Robert Graves's 'What I Believe About Ghosts', *Picture Post*, 27 December 1941.

15 'Bill Brandt visits the Brontë country', *Lilliput*, May 1945.

16 *Lilliput*, May 1946, June 1948, March 1948. 'Over the Sea to Skye' (*Lilliput*, November 1947) was not conceived as a literary story, but provided images for *Literary Britain* of Johnson and Boswell's tour to the Hebrides.

17 Wilson was a co-editor of *The Focal Encyclopedia of Photography*.

18 An extreme case was Brassaï's 'Ciel Postiche', where a female nude in the foreground mirrors the skyline of hills behind. This appeared facing Brandt's pictures of the Scilly Isles in *Minotaure* 6 (December 1934).

19 One exception was Brandt's moonlight pictures from the Blitz, where London appeared as a landscape in its own right.

22 Deep Focus

1 Stephen Dwoskin, interview with the author.

2 The first significant collection was by Bertram Park and Yvonne Gregory, *The Beauty of the Female Form* (1934).

3 In the introduction to *Nudes 1945–1980* (London: Gordon Fraser, 1980), Michael Hiley reports that Brandt first saw *Kane* in 1943, but this was probably a memory lapse. Welles's *The Magnificent Ambersons* (also an important film for Brandt) had its London premiere in March 1943.

4   David Thomson goes so far as to say that 'there was more going on in the photography of *Kane* than Welles grasped in a lifetime'. *Rosebud: The Story of Orson Welles* (London: Little, Brown, 1996), p. 160.

5   Thomson, pp. 160–1. Many of the book illustrations that one sees of *Kane* were taken on set with a still camera, so it is essential to view the actual film to understand Thomson's description.

6   Taken in 1947, this is an example of Brandt taking the typical composition of a *Kane* shot and applying it to landscape photography.

7   Pauline Kael, 'Raising Kane', in *The Citizen Kane Book* (London: Methuen, 1985), p. 73.

8   'The Tay Bridge Disaster' (20 September 1941); 'When Britain Fought Europe' (8 November 1941); 'A Cartoonist's Joke Becomes a Film Hero' (19 December 1942). In 1963 Brandt did a portrait of Donald Pleasance and took other stills on the set of the film of Pinter's *The Caretaker*.

9   Wiene's most famous film was *The Cabinet of Dr Caligari* (1920). The German original of *Mad Love* was called *The Hands of Orlac* (1924).

10   *Shadows from Light*, dir. Steven Dwoskin (Arts Council, 1983).

11   'Notes on Perspective of Nudes'; Nigel Warburton, *Bill Brandt*, p. 122.

12   Mark Haworth-Booth, *Bill Brandt Behind the Camera*, p. 62. The camera used ASA 400 sheet film.

13   On Tenniel's illustrations for *Alice in Wonderland* and Brandt's 'Portrait of a Young Girl, Eaton Place, 1955', see Mellor, *Bill Brandt*, The R.P.S. National Centre of Photography, Bath (1981), p. 14.

14   The first book collection of Weegee's pictures, *Naked City*, was published in 1945. Weegee did not use a 'police camera', however, but a Speed Graphic.

15   See the nude by Pulham in Val Williams (ed.), *Too Short a Summer: The Photographs of Peter Rose Pulham 1910-1956* (York: Impressions Gallery, 1979), p. 20.

16   The model's fingers are so close to the lens as to be out of focus, and they appear to have been re-touched.

23 The Policeman's Daughter

1   *Ecstasy* appeared in 1933, starring the Viennese actress Hedy Kiesler; her name was changed to Lamarr when she moved to Hollywood.

2   The caption was from Richard Crashaw: 'Who'er she be, that not impossible she.'

3   In the archive there is another semi-nude picture of Lyena in the same bathing suit. The January 1943 *Lilliput* has a bare-breasted skier that may be by Brandt.

4   'Notes on *Perspective of Nudes*' (1961); Nigel Warburton, *Bill Brandt*, p. 121. Brandt says that *The Saturday Book* project came up after the war; but he was already taking pictures along these lines in 1944 and early 1945.

5   Around the time he was beginning these indoor nudes, Brandt photographed 'The Brontë Country' for *Lilliput* (May 1945).

6   The captions are uncredited, but payment to Dylan Thomas is recorded in the file copy, Hulton Getty Archive.

7   The artists were Picasso, Dalí, Edouard Mesens, Derain, Ernst, Balthus, Eugene Berman and Cocteau.

8   Theodora Fitzgibbon, *With Love* (London: Century, 1982), p. 103. Brandt was very impressed by Pulham's ideas on vision and the camera lens: 'Nothing is less true than the notion that the camera cannot lie: on the contrary, it is incapable of telling the truth, it cannot even reproduce human vision, and as our idea of human vision is itself a convention, a photograph is twice removed from any possible reality: it can only present one of the myriad facets of a possible truth. Which facet it shows depends on the photographer.' Peter Rose Pulham, 'The Camera and the Artist' (*The Listener*, 24 January 1952); reprinted in Val Williams, *Too Short a Summer*, p. 16.

9   The former is reproduced in Fitzgibbon, the latter in Williams, p. 12.

10   For a series of winter pictures, of which two were by Brandt: *Lilliput*, January 1942. In June 1945 Thomas was hired by *Lilliput* to write captions for a zoo story called 'What Animals Think'; he commented, 'I don't know if it's Brandt, rather hope not' (Brandt did not do the story). It is not known what Thomas held against Brandt, but the two men could hardly have been more different in temperament. *The Collected Letters of Dylan Thomas*, ed. Paul Ferris (London: Dent, 1985), p. 556.

11   The models for Degas's painting were Ellen Andrée and Marcellin Desboutin: an actress and an artist, like Rosling and Pulham. The picture was also included in Brandt's Chelsea story.

12   Sheila Hardy, interview with the author.

13   The street was featured in Brandt's *Lilliput* story 'Hampstead Under Snow' (February 1946). There is another unpublished nude taken by Brandt in the same room, for which Mary Pulham was the model.

14   Frances Rice and David Mellor both reported Brandt's use of this name, though they had no explanation for it.

15   Eventually published in Cecil Y. Lang (ed.), *Swinburne: Unpublished Writings* (Syracuse: Syracuse University Press, 1964). Lafourcade saw a manuscript version of the work in the collection of Thomas J. Wise, later acquired by the British Library.

16   There is also a policeman's daughter who helps a young man falsely accused of murder in Hitchcock's *Young and Innocent* (1937).

17   Buñuel wanted to make a film of it after finishing *L'Age d'or*. He eventually made a Mexican adaptation, *Abismos de Pasion*, in 1954.

18   The caption for the picture is 'Cathy and I escaped from the wash-house to have a ramble of liberty'.

19   Brandt made his own version of Man Ray's picture, a semi-nude holding an apple.

20   David Mellor, interview with the author. Sheila Hardy, Bert Hardy's widow, could not confirm this story and considered it somewhat unlikely.

21   One appears in Ian Jeffrey, *Bill Brandt: Photographs 1928-1983*, p. 168.

22   Frances Rice recalls seeing another version of this picture with a rubber glove visible on the left.

23   *Lilliput*, March 1949.

24   See Chapter 25. A similar carved chair also appears in the nude 'Blue-stocking' (*Lilliput*, May 1947).

25   July 1948. Brandt used the same model for 'The Watcher' (*Lilliput*, June 1946). I am assuming that he chose the caption personally, because he was usually treated with great deference by Tom Hopkinson and sometimes wrote his own lengthy captions for photo-stories. It is just possible that the picture was casually captioned by *Lilliput*'s editorial staff because the model is posed against a wood-panelled wall. A few months earlier another nude, not by Brandt, had been captioned 'Santa's Daughter'.

26   Millais's painting was inspired by Coventry Patmore's poem of the same title. There, the daughter is abandoned by her aristocratic lover after she becomes pregnant. She drowns her baby and goes mad. But Millais was free to modify his original, and his painting created a scandal when it was shown.

27   Brandt routinely introduced such props. In a story for *Lilliput*, for example, about a man who raised eagles at his home, Brandt carried one of his own lamps from London to Lancashire. The lamp had a picture of a bird on its base.

28   Frances Rice, interview with the author.

29   *Picture Post*, 20 August 1949. See Jeffrey, pp. 162, 170.

30   Also two of Rolf's other step-daughters, and a daughter of Dorothy Kingsmill, who became Tom Hopkinson's third wife after the war.

31   Usually these foreground figures in *Kane* are observers, who give the film's viewers a stand-in inside the frame.

24 The End of Photo-Journalism

1   Nigel Warburton, *Bill Brandt*, p. 91.

2   For example, Brandt's first appearance in *Lilliput* was 'Beggar in Spain' (November 1937), which had been taken in Barcelona in the spring of 1932. Another picture of Barcelona appeared in *Lilliput* as late as August 1944.

3   After 1948 Brandt did work regularly on commission, but usually only for portraits.

4   Brandt, 'A Statement' (1970). Warburton p. 30.

5   'The Forgotten Gorbals', *Picture Post*, 31 January 1948.

6   Bert Hardy, *My Life*, p. 104.

7   'Pull Down the Slums' was the title of a story in *Weekly Illustrated*, 17 November 1934. Brandt's East End story was in *Picture Post*, 9 March 1946.

8   *Picture Post*, 18 January and 19 April 1947. The special issue on 'Where Stands Britain?' used Brandt's 'Stonehenge under Snow' for its cover.

9   *Picture Post*, 1 May 1948.

10   *Picture Post*, 8 April 1950.

11   Introduction to *Camera in London*: Warburton, pp. 89-90.

12   *Camera in London*, p. 43.

13   'Box-office Boys', on theatre producers. Until this story, he had gone for thirteen months without having anything in *Lilliput*.

14   Ian Jeffrey lists Brandt as a contributor to the 'All London Issue' of 26 May 1951, but there are no contact sheets attributed to Brandt in the story folder at Hulton Getty.

15   Marjorie also did some general features for *Picture Post*, such as 'Old Bath is Born Anew' (8 May 1948). Brandt had photographed the 'Baedeker raid' on Bath for *Picture Post* (4 July 1942), but the photographer for Marjorie's story was Kurt Hutton.

16   See Chapter 10, '*Picture Post*'s Decline', in *Bert Hardy: My Life*. *Lilliput* survived until the early 1960s.

17   Edward Hulton had supported Labour in 1945, but by 1948 he was writing editorials in *Picture Post* calling for their defeat at the next election.

18   The slogan was used for Macmillan's successful 1959 election campaign.

19   Magazines suffered further from competition for advertising revenue when commercial television began in September 1955.

20   The first of these was the *Sunday Times Colour Section*, later the *Sunday Times Magazine*; in 1964 the *Observer* and the *Sunday Telegraph* followed suit. *Picture Post* had begun publishing a few colour pictures in the 1940s, usually of static subjects.

21   Title of a chapter in John Berger's *About Looking* (London: Writers and Readers, 1980).

22   See Horst Faas and Tim Page (eds), *Requiem: By the Photographers Who Died in Vietnam and Indochina* (London: Jonathan Cape, 1997).

23   Brandt did a series of pictures on Eton in the mid-1950s, but they do not seem to have been published. For Brandt as an English classic, see *The Independent Magazine*, 30 October 1999. Tributes to Brandt in this issue include one by Don McCullin: 'Many years ago, when I was a young photographer, I was introduced to Brandt, through a friend of Norman Hall who ran a magazine called *Photography*, and since then I have admired his work. As a man I found him gentle, kind and frail, which I thought odd because photography demands a lot of energy. But his social documentary pictures had tremendous strength and sympathy. The question I often asked myself about Brandt was: who did he feel comfortable with, the poor in their houses with that pervasive smell of poverty, or the rich in Mayfair? I grew up in a poor background and I always felt happiest being around normal, struggling, everyday people. Looking at this miner, it reminds you that this was one of the most powerful societies in the world, and coal kept the country alive. The miners were heroes, working in adverse conditions. We can see the factories and the chimneys and the smog of the London

photographs as dramatic. But remember, the atmosphere was living death for some people. My father was asthmatic and it killed him. That is the difference, I suppose. Bill had the mind of a creative artist, whereas I see myself as a photographer. Later on in life I was confronted by him. He said, "Is it Don?" and as I said yes, I realised I was trembling; like meeting an old headmaster. He was a gentleman, an artist and a friendly soul, who left a considerable legacy.'

25 Farewell to Eva

1   Anne Scott-James, interview with the author.

2   His last contribution was a portrait of the cellist Pablo Casals (which also appeared later in the New York *Harper's Bazaar*); his advertising pictures for Rima gowns continued until December 1948.

3   *Picture Post*, 19 May 1945.

4   The devaluation of the pound to $2.80 in 1949 made it even more attractive to earn US income.

5   *Harper's Bazaar*, June 1947, July 1948, January 1951.

6   John Berger, review of the 1966 edition of *Shadow of Light*, in Nigel Warburton, *Bill Brandt*, p. 128.

7   Angela Phillips / Robert Adkinson, 3 April 1996. Brandt papers, Victoria and Albert Museum.

8   Its great depth of field suggests that it may have been taken with the police camera – like the 'Belgravia' nudes of 1951 and 1955, which were also taken in Eva's flat. *Nudes 1945-1980*, pl. 8, 20.

9   David Mellor in *Bill Brandt Behind the Camera*, p. 92.

10   Ester Cotton, interview with the author.

11   Warburton, p. 85.

12   See Ian Fraser, 'A Close-up of the Holland Park Flat of Influential Photographer Bill Brandt', *The World of Interiors*, February 1983.

13   Warburton, frontispiece.

14   Apart from pre-war visits, Brandt went to Catalonia in 1957, for a portrait of Salvador Dalí, and to Majorca for Miró in 1968 and Robert Graves in 1978.

15   Obvious occasions would have been shows of his work at Rochester, New York, in 1963 and the Museum of Modern Art in 1969; according to Lyena Dodge, Brandt feared the attentions of the American press.

16   Patrick Roegiers, *Bill Brandt*, p. 166.

17   The Picasso portrait was achieved only after many delays, as Brandt recounts in 'Photographing Picasso', in Warburton, pp. 114-16.

18   The diary, held by the Brandt archive, runs from 16 June 1949 to June 1951.

19   Eva's 'The End of the Poem' was in New York *Harper's Bazaar* in April 1950; Marjorie probably helped to place it there, through her friendship with the editor, Carmel Snow.

20   Marjorie Beckett, diary, 3 January 1950. George Orwell died eighteen days later, as a result of being allergic to streptomycin, which otherwise would have cured his TB. A pneumothorax – the collapsing of one lung by injecting nitrogen into the cavity between lung and chest – had to be periodically topped up with more nitrogen.

26 Perspective of Nudes

1   In May 1951, New York *Harper's Bazaar* had published four pictures from *Literary Britain*, and in July it ran 'Still Van Gogh's Provence', from the September 1948 *Lilliput* story. This suggests that Brandt was working on a kind of mini-sequel to *Literary Britain*, which might have been called 'Literary Normandy'. But none of the Normandy pictures were published. Another abortive project, in 1955, was a book on Spain by Cyril Connolly, to be illustrated by Brandt. See Jeremy Lewis, *Cyril Connolly: A Life* (London: Jonathan Cape, 1998), p. 473.

2   Marjorie Beckett, diary.

3   Brandt returned to the Sussex coast as a setting for some of his late nudes in 1977-9.

4   Brandt's geological photo-essay, 'History in Rocks', appeared in *Lilliput*, August 1948.

5   In *Nudes 1945–1980* the outdoor nudes of the Fifties are all placed together in section 3; in *Perspective of Nudes* (London: Bodley Head, 1961) they are in a different order and divided between two sections, one in the middle and one at the end of the book. Additional nudes appear for the first time in *Brandt: The Photography of Bill Brandt*.

6   'Notes on *Perspective of Nudes*'; Nigel Warburton, *Bill Brandt*, p. 123.

7   Brandt used Rolf's studio to take several indoor nudes in the Fifties.

8   Eygalières is near St-Rémy, which Brandt had visited in 1948 for his story on Van Gogh.

9   *Nudes 1945-1980*, pls 23, 53.

10   Sections five and six comprise the late nudes, discussed in Chapter 29 below.

11   Judith (now Savita) Brandt remembers a long set-up with the police camera, after which Brandt made only two exposures: 'It was all pre-arranged, he knew what he wanted' (interview with the author, August 2002). Technical details are given in *International Photography Yearbook 1957* (New York: St Martin's Press, 1956), p. 179: 'Bill Brandt … had to stop down to f/32 on his Kodak camera to get the depth of field. The exposure, as one might expect, was two seconds on HP3 and the film was developed in Microphen. A rather contrasty print was made on ordinary bromide paper to achieve the effect.'

12   Twelve of the pictures appeared in *Le Sourire* (Paris), 2 March 1933. See Pierre Borhan, 'Distortions 1933', in Pierre Borhan (ed.), *André Kertész: His Life and Work*, pp. 197-201.

13   In several nudes, the model has four arms crossed in front of her; according to Ruth Goodall, these were made by exposing for thirty seconds, replacing the cap on the lens, then exposing again after the arms had been crossed in a new position. See, for example, *Nudes 1945-1980*, pl. 18.

14   *Perspective of Nudes*, introduction. Mortimer was married to Frances Rice at this time, and was a member of Brandt's inner circle.

15   Mortimer reports, also, that Brandt associated plate 41 with Baudelaire's lines:

> *Au temps que la nature en sa verve puissante*
> *Concevait chaque jour des enfants monstrueux*
> *J'eusse aimé vivre auprès d'une jeune géante*
> *Comme aux pieds d'une reine un chat voluptueux.*

16   By Robert Waelder.

17   For the history of this group, see Russell Jacoby, *The Repression of Psychoanalysis: Otto Fenichel and the Political Freudians* (New York: Basic Books, 1983). On the dissolution of German psychoanalysis, see Karen Brecht et al., '*Hier Geht das Leben auf Eine …*' (Hamburg: Verlag Michael Kellner, 1985), which has some incidental information about Lantos.

18   See Pearl King and Ricardo Steiner (eds), *The Freud-Klein Controversies 1941-45* (London: Tavistock/Routledge, 1991); Phyllis Grosskurth, *Melanie Klein: Her World and Her Work* (New York: Knopf, 1986).

19   'On the Motivation of Human Relationships', *International Journal of Psychoanalysis* 36 (1955), p. 286.

20 Susan Brandt, interview with the author.

21 The story was 'The End of the Poem'; see p. 55 above.

22 In the novel, the heroine is twenty-one when she is admitted to the sanatorium in June 1934. Eva herself was twenty-seven on that date and just moving to London from Vienna with Brandt. Eva was in a Budapest sanatorium around the age of twenty, in 1927.

27 Private Life

1 Introduction, Edward Steichen, *The Family of Man* (New York: Simon & Schuster, 1955).

2 Roland Barthes, in *Mythologies* (Paris: Seuil, 1957), wrote one of the most cogent leftist critiques of the show. Rightists, on the other hand, objected to the sentimental treatment of Russians and Chinese as 'basically the same as us'.

3 Nigel Warburton, *Bill Brandt*, p. 92.

4 The buildings are the NatWest tower for Seifert, the National Theatre for Lasdun.

5 There was also a residual income as property leases fell due on the Hamburg estate.

6 When Eva died in 1988 her estate was worth about £550,000.

7 An exception was Brandt's portrait of Picasso, commissioned by *Harper's Bazaar*. It required two trips to Antibes, the first of which involved three weeks of waiting and no picture; see his account in Warburton, pp. 114-16.

8 *Perspective of Nudes*, introduction.

9 The 1945 Hampstead nude belonged in this category, but was not published before *Perspective of Nudes*.

10 The printers were Héliographia of Lausanne, and Brandt travelled there to supervise their work. For the more contrasty style of the later English printing, by Westerham Press, see Chapter 29.

11 'The child' was presumably Durrell's ten-year-old daughter, Sappho Jane. He goes on to say of Brandt that he 'broods over the nature of things and makes a quiet poetic transcript of them; his work is a prolonged meditation on the mystery of forms … There is nobody o f his stature in England today.'

12 Tom Hopkinson, 'Great Photographers of the World 2: Bill Brandt', *Daily Telegraph Magazine*, 24 April 1970, p. 47.

13 Hopkinson's articles, listed in Warburton's bibliography, appeared in *Lilliput* (August 1942); *Photography* (April 1954); and *Caméra* (April 1954). He also reviewed *Perspective of Nudes* in the *Observer* (2 May and 21 May 1961).

14 Photography, June 1959.

15 *Caméra*, April 1961, p. 6. The original reads: '*Bill Brandt, 55 ans, le plus grand photographe britannique contemporain, a commencé son apprentissage dans un studio de portraits en Suisse. Vers 1929/30 il se rend à Paris, il y séjourne plusieurs années et travaille quelque temps avec Man Ray. De retour à Londres, où sa collaboration est fort recherchée par les plus importantes revues et magazines d'Angleterre, il fait du photo-journalisme.*' Brandt was actually fifty-six at the time of publication of this note. The author's note for *Camera in London* (1948) had read: 'BILL BRANDT is forty-two years old. He became interested in photography in his early twenties and, attracted by the school of modern French photography, went to Paris, where he was much influenced by the work of Atget and Man Ray and by the surrealist films of that time.'

16 Brandt the politician was originally from Lübeck; his name was a pseudonym, taken during the anti-Nazi resistance. He became Chancellor of Germany in 1969.

17 *The British Journal of Photography*, 25 February 1966, p. 155.

18 David Bruxner, 'Bill Brandt: A Profile', *The British Journal of Photography*, 25 February 1966, pp. 155-6.

19 *Caméra* (April 1954), pp. 175-7. Tom Hopkinson's article on Brandt appeared in the same issue.

20 Bill Brandt interview with Frantz André Burguet in *L'Arc: Photographie* (1990), 'Dialogue avec les Faiseurs d'Images', pp. 6-33.

21 All Cartier-Bresson quotations are from 'The Moment of Truth' in *Caméra*.

22 Bill Brandt, interview with Franz André Burguet.

23 Bill Jay, 'Bill Brandt – The Best from Britain', *Creative Camera Owner* 38 (August 1967), p. 161.

24 Cartier-Bresson and Walker Evans both experimented with cameras rigged with ninety-degree viewfinders, so that their subjects would not realise when the photographer was aiming at them. Cartier-Bresson also objected to pictures taken with flash, 'if only out of respect for the actual light – even when there isn't any of it'.

25 Under the title *Ombres d'une Île*, with an introduction by the novelist Michel Butor.

26 Introduction to *Shadow of Light*.

27 Connolly had published Brandt's shelter pictures in *Horizon* that year.

28 On the status of photography, see Pierre Bourdieu, with Luc Boltanski, *Photography: A Middle-brow Art* (Stanford: Stanford University Press, 1990).

29 The exhibition was at the Kinsman Morrison Gallery in 1974; thirty-one pieces were shown at the Reed's Wharf Gallery in 1993. These are reproduced in Zelda Cheatle and Adam Lowe (eds), *Bill Brandt: The Assemblages* (Kyoto: Kyoto Shoin, 1993).

30 Brassaï, also, was an avid collector of curious natural and man-made objects.

31 Walker Evans wrote about Pratt and her colleague serving dinner, in L. Kronenberger (ed.), *Quality: Its Image in the Arts* (New York: Atheneum, 1969), pp. 186-7. Frank's praise of 'the spell of Brandt's work' appeared in *Creative Camera* 66 (December 1969), p. 414.

32 See 'Bill Brandt Today … and Yesterday', *Photography* 14, No. 6 (June 1959), pp. 4, 20-33.

33 For a recent reappraisal, see David Mellor, *Cecil Beaton* (London: Weidenfeld & Nicolson, 1986). Brandt took a somewhat languid portrait of Beaton in 1945, and another for *Harper's Bazaar* in 1953.

34 Gail Buckland, interview with the author, June 2003. Beaton also treated Brandt generously in *The Magic Image*, the history of photography on which Beaton and Buckland collaborated.

28 Noya

1 Derry Moore, now Earl of Drogheda, has become a leading professional photographer.

2 Ruth Pitman also mentions a female student of Brandt who took pictures of her at Hillfield Court.

3 Brandt put Moore in touch with a music student to model for him – perhaps Diana, whom he had used for several pictures in *Perspective of Nudes*; see p. 242 above.

4 Jim Marsh (Rakos's son-in-law), interview with the author.

5 This might have had something to do with Eva's scruples as a Catholic: in the eyes of the Church, a civil divorce did not free either of them to re-marry. By the time of her marriage to Rakos, Eva presumably no longer felt bound by Catholic doctrine.

6 Bill Brandt / Noya Kernot, 11 September 1972.

7 Bill Brandt / Noya Kernot, 21 June 1972.

8 Bill Brandt / Noya Kernot, 30 July 1972.

9 Bill Brandt / Noya Kernot, 15 August 1972.

10 Bill Brandt / Noya Kernot, 25 August 1972.

11 Bill Brandt / Noya Kernot, 18 August 1972.

12 Eva Rakos / Noya Kernot, 11 October [1972].

13 Noya Brandt, interview with the author.

14 Lyena Dodge, interview with the author. On another occasion, Noya recalls, they were going to visit a niece who had a new baby, and Brandt did not realise that he should take a present.

15 Noya Brandt, interview with the author.

16 John le Carré, filmed interview with Aysha Rafaele, 2001.

29 Paint It Black

1 *Shadow of Light* (1977), pl. 119, 120, 62a, 67.

2 *Lilliput* was printed by Hazell, Watson and Viney; *Picture Post* by the Sun Press.

3 My discussion of the later printings is based on an interview with John Parfitt, 28 July 1998.

4 Blocking-out fluid was lead-based; in effect, it meant that nothing would print from the areas it covered.

5 Or perhaps added smoke from another negative, a technique commonly used to add clouds. See *The Ilford Manual of Photography* (London: Ilford, 1949), p. 296.

6 The alternative is that the smoke was touched out for *Lilliput*; but there seems no good reason for doing this, and smoke drifts atmospherically across the *Lilliput* facing page.

7 Parfitt mentions as an example plate 29 of the 1977 *Shadow of Light*, 'Policeman in a Docklands Alley, Bermondsey'. This picture was taken by daylight, then printed dark to give a night-time effect.

8 The books were *Shadow of Light* (1977); *Nudes 1945-1980* (1980); *Portraits* (1982); *London in the Thirties* (1983); *Literary Britain* (1986). Gordon Fraser also published Brandt's selection of landscape photography, *The Land* (1975).

9 See Nigel Warburton, *Bill Brandt*, p. 15; for a general survey of this question, see also Warburton's note, 'Brandt's Printing Styles', in *Brandt: The Photography of Bill Brandt*, pp. 316-19.

10 *Picture Post* photographers were encouraged to underexpose slightly, to get a better result

in photogravure.

11   Warburton, p. 32.

12   Tom Hopkinson, the great patron of Brandt's photo-journalism, deplored his later style: 'I have thought for several years that he is going too far in his blocking out and overemphasis of black and white; that he is destroying what was genuinely photographic in his own earlier work to achieve effects which are: 1. not truly photographic 2. obvious.' Letter to Mark Haworth-Booth, 5 January 1981, Victoria and Albert Museum.

13   David Mellor in *Camera Arts*, May 1983.

14   *The Photography of Bill Brandt*, pp. 316, 319.

15   *Shadow of Light* (1977), pl. 134. The picture was not included in the first edition.

16   There was sometimes a contemporary difference in format; for example, Brandt's series on Doré's London appeared in December 1938 in *Verve*, a high modernist journal that sold for sixty francs, and six months later in the mass-circulation *Lilliput*.

17   Apart from the thirty-four late nudes in *Nudes 1945-1980* there are about fifteen unpublished ones in the Brandt archive. These seem only to be rejects, however; they are not substantially different from the published ones.

18   Props were also a standard feature of nudes in contemporary fetish magazines, such as *Bizarre*, in which Brandt took an interest.

19   The original Venus de Milo had arms, which were lost. On the misogynistic tradition, see Bram Dijkstra, *Idols of Perversity: Fantasies of Feminine Evil in Fin-De-Siècle Culture* (New York: Oxford University Press, 1986).

20   See Rosalind Krauss and Jane Livingston, *L'Amour Fou: Photography & Surrealism*; Sue Taylor, *Hans Bellmer: The Anatomy of Anxiety* (Cambridge, Mass.: MIT Press, 2000).

21   Noya Brandt remembers that Brandt 'thought he was being trendy' by photographing women masked or tied up. In 1973 four people in Sweden, after being held prisoner by bank robbers for six days, took the side of their captors. They resisted the police who rescued them, and one young woman later became engaged to one of the robbers. This episode created the term 'Stockholm Syndrome'. The following year, Patti Hearst acted similarly after being kidnapped by the Symbionese Liberation Army. There were also such headline events as the hostage-taking at the Munich Olympics of 1972 and the Air France hijacking at Entebbe in the summer of 1976. The woman under restraint on page 274 has her head blacked in so that it looks like a terrorist's balaclava helmet.

22   Bill Brandt / Noya Kernot, 31 August 1972. 'Persecution mania' is an old-fashioned term for what would now be called a paranoid personality disorder. Such disorders usually start in early adulthood; in Brandt's case, probably when he was sent away to school at Elmshorn. His paranoia became more acute in the last decade of his life, after Marjorie died.

23   Page 210 above

24   *Nudes 1945–1980*, p. 68. In plate 86, taken in the same year as the armless nude, the model's right arm ends in a bird's wing.

25   In plate 66 the model's nipples seem to take the place of her eyes, as in Shelley's hallucination about Mary Godwin. Magritte's 'Le Viol' used a similar image.

26   Andy Grundberg, 'Books in Review,' *Modern Photography* 45, no. 10 (October 1981), p. 188.

27   Pl. 68, 70, 72, 76 and 90.

28   Pl. 73.

29   John Fowles's novel *The Collector* (1963), about a young woman held hostage, was filmed in 1965.

30   A few of these nudes, such as those taken on the beach in Sussex, return to the style of the nudes of the Fifties, without any obsessional baggage. One of the Sussex nudes, where the model is draped in seaweed on a shipwreck, was not published. Two other unpublished nudes, of a woman washing herself, show Brandt's interest in bathroom nudes; published examples include plates 4, 19 and 71. There was a precedent for such pictures in the great Impressionist paintings of women at the bath, but Brandt could never bring out much warmth in the tile and chrome decor of modern bathrooms. The archive also has a picture of a chorus girl in the shower, probably an out-take from Brandt's 'Backstage at the Windmill', *Lilliput*, October 1942.

31   See the discussion in Sue Taylor, *Hans Bellmer*, pp. 6-7.

30 Last Years

1   Helena Srakocic-Kovac interpreted for them. Interview with the author, May 2003.

2   27 March-17 April in New York, November-December in London.

3   Marlborough also bought prints for stock. In

some cases Brandt made the first print and then successive prints were made commercially.

4   Haworth-Booth is currently director of the Photography Division of the Victoria and Albert Museum; Mellor is Professor of Art History, University of Sussex; Jeffrey a freelance curator and critic.

5   David Mellor, interview with the author, 26 March 1997.

6   In 1975, an Arts Council touring exhibition helped to turn the spotlight towards the Thirties work: *Bill Brandt: Early Photographs 1930-1942*.

7   Also published as a book in the same year: M. Haworth-Booth (ed.), *The Land: Twentieth Century Landscape Photographs Selected by Bill Brandt* (London: Gordon Fraser, 1975).

8   This only counts exhibitions preceding Brandt's death in 1983; for a fuller listing see Nigel Warburton, *Bill Brandt*.

9   Brandt archive.

10   The *Who's Who* entry may have been drafted by Marjorie.

11   Brandt did a portrait of Lartigue in 1974 and of Brassaï in 1978; both are included in *Portraits*. Noya Brandt recalls that the Lartigues did not get on well with Marjorie, but were friendly with her.

12   Quoted in Warburton, p. 8. Warburton goes on to defend Brandt's practices.

13   Three years later he was made an Honorary Member of the Royal Photographic Society.

14   John-Paul Kernot recalls that when assigned to do a portrait, Brandt would study the works of his subject – Alain Robbe-Grillet's novels, for example – to help him decide on an approach.

15   The commission was from the Victoria and Albert Museum, for its exhibition *The Open and the Closed Book*.

16   Roy Strong, 'Bill Brandt: Portraits', *Creative Camera* 210 (June 1982), p. 538. Privately, Strong thought the picture was a complete botch.

17   Brandt made Tippett's first portrait in 1946, when he was forty-one; Pinter's in 1961, at thirty-one.

18   David Mellor's biographical essay, for a 1981 retrospective exhibition in Bath, skirted the most sensitive issues by making no reference to Brandt's German childhood or his years in Vienna.

19   Brandt also gave a copy of *The Go-Between* to his niece Judith.

20   John-Paul Kernot, interview with the author, March 1997.

21   This was not the best introduction, because Brandt made a string of exposures before he realised that there was no film in the camera. He told Lartigue that he wanted to take a few more, and surreptitiously re-loaded.

22   This was the room shown in plate 75 of *Nudes 1945-1980*, where Brandt kept the materials for his collages.

23   Martin Breese, interview with the author, November 2000.

24   Barbara Lloyd, who had been made trustee of the estate, resigned her position rather than be a party to the conflict. Since Brandt's rights were under litigation, the Marlborough could no longer represent him.

25   There was also a late nude of a model wearing a Chinese mask, like the one used for the picture of Ester in Hamburg in the early Thirties.

26   Since demolished and re-built as the Chelsea and Westminster Hospital.

27   Noya Brandt notebook, Brandt archive.

28   Ibid.

Afterword

1   Patrick McGrath has acknowledged Brandt's influence on his novel *Spider*, recently filmed by David Cronenberg.

2   'The Photograph and the Mental Image', in *Animal Faith and Spiritual Life: Previously Unpublished Writings by George Santayana* (New York: Appleton Century Crofts, 1967), pp. 394, 402.

Bibliography

The most complete listing of Brandt's work and writing about it (up to 1993) is in Nigel Warburton (ed.), *Bill Brandt: Selected Texts and Bibliography*. This should be supplemented with the lists of Brandt's magazine contributions in Ian Jeffrey, *Bill Brandt: Photographs 1928-1983*.

Abbott, Berenice, *Berenice Abbott*, New York: Aperture, 1988.

Amburger, Eric, *Die Familie Brandt: Hamburg – Archangel – St Petersburg – London*, Groitzsch: G. Reichardt, 1937.

Atget, Eugène, *Atget, Photographe de Paris*, preface by Pierre Mac Orlan, Paris: H. Jonquières, 1930.

The Work of Atget. Volume IV: Modern Times, ed. John Szarkowski and Maria Morris Hambourg, New York: Museum of Modern Art, 1981.

Auer, Anna, *Trude Fleischmann, Fotografien 1918-1938*, Vienna: Galerie Faber, 1988.

Barman, Christian, *The Man Who Built London Transport: A Biography of Frank Pick*, Newton Abbot: David & Charles, 1979.

Barthes, Roland, *The Grain of the Voice: Interviews 1962–1980*, tr. Linda Coverdale, New York: Hill & Wang, 1985.

'La Grande Famille des Hommes' in *Mythologies*, Paris: Seuil, 1957.

Berger, John, *About Looking*, London: Writers and Readers, 1980.

Bernhard, Thomas, *Gathering Evidence*, New York: Knopf, 1985.

Borhan, Pierre (ed.), *André Kertész: His Life and Work*, Boston: Little, Brown, 1994.

Boros, Eva, 'The End of the Poem', *Harper's Bazaar*, New York, April 1950.

The Mermaids, London: Rupert Hart-Davis, 1956.

Bourdieu, Pierre, with Luc Boltanski, *Photography: A Middle-brow Art*, Stanford: Stanford University Press, 1990.

Brandt, Bill, *Bill Brandt: The Assemblages*, (eds), Zelda Cheatle and Adam Lowe, Kyoto: Kyoto Shoin, 1993.

Bill Brandt: London in the Thirties, London: Gordon Fraser, 1983.

Bill Brandt: Nudes 1945-1980, London: Gordon Fraser, 1980.

Bill Brandt: Portraits, London: Gordon Fraser, 1982.

'Bill Brandt Today ... and Yesterday', *Photography* 14, no. 6 (June 1959), pp. 20-33.

Brandt: The Photography of Bill Brandt, New York: Abrams, 1999.

Camera in London, London: Focal Press, 1948.

The English at Home, London: Batsford, 1936.

Exhibition catalogue, Galerie Municipale de Toulouse, 1976.

Literary Britain, London: Gordon Fraser, 1986.

A Night in London, London: Country Life, 1938.

Perspective of Nudes, London: Bodley Head, 1961.

'Pictures by Night', in L. A. Mannheim (ed.), *The Rollei Way*, London: Focal Press, 1952. Reprinted in Nigel Warburton, *Bill Brandt*, pp. 41-6.

Shadow of Light, London: Bodley Head, 1966.

Shadow of Light, London: Gordon Fraser, 1977.

Brassaï, *Henry Miller: The Paris Years*, New York: Arcade, 1995.

The Monograph, Boston, Bulfinch, 2000.

Paris de Nuit, Paris: Arts et Métiers Graphiques, 1932.

Paris After Dark, London: Batsford, 1933.

The Secret Paris of the 30's, tr. Richard Miller. London: Thames & Hudson, 1976. Originally published as *Le Paris Secret des Années 30*, Paris: Gallimard, 1976.

Brecht, Karen et al., '*Hier Geht das Leben auf Eine …*', Hamburg: Verlag Michael Kellner, 1985.

Bruxner, David, 'Bill Brandt: A Profile', *The British Journal of Photography*, 25 February 1966.

Buot, François, *René Crevel: Biographie*, Paris: Grasset, 1991.

Burguet, Frantz André, 'Dialogue avec les Faiseurs d'Images', *L'Arc: Photographie* (1990).

Buzard, James, 'Mass-Observation, Modernism, and Auto-Ethnography', *MODERNISM / modernity* 4, no. 3 (September 1997), pp. 93-122.

Cartier-Bresson, Henri, 'The Moment of Truth', *Caméra* (April 1954).

Centre Georges Pompidou, *Atelier Man Ray: Berenice Abbott, Jacques-André Boiffard, Bill Brandt, Lee Miller, 1920-1935*, Paris: Philippe Sers, 1982.

Chorley, W. R., *Royal Air Force Bomber Command Losses of the Second World War, Vol. 3: 1942*, Leicester: Midland Counties, 1994.

Cohen-Portheim, Paul, *The Spirit of London*, London: Batsford, 1935.

Crevel, René, *L'Esprit Contre la Raison*, Paris: Pauvert, 1986.

'La Grande Mannequin Cherche et Trouve sa Peau', *Minotaure* 5 (May 1934).

Crick, Bernard, *George Orwell*, Harmondsworth: Penguin, 1982.

Cunningham, Valentine, *British Writers of the Thirties*, Oxford: Oxford University Press, 1988.

Deichmann, H., *Objects: A Chronicle of Subversion in Nazi Germany and Fascist Italy*, New York: Marsilio, 1997.

Dijkstra, Bram, *Idols of Perversity: Fantasies of Feminine Evil in Fin-De-Siècle Culture*, New York: Oxford University Press, 1986.

Doré, Gustave, and Jerrold, Blanchard, *London: A Pilgrimage*, London: Grant & Co., 1872.

Faas, Horst, and Page, Tim (eds), *Requiem: By the Photographers Who Died in Vietnam and Indochina*, London: Jonathan Cape, 1997.

Faber, Monika, *Divas and Lovers: Photographic Fantasies from Vienna Between the Wars*, London: Thames & Hudson, 1998.

Fitzgibbon, Theodora (née Rosling), *With Love*, London: Century, 1982.

Fraser, Ian, 'A Close-up of the Holland Park Flat of Influential Photographer Bill Brandt', *The World of Interiors*, February 1983.

Freud, Anna, *Anna Freud's Letters to Eva Rosenfeld* (ed.), Peter Heller, Madison, Conn.: International Universities Press, 1992.

Gasser, Martin, 'Bill Brandt in Switzerland and Austria: Shadows of Life', *History of Photography* 21, no. 4 (Winter 1997), p. 4.

Gräff, Werner, *Es Kommt der Neue Fotograf!* Berlin: Reckendorf, 1929.

Grosskurth, Phyllis, *Melanie Klein: Her World and Her Work*, New York: Knopf, 1986.

Hardy, Bert, *Bert Hardy: My Life*, London: Gordon Fraser, 1985.

Harrisson, Tom, *Living Through the Blitz*, London: Collins, 1976.

Hart, Edith Tudor, *The Eye of Conscience*, London: Nishen, 1987.

Haworth-Booth, Mark, *Bill Brandt Behind the Camera*, Oxford: Phaidon, 1985.

(ed.), *The Land: Twentieth Century Landscape Photographs Selected by Bill Brandt*, London: Gordon Fraser, 1976.

Hewison, Robert, *Under Siege: Literary Life in London 1939-45*, New York: Oxford University Press, 1977.

Hopkinson, Lyndall Passerini, *Nothing to Forgive: A Daughter's Story of Antonia White*, London: Chatto & Windus, 1988.

Hopkinson, Tom, 'Bill Brandt – Photographer', *Creative Camera* 211 (July/August 1982), p. 600.

'Great Photographers of the World 2: Bill Brandt', *Daily Telegraph Magazine*, 24 April 1970.

Of This Our Time: A Journalist's Story 1905–1950, London: Hutchinson, 1982.

Hutton, Kurt, *Speaking Likeness*, London: Focal Press, 1947.

The Ilford Manual of Photography, ed. J. Mitchell, London: Ilford, 1949.

Jacoby, Russell, *The Repression of Psychoanalysis: Otto Fenichel and the Political Freudians*, New York: Basic Books, 1983.

Jay, Bill, 'Bill Brandt – The Best from Britain', *Creative Camera Owner* 38 (August 1967).

Jeffrey, Ian, *Bill Brandt: Photographs 1928–1983*, London: Thames & Hudson, 1993.

Karlen, Arno, *Threesomes: Studies in Sex, Power, and Intimacy*, New York: Beech Tree Books, 1988.

Kertész, André, *Paris Vu Par André Kertész*, preface by Pierre Mac Orlan, Paris: Plon, 1934.

King, Pearl and Steiner, Ricardo (eds), *The Freud-Klein Controversies 1941–45*, London: Tavistock /Routledge, 1991.

Kitaj, R. B., 'R B Kitaj and Two Faces of Ezra Pound', *Creative Camera* 210 (June 1982), p. 536.

Koestler, Arthur, *Arrow in the Blue*, New York: Macmillan, 1961.

Krauss, Rosalind and Livingston, Jane, *L'Amour Fou: Photography & Surrealism*, New York: Abbeville Press, 1985.

Lafourcade, Georges, 'Swinburne Romancier Où La Fille du Policeman', *Minotaure* 7 (June 1935), pp. 62–5.

Lantos, Barbara, 'On the Motivation of Human Relationships', *International Journal of Psychoanalysis* 36 (1955).

Levy, Julian, *Surrealism*, New York: Arno / Worldwide, 1968.

Lewis, Alun, *Alun Lewis: Letters to my Wife*, Bridgend: Seren Books, 1989.

Lewis, Jeremy, *Cyril Connolly: A Life*, London: Jonathan Cape, 1998.

Lyon, Christopher (ed.), *The International Dictionary of Films and Filmmakers: Volume II: Directors/Filmmakers*, New York: Perigee, 1984.

Mac Orlan, Pierre, *La Lanterne Sourde*, Paris: Gallimard, 1982.

Malinowski, Bronislaw, *Argonauts of the Western Pacific*, New York: Dutton, 1961; first published 1922.

Mann, Thomas, *Buddenbrooks: The Decline of a Family*, tr. John E. Woods, New York: Knopf, 1993.

Death in Venice and Seven Other Stories, New York: Vintage, 1954.

The Magic Mountain, tr. H. T. Lowe-Porter, New York: Knopf, 1944.

Man Ray, *Man Ray 1890–1976*, New York: H. N. Abrams, 1994.

Self Portrait, Boston: Little, Brown, 1963.

Martin, Tim, *Essential Surrealists*, London: Dempsey Parr, 1999.

Matless, David, *Landscape and Englishness*, London: Reaktion Books, 1998.

Mellor, David, *Bill Brandt*, The R.P.S. National Centre of Photography, Bath, 1981.

'Brandt's Phantasms', in Mark Haworth-Booth, *Bill Brandt Behind the Camera: Photographs 1928–1983*, Oxford: Phaidon, 1985, pp. 71–97.

Cecil Beaton, London: Weidenfeld & Nicolson, 1986.

Moholy-Nagy, László. *Malerei, Fotografie, Film*, Munich: Albert Langen, 1925.

von Moltke, Helmuth, *Letters to Freya*, New York: Knopf, 1990.

Musil, Robert, *Briefe 1901–1942*, Hamburg: Rowohlt, 1981.

Selected Writings, ed. Burton Pike, New York: Continuum, 1986.

Tagebücher I, Hamburg: Rowohlt, 1983.

Newhall, Beaumont (ed.), *Photography: Essays and Images*, New York: Museum of Modern Art, 1980.

Park, Bertram and Gregory, Yvonne, *The Beauty of the Female Form*, London: Routledge, 1934.

Penrose, Anthony, *The Lives of Lee Miller*, London: Thames & Hudson, 1985.

Piper, John, *English Romantic Artists*, London: Collins, 1942.

Powell, Anthony, *Hearing Secret Harmonies*, London: Heinemann, 1975.

Priestley, J. B., *English Journey*, London: Heinemann, 1968.

Roazen, Paul, *How Freud Worked: First-Hand Accounts of Patients*, Northvale, NJ: Jason Aronson, 1995.

Rodger, George, *The Blitz: The Photography of George*

Rodger, London: Bloomsbury Books, 1994.

Roegiers, Patrick, *Bill Brandt*, Paris: Pierre Belfond, 1990.

Sachs, Harvey, Profile of Hans Deichmann, *The New Yorker*, 4 June 1990.

Santayana, George, 'The Photograph and the Mental Image,' in *Animal Faith and Spiritual Life: Previously Unpublished Writings by George Santayana*, New York: Appleton Century Crofts, 1967.

Sayag, Alain and Annick, Lionel-Marie (eds), *Brassaï: The Monograph*, Boston: Little, Brown, 2000.

Sichel, Kim, *Germaine Krull: Photographer of Modernity*, Cambridge, Mass.: MIT Press, 1999.

Smith, F. B., *The Retreat of Tuberculosis 1850–1950*, London: Croom Helm, 1988.

Spender, Humphrey, *Humphrey Spender's Humanist Landscapes*, ed. D. Frizzell, New Haven: Yale Center for British Art, 1997.

Spender, Stephen, *World Within World*, London: Readers Union, 1953.

Steichen, Edward, *The Family of Man*, New York: Simon & Schuster, 1955.

Stekel, W., *The Autobiography of Wilhelm Stekel*, New York: Liveright, 1950.

Sadismus und Masochismus: Für Ärzte und Kriminalogen Dargestellt, Berlin, Urban & Schwarzenberg, 1925.

Sexual Aberrations: The Phenomena of Fetishism in Relation to Sex, London: Vision Press, 1953; the German original was published in 1923.

Swinburne, A. C., *La Fille du Policeman*, in Cecil Y. Lang (ed.), *Swinburne: Unpublished Writings*, Syracuse: Syracuse University Press, 1964.

Taylor, John, *A Dream of England: Landscape, Photography and the Tourist's Imagination*, Manchester: Manchester University Press, 1994.

Taylor, Sue, *Hans Bellmer: The Anatomy of Anxiety*, Cambridge, Mass.: MIT Press, 2000.

Theweleit, Klaus, *Male Fantasies*, tr. Stephen Conway, Minneapolis: University of Minnesota Press, 1987.

Thomas, Dylan, *The Collected Letters of Dylan Thomas*, ed. Paul Ferris. London: Dent, 1985.

Thomson, David, *Rosebud: The Story of Orson Welles*, London: Little, Brown, 1996.

Tucker, Anne, *Brassaï: The Eye of Paris*, Houston: Museum of Fine Arts, 1999.

Tynan, Kenneth, *Profiles*. London: Nick Hern Books, 1989.

Waelder, Robert, *The Living Thoughts of Freud*, London: Cassell, 1942.

Warburton, Nigel (ed.), *Bill Brandt: Selected Texts and Bibliography*, New York: G. K. Hall, 1993.

'Bill Brandt's Cathedral Interiors', *History of Photography* 17, no. 3 (Autumn 1993), pp. 263–76.

Weightman, Gavin, *Picture Post Britain*, London: Collins & Brown, 1991.

Westerbeck, Colin and Meyerowitz, Joel, *Bystander: A History of Street Photography*, Boston: Little, Brown, 1994.

White, Antonia, *Diaries 1926–1957*, London: Constable, 1991.

Williams, Val (ed.), *Too Short a Summer: The Photographs of Peter Rose Pulham 1910–1956*, York: Impressions Gallery, 1979.

Woolf, Virginia, *Letters VI*, London: Chatto & Windus, 1983.

Acknowledgements

Because I never knew Bill Brandt, my first debt in giving an account of his life must be to those who did. His widow, Noya Brandt, encouraged me to go ahead, spoke freely of her life with Brandt and supplied a wealth of information without trying to impose her views on my narrative. I am deeply grateful for her support. Equally crucial was the help given to me by those who first knew Brandt in the Twenties and Thirties, and who remain devoted to his memory: Lyena (Barjansky) Dodge of New York; Ester Cotton of Cambridge, the first wife of Rolf Brandt; Freya von Moltke of Norwich, Vermont; and Frances Rice of London. All sat patiently through long interviews and gave me access to pictures. For interviews, correspondence and precious information about the Brandt family I thank Susan Brandt, Ruth Pitman, Peter Brandt, Nigel Brandt, Savita Brandt and Dennis Brandt. Other personal friends or associates of Brandt who brought me closer to understanding his personality and working methods include Dorothy Bohm (who also gave me access to her extraordinary photographic library), Bob Cotton, Stephen Dwoskin, John Parfitt, Dr Paul Ignotus, Barbara Lloyd, Derry Moore, Wolfgang Suschitzky, Helen Srakocic-Kovac, Gail Buckland, Jim and Griffi Marsh, John Ryan, David and Peggy Godfrey. John and Jack Dawson and Mary Price told me about modelling for Brandt in Birmingham during the war.

I could barely have started on this project without the generosity and support of four scholars who founded the study of Brandt's work, and of the British photographic culture to which he belonged. They are Mark Haworth-Booth of the Victoria and Albert Museum; Ian Jeffrey; David Mellor of the University of Sussex; and Nigel Warburton of the Open University. Almost every page of my book has benefited from their work and their friendship. Other scholars who went out of their way to give personal help are Monika Faber of the Albertina Museum, Vienna; Martin Gasser in Zurich; Henri Coudoux of the Maison Européenne de la Photographie, Paris. I am also greatly indebted to Patrick Roegiers, Francis Hodgson, Colin Ford, Deborah Frizzell, David Travis, Anne Tucker and Edwynn Houk. Aysha Rafaele and Penny Bowles shared with me their work on Brandt for the BBC. I am indebted in various ways to Robert Streibel, Dr Tony Toszeghi, Beata and Michael Dobo, Stuart Alexander, Humphrey Spender, Martin Breese, David Cornwell, Paul Roazen, Roy Strong and Dorothy Tutin.

For insight into Brandt's career as a photo-journalist I am indebted to the late Stefan Lorant, Sheila Hardy, Sallie Hopkinson, the late Richard Bennett, John

Chillingworth, Brian Dowling, Michael Hallett, Sallie Hopkinson, Peter James, Colin Osman and Anne-Scott-James (Lady Lancaster).

Dorotheé Portmann was my host and guide at Davos. Mrs Sally Fry shared her memories of Brandt as a resident of Hillfield Court, and Mrs Valerie B. Lawrence showed me number 58. For information about Barbara Lantos I thank Peter Lantos, and Jill Duncan of the British Psychoanalytic Institute. I would also like to thank the records department of the King Edward VII Hospital, Midhurst; Anne Tobé at the Plateau d'Assy; Hartwig Forck of the Bismarckschule, Elmshorn; Gunther at the office of the General Registrar, Hamburg; Herbert Koch at the Magistrat of the City of Vienna; Françoise Reynaud at the Musée Carnavalet; and the proprietors of the Hotel Cottage on the Hasenauerstrasse, Vienna.

For support of my work on this biography I am indebted to Clare Hall, Cambridge, for a visiting fellowship in 1999; to the late Peter Copek and Wendy Madar at the Center for the Humanities, Oregon State University, where I was a research fellow in 2000; to the Hasselblad Foundation for a research grant; to the Social Sciences and Humanities Research Council for travel funding; and to my home institution, Simon Fraser University, for many kinds of assistance. Maggie Nicholson and Carla Cesarone provided both enthusiasm and practical help. Thanks to Pryor Dodge, who supplied most of the early photographs of Brandt and his friends. I owe a great deal to my agents: Georges Borchardt in New York and Bruce Hunter in London. Mark Holborn has been a great editor and also a teacher at Jonathan Cape. John-Paul Kernot, on behalf of the Bill Brandt Estate, has been generous with his time, materials and access to the surviving records of Brandt's life. He has facilitated my project, but left me free to tell the story as I see it.

Friends with whom I have discussed photography, and who have helped me along the way, include Ed Hundert, Roger and Barbara Seamon, Bob Anderson, Kathy Mezei, Graham Good, Torsten Kehler, Maria Tippett and Ralph Maud. Barbara Wood showed me how to take pictures, and how to be in them. Jasmine Nicholsfiguieredo put things in order and made sure that no moment was dull. Paul and Catherine Lawton, David and Anne Murray, Judith Murray and James Tayler were my refuge in France and England. Elspeth McVeigh was there at the beginning, and knows the length of the journey.

Vancouver
June 2003

Index

References to illustrations and photos are shown in italic. Bill Brandt (B. B.)'s individual photographs are indexed under 'Brandt Bill: PHOTOS BY'.

Credits

Published by Jonathan Cape 2004

2 4 6 8 10 9 7 5 3 1

First published in Great Britain in 2004 by
Jonathan Cape
Random House, 20 Vauxhall Bridge Road,
London SW1V 2SA

Random House Australia (Pty) Limited
20 Alfred Street, Milsons Point, Sydney, New South Wales
2061, Australia

Random House New Zealand Limited
18 Poland Road, Glenfield, Auckland 10, New Zealand

Random House (Pty) Limited
Endulini, 5A Jubilee Road, Parktown 2193, South Africa

The Random House Group Limited Reg. No 954009
www.randomhouse.co.uk

A CIP catalogue record for this book is available
from the British Library

ISBN 0 224 05280 2: Cape
ISBN 0 7126 6542 0: Pimlico

Papers used by Random House are natural, recyclable
products made from wood grown in sustainable forests;
the manufacturing processes conform to the environmental
regulations of the country of origin

Printed and bound in China by C&C Offset
Printing Co. Ltd

Design by Antigone Konstantinidou and Mark Holborn
Production Controller: Simon Rhodes